I0754610

[Frontispiece.]

BUFFALO CHASE.

JOURNAL

OF

ARMY LIFE.

By R. GLISAN.

San Francisco:
A. L. BANCROFT AND COMPANY.
1874.

PREFACE.

ALTHOUGH the following extracts from my private journal are confined mostly to personal details of nine years service in the Military Department of the Government, at a period when there were no conflicts excepting with the Indians, still, they may interest a few readers who are curious to learn something of Garrison life on the border; and of Oregon and Washington Territorial Indian wars from 1855 to 1858.

They may also serve to enlighten such persons as are ignorant of the privations and occasional hardships endured by military men in the intervening periods of great wars; and others, who imagine that the army, as a peace establishment, is only an expensive luxury, kept up for display.

These people do not seem to be aware that even during the most profound national quietude, the troops are divided up into small detachments and garrisons, to stand guard on our extensive frontier, with the red men of the forest on the one side, and the pioneer settlers on the other; and that through their constant vigilance many bloody strifes between these ever-conflicting classes are prevented.

In regard to the Washington and Oregon Territorial Indian wars, it will be observed that details are given of the campaign only in which I had some actual knowledge and experience; although general reference is made to many other engagements with the Indians by the regulars and volunteers.

A mere summary of the incidents of Colonel Buchanan's campaign, would probably be more interesting to the general reader than the tedious details given in my journal; but there doubtless are some persons who are desirous of knowing all the particulars of the last sanguinary struggle that the Government has ever had, or probably ever will have, with the once warlike bands of red men of the northwest coast, who contended so fearlessly and savagely with the pioneer settlers.

Yes, the last struggle—for the Snake and Modoc Indians, who have subsequently given trouble, were not among the belligerents in the general Indian war that harassed the border settlements of Oregon and Washington Territories, from 1855 to 1858.

R. GLISAN.

Portland, Oregon, April 15, 1874.

CONTENTS.

CHAPTER I.

CHAPTER IX.

CHAPTER X.

CHAPTER XI.

CHAPTER XII.

CHAPTER XIII.

CHAPTER XIV.

CHAPTER XV.

CHAPTER XVI.

CHAPTER XVII.

CHAPTER XVIII.

CHAPTER XIX.

CHAPTER XX.

CHAPTER XXI.

CHAPTER XXII.

CHAPTER XXIII.

CHAPTER XXIV.

CHAPTER XXV.

CHAPTER XXVI.

CHAPTER XXVII.

CHAPTER XXVIII.

CHAPTER XXIX.

CHAPTER XXX.

CHAPTER XXXI.

CHAPTER XXXII.

CHAPTER XXXIII.

JOURNAL OF ARMY LIFE.

CHAPTER I.

COMMENCEMENT OF ARMY LIFE.

Army Medical Board—Grades in Medical Corps—The Examination a Severe Ordeal—Depression on severing Old Ties and Associations—Not to remain in Army for Life—Acting as Aid to General Childs--Pleasant Society at Fort McHenry and Carlisle Barracks—Comanche Charge.

CARLISLE BARRACKS, PENNSYLVANIA, July 2d, 1850.

HAVING received a diploma as M. D., from the University of Maryland on the 20th of March, A. D., 1849, I shortly afterward opened an office in Broadway, Baltimore, Maryland, where I practiced medicine until the second of May in the following year, when I received a commission of Assistant Surgeon in the United States Army—having passed the necessary examination before a Board of Army Surgeons, convened in Philadelphia on the 15th of October, 1849.

There are three grades in the medical corps—Surgeon General, Surgeon and Assistant Surgeon; the first has the rank of Colonel, the second of Major, and the third of First Lieutenant, during the first five years of service, afterward of Captain until promotion to the grade of Surgeon. This rank is not merely assimulative, but real; and avails its possessor in the selection of quarters, in the matter of precedence where serving on mixed Boards, Councils of Administration, Courts Martial; and in everything except commanding troops when a line officer is present.

The duties of Surgeons and Assistant Surgeons are essentially the same. When acting together, which is rarely the case, owing to the numerous garrisons and detachments into which our army is distributed, the former, of course, rank the latter. So does seniority in either grade give precedence over juniors.

During the Revolutionary war, and for many subsequent years, the medical corps had a very different, and far less efficient organization than at present. The Surgeons, and Surgeons' Mates, as the Assistant Surgeons were then designated, were attached to posts or regiments permanently; now medical officers belong to the general staff, and are liable for duty in any arm or branch of service.

Few persons out of the medical profession have a just appreciation of the severe ordeal through which medical officers of the army have to pass before obtaining their commissions. Until July 7th, 1832, political influence alone was sufficient to enable one to enter the medical corps of the army, at which time Lewis Cass, Secretary of War, issued an order reiterating a clause of the army regulations for 1825, prohibiting appointments into this corps until after an examination by a properly authorized Medical Board.

Prior to the Secretary's order this regulation had never been carried out on account of the difficulty of detailing medical officers to constitute the Board; but ever since then it has been strictly enforced. The Board has generally been convened about once a year, either at New York, Philadelphia or Baltimore—these cities being the great centers of medical education. Due notice of the meeting of the Board has always been given in the public press several months before its session; likewise an invitation to all persons desirous of being candidates for appointment into the medical staff, to appear before the Board.

The only preliminary step required is to obtain a permit from the Secretary of War—this being readily granted to all applicants of good, moral, and social standing within the prescribed ages, from twenty-one to twenty-eight.

The examination is always critical and severe, and but a small proportion of the applicants successfully pass the ordeal. Having determined to stand my chances either before the Army or Naval Board, I devoted my whole leisure time, after graduating, to the study of my profession, and such collateral branches as appertain to a liberal medical education. Not wishing to lose what practice I had in Baltimore, by too long an absence, I wrote to the President of the Board to know about what time it would be ready to examine me. Having received a satisfactory reply, I reported in person at the designated time, and was told to be ready on the following day.

The Board was composed of Surgeons Thomas G. Mower, Richard S. Satterlee, and Assistant Surgeon Robert Southgate, and held its session at Jones' Hotel, Philadelphia.

The members were entire strangers to me, but being convinced of the impartiality of their examination, I felt no fears on that score. The only letters that I presented related mostly to my moral and social standing, as I well knew that the Board would prefer to ascertain, by an examination, my scientific and scholastic acquirements.

It was well for me, perhaps, that I was fortified with testimony as to character, for, as ill-luck would have it, I received a severe bruise on the cheek by accidentally striking my face against the bedstead the night previous to my examination. The Board was somewhat shocked at my appearance, but seemed satisfied with my explanation. My examination lasted three days.

On the first day the questions were of a general character, having as much reference to educational as scientific attainments. The Board, being satisfied on these points, handed me a subject for a thesis, scorbutus or scurvy, and placed me in an adjoining room to write it. I was prohibited from referring to any books for information. This being a very rare disease in the Atlantic cities, I had never seen a case of it, or heard a lecture upon this subject. Nevertheless, I was familiar with the history and theory of the disease from medical books, and consequently wrote what the examining board considered a good thesis.

On the second and third days I underwent a very searching examination in the various branches of medicine. As I had satisfactorily answered nearly all of the questions propounded, I felt sanguine of success, but did not, of course, make any inquiries in relation thereto, as I knew that the Board could not divulge any part of its proceedings until making a report to the Surgeon General, at Washington City.

In due course of time I received a letter from the War Department informing me that having passed a successful examination, I should be commissioned as soon as a vacancy occurred. There were six other successful candidates, I being the only one from Maryland, although there were quite a number of candidates from this State. I subsequently ascertained, at the Surgeon General's office, that the Board made an unusually complimentary report as to the qualifications of the successful candidates. Very few of my friends knew that I had appeared before the Board until I had been officially informed of my success—not even my relations.

The first impressions of delight on the reception of my commission being over, I began to look forward to my new career with feelings a little tinctured with regret at having to sever old ties and associations in a city that I loved so well, to enter upon a field of duty so different from anything in civil life. The gilt button, which is all the rage since the Mexican war, had no charms for me. Still I looked upon my new position as one of honor—and knew whilst it afforded me a sure livelihood, I should also have facilities of acquiring much useful information, both professional and otherwise, not to be obtained in civil practice. Yet, however much I may like army-life, it is not my intention to remain in it for life.

My first assignment to duty was at Fort McHenry, near Baltimore—which was then garrisoned by two companies of light artillery—Brevet-majors Hays and

Sedgwick's—and commanded by Brigadier General Thomas Childs. I was stationed there temporarily during the absence of Surgeon Robert C. Wood at West Point, where he had gone as a member of a Board for the physical examination of Cadets.

Besides my duties at the post, I had to visit the recruiting rendezvous, in Baltimore, daily, to examine recruits. Medical officers of the army, although to a certain extent under the control of commanding officers of posts, or of commanders of departments, or divisions, or of an army in the field, have their duties so well defined by the "regulations," that it is very rare indeed for them to receive orders except from the head of their own department. They belong, however, to the general staff, and are consequently liable in an emergency to almost any kind of duty required of staff officers. For instance, at the first "general inspection and muster" at Fort McHenry, that occurred after my arrival, I was required to act as aide-de-camp to the general, Mr. Rhett being ill. These "reviews" are generally attended by a great many spectators.

Owing to the beauty of the day, and a special invitation from General Childs to his city friends, there were present on this occasion an unusually large number of gentlemen and ladies from Baltimore. After having reviewed and inspected the troops, we dismounted, and turning our horses over to an orderly to hold, joined the lady spectators to witness the drill. Whilst I was proceeding *faire l'aimable* to a very charming demoiselle, the General turned to me and said, "give my compliments to Major Sedgwick—he will cease firing." Not fully appreciating all the duties of an aid-de-camp, I was at first a little disconcerted, but, remounting my horse, I delivered the General's order, which was, of course, promptly obeyed by the Major. The review being over, we joined the invited guests, and partook of refreshments at the General's residence.

A happy combination of circumstances rendered the six weeks of my sojourn at Fort McHenry a delightful recreation. It was in the lovely months of May and June, when the rural scenery of Maryland presents its most enchanting view. The season when the over-worked denizens of large and crowded towns should bid adieu, for a time, to the heat, smoke and unhealthy miasma of a city atmosphere, and hie to the country.

Fort McHenry is about a mile from the suburbs of Baltimore, and being situated in a somewhat triangular neck of land (a peninsula), with one of its sides washed by the river Patapsco, and the other by the basin or harbor of Baltimore, it affords a very agreeable, quiet country-like retreat, where the exhausted and weary student, or professional man, can inhale the invigorating sea and country air, and enjoy a comparative freedom from the cares of busy life.

I did not, however, lead the life of a sluggard. My professional duties were promptly attended to, and the most of my leisure hours devoted to mental culture. Still the stream of my life had begun to run in a channel so quiet and smooth, in comparison to the never-ceasing toil of my student life, that I began to think, after all, the lot of an army medical officer was quite as good as a young man with moderate aspirations could desire.

The society of the garrison, consisting of the officers and their families, was congenial and agreeable, and nothing occurred during my short stay to render me discontented; still, for some reason or other, when orders came for my departure to a rougher and more distant field of duty, I felt delighted. Curiosity and desire to experience the various vicissitudes of army life, had doubtless much to do in rendering me so willing to cut loose from the many pleasant reminiscences of old Fort McHenry.

On the 28th of June, 1850, I received orders from the War Department to proceed to Carlisle Barracks, Pennsylvania, and accompany thence a detachment of recruits to Jefferson Barracks, Missouri; thence to go to Fort Smith, in Arkansas, and report myself for duty to the commanding officer of Military Department No. 7, to be sent by him to a new post about being established on the Canadian river.

Nothing of peculiar interest occurred on my trip from Fort McHenry to York—whither I went by railroad—excepting being somewhat annoyed by the frequent clouds of embers from the engine. At York I took the stage. It being a delightfully cool evening, and having a beautiful range of country to pass through, I was most agreeably disappointed as to the unpleasantness of this mode of travel. Arriving at Carlisle at 7 P.M., I took lodgings at the Mansion House. On the following morning I came to the Barracks, which are only a mile from town. Here I found the officers engaged in the muster and inspection of troops, which is required by the army regulations every two months. Besides these there are, of course, monthly and other minor inspections.

The beauty of everything in this region, at this season of the year, and of the barracks themselves, together with the brotherly kindness with which I was received by the officers of the garrison, caused me to feel perfectly at home. This post is a depot and school of practice for recruits, to fit them for the dragoon service, and is at present commanded by Brevet-lieutenant Colonel P. St. George Cooke. The regimental band at this place is a very excellent one ; and being the only one in this part of the country, is much sought after by various parties and celebrations.

There are but few, I imagine, who could not appreciate the comforts of a garrison like this. The barracks are located in the heart of a beautiful valley, equidistant from two ranges of mountains, which form parts of the great Apalachian Range. They are built in a rectangular form, with neat and comfortable quarters for men and officers, and constitute the greatest attraction in the neighborhood.

During my stay here I have enjoyed myself in a quiet way. I called on a few ladies in Carlisle, and was one of a social company who assembled at Captain Buford's the other evening, where we had a most delightful party. In truth, the several parties in the garrison, both here and at Fort McHenry, to which I had the honor of an invitation, equaled, if not excelled in elegance, many of those given in Baltimore. Army people, stationed at the forts in the vicinity of our large cities, are the ever-welcome guests of all the parties, balls, and other like gatherings in the fashionable world. But, as it is well known that their pay is small, they are rarely expected to give large entertainments to their friends in return for the civilities extended to them. When, however, they do have a military party, it is generally well gotten up, even though it exhausts several month's pay to foot the bills.

Yesterday, desiring to take a gallop over the hills and dales of this enchanting valley, I borrowed a dragoon horse, that is in the habit of starting on the instant the rider gets his foot in the stirrup. Not being informed of this trick, I attempted leisurely to mount him, and to my surprise, instead of lighting in the saddle I found myself behind it, with only my left foot in the stirrup, and the horse running at full speed. I sailed along in this condition in full view of the whole garrison, who happened to be on parade at the time, for a distance of several hundred yards, before I could adjust myself in the saddle, and bring my pegasus under proper control. The high cantel of the dragoon saddle added greatly to the difficulty of gaining my seat. On my return, seeing a slight disposition on the part of the officers to rally me, I told them that I was practicing the Comanche Charge.

CHAPTER II.

FROM CARLISLE TO JEFFERSON BARRACKS.

Accompanying Recruits from Carlisle to Jefferson Barracks—By Rail, Canal and Steamboat—Beauty of Scenery—Prevalence of the Cholera—St. Louis a Great Military Place.

JEFFERSON BARRACKS, MISSOURI, July 23d, 1850.

Having left Carlisle on the eleventh, we arrived here yesterday.

We started from the former place with fifty recruits, to which number were added at New Post Barracks 130 more—making a total of 180.

Our commissioned officers are—Captain Abraham Buford, of the First Dragoons, in command; Captain Lorimer Graham, First Dragoons; Lieutenant Henry B. Schroeder, Third Infantry; Lieutenant Alfred Pleasanton, of the Second Dragoons, and myself.

On bidding farewell to our friends in the town of Carlisle, we were cheered repeatedly. Arriving at Harrisburg about 2 P. M., we found our way to the best hotel in the place, and partook of a hearty dinner. That town, though not large, is a very neat looking place. The bridges which span the Susquehanna below and above the city, are very lengthy, the first being a mile long, and the other about half that length.

At Harrisburg we took the cars for Huntington, which we reached at dusk—passing on the way many small and uninteresting villages. The road runs through a mountainous and picturesque country. To our right for many miles lay the beautiful Susquehanna river, a broad and noble stream, taking its meandering course along and between many spurs of mountains, covered with trees in full foliage—thus forming a charming landscape.

At Huntington we were transferred to a canal boat, running to Hollydaysburg, where we again took the cars at 9 A. M., on the following day. The railroad crossing the Alleghany mountains at this point, forms a connection with a canal at Johnsburg. The country traversed is the most romantic I have yet seen. The road has ten inclined planes—five each side of the summit—and passes through a long tunnel a little west of the latter. The cars are moved on these heavy grades by stationary engines, located at the highest point of each.

Reaching Pittsburg on Saturday we engaged passage on the steamboat Asia, a noble vessel, which was to have started on the next morning, but did not get off until the Monday following. Pittsburg contains about seventy-eight thousand inhabitants, and is the smokiest and dirtiest place for its size in the Union. Every house is blackened by the dense smoke and gas being constantly belched forth from its many iron and other factories. The cholera is quite prevalent along the Ohio and Mississippi rivers. It is very fatal in St. Louis and Cincinnati, and had just made its appearance in Pittsburg when we were there.

On our way down the Ohio river one of our men was taken with this disease, but recovered. Just before reaching this place, however, we lost one man from the malady. I find the hospitals here crowded with cases of this frightful complaint. Arriving at Wheeling, Virginia, on the 16th of July, we took a stroll through the town, and then continued on to New Port Barracks, Kentucky, where we arrived on the eighteenth, and got about one hundred and thirty more recruits ; all of whom, together with those we already had, were put on board a small and very old steamboat, on which we took passage to Louisville, Kentucky. When the boat started we sat down to supper, but ate very little, being thoroughly disgusted with the boat, and the appearance of the unclean supper table in particular. A waiter, in serving coffee, unfortunately capsized a tray full of this beverage on Captain Graham's shoulders, which accident caused this gentleman to leave the table in a towering passion.

At Louisville, the United States Quartermaster furnished us with one of the most superb boats on the western rivers—the Fashion. Being mentally fatigued one evening from reading, and seating myself in an arm-chair in the forward part of the boat, with the gentle zephyrs fanning my brow ; the silvery moon shedding through the sky her mellow light ; the twinkling stars shining forth with unusual brilliancy from the diamond-vaulted heavens, I gave my mind up to reverie, and soon lived over again the days of my boyhood—

"Ah, then how sweetly closed those crowded days !
The minutes parting one by one like rays,
    That fade upon a summer's eve.
But O, what charm or magic numbers
Can give me back the gentle slumbers
    Those weary, happy days did leave ?

Where by my bed I saw my mother kneel,
And with her blessing took her nightly kiss ;
Whatever Time destroys, he cannot this :—
E'en now that nameless kiss I feel."

On our way up the Mississippi, we saw a flock of wild turkeys, who, on perceiving the boat, marched quietly off into a neighboring thicket. The first sight of these noble birds in their wild condition, made me long for a good shotgun, and a few hours ashore. Such an opportunity may, however, not occur until I reach my new home in the Indian Territory.

Being unable to secure quarters for our men at this Post, we encamped in the vicinity.

Jefferson Barracks is a general depot for recruits and army supplies, and bears the same relation to the more distant frontier stations, camps, and forts, that the city of St. Louis does to the numerous villages and towns along the tributaries of the great Father of Waters —the Mississippi River. It is also a school of practice and drill for troops of all arms of this service, when for any reason they are not required immediately at the more western points.

At present the garrison is very much crowded. Hence General Newman S. Clark, now in command of Military Department No. 6, has ordered all the recruits intended for New Mexico, including our detachment, and another which arrived subsequently, to start forthwith for their destination.

My orders from the Secretary of War required me to accompany a body of recruits to Jefferson Barraeks, and then proceed to Fort Smith and report myself to the General commanding Military Department No. 7, for duty at the new post about to be established in the Indian Territory.

General Clark modified this general order by directing me to continue with the detachment of recruits, with which I came, as far as Fort Leavenworth, and then obey the general order.

Subordinate officers have a right to change the orders of their superiors when an "emergency of service" arises—the prevalence of the cholera being the emergency under which General Clark is acting in sending me to Fort Leavenworth.

St. Louis, being only a pleasant hours drive from Jefferson Barracks, is the constant resort of the younger officers when not on duty. It is probably the greatest army place in the United States. The young ladies there are most accomplished coquettes, and turn the heads and break the hearts of almost every Second Lieutenant who chances to come this way. In order to keep up appearances in this gay society, many of the young men, fresh from West Point, hypothecate or sell their pay accounts several months in advance; and are then compelled, when they join their companies at some out of the way post, to live as economically as possible, in order to replenish their exchequer.

When, however, these young sons of Mars have rich papas to draw upon, they sometimes live a fast life at this place. Perhaps the most lucky one here in this respect is Lieutenant Mathew R. Stevenson, of the seventh regiment of infantry, whose father, Col. Stevenson of San Francisco, California, allows his favorite son Mat. five thousand dollars per annum as extra "pin money." Of course the latter is a lion among his fellow chums at present—as he spends his money with a lavish hand.

Many of the older officers think that Mat. is becoming a spoiled child, and that his father would do better to lay by his surplus cash for some rainy day, when it might serve them both more profitably.

There being a large number of officers with their families stationed at this post, and so many new arrivals, the society in garrison is of course much more lively than at most other military places.

Having paid my respects, as required by the army regulations, to the commanding officer, Brevet Brig. General Richard B. Mason, and returned the courtesies of other officers who called upon me, I shall make no further effort to mingle in the gay society of this place or St. Louis—especially as my sojourn is to be of such short duration.

CHAPTER III.

ON TO FORT LEAVENWORTH.

By Steamboat to Fort Leavenworth—Military Stations being nuclei for Settlements—The frequent removal of Indians by the Government, and their Final Fate—Alcohol the Firebrand of Indian Disturbances—Col. B. of the Dragoons—Union of the Missouri and Mississippi Rivers—Panic of the Recruits at the great prevalence of the Cholera—Mexican Veterans would rather face a Battery than Asiatic Cholera—Death of General Mason by this Disease.

FORT LEAVENWORTH, August 17th, 1850.

WE reached this place on the evening of the twenty-seventh ultimo, after a four days trip by steamboat from Jefferson Barracks. This fort was built by General Leavenworth, from whom it takes its name, and is located on the west bank of the Missouri River, in Kansas Territory. It is a most charming spot, and surrounded by one of the richest agricultural regions in the United States. It is distant by water from St. Louis six hundred miles.

Only a few years ago, this post was considered in the very heart of the Indian country. But settlements spring up so fast in the vicinity of military stations, when not prohibited by Government, that the whole aspect of this region is being rapidly changed by the small homes of the pioneer settlers.

The overland emigration to New Mexico, Utah, and California, passing near here, gives an increased impetus to this section of country.

The many small bands of Indians, removed to this part of our territory a few years ago, to give room for the great expansion of the white settlements, will find that they must soon pack up for another pilgrimage. before the *avant couriers* of civilization press them too closely.

Thus it ever is; the red man of the Atlantic slope must be crowded further west, whilst his race on the far-off Pacific shores, are jostled and pushed towards the rising sun. When at last the great tides of immigration meet midway between the two oceans, the remnants of the sixteen millions of those native lords of the soil, that once roamed over this broad land, who shall not have left their bones bleaching on the plains behind, will be engulphed forever beneath the waves of advancing civilization. One shudders at the thought of the many bloody conflicts yet to occur between these contending races of human beings.

If we are to take history as our guide in divining the future, the right and wrong of these cruel encounters will not always rest exclusively on either side—but one time with the red man—at another with his pale-face brother. Yet, as in the past, the innocent many will often have to suffer for the guilty few. He who sows the wind does not always reap the whirlwind.

The small tribes of Indians living in the vicinity of, or who visit, this post for the purposes of trade at the sutler's store—the transaction of official business with the government—or out of idle curiosity, are the Omahas, Ottoes, Konzas, Pawnees, Delawares, Weahs, Shawanos, Potawatamies, Kickapoos and Ioways.

In the scale of civilization they range from the primitive savage to the half civilized Indian. They have many troubles among themselves, and with the pioneer settlers, that can only be arranged by an appeal to the military commander at this post. Such interviews on the part of these children of the forest with the government officers at all the frontier stations are numerous, and require the possession of great patience and tact in the latter, in order to produce good results.

Alcohol is the fire-brand that creates more disturbances among them and their neighbors than all other causes combined. However strict the government may be in its laws, concerning the introduction of spirituous liquors on Indian reservations, there is always a class of bad white men, and of half-breed Indians, who defy all regulations upon the subject.

In view of more easily controlling the sale of contraband articles to the Indians, and to the soldiers occupying military reserves in the Indian country, the govment has found it convenient and wise, to appoint at almost every frontier station a post sutler — who is simply a merchant, under certain military restrictions. The following extracts from the army regulations, relating to him, explain themselves:—

"Every military post may have one sutler, to be appointed by the Secretary of War, on the recommendation of the council of administration, approved by the commanding officer.

* * * * * * *

No tax or burden in any shape, other than the authorized assessment for the post fund, will be imposed on the sutler. If there be a spare building, the use may be allowed him, he being responsible that it is kept in repair. If there be no such building, he may be allowed to erect one; but this article gives the sutler no claim to quarters, transportation of himself or goods, or to any military allowance whatever. The tariff of prices fixed by the council of administration, shall be exposed in a conspicuous place in the sutler's store. No difference of prices will be allowed on cash or credit sales. Sutlers are not allowed to keep ardent spirits, or other intoxicating drinks, under penalty of losing their situations."

A sutler's store at a frontier post is a very popular place of resort, not only for members of the garrison off duty, but for the inhabitants of the surrounding country far and near. Although prohibited from selling ardent spirits, he is allowed to keep it for his own use and that of his friends. Of course his hospitality is often called into requisition by such of the officers as use this beverage—the number who do not, to some extent, is small indeed—I find myself in this respect an exception almost everywhere. At present there are a few officers at this post who indulge quite too freely for their own health, or the comfort of their friends. The most remarkable one in this respect is Colonel B——, of the Dragoons, who can sit up night after night for a week imbibing his toddy, and relating anecdotes by the thousand. The old gentlemen's vivacity, wit, and humor, are exceedingly entertaining to strangers. Some of his subordinates, however, who have been stationed at the same post with him for several years, say, that after he begins to relate over his anecdotes a few times, they cease to excite any mirth, and become a nuisance. Good story-tellers should endeavor to repeat but seldom their mirth exciting narrations, to the same auditors, if they wish to avoid being voted a bore. As good jokes, like strawberries and cream, are only relished when not served too often.

On our trip from Jefferson Barracks to this place, we had the pleasure of seeing what Thomas Jefferson once said was worth a journey from Washington City to behold. That is, the union of the waters of the Mississippi and Missouri rivers. They run for miles without mixing. The water of the former, at this season of the year, being limpid, and that of the latter muddy. This turbid appearance is produced by the falling in of the rich alluvial banks of the river, which is unceasingly changing its course, by making on one side and losing on the other. Though always muddy, it is, of course, more so during the spring freshets. What may be called the bottom land of the Missouri river is formed by the ever-varying course of this whimsical stream, and has an average width of about nine miles. This is covered at many places with gloomy forests of lofty cotton-wood. Its soil is rich and productive in the highest degree.

On either side of this lowland of the river, are the boundless prairies, whose summit levels are several hundred feet above the bottom. In many places these natural meadows slope gently down to the water's edge, uncovered except by a green carpet of grass—thus affording a charming landscape.

General Clarke acted wisely in not permitting the four hundred recruits at Jefferson Barracks to be crowded on a single boat with only one medical officer; and in dividing them into two detachments, having Dr. Elisha P. Langworthy with one, and myself with the other; because, as he feared, of the presence of the epidemic, or Asiatic cholera.

This frightful disease broke out among the troops on the first day of our departure, and spread with fearful rapidity. Nearly every man in the command was taken sick with it, in some of its stages, before our arrival at Fort Leavenworth. None of the cases, however, proved fatal until the night we reached the fort, when several died. The men were panic-stricken at the appearance of this complaint among them, and besought me to recommend the officer in command to let them march overland to their destination. Of course there were powerful reasons why I declined to acquiesce in their petition. I well knew that such a trip in a torrid July sun, after the system had once been infected, would have sounded the death-knell of almost the entire command. The captain of the boat was requested to push on to Fort Leavenworth as fast as steam could carry him; and to stop for wood as seldom as possible. Whenever he did make a landing the commissioned officers had to stand guard, pistol and sword in hand, to prevent a general desertion of such of the recruits as were able to be on their feet.

We placed the sick in the most comfortable parts of vessel, reserving to ourselves, and other cabin passengers, barely room for the dining table. Although the officers escaped the scourge, yet the groans of its victims were anything but sedatives to their nerves. They had all been in the Mexican war—where one of them was badly wounded—yet acknowledged that they would far rather be under fire, where the stimuli of the din of battle and military renown keep off fear, than spectators of the silent, though deadly, onslaught of the Asiatic cholera.

On arriving here, we found this pestilence in full force, and have just heard the sad news of the death, at Jefferson Barracks, of Brevet Brig.-General Richard P. Mason, Colonel of the First Dragoons, and commandant of the post, from cholera. He died on the twenty-fifth ultimo. Only three weeks ago I saw him surrounded by a doting and happy family, all unconscious that the angel of death was hovering near.

> "O, why should the spirit of mortal be proud?
> Like a swift-fleeting meteor, a fast-flying cloud,
> A flash of the lightning, a break of the wave,
> Man passes from life to his rest in the grave.
> The leaves of the oak and the willow shall fade,
> Be scattered around, and together be laid;
> And the young and the old, and the low and the high,
> Shall moulder to dust, and together shall lie.
> The hand of the king that the sceptre hath borne;
> The brow of the priest that the mitre hath worn;
> The eye of the sage and the heart of the brave,
> Are hidden and lost in the depth of the grave."

While sympathizing deeply in the bereavement of the many happy homes caused by the cholera, I cannot but feel a professional pride in having been able to see this disease for myself, an opportunity that may never again be afforded me, although I should live to a good old age; for it is a malady that invades this country only at long intervals. Its native home is India, where it prevails both sporadically and epidemically. Commencing its devastating march from Bengal in 1817, it gradually spead, with numerous halts, until it had invaded almost the entire world.

It did not reach the American continent until 1832. It appeared first at Quebec on the 8th of June, and at Montreal on the 10th; thence moved rapidly along the St. Lawrence river, and the great chain of lakes, to the Mississippi valley, extending southerly so far as New

Orleans, attacking on its way the United States troops who were being concentrated near the lake for a campaign against the hostile Indians under Black Hawk, living in the present State of Wisconsin, who commenced warfare upon the frontier settlers of Illinois.

This fearful disease nearly paralyzed the efforts of the troops for the time being. Like an invading army it did not confine itself to a single point of attack, but sent off a detachment from the main line of invasion to strike terror into the hearts of the citizens of New York, where the disease broke out on the 24th of June. Thence it radiated northerly up the Hudson river as far as Albany, and southerly to Philadelphia and Baltimore, and other places on the Delaware and Chesepeake bays.

Before the end of 1832 it had spread to Charleston, South Carolina; Havana, in Cuba; and to Mexico. In the United States there were partial returns of the complaint in 1833 and 1834; when it disappeared from North America entirely.

The rising generations of physicians in this country have never had an opportunity to see the disease until its second great visitation in 1849 and 1850. They will now be able to behold and investigate it for themselves; and after trying such remedies as their forefathers have sometimes found beneficial, yet often powerless, can seek for the, as yet undiscovered, specific in epidemic cholera.

CHAPTER IV.

FORT LEAVENWORTH TO FORT SMITH.

Trip from Fort Leavenworth to Fort Smith—Thoughts on Benton, Clay, Calhoun and Webster—Hot weather at Memphis—Tedious Journey up the Arkansas—A Row between Passengers and Captain—Numerous Doctors at Little Rock—Pat desires to be his own Heir—Rough Stage Traveling and several Accidents—Arrival at Fort Smith—The Interposition of United States Troops often required to settle disturbances among the Cherokees, and between the latter and their Arkansas neighbors—The Cherokees a Warlike Race.

FORT SMITH, ARKANSAS, September 3d, 1850.

I REACHED here on the twenty-third of last month, after a tedious journey from Fort Leavenworth. As my children, if I ever have any, will fly through this country on the swift railroad car; and my grandchildren, sail over it in some ethereal balloon, or flash across it in a pneumatic tube, and may have a curiosity of knowing the slow, plodding modes of travel now in vogue; which, by the way, are fast in comparison to those of our forefathers, I shall dedicate to them the following account of my trip:—

Having obeyed the order of General Clarke, in accompanying a detachment of recruits to Fort Leavenworth, it became my duty to follow the general instructions from the War Department, to report for duty to the commanding General of Department No. 7, at Fort Smith. The only practical route being via. St. Louis, I determined to take passage on the first steamboat for that city. As the first upward-bound boat, the Sacramento, touched at the fort just long enough to land the mails, and then continued up the river to St. Joseph, I became fearful that she might not, on returning, give me time to get aboard. So I concluded to go up the river some five miles to a little town called Weston, on the eastern side of the river, and there await her return, as she would tarry a few hours at that place.

On my way thither I passed through a forest of noble cottonwood, the cooling shade of which is very refreshing in this hot summer weather. On reaching the ferry I had to wait until the captain extricated some unfortunate cattle who had strayed into the mire. Crossing over to Weston I remained there for a few days ; and on the first of August took passage on the Sacramento, and arrived at St. Louis on the fifth.

After securing a room at the Planter's House, I strolled by gaslight around the city; which was in a ferment over the result of an election that had just taken place, and that foreshadowed the political downfall of Thomas H. Benton; who had represented Missouri in the United States Senate continuously since her admission into the Union in 1821. His term will expire next winter. Thirty years in the Senate with those intellectual giants, Webster, Clay and Calhoun! Such honor rarely falls to the lot of man.

The greatest privilege of my life was being able to visit the senate-chamber last winter, and to hear these renowned men discuss the last great compromise measure of Henry Clay.

I was saddened by the impression that when they shall have been called off the stage of life (Calhoun lately gone,) there would be no others to take their places. Only a few such senators lived in the palmiest days of Rome.

When in Oregon and California, the forests of the stately fir, and majestic redwood perish by fire, they are succeeded by thickets of hazel, vine, maple and scrub oak. Let us pray that this botanical law will not have a parallel in the congress of our great nation; and that when the giant minds that now illuminate our political sky, like the sunbeams from heaven do our snow-clad mountain peaks, shall have burned out in the intensity of the fires of their own genius, they may not be followed by a race of moral and intellectual pigmies.

We must, however, be on the alert. 'Tis not the mere expansion of territory—or the cultivation of science or morals to the highest degree by a few—or the possession of great wealth by the many—or yet the right of suffrage by all, that can preserve in the councils of our nation the wisest and most noble of our race. "Eternal vigilance is the price of liberty."

St. Louis was settled by the French in 1764, while Missouri formed a part of the vast territory of Louisiana, which was purchased from the French during the reign of Napoleon in 1803. It remained a sort of trading post until 1804, when the territorial government of the United States was extended over Missouri. The growth of the town, for the first few years after it came into our possession, was necessarily slow; but it is now, as all the world knows, fast developing into a magnificent commercial mart.

When many of those great arteries of commerce—the railroads—shall have centred in this well-located city, her increased prosperity will astound the most sanguine. Although the grades of the wholesale business streets are about forty feet above low water mark, they are sometimes overflowed by the Mississippi River. There have been several destructive fires in this part of the city during the last few years — having their origin in the steamboats lying along the wharf. It is said there was not a breath of air stirring at the beginning of the last great fire; but that the heat of the first burning boat created a sufficient breeze to carry the vessel among the other boats and set them on fire, which thence spread to the warehouses in the vicinity.

Leaving St. Louis on the steamboat "Concordia," we passed slowly down the Mississippi, seeing but little to attract attention. At the mouth of the Ohio we witnessed a similar phenomenon to that of the union of the Missouri and Mississppi—I allude to the junction of the Ohio with the latter river. This being below the entrance of the Missouri, the Mississippi is of course turbid, whilst the Ohio is, at this season, as transparent as a crystal.

Arriving at Memphis, Tennessee, the Captain informed us that he would remain there at least a day, in order to discharge and take in freight. The boats coming down the Missouri are laden principally with hemp, whilst those running from St. Louis to New Orleans, unless they secure full cargoes at the former city, take in cotton and sugar along the river.

In the vicinity of Memphis I had an opportunity of seeing plantations of this great staple production of the South—cotton. I have never experienced such warm weather as at Memphis. The thermometer

(Fahrenheit's) on the boat was at 2 P. M. generally 103 in the shade. This, however, is an unusually warm summer in the South.

Memphis contains about thirteen thousand inhabitants; but will never grow very rapidly until she secures good railway connections. The most important public work in the vicinity is a United States Navy Yard; which of course gives employment to a vast number of laborers and mechanics. A short distance out of town there was in course of erection a very fine cotton factory.

After being here a day, the Captain informed us that he would certainly leave in a few hours, and that we had better remain on board. We were detained a day longer; and he would not have started then, had not an opposition boat come puffing down the river; when he suddenly fired up and started, leaving quite a number of his passengers behind.

We arrived at Napoleon, at the mouth of the Arkansas River, on the eleventh of August. This is the sorriest excuse for a town I have ever seen. I was very fortunate in finding here five very agreeable young gentlemen, awaiting conveyance up the Arkansas. Col. Philip St. George Cooke had informed me, when at Carlisle Barracks, that I should find on the Arkansas River only a set of gamblers and cut-throats. The gentlemen mentioned were merchants and planters traveling on business into the interior of Arkansas.

We left there on the fourteenth in a very small steamboat; and after going about one hundred miles, were transferred to a still smaller one. We had not gone far on the latter ere she stranded on a sand-bar. Here we lay for half a day.

On reaching Pine Bluffs, the Captain told us that he could not go to Little Rock and return in time for the next mail, and that we might either remain aboard and return for the mail in the course of two days, and then go up; or take the mail stage at this place, and he would refund a part of our boat fare; for we had paid through to Little Rock. After five of our party had hired a private conveyance, the Captain not only refused to refund any part of the boat fare, but stoutly denied ever having promised to do so. A row, between the passengers on one side, and the boat's officers and crew on the other, seemed for a while inevitable; but, after blustering for a few minutes, the Captain paid back a part of the fare. As the private conveyance and the stage were too much crowded, some of the passengers, including myself, remained aboard the boat until she returned for the mail, and finally reached Little Rock. On her way up she was grounded on sand-bars a great many times.

At Little Rock I put up at the Anthony House, where I remained three days. The hotel being crowded, Major Robert S. Garnett, of the seventh infantry and myself had to occupy the same room and the same bed. This town of two thousand inhabitants, is full of lawyers and doctors; there being about thirty of the former, and fourteen of the latter.

One morning, quite a number of gentlemen were sitting in front of the hotel, enjoying their *otium cum dignitate*, when a man came up and said, "Doctor, a boy is waiting at your office for you." Instantly three or four gentlemen got up, when one of the party remarked, "for Heaven's sake, don't all go." It appears that it was Dr. Webb who was wanted. He is a very comical gentleman. At a small town where he had previously been, he happened to be both doctor and judge. An Irishman, leaving the place for New Orleans, and not returning for a long time, it got into the papers that he was dead. His estate was settled, and the property turned over to his heirs. Pat, returning in the meantime, demanded of Judge Webb his goods and chattels; but was informed by his honor that his estate had been administered upon in due form, and the property divided among the heirs, and that he could not go behind the record. "Faith," says Pat, "and can't I be one of the heirs then?"

Between Little Rock and Fort Smith we traveled in a stage-coach, which was heavily laden with the United States mail, besides a number of passengers, We got along slowly and roughly for about thirty miles, when in being ferried across a narrow but exceedingly deep stream, we narrowly escaped drowning. It was 2 A. M.—the moon having gone down—and the place surrounded with thick woods, darkness reigned supreme. Having crossed over, our team, owing to the steepness and slipperiness of the bank, and the heavy load, were unable to pull up the hill, and let the stage run suddenly back against the boat; thus breaking some of the fastenings, and knocking the latter several feet from the shore. Had the main rope given way, the stage and team, at least, would have sunk to the bottom of the slough. After much toil and tribulation, we managed to extricate the vehicle from its perilous situation, and proceeded on our journey.

In getting over, we found that the only damage

done to the stage was the breaking of several spokes of one of the wheels. This gave us much uneasiness, as we had yet to travel in this conveyance twenty miles. The driver told me that he would be compelled to put out some of the baggage. Having paid extra fare on account of it, I was determined that he should do no such thing, especially as I had already walked up every hill, because there were only two horses to the stage, when the company should have sent at least four.

The Stage Company's contract with the United States for carrying the mail is said to be very lucrative; hence there is no excuse for such miserable coaches and teams as are now employed on this route. The next vehicle to which we were transferred broke down after a few miles travel. The third one, having no rubbers or brakes to the wheels, went so fast, down a steep hill, that the driver was thrown from his seat, and would have been crushed to death, but for the fortunate circumstance of his throwing his weight on the foot-board, or sweep, which being iron, bent and caught a spoke of the right fore wheel—thus checking the stage.

The greatest inconvenience of traveling over this route is, that one is three days without any sleep. In fact, they hurry us on day and night, over one of the roughest roads any poor mortal ever journeyed—not even allowing sufficient time for meals. An occasional glimpse at a flock of wild turkeys, or a swift bounding deer, made me wish for an opportunity to try my luck at hunting this species of game.

Arriving at the town of Fort Smith about eleven

o'clock at night, we stopped at Captain Roger's hotel. Our host is a fat, jolly old pioneer, and is the original town proprietor. The place numbers about one thousand inhabitants, and is growing slowly. It takes its name from a fort in its immediate vicinity. After a good night's rest—being the first since leaving Little Rock—I donned my uniform and reported myself to the Commanding General of Department No. 7—General Mathew Arbuckle—who told me to remain at Fort Smith until he could secure me a small escort on my journey to the new post about to be established in the Indian Territory. In due course of time I was of course invited to dine with the General, and subsequently with each of his staff officers. Several pleasant families in the adjoining town also extended to me invitations to parties; thus enabling me to form the acquaintance of some very agreeable people.

The Surgeon of the post, Dr. Joseph H. Bailey, very kindly accompanied me in a few gallops around the country. On our return from one of these trips, we were attracted by a crowd of persons on Water street, looking very intently at the freaks of two drunken Cherokee Indians—a man and his wife—who were crossing the Arkansas River opposite the town. They would have drowned, had not timely assistance been extended to them by a couple of the spectators.

In defiance of stringent United States laws against selling liquor to Indians, they frequently obtain it in large quantities; hence many bloody frays among themselves and with the border settlers. The interposition of the troops stationed at Fort Smith and Fort Gibson becomes frequently necessary, to preserve law and order among the Cherokees and their Arkansas neighbors. The former station is on the border line between the State of Arkansas and the Indian Territory; and the latter is about sixty miles northw-est of Fort Smith.

It will be remembered that the Cherokees lately resided in the State of Georgia, and have quite recently been removed to this section of country, where they are farming on a small and rude scale. Many of them still refuse to do anything except fish and hunt, opportunities for which abound in this beautiful prairie country. These Indians for many years inhabited the upper portion of the State of Georgia, one of the finest regions of the United States. They were at one time a very warlike people, and after numerous conflicts with neighboring tribes—especially the Shawnees, whom they drove out of that part of the country about the year 1600—they finally established their possessory right to the soil, and were supported in this claim by a solemn treaty of the United States.

The Cherokees assisted the Colonies in the capture of Fort Du Quesne (the present site of Pittsburg) in 1758, but soon after became embroiled in a border war with the English settlers of Virginia. Peace was made with them in 1761. During the war of the Revolution they sided against the Colonies, and in favor of the British. In the war of 1812, however, they aided the United States, and did good service in helping to subjugate the hostile Creek Indians. They were gradually advancing in civilization when the State of Georgia demanded their removal from the homes and graves of their kindred to their present abode in the

Far West. At first, only about one third of them could be induced to emigrate; the remainder, under their head chief, John Ross, obstinately refusing for several years to leave the soil of their forefathers.

They are now, however, all established in a beautiful section of the Indian Territory, lying west of the State of Arkansas, under the government of their old chief, John Ross, who is an educated, and, in many respects, a remarkable man.

CHAPTER V.

INTO THE INDIAN COUNTRY.

Departure from Fort Smith into the Indian Country with only a stupid Teamster—First effort at making Coffee—Choctaw Ball-play—Remarks concerning these Indians—A dreary Travel in the Dark—Charming Landscape—Supper on broiled Squirrel and stony Biscuit—Knowing winks of the roguish Mules—The Teamster's Nightmare—Left alone all night without Weapons in a dismal Forest, and serenaded by Wild Beasts——Arrival at Fort Washita.

CAMP ARBUCKLE, INDIAN TERRITORY, September 22d, 1850.

THE commanding general not being able to furnish me with the small escort promised, I concluded to proceed to my station via Fort Washita, which made my journey a little longer than the direct route would have been. I accordingly left Fort Smith on the seventh inst., mounted on a horse, which I purchased in the town, accompanied by the quartermaster's wagon, containing among other things my baggage.

After traveling about three miles my driver informed me that he would have to await for another teamster as he was sick. It appears that before leaving Fort Smith he had reported to Captain Alexander Montgomery, the quartermaster, his inability to undergo the fatigue of the trip, and that the latter told him to drive a few miles, and in the meantime he would secure a substitute, who would overtake and relieve him.

In a short time he was relieved by the arrival of the new teamster. The change, as the sequel will prove, turned out to be a bad one for me. For the last driver, being obtained in a hurry, soon gave evidence of his total unfitness for the position. He was green and awkward, and totally unacquainted with the road. He drove a slight distance, when bang went the wagon against a tree, that the mules themselves would have avoided had they been uncontrolled. The result of this carelessness was a cracked wagon-tongue.

Having started at noon we made only thirteen miles the first day, and encamped for the night near a little stream, which furnished water for our team, and for a pot of coffee, which I made to the best of my ability, whilst the teamster cared for his animals. This, my first effort at coffee-making, was conducted more upon pharmaceutical principles, than the art *de cuisine*. I succeeded in a primitive way in making at least a decoction, that, when duly sweetened, was palatable to hungry palates.

Experienced travelers on the prairies generally lay in a stock of useful kitchen utensils, and other things indispensable to convenience in preparing meals at the camp-fire; but for some reason or other I failed to have anything in the culinary line except a tin coffee-pot and frying-pan. As, however, I had a moderate supply of crackers and ham, we managed to enjoy our frugal repast very much.

Next morning we started at seven, and moved on quite briskly to the Choctaw agency, where we inquired of a negro the route to Fort Washita. He informed us that he knew the way very well; and that we must take the left hand road on reaching the fork at the border of the first woods. His advice was followed, but contrary to our own judgment; for the right hand road was much plainer, and more traveled, and corresponded in these particulars to the information I had gained upon the subject before starting from Fort Smith. After traveling the left hand road some five miles, we came across a party of Choctaw Indians engaged in their national pastime, the ball-play; and were told by them that we were on the Fort Towson, instead of the Fort Washita, road. However we did not regret the colored man's blunder, as it gave us an opportunity to witness one of the most interesting scenes in the world.

Before us were several hundred athletic Indian men, divested of all clothing, save ornamental breech-cloths, fastened by beautiful bead belts around their waists, and with tails of feathers or white horsehairs; and manes, on their necks, of horsehair of varigated colors—their bodies being painted in the most brilliant of colors—all screaming, yelling, barking, howling, springing, running, jumping, tumbling, rolling, struggling, and striking at a ball with might and main.

In the noise and confusion I was greatly puzzled at first to understand the principles of their truly interesting game. There are two goals, about three hundred yards apart, each of which is formed by two upright poles, fifteen or eighteen feet in height, and seven or eight feet apart, set in the ground, with a cross-piece on top. Half way between the goals is the starting point, where the ball is thrown up at a certain signal—generally the report of a gun — when the struggle begins.

The sticks with which they play are somewhat spoon-fashioned—made by taking a green stick, about three feet in length, and an inch and-a-half thick, and

INDIAN BALL-PLAYING.—Page 38.

bending the end in an oblong or oval shape, with a net work of thongs on one side of this bent portion, so as to prevent the ball's passing through when caught. With these sticks the players can hurl the ball with fearful force. But there are so many ready to catch it that it sometimes takes a long time for any one side to pass the ball across its goal, and thus count one point in the game, which consists of one hundred points. Judging from the excited and turbulent manner in which the players go to work in this game, there must often be many sore shins, limbs and heads before the play is ended.

I may add here that our route from Fort Smith to Camp Arbuckle lay in the Choctaw country, an immense territory ceded to the Choctaws by the United States, in 1831, and lying south of, and adjacent to, the country of the Greeks and Cherokees. These Indians occupy but a very small part of their land, which extends from the western border of Arkansas five and a half degrees west, and is bounded on the north by the Canadian, and on the south by the Red river; the west half of it being within the range of the wild Indians of the prairies—especially the Comanches, whom they fear almost as much as the white settlers of Texas and New Mexico do. In fact it is mainly with the view of preventing hostilities between these partly civilized Indians, and the wild tribes, that our new post is to be established, the United States having stipulated, in its treaty with the Choctaws, to keep up a certain number of military stations on the borders of their country for a specified time.

The Choctaws number about twenty-two thousand

in population, and are gradually becoming civilized. They once lived upon the Gulf of Mexico, just west of the Mississippi river, and have always been, as a tribe, peacefully disposed. Some of them have fine farms, on which they raise wheat, potatoes, melons, squash and corn. The great majority, however, appear to lead an idle, dissolute life, depending on the small annuities allowed them by our government, and on such game as they may chance to find in their hunting expeditions. Their laws are similar to those of the United States, but are seldom rigidly enforced. They have one pretty good school; and support a small newspaper, published in their own language.

The fact of these Indians living so many years in Mississippi, and Alabama, in communication with the whites, and being no further advanced in the simple arts and sciences, is proof that civilization is a process requiring more than one generation for even moderate development.

Having satisfied our curiosity concerning the ball-play, we, in accordance with information gained from one of the chiefs, retraced our steps a mile, and striking across a prairie, soon regained the Washita road; along which we hurried in order to reach a house called the "Bluffs," kept by a half-breed Indian. Night coming on, we passed the place unknowingly; and soon found ourselves in a large timbered bottom, where it was so dark that the driver, being unable to guide his mules, gave them a loose rein to find the road themselves. After groping along in this manner for several miles, we encamped on the margin of a prairie, both of us sleeping in the wagon, as on the previous night.

MIDNIGHT SERENADE ON THE PLAINS.—Page 43.

We made an early start on the third day. The country grew gradually more and more interesting. The gracefully undulating prairies covered with green grass, and a profusion of wild flowers of variegated colors, and bounded in the dim distance by azure mountain hues, gave the landscape an indescribable charm.

When the novelty wore off, these picturesque scenes became somewhat monotonous; but the intense enjoyment their first appearance produced, afforded us a realizing sense of the true beauties of nature.

Having killed a few squirrels during the day, I commenced, on our arrival in camp, to cook them for our evening's repast. They were split open, and spread upon forked sticks, and broiled by the fire.

The mules having poked their heads into the wagon on the night previous, and devoured all my crackers and salt, it became necessary for me to try my hand at baking biscuit. I have often heard of the festival of unleavened bread, celebrated by our Jewish brethren in commemoration of the Passover, but fail to understand how they can work themselves into a very thankful frame of mind on such bread as I manufactured on that particular occasion. It was so hard that the roguish mules, who devoured my crackers, winked knowingly at each other, as I carefully put away the remnants for next morning's early breakfast; and seemed to say, Doctor, you have no need to fear our foraging propensities to-night, if that be your best effort in the art of baking bread.

My teamster evidently did not belong to the family of croakers, as he partook of the frugal meal set before us, of broiled squirrel, without salt; stony biscuit, minus butter; and a decoction of coffee, with no milk; as though it were good enough for a prince. That night he came near stampeding the team by his horrid yells, in a paroxysm of the nightmare. I don't believe, however, that the poor fellow realized, as I did, that his attack was produced by too much hard biscuit in the stomach.

The fourth, fifth and sixth days passed over without any unusual occurrence; and also the seventh, until night. We were then within twelve miles of Fort Washita; but as we had traveled hard all day, it was deemed advisable to encamp on what we supposed to be Blue river. The sun being an hour high, and the mules needing grass, the driver tied them in pairs, and turned them loose to graze. I cautioned him not to allow them to get out of sight. After bathing myself in the river, and returning to the wagon, I was surprised at not being able to see the animals; but, on being assured by the man that he had just been to look after them, and found them and my horse quietly grazing in a small prairie not far off, I dressed myself leisurely, and then started to look after the mules. But to my great disappointment could find neither them or the prairie.

It was very evident that the fellow had lied to me. I went back and ordered him to hunt after the animals as speedily as possible. He asked the loan of my shotgun, which I permitted him to take. Hour after hour passed away without the return of the teamster. I began to feel uneasy both for his and my own safety. There I was alone at midnight in a dense forest, in an Indian country, without weapons of defense, far from any white habitations, and within the range of the wild Indians of the prairies. As the man failed to report himself by one o'clock at night, I concluded to retire. I was awakened from my first nap by a serenade from hundreds of wild birds and beasts. I had read of Indians imitating the cries of animals, and at first imagined that some of the Choctaws might have known of my lonely situation, and were getting up a little fun at my expense. There must have been at least a dozen kinds of wild birds and beasts represented in this forest menagerie—all quacking, hooting, barking, yelping, growling, screaming and howling at the same time. I could distinguish the noise of ducks, cranes, owls, wolves, and perhaps panthers and bears. Whether such gatherings of wild animals were ever heard of in this dark and dismal forest before, I know not; nor do I care to be again a lonely auditor of their tartarean chants.

It is a common thing for wolves to entertain travelers by howling in the dead hour of the night; but when they do, other animals, and wild birds, are usually silent. They must have been holding a peace convention on that particular occasion. I fancy that a discharge from a double-barreled fowling-piece might have created quite a commotion among my uninvited guests. But being minus the very essential weapon, I remained quietly in bed until the noise ceased, and then fell asleep, to be disturbed no further, except by those pests of warm climates, the mosquitoes. 'Tis said that wild Indians sometimes torture their prisoners almost to death by stripping them naked, and securing their hands and feet together, and then tying them up to a stake, to the mercy of these annoying insects. Let him who believes this to be a mild kind of punishment try the experiment of sleeping in the open air without a mosquito bar, on the banks of some of our southwestern streams, in the latter part of summer, or beginning of autumn.

On the following morning, after partaking of a cup of coffee and a few bites of my unleavened biscuit, I started on a tour of reconnoisance; but could see or learn nothing of my driver or the mules. Neither could I ascertain anything in relation to the vast assemblage of wild animals around my camp-fire on the night previous—unless the burning of the neighboring prairies had driven them into the timber for shelter. Saving the barking of squirrels, and the chirping of small birds, everything was supremely quiet, all nature seemed at rest. Had there been no other valuables in the wagon than my own baggage, I would have proceeded on foot to Fort Washita for assistance; but under the circumstances concluded to stand guard over the things until some one made an appearance.

Late in the afternoon I was delighted to perceive coming along the road, in a two-horse ambulance, a couple of gentlemen; who proved to be Lieutenant Edward F. Abbott, of the Fifth Infantry, and Doctor Elisha J. Bailey, of the army. They informed me that my driver had found his way into Fort Washita about ten o'clock that morning, and that they had come to take me in; and that the quartermaster had sent along four horses to haul in the wagon. The horses were soon in sight—also the mules, the driver having found them on his way back. The horse he had caught the night before, and ridden him as far as an Indian hut, three miles from our place of encampment, where he staid until the next morning, and then went to the fort in pursuit of the mules. The driver had lived all his life on the border, and consequently felt unconcerned about his own safety—especially as he had my gun—but had never before been employed in any capacity in the military service, or else he would have deemed it his duty, on not finding the stray animals on the night previous, to have returned to camp, and reported accordingly.

On arriving at Fort Washita I was the guest of Dr. Bailey and his estimable wife; under whose kind hospitalities I soon felt like a new man. I believe it is a well-established maxim of etiquette that one can pay no greater compliment to the hostess than by showing a proper relish of her viands. Mrs. Bailey, I am certain, will bear me out in the assertion, that I proved myself in this respect, on the evening of my first meal at her table, exceedingly complimentary.

During my short stay at that post I was invited to several very pleasant little garrison parties. I soon learned that one of the gentlemen, Lieutenant Abbott, who so kindly assisted me out of my late trouble, was an acknowledged practical joker. How it happened that he allowed so splendid an opportunity to pass by of playing a joke upon me, on coming to my rescue, I cannot understand. Perhaps his companion, Dr. Bailey, having the honor of the medical corps at heart, held this fun-loving son of Mars in check, by introducing themselves before any trick could be played upon me. I was delighted to find that the commanding officer of Fort Washita, Colonel Dixon S. Miles, was an old Baltimorean. I had also the satisfaction of meeting here Captain Randolph B. Marcy—the commander of the camp whence I was bound. He told me that we would start for our new home in three days; it being distant from Fort Washita in a nearly western direction about seventy miles.

Fort Washita is in the Choctaw country, not far from the northern boundary of Texas. It was established a few years ago in accordance with a treaty stipulation with these Indians; and also to preserve order on the frontier of Texas. A little village has sprung up near the post called Rucklesville, but can never grow into that importance that such nuclei of larger towns near military stations, sometimes asésume. The site of the post commands a fine landscape view of the surrounding country, which is mainly a succession of rolling prairies. Over these great natural meadows vast herds of buffalo were wont to roam; and that too until within a very few years.

It was near that place where the gallant General Leavenworth lost his life a short time ago, from a spell of sickness which had its pre-disposing origin in a fall he received whilst pursuing a herd of buffalo. This officer was in command, at the time, of the first regiment of Dragoons, which was going on a reconnoiteriug tour through the wild Indian country, in order to cultivate the acquaintance of those arabs of the western prairies—the war-like Comanches. The latter Indians, and the Pawnees, have until quite recently been the terror of this section of country.

The fate that Judge Martin met at the hands of one of these tribes a few years ago, may serve as a warning to adventurous frontiermen. This wealthy, but rather eccentric, gentleman was in the habit of taking his children and colored servants every summer out on these wild plains, and spending several months in chasing the buffalo. A roaming party of Indians at last came upon the Judge and killed him—and took his son into captivity. This circumstance is mentioned as a mere sample of many somewhat similar occurrences in border life in this charmingly beautiful, yet dangerous, region.

Our route from Fort Washita to this camp lay mostly through lovely undulating prairies, covered with nature's carpet of green grass and wild flowers in profusion, except where the fire-fiend had blackened the earth with his foul and consuming breath.

The view on these great natural meadows seemed to be confined only by streaks of cottonwood along the streams, and occasional groves of oak on the high grounds. Interspersed at intervals of a few miles were also patches or thickets of wild plum trees. The soil of this magnificent country is deep and rich, affording a future home for thousands of agriculturists, but at present rarely traveled over even by the owners of the soil—the Choctaws.

After one gets a few miles westward of Fort Washita, there is not to be seen a single hut, or other evidence of settlement, by these Indians. The nomades of the prairie have it all to themselves. I found Captain Marcy a very entertaining traveling companion—full of narrations of wild border life. It was truly amusing to hear him tell some of his choice anecdotes; which he always did without a ripple on his smooth countenance until he found the story appreciated by his auditors—then his expressive eyes and smiling face indicated a keen relish for the ludicrous aspect of human life. He is not much given to practical jokes; but, during the first night of our journey, as we were quietly passing through a cottonwood bottom, the almost human-like hooting of an owl caused him to suddenly halt, and exclaim in a low mysterious voice—Indians! Indians! There were several of us in company, but being the latest arrival in the Indian country, I thought it was done to try my courage. So I laughingly remarked that the people born in the woods ought not to be frightened by an owl.

We arrived at our present camp on the night of our second day out from Fort Washita, and found everybody but the guard asleep. The officers soon got up, and welcomed us by a jolly shake of the hand; and the offer of something to drink. Every one but myself joined in a social glass.

"What! a *tee-to-taler?*" exclaimed the sutler. "My dear sir, you will lay this abstinence all aside after being in this dull place a few months." I took the remarks as intended, as a mere bit of pleasantry, but will here state, that although I have seen a good deal of drinking among the officers of the army, yet, as a class, they are gentlemanly polite even when largely under the influence of liquor, and rarely make rude and offensive remarks to persons differing from them in tastes, habits, inclinations, or principles.

Our camp is named after the commanding general of this military department—Camp Arbuckle—and was selected by Captain Marcy under general instructions from the War Department; but the site does not meet the approval of General Arbuckle, who desires it to be established further south. We are consequently living in tents, awaiting further orders from our superior officer, before erecting log cabins for quarters. Everything, as yet, in and around camp appears strange and novel to me. How I shall fancy this isolated life cannot yet be determined. I think it prudent to cultivate a taste for hunting, as Captain Marcy is a pupil of the celebrated Captain Martin Scott, and can initiate me me into the mysteries of western sportsmanship.

By the by, I must relate a good joke I accidently played on the Captain the other day. He, with other officers, was practicing rifle shooting at a target, placed some seventy-five yards off. After they had all fired without striking the "bull's-eye," the Captain turned around and said to me, whilst casting significant glances at the other officers, perhaps, Doctor, you can be more successful. Although a good shot with a bird-gun, I never had much experience with the rifle, yet concluded to try my luck. So nerving myself for a master stroke, I knocked a hole through the very center of the mark. The Captain was evidently puzzled at this remarkable shot from a city novice, and urged me to try again. Having luckily shifted the joke upon him, I prudently and politely declined to make any further display of my marksmanship, but rested on my laurels—knowing full well that it would be impossible for me to sustain my sudden, and accidental, reputation of being a crack marksman. I think, however, that the officers shrewdly suspected that my shot was what is called, among billiard players, "a scratch."

Having alluded to Captain Martin Scott I shall here relate one of the many anecdotes told of him by Marcy. Captain Scott and several friends, being out hunting, discovered on the top of a very tall tree a raccoon. All of the latter separately took a pop at the coon without effect. Finally Captain Scott concluded to try his luck. He elevated his rifle, and was on the eve of pulling the trigger, when the coon said "hold on—who are you?" "My name is Scott," replied the captain. "What Scott?" inquired the coon. "Why, Captain Scott." "Are you Captain Martin Scott?" "Yes." "Then don't shoot—I'll come down."

AN ARMY CAMP BEYOND THE BORDER.—Page 51.

CHAPTER VI.

AT CAMP ARBUCKLE.

Living in Tents and temporary Log Cabins—Commissioned Officers mess together—Mrs. Marcy's first attempt at cooking—Love in a Cottage and Love in a Frontier Cabin contrasted—Proposed exchange of Wives between an Indian Chief and Marcy—Too much hard work and not enough Military Instruction—Hunting instead of Fatigue Parties—Several Hunting Trips—Killed the first deer—Alarmed by Indians and swim the River—Lost my way—Headed off by two Wild Indians—Hunting Deer with a Hog—Kill another Deer, which was claimed by Updegraff—Almost Frozen to Death—Christmas Bill of Fare—Army and Navy Mess—Cherokees and their Negro Prisoners—Cherokees and Creeks—Burning Hay to save it: Hey!—Genuine Prairie Fire—Rattlesnakes, Centipedes and Tarantulas—Compass Plant—Sad news from Home.

CAMP ARBUCKLE, INDIAN TERRITORY, April 2d, 1851.

WE are still at the camp established last autumn, one mile south of the main branch of the Canadian River, but anticipate removing to a new site on Wild Horse Creek, a tributary of the False Washita River, in the latter part of this month.

Our command, consisting of Company D, fifth infantry, lived in tents until last December, when the expected orders for changing our location not having arrived, we hastily constructed rude log cabins for winter quarters. These are one story high, with floors of puncheons, and roofs of clapboards, in lieu of shingles. The chinks, or spaces between the logs, are filled in with strips of wood, on which is spread, both within and without, mud mixed with straw. Our chimneys are constructed of short pieces of puncheons, and are well plastered inside and out with a kind of clayey loam. The men occupy a long building about twenty-five by two hundred feet, divided into about four rooms, besides the kitchen. They sleep on rude bunks, made of split logs and clapboards, placed two and a half feet from the floor. There are four of these log huts for the commissioned officers. A double one for the commanding officer, Captain Marcy, and a single one, or cabins with only one room, for each of the Lieutenants—Frederick Myers and Joseph Updergraff—and myself.

We all mess together at Captain Marcy's quarters; where our meals are superintended by that jewel of a lady—his wife. She has been with us only a few months, and expects soon to take her departure east; as the wild and isolated country whither we are ordered, would be too uncomfortable for even such a veteran as herself. Being reared in ease, elegance, and social refinement, she had many hardships to contend with in early married life, whilst accompanying her gallant husband in frontier service. Yet, among all her difficulties, nothing ever occurred to mar—for the time being—her domestic happiness so much, as an utter inability, on one occasion shortly after marriage, to prepare a meal for her liege lord and a few invited guests, when her servant had suddenly left her; as this class of persons are so apt to do when most needed. Although she failed to cook well, she wept to perfection, on beholding the meanly-cooked dinner that had been prepared after so much tribulation.

Her husband, like a perfect gentleman as he is, instead of expressing any disappointment at her want of success, as married men sometimes do, consoled his loving wife with the assurance that his guests and himself relished the meal very much, and with a little further experience she would be able to cook as well as anybody.

The young officer of the army is not always so fortunate as Captain Marcy, but sometimes marries one of those gay butterflies of fashion, who love so well to flutter and flirt as ball-room belles. And he finds, that while love in a cottage, surrounded by all the comforts of wealth and society, may be poetical and delightful to his bride, yet when the honeymoon is spent in a log cabin on the frontier, with occasionally nothing to eat but pork and beans—no music save the fife and drum—few visitors, except the naked and hungry savages—romance often gives way to sad repinings on the part of his young wife. However, a true and noble woman will always adapt herself, as Mrs. Marcy did, to the new condition of things.

While officers of the army do not need their wives to be mere cooks, but, as educated gentlemen, should marry elegant and refined women, if they marry at all; yet these ladies ought to have some practical knowledge of that most essential part of housekeeping—cooking—so as to superintend the preparation of meals; and, in rare emergencies, be able and willing to try their own delicate hands in the culinary arts. It is useful, and frequently necessary, for officers themselves to have a knowledge of cooking, so that they can know when their men are properly cared for by the company cooks.

Shortly after Mrs. Marcy arrived here, last winter, a band of wild Indians of the prairie made us a call.

It being their first visit to the abode of the pale faces, almost anything they saw excited their curiosity. One of them was particularly charmed with some of Mrs. Marcy's embroidery, which she happened to exhibit to him, and proposed to her husband an exchange of wives. Although feeling highly complimented, the Captain politely declined the proposition.

In the erection of our temporary quarters we had the assistance of a few carpenters; yet most of the work was performed by the soldiers. I am satisfied, from my short experience in the service, that it is a mistaken economy to keep the men so steadily at hard labor, instead of drilling them more thoroughly in the most essential of all the principles of military tactics, the art of shooting well.

If the Government desires to expend as little as possible on the army, let her adopt the plan of organizing among the troops hunting parties instead of fatigue parties, whose duty it shall be to supply the garrison with fresh meat. This would be a real saving at frontier stations like ours—within easy range of the buffalo, and all other wild animals of the western plains. Give all the men, by turn, a chance at this sort of duty, and they will soon learn to use firearms with precision, and at the same time save more in the commissary department than they can possibly do in the quartermaster's department by hard work in the erection of quarters, and the making of roads and bridges.

This idea is original with myself, and may be as impracticable as novel—yet I should like to see it tested. At all events, if I were at the head of the war department, the army should be ordered to do less work, and more shooting—if only at a target. For most of the recruits being foreigners, who never handled a gun before enlisting into the United States service, could not hit a man at the distance of thirty yards, in a dozen trials. What sort of troops are these for Indian fighting? Of course the older soldiers can shoot better than the raw recruits; but the manner in which they learn to handle firearms with effect is by hunting, at spare hours, thus proving the correctness of my theory.

The commissioned officers, as a class, are far superior shots to the rank and file, simply because they have more leisure, and can afford to buy more ammunition. The soldiers should at least be allowed one day in every week to hunt; and their ammunition furnished them by the government. Hunting is the handmaid of war. Search the wide world over, and it will be found that those nations or races of mankind who follow hunting, either for pleasure or subsistence, are the most formidable in war. This is the reason why our hearty frontiersmen, when properly disciplined, make the best troops for Indian service. The Indians of the plains are natural soldiers, because they subsist by means of the chase. Such sport is conducive to contentment and health. Show me the man who is fond of such sport, and I will promise you that whereever he may be placed—whether in the jungles of India, or the wilds of America—he will be far more satisfied with his exile from home and society, than the inactive drone, who lounges at the saloons of stations near a town, or at the sutler's store, if in garrison, and croaks upon his hard fate, and the ingratitude of the government at placing his wonderful self at such out of the way stations. As fond as I am of professional study and miscellaneous reading, I feel confident that the hum-drum life of frontier garrisons would be perfectly intolerable if the chase had no attraction for me.

It is fortunate that there is at this camp another officer, besides myself, who loves this species of amusement—Captain Marcy. We occasionally go out together, but as the game of this country—deer, wild turkeys, geese, ducks, grouse, and bears—are more easily reached by the light and cautious approach of a single sportsman, than by the almost inevitable noise of two or more hunters in company, we have mostly gone out alone. We keep the mess supplied with game. Hunting parties of the wild Indians, as well as of the partially civilized Choctaws, Chickisaws, Cherokees, Creeks, Seminoles, Delawares, and Kickapoos, have roamed over this section of the Choctaw country so frequently, that the larger species of game, particularly deer, have become very scarce. So much so indeed that Captain Marcy, as experienced as he is, began to despair of securing by his own efforts one of these animals for the table. In fact, a lucky chance gave me the opportunity of carrying off the palm in this respect. I made my arrangements, by an early sick call at the hospital, to leave garrison one morning at daylight for a stream some seven miles from camp, where it was highly probable abundance of those delicious ducks, called mallards, could be found.

The lowering clouds gave strong indications of a storm at the hour of starting, but my feverish eager-

THE WILD DENIZENS OF THE PLAINS.—Page 55.
(The proper targets for recruits.)

ness for a few good shots at these wild birds, made me heedless of all else except my game. So mounting my fine Comanche hunter, I galloped to within a convenient distance of the hunting ground, then dismounting and approaching the creek on foot, was greatly excited by the quacking of hundreds of ducks. In the meantime the rain began pouring down in torrents—fortunately I succeeded in keeping my ammunition dry—and, under cover of trees, managed to get within good range of my game. Discharging one barrel at the ducks whilst thickly huddled together in an eddy of the stream, and the other as they arose in a mass so dense that it seemed impossible for a single shot to go astray, I was delighted to find the water was covered with trophies of my hunt. Whilst rapidly reloading I beheld, a few hundred yards up the creek, a deer, stalking deliberately, but carefully, down the current. Fearing that he might not continue his course so as to come within shooting distance, I cautiously changed my position a hundred paces nearer him; and, standing behind an oak tree, watched my opportunity to fire just as he moved clear of a bluff bank, which screened me from his keen gaze. He scented me, but as I was to his leeward, and he was sniffing the breeze to the windward, I had a fine opportunity to plunge a whole charge of duck shot into his side, over the region of the heart.

He made a few leaps on three legs for the bank on the other side of the creek, when a discharge from the second barrel brought him quickly to the ground. I crossed over; and after cutting the body in two without severing the skin, endeavored to throw him in a mill-bag style across my saddle—but being a very large buck, his weight baffled my efforts. Putting one of my feet into the stirrup, so as to make a fulcrum out of my knee, I managed to draw each half, in regular succession, up high enough to be tied to the front rings of the saddle—a half on each side of the horse. In the meantime I could distinctly hear the yelping of dogs, the sharp cracks of rifles, and the yelling of Indians, in the timber a short distance up the creek. The deer that I had just killed had evidently been pursued by them; and had taken to the water to elude the scent of their dogs. In fact there was a slight and recent flesh-wound in one of his hips made by a rifle ball or an arrow.

I hurriedly recrossed the stream, and after securing such of my ducks as had not been carried down the current, galloped towards the garrison, glancing back repeatedly to see if I was pursued; for the Indians must have been almost in sight when I started. I presume, from the fact of their using rifles, that they were what is known as partially civilized Indians. Could I have been certain of that, of course there would have been but little occasion for alarm—but some of the hostile Indians use guns also.

On reaching the Canadian river, I found that it had risen several feet, and would undoubtedly swim my horse, who, being so heavily packed with game, would have a severe struggle to reach the opposite bank. To have cut loose the ducks and deer would have rendered his crossing over an easy matter. But then the Indians or the wolves would have glutted over my misfortune; and my companions in camp might have been a little incredulous concerning the killing of so much game. So I resolved to take the chances, and plunged into the swift and whirling current, holding my horse's head well up stream, and guiding him more by my hand than the bridle. Comanche brought me out on the opposite side some distance below where I aimed to reach. The gallant brute had evidently swam many a stream whilst in the possession of his savage master, from whom I purchased him, or he could not have struggled across the Canadian with such a load as I had upon him. Vive la Comanche. I marched into garrison as proudly as an Indian warrior with his dozen scalps dangling to the breeze.

Marcy had hitherto hunted exclusively with a rifle—of which he had two, one having a double barrel, and the other being a very heavy and costly gun, with an elevating back sight for shooting at great distances—but for some time after my successful hunt he borrowed my shotgun, thinking that it was, as some of the northwestern Indians say, "big medicine." But although killing a great many ducks with it, he failed to secure a deer, and returned to his first love—the rifle. The latter was also my favorite gun for hunting the larger game; and I soon learned to handle it well and effectively. A few more incidents connected with my many hunting trips during our sojourn at this camp may not be entirely devoid of interest.

On one occasion, shortly after my arrival in garrison, I went some six miles from camp down the bed of the Canadian river, which is nearly dry in the latter part of summer and beginning of autumn, and night coming on earlier than anticipated, I attempted to reach home by a shorter route than the river. Taking an Indian trail, which I correctly supposed led toward the garrison, I journeyed along the same for about two miles, when it turned, as it appeared to me, in a wrong direction. As darkness was setting in, it was impossible to retrace my steps; so trusting to the well known sagacity of my horse, I gave him a loose rein, and after traveling in great suspense for about an hour, I was gladdened with the sight of the garrison lights. The officers had felt alarmed for my safety. Mrs. Marcy said that if I ever frightened them so again she would urge her husband to forbid my going out alone so far from camp.

Last summer, whilst returning from a hunting trip up the almost dry bed of the Canadian river, my horse suddenly pricked up his ears and dashed off in an excited manner. On looking around to discover the cause of his excitement, I beheld two mounted Indians approaching from the opposite bank of the river at full speed, and endeavoring, as I thought, to cut off my retreat to the garrison by the only trail near by. They were naked, with the exception of moccasins, leggins and breech-cloth; and painted in the most hideous colors; being also well armed with bows and arrows. They were so suddenly upon me that I saw at a glance that there was more danger in running than fighting. So cocking my rifle—one of Hall's breech-loaders—I kept steadily on my course. My rifle was very hard on the trigger or I would not have cocked it, because there would have been danger of a premature discharge by the jolting of the horse.

As I reached the trail leading from the river to the

STILL-HUNTING.

garrison, the two Indians halted ahead of me, and set up a most fearful whoop. To state that I was not alarmed would be untrue; but I acted far more coolly than I ever thought possible under the circumstances—feeling determined if they attacked me, to get at least one good shot at them. They inquired, by gestures or pantomime, the distance to garrison, and then beckoned me to go ahead. I made motions for one of them to take the lead, which was finally reluctantly done. Under pretense of a friendly chat—in signs of course—I kept my eyes on both of them. I saw, by an exchange of significant glances, that they knew my rifle was ready for action if necessary. After thus marching along in single file for a few hundred yards, my stranger friends suddenly galloped off into the thicket, without even bidding me adieu.

On returning to garrison, I related the occurrence to Black Beaver, a famous Delaware guide, who chanced to be there on a visit. From my description he recognized the Indians as belonging to a band of hostile Comanches, at that time roaming in the vicinity, and said that I had made a narrow escape. In one of my hunting rambles I was followed by a pet hog belonging to the teamsters. I repeatedly endeavored to drive him back, but without success. Finding it impossible to hunt deer with a hog grunting at my heels, I was on the eve of returning to the camp, when I saw a fine deer running up the ravine. As he was passing within fifty yards of me, the hog gave a grunt, which caused the deer to halt suddenly, and gaze curiously at his hogship for several moments. Having no time to dismount, I fired from the saddle. As my horse was unusually restless, I failed to make a mortal shot, but wounded the deer, which I tracked by his blood for several miles. Had I had a good dog with me, in lieu of the hog, I would in all probability have finally captured my game, instead of leaving him to become a prey to wolves. Unless a deer be struck in a vital part, he is almost certain to elude the hunter—provided, of course, that the latter has no dog with him. He will do this even though one of his legs be broken.

As one of many cases in illustration of this point, it is only necessary to relate that during the past winter, being surprised by the fall of a deep snow—a very unusual occurrence for this section of the country—we started out in three parties a deer-stalking. Captain Marcy went in one direction, Lieutenant Updegraff, and James Stephens, the post sutler, in another course, and I took a third route. After a hard and unsuccessful day's hunt, I was returning home a little out of my beat, when I espied fresh tracks of a deer. Following cautiously in pursuit, I soon perceived, from crimson spots here and there in the snow, that the deer had been wounded. I had gone only a few hundred paces, when I beheld him lying down behind a clump of bushes. I sent a half ounce ball crushing into the only visible part—his rump. He arose and ran a few steps, and fell. On coming up, it became necessary to strike him in the head with the butt end of my rifle, and to cut his throat besides, before he would give under. In fact, he showed a desperate disposition to fight. He was a very large buck. On examination, I found that one of his fore legs had lately been broken by a rifle ball. While skinning him, Lieutenant Updegraff and Jim Stevens came riding along, and claimed the deer, because they had drawn the first blood. I think it very doubtful, however, from the noisy manner in which they pursued him, whether they could have ever obtained a second shot; and as they had no dogs, of course their pursuit would otherwise have been fruitless. Captain Marcy, on the same day, broke a deer's leg, and trailed him afterwards to the distance of eight miles, without success.

After the deep snow just alluded to, the weather grew very cold. The freezing temperature did not cool my ardor for hunting in the least. So, a few days subsequent to my last jaunt, I sallied forth again in the snow. Several miles from camp, I beheld at a distance a large flock of geese, all huddled together in a small unfrozen spot—a springhead—in a pond situated in the bottom of the Canadian. There being no bushes or trees to hide my approach, I resolved to crawl on all fours over the frozen and snow-covered ground to a bunch of tall grass within good gun-shot range of the coveted prize. I was so benumbed by the intense cold that, having reached the designated place, and risen to fire, I fainted just as the gun went off. Although everything grew dim and blurred before me, and I felt a strong desire to sleep, there was just perception enough left me to know that unless I should make a powerful effort to arouse myself, and keep in motion, death from freezing would be the result. If insensible at all, it must have been only for a few minutes; for, after rubbing myself a little, I soon found strength sufficient to reach my horse, and ride home. My friends in garrison did not fail to observe the death-like pallor of my blanched cheeks on my arrival in camp. Frost-bitten feet was the consequence of this foolish trip; and now that warm weather has set in, they itch and burn very much; and they will, in all probability, be hereafter more susceptible to chillblains.

Although hunting was our chief amusement, yet when young officers from neighboring posts visited our camp, we would occasionally mount our fleetest horses, and try their speed over the prairies; and, sometimes, attempt to run down wolves when we chanced to meet them far from ravines or woods. These contests were rarely premeditated, but gotten up on the spur of the moment. Yet occasionally we would have a regular race, except that there was no betting—at least none by myself. When I first purchased my Comanche hunter; before he had recovered from the hard usage given him by the Indian of whom he was bought, Lieutenant Myers bantered me for a race with a fine horse of the sutler; he to ride one horse—and I the other. On reaching the goal he was half a neck ahead. It might be inferred from my remarks about hunting, that our mess table was kept well supplied with fresh game, however much we lacked many of the delicacies to be found in a large city market.

On last Christmas we had on our bill of fare, bear meat, buffalo tongue, prairie hen or grouse, venison, wild turkey, duck, goose, quail, and pigeons. Usually, however, we have only one or two kinds of game at a time. Pigeons are rarely to be found in this vicinity; but occasionally make their appearance in vast flocks, as was the case for a few days in the latter part of last December. They were attracted hither by the mast or post-oak acorns, to be found in the oak groves in this country. In mess arrangements, there is a marked distinction between the army and navy. In the latter, there are several grades and divisions of messes even among the commissioned officers—such as the steerage mess, embracing mostly the midshipmen and assistant engineers; the wardroom mess, including medical officers, paymasters or pursers, chief engineers, chaplain, sailing-master and lieutenants; the captain's mess—and if a flag-ship, the commodore's mess. In the former all commissioned officers are welcomed to the mess—although in some garrisons the commanding officer lives by himself. The army regulations seem to contemplate this action on the part of the officer in command, as it allows him extra pay in the form of double rations for the purpose of entertainment. Most of the entertaining, however, is generally done by the officers' mess, whether the double rationed individual happens to be a member or not. Of course no non-commissioned officer, or other person below the grade of brevet-lieutenant, ever becomes a member of the mess.

We have not yet received many calls from the wild Indians of the prairies, but frequently see small parties of Delawares, Kickapoos, Osages, Choctaws, Chickasaws, Cherokees, Seminoles and Creeks. A large band of the latter tribe passed our camp on the twenty-third of last October, having in custody some sixty colored slaves, who had run away from their masters, the Creeks, and followed Wild Cat, a Seminole chief of Floridian notoriety, through the wild Indian country toward Mexico. When their masters found them they were prisoners of the Comanches, who demanded, and received, a ransom for giving them up. The darkeys, on being redeemed from capture, declined to return with their masters in a peaceable manner, and made an abortive attempt to escape. Their obstinancy provoked a bloody encounter with the Creeks, as was evinced by the number of wounded I saw among the negroes.

The Creeks and Seminoles are our nearest neighbors, yet have no settlement in the immediate vicinity of the garrison. Most of the latter tribe have left the hammocks and swamps of Florida, where they cost the government so many valuable lives and millions of money, and are living in a country just south of that lately set apart for the Creeks, who are, in their turn, south of the Cherokees. It was owing to an attempt by the United States to remove the Seminole Indians to the district now occupied by them, that induced these Indians, under their head sachem, Micanopy, to begin in 1835 a most harassing war upon the white settlers of Florida and Georgia.

Notwithstanding the large number of United States troops sent to quell the disturbances, the war lasted for nearly seven years.

The Creeks also gave the government trouble when about being sent from Georgia and Alabama to their present abode; and at one time made common cause with their neighbors, the hostile Seminoles. There are still a few of the latter Indians in the swamps and everglades of Florida. It will not be long before all of them will be induced to come to this new country. Major Garnott, United States army, whom I met at

Little Rock, and again at Fort Smith, had a few of them with him.

In conversation the other day with one of their head chiefs he told me he remembered me well; as he often saw me in Florida during the war. As I had previously considered myself a very youthful person, I immediately consulted my glass for evidence of old age. But finally came to the conclusion that my visitor had poor eyesight.

The Seminoles and Creeks speak the same language, and in fact belong to the same nation. The former word in their tongue signifying runaways, because they separated in a body from the rest of their people when living east of the Mississippi river; and emigrated further south, into the region now embraced in the State of Florida, where they gradually extended their dominion until they had nearly annihilated a numerous band of Indians called the Euchees—a remnant of whom they subsequently adopted as a part of their own tribe.

The band of Creeks, which passed our camp last October, fired the prairie near by. The government, and officers, myself among the number, having a large supply of hay endangered by the fire, Lieutenant Updegraff was ordered by Captain Marcy to take a few men and fire a broad circle around the hay, so as to prevent its burning up. He was strictly enjoined to be cautious to keep the fire, to be made by his party, well under command; and in order to do so, it was suggested to him to burn very small patches at a time. The Lieutenant desired to know if the commanding officer thought that he, who had been raised in the west, and read Shakspeare all his life, was devoid of common practical sense.

The upshot of the whole matter was, that owing to a sudden change in the wind, and the grass not being very dry, the prairie fire did not come near the ricks of hay, but Updegraff's fire did, and consumed them all. After that incident, if one happened, in conversation with the Lieutenant, to use the interjection *hey!* he would boil over in a moment.

After witnessing the feeble flickering of the prairie fire just mentioned, I began to suspect that travelers had drawn largely on their imaginations to call such conflagrations sublime. I did not make sufficient allowance for the greenness of the grass, the absence of strong winds, and the presence of daylight. A few weeks subsequently, when the grass had become withered and parched, the surrounding prairies caught fire in various places. The strong wind prevailing at the time was soon accelerated by the heat into a hurricane—thus causing the fiery element to spread with amazing rapidity, forming almost an unbroken circle around the camp as a common focus. It being a dark and cloudy night, the sea of fire illuminated the heavens with a reddish yellow glare, as though the very elements were about to melt in fervent heat. Oh, that I had the power to convey some faint idea of this sublime sight. Imagine the ocean lashed in billows by the tempest; until the crests of her dashing, roaring, thundering mountain billows seem to reach the sky—instead of water let these swelling waves be flames of liquid fire rolling in wild fury over all barriers; and you may then have some idea of the awful grandeur of the scene of a prairie on fire on a dark stormy night.

Under such circumstances one is vividly impressed with the sublimity of the following lines of the poet:

> "When wrapt in flames the realms of ether glow,
> And heaven's last thunder shakes the world below.

To add to the wildness of the scene, on the night in question, vast flocks of white cranes, of swan, and wild geese, flew to and fro over the lurid flames in utter bewilderment and consternation. Although these fires are sometimes started by accident, yet they are more frequently kindled to afford easier traveling for the Indians, and to secure a fresh crop of grass for their horses.

Before the commanding officer could decide definitely the exact location of the new post to be established on Wild Horse Creek, a tributary of the false Washita river—some twenty-five miles in a direct line south of our present camp—it became necessary for me, as medical officer, to report upon its medical topography, and probable healthfulness.

Accordingly Updegraff and I made the trip there and back, without even seeing a wild Indian, although it was apprehended at the time of our starting that we might be ambushed by roaming bands of Comanches. Sleeping on the ground, wrapped in a blanket, is not at all unpleasant in moderately fine weather, except when mosquitos, tarantulas, centipedes, scorpions, or snakes, become too sociable.

This whole region abounds in insects and reptiles. It is no uncommon occurrence for a traveler in this country, on awaking in the morning, to find a rattlesnake in his bed, or a centipede in his hat, or a most hideous chill-inspiring tarantula in his boot. Everybody knows how venomous the bites of these horrid creatures are. Horses have an instinctive dread of them—especially of the rattlesnake. My Comanche horse will jump ten feet at the sudden rattle of one of these reptiles. And, if made to approach within a few feet of one, will tremble like an aspen leaf. A very common plant in these western prairies is one known as the rattle-weed, which derives its name from the fact that its pod is full of loose seed, and makes a rattling noise when dry, if touched by the passer-by. Both man and beast are often frightened at the similarity of sound of this insignificant weed to that produced by the dreaded rattlesnake. I presume that the rattle-weed, like hundreds of more beautiful flowers that decorate our south-western prairies, and render this region more entitled to the name of the land of flowers than even Florida itself, has its use, although as yet unknown.

There is on these vast natural meadows a very useful, as well as curious, plant, called the compass-plant, because the edges of its broad leaves point due north and south—thus enabling the traveler, by observing their general direction, to know what course to pursue. I have never heard any explanation of this phenomenon, but presume it is owing to the fact that the strongest and most prevalent winds are from the south during the early growth of the plant, and that the leaves are thus forced to present their edges, instead of their broad faces to the breeze.

The traveler in the prairie, if without a compass, will observe this plant by day, and the heavenly dipper by night—whereas the person who is trying to find his way through the woods in the timbered bottoms, will look on which part of the trees the moss is generally found, knowing that it grows most abundantly on the north side. Observations on these natural phenomena are often indispensable to the backwoodsman or prairie traveler.

Every officer, private soldier, and other employee of the government, with the exception of myself, at this camp, have had a spell of some form of malarious fever, during our short sojourn at this place. Of course, they were not all sick at the same time; although at one period last autumn there were hardly well ones enough to carry on the regular routine of garrison duties. In this connection I am forcibly reminded of the trip of the First Regiment of Dragoons, under General Leavenworth, a few years ago, through this region to the heart of the Comanche country; and of its sufferings from a low type of malarial or intermittent and remittent fevers.

Before the return of the expedition to Fort Gibson, several commissioned officers, and a large number of the men, sickened and died. The gallant commander himself might have recovered from an injury received in pursuit of a buffalo, as already mentioned, had not a miasmatic fever complicated his disease.

A fort established by the Dragoons, several years ago, on the Canadian river, between here and Fort Gibson, had soon to be abandoned on account of the extreme prevalence of malarial fevers. How we shall fare in this respect at our new camp remains to be seen. We receive the mail here, by an expressman sent to Fort Washita, every two weeks. Only those persons exiled as we are, from society, friends, home and the daily activity of the great world, can fully realize the intense interest we all take in the arrival of the mail-carrier. After reading our letters, and perusing the leading newspapers, and magazines, of the day, we feel as though there are many things in this great world of more importance than hunting; or standing guard on the frontier, to prevent encroachments of a lot of naked and wild savages against others of their race, removed only a few degrees higher in the scale of civilization—such as the partially civilized Chickasaws, Choctaws, Creeks and Cherokees.

Our letters, of course, do not always bring good news, but occasionally tidings of bereavement and death. In my last letter from home is the sad announcement that grandfather Glisan is no more. He lived to the mature old age of eighty-nine. By his industry and thrift he accumulated vast wealth for a farmer; yet never traveled beyond the limits of his native State of Maryland. He owned at one period a large number of negroes, but emancipated them all before his death, and bequeathed to each of them, living at his decease, a handsome legacy. He was an honest, intelligent, useful and charitable man—and will be greatly missed in the community where he lived and died.

INDIAN GRAVE ON THE PLAINS.—Page 111.

CHAPTER VII.

ESTABLISHMENT OF FORT ARBUCKLE.

Change of Location—View of the Washita Valley—Graves of Comanches—Habits and Customs of these Indians—Their Hostility to the Government—and Threats to Drive everybody out of the Country—An Unoccupied Field for Missionaries among them—To Chastise them Mounted Troops Indispensable—Recruits Worthless—Comanches at home on Horseback—How they Subsist and Clothe themselves—They Approach both Friend and Foe in a Run.

FORT ARBUCKLE, INDIAN TERRITORY, April 25th, 1851.

WE are now encamped in a beautiful oak grove, near Wild Horse Creek, and south of our late camp on the Canadian, twenty-five, and of the Washita river four miles; west of the State of Arkansas two hundred, and north of Texas forty miles.

It is here that we are ordered to build a permanent post, which is to be called Fort Arbuckle, although not yet officially recognized by this name. Our latitude is 34° 27′ north, and longitude 97° 09′ west of Greenwich. East and west of us are lovely undulating prairies swelling gradually southward into mountain ridges, with an elevation of five hundred feet above the bed of the Washita.

To-day several friends and myself rode to the summits of several of these mountain peaks, and enjoyed one of the most enchanting landscape views in the world. Below us lay an almost boundless plain, with gracefully swelling mounds and ridges here and there, and fringes of timber skirting the Washita, Wild Horse Creek, and other streams. We could take in at a *coup-d'œil*, a scope of about fifty miles. Although we were twenty-five miles in a direct line from old Camp Arbuckle, yet we could distinctly see a grove of oak in its immediate vicinity.

On these mountains we found several mounds of stone, where had been deposited from time to time the last remains of many of the primeval lords of the soil —probably Comanches; as the skeletons, though disturbed by the wolves, indicate that the dead were originally placed with their faces toward the rising sun. These people always bury their warriors on the summits of the highest hills and mountain spurs, facing to the east—probably out of respect to the sun, which they worship as a mediator between them and their Heavenly Chief.

The Comanche Heaven is a great plain, covered with grass forever green, and dotted over with vast herds of antelope, deer, and buffalo. There the greatest degree of happiness is allowed to the man who has stolen the most horses, and taken the largest number of scalps in this world.

In the plain below us were the bleached skeletons of numerous buffaloes. Although a few of these noble animals are still occasionally seen in this neighborhood, they no longer come here in vast herds, as has been the case until quite recently. Could the warriors who now lie sleeping in their mountain graves come forth and tell us of the scenes they have beheld in the vale below, we should probably hear not only of many exciting chases after buffalo, but of great battles that have been lost and won by contending tribes of red men. Doubtless the green carpet of grass that now covers the surrounding valley, has often been crimsoned o'er by the life-current of thousands of these benighted but brave human beings. 'Tis sad to think that there is no place on God's earth so beautiful and retired, that the demon of war, with all his destructive train, dare not enter. If the poor Indian could live in peace and harmony, what an Eden he would have in this lovely country.

The evil genii of war, pestilence, and famine accompany man in all stages of civilization, from the savage Comanche, who roams over the vast plains between here and the Rocky Mountains, up to the inhabitants of civilized Europe, who are surrounded by all the appliances of intellectual, moral, and Christian developments. Thus it has ever been and must forever be, until the Archangel's trump shall sound the resurrection morn. My heart almost bleeds when I think of man's inhumanity to man. 'Tis so strange that we cannot live out our short span of threescore years and ten in peace and harmony, but must always be contending with our fellow-travelers along the journey of life.

Christianity has done much to soften the asperities of human nature; but a vast field of labor still invites her energy and constant vigilance, before the world can be ready for the millenium. There is as yet an untried field for the work of our missionaries among the Indians of the south-western plains, who have never heard a word of the gospel of our Lord and Saviour. The Sioux, Pawnees, and Blackfeet in the northwest, and the Nez Perces, Walla Wallas, Umatillas, Palouses, and Cœur-de-lanes, of the Territory of

Oregon, have had missionaries sent among them by the General Missionary Board; but, so far as I have been enabled to learn, no one has ever tried to hoist the Cross among the Comanches, Apaches, and other large tribes roaming over the extensive south-western plains; for the reason, I presume, that these Indians are dangerously hostile nearly all the time. They consider stealing one of the cardinal virtues—especially purloining mules and horses from Mexico, whom the United States is bound by treaty to protect from their depredations. They also look upon New Mexico and Texas as natural fields for their predatory operations. Possessed of these false notions of right and wrong, and knowing little, and caring less, of the power of the United States, they are continually bringing themselves into disrepute and open hostilities with the Government.

Shortly after General Leavenworth's expedition among the Comanches, a few years ago, they solicited and allowed traders to come into their country; but recently these venturesome merchants have been plundered, murdered, or forced to flee for their lives. Not even Choctaws, Chickasaws, Cherokees, Delawares or Kickapoos, dare go among them at present.

Whether it is more desirable to attempt conciliating these savage freebooters, or send a large force into their country, and teach them to respect the government of the United States, and afterward offer them terms of peace and friendship, is a hard problem for the Indian and War Departments to solve. My old professor of physiology used to say: "Gentlemen, the first step in digestion is not, as laid down in the books,

COMANCHE HORSEMEN.—Page 78.

'mastication,' but 'food to masticate.'" So, if we go to war with the Comanches, the first step in thrashing them is to catch them. This cannot be done by infantry or foot soldiers alone.

Ten regiments of this species of troops might be sent into the Comanche country, and kept there for years, without even seeing one of these Indians, unless he choose to exhibit himself—for the simple reason that they are the most superior riders in the world, and can elude the enemy as often as they please. All they have to do is to station here and there behind the little hillocks in the prairie, sentinels, who have their horses screened from view near by; and, as the slow procession of blue coats and blue buttons, moves onward with burnished muskets flashing their reflected light from the sun far and near, like so many calcium illuminators, and with their long train of baggage wagons and noisy teamsters bringing up the rear, the Comanche guard peeps through a bunch of prairie grass held up before his keen visage, and notes the progress of Uncle Sam's warriors so long as he pleases, and then adroitly mounts his fleet horse, and sails, undiscovered, over the prairie, to report the result of his reconnoissance to his chief; who lets his band either remain where they are, or prepares them to fight or flee as the emergency seems to dictate.

The infantry are suitable enough to guard the cordon of posts now being established along our southwestern frontier; but for an effective campaign against these Arabs of the southwest, we must send mostly cavalry, with a small proportion of artillery and infantry; also, a few companies of Texas Rangers or other western troops well trained in riding and the use of firearms.

In such an expedition it is better not to be encumbered with raw recruits, who should be left in garrison with the assurance, that when the dead march is played over their coffins, they will be in possession of their scalps; which happy condition might not obtain, were they to come in contact with those tonsorial manipulators of the occipital protuberance, whose affection for their pale face brothers is so deep, that they are desirous of its perpetual remembrance by such affecting souvenirs as locks of hair.

The natural home of the Comanche is on horseback. He is trained to ride from early infancy. On foot his gait is clumsy in the extreme. He walks very much like an old sailor who has not been ashore sufficiently long to divest him of his sea-legs. That is, he steps as though the earth were moving to and fro under him, and might trip him up, if not on his guard. So the sailor, when first on shore, perambulates in a kind of jogging, spread-leg style to keep his centre of gravity, the same as though he were on the deck of his vessel in a storm, with her bow and stern alternately rising up and bobbing down, in riding over the billows—with an occasional lurch sideways as she trembles in the trough of the sea.

The most remarkable of all their equestrian feats is the ability of dropping the body on either side of the horse under full speed, and thus screening every part of the person from the enemy on the opposite side, excepting the heel of one foot, which is left hanging over the horse's back. While in this posture the rider has the power of throwing his arrow, or using his lance, over or under the animal's neck. He is assisted in retaining his position by allowing one of his arms to fall through a hair loop, or sling, attached to the horse's mane.

These Indians number about sixteen thousand souls. Fresh meat, with occasionally a few berries, or wild plants, is their only food. The buffaloes afford them food, raiment and skins, with which to construct their lodges. Antelopes, deer, and other small animals are also eaten by them, and in times of great scarcity of wild game, they use the flesh of their horses, mules and dogs. The skins of the smaller animals, when dressed, make them good moccasins, leggins, and breech-clouts. The warriors use only the latter articles of clothing when on the war path—but, at other times, cover the upper portion of their bodies with dressed buffalo skins or robes.

With rare exceptions they have not yet learned the use of firearms, but hunt and fight with the bow and arrow, and lance, which they wield with wondrous expertness. They are trained to the use of these weapons from childhood. They hunt and fight on horseback. Dashing into a herd of buffalo they ride along side of their victims until an opportunity occurs for a fair shot, when the swift arrows are sent whizzing into the vitals of the poor animals, who soon tumble to the ground with their life-blood spurting in red currents from the mortal wounds.

As none of the men are considered of any account until after they have stolen a few mules or horses, and taken several scalps, it is very dangerous for a white man to meet two or three, or a small party, of young fellows on the prairie, even at times when the main body of these people profess to be friendly. The Comanches, and the prairie Indians generally, have a disagreeable custom of approaching strangers with their horses in a run, both when they are friendly and when hostile.

They should never be allowed to come too near until they have shown by pantomimic signs that they are friendly, and not even then if the party approached has any doubts of their friendship, or if he is alone; in which event it is better to make signs to them to keep away. If they pay no attention to his signals, and he be mounted, he should retreat for the nearest thicket or woods. If too closely pursued he might wheel and point his gun at the foremost, but not fire unless his gun has a revolving chamber with more than one load. For his pursuers are far more apt to continue the chase after the discharge of the weapon than before, as there can be no chance to reload. Still a general rule will not apply to all cases. A person must act in accordance with the particular circumstances attending each case. If there be only two or three Indians, and they come upon you unawares, and cut off your retreat, it is better to act as I did in a similar emergency, as related a few pages back.

INDIAN PONY IN AUTUMN.

IN SPRING.—Page 80.

CHAPTER VIII.

BUILDING THE FORT—HUNTING ADVENTURES.

Erection of Quarters—Whisky Dealers—Hospital Steward—Reflections upon the Evils of Intemperance—The Fifth Infantry to be relieved by the Seventh—Separation of Families—Vow of Celibacy while in the Army—Violent Storms—Rattlesnakes seek shelter in Mess Tent, and beneath my Bed—The Wild Indians threaten to combine and drive us out of the Country—Death of two Officers of the Fifth Infantry—Fish, Birds and Animals—My Hunting Companion, Lieutenant Pearce; He frightens me terribly by screaming at a Rattlesnake; Our Turkey Hunt; Delaware and Shawnee Indians as Guides—The Kickapoos—First Lady in Garrison—Respect for Females by Civilized and Uncivilized People.

FORT ARBUCKLE, INDIAN TERRITORY, May 12th, 1851.

WE are living, and are expecting to live for some months, in tents. The carpenters and extra-duty men are engaged in erecting the men's barracks; which will be built of hewn logs, with the chinks stopped with small pieces of wood and clay loam. The floors will be of puncheons, and the roofs of clapboards. The chimneys will be constructed of stone and clay. The buildings will be arranged into an oblong rectangular parallelogram, with a line of barracks on each side for the men—the commissary and quartermaster buildings at one end, and the officers' quarters at the other. The hospital, which will be erected so soon as the private soldiers are under cover, will be a long one-story log building, divided into four compartments—one of which will be used as a dispensary, with the steward's room adjoining—the next two as wards for the sick—and the fourth as a kitchen. This building will be erected a short distance outside of the garrison.

The sutler's store is about a hundred yards north of the commissary buildings. Just under the brow of the hill is a limpid spring of icy water, gushing forth in a stream powerful enough for a first-class water power. It would be a great blessing if the men were content with this wholesome beverage of nature; but such is not the case. Although they, in common with their officers, are here to uphold the laws of their country in preventing the introduction of spirituous liquors into the Indian country, some of them not only connive at its being brought here, but solicit its illicit sale—at least to themselves. However faithful soldiers may be in all other respects, there is no dependence to be placed in many of them in regard to the indulgence in strong drink.

There are always a few reckless itinerant whisky dealers who know when pay-day comes, and by secreting themselves in the vicinity of the post, manage to rob the men of their money, their senses and health, in defiance of the utmost vigilance of the officers. Uncle Sam's soldiers are not famous for strictly temperate principles. Fortunately the price of intoxicating spirits is, in this isolated place, so high that even the most inveterate tiplers cannot afford the indulgence of a big spree very frequently.

Most of the Comanches, and several other tribes of wild Indians, have not yet acquired the habit of strong drink. 'Tis sad to think that it will be one of the first lessons taught them by the march of civilization. For they learn the white man's bad habits much more readily and quickly than his good ones.

To-day I had to reduce my Hospital Steward to the ranks. This is very discouraging to me; as, independently of other inconvenience arising from this necessity, I shall have to undertake the tedious duty of educating another person into the profession of apothecary. The history of this man is a sad warning to the devotees of Bacchus. He is reported to be of good parentage, and very respectably connected. At one time he was an officer in the British navy; from which he was dismissed on account of his habits of intemperance. How and when he came to the United States I do not know. He has served for several years as a private soldier in our army. His only brother is one of the most eminent physicians in Texas.

On joining this command I was truly gratified to find so intelligent and capable a man as steward. It appears that he was then under an oath not to drink for six months. In a very short time, however, he commenced using the hospital liquors to excess. Upon being discovered and reprimanded, he promised faithfully never to drink any more. It was not long ere he got on another spree, and, in the absence of other stimulants, drank hospital alcohol. Being reduced to the position of a private soldier for this offense, and seeming so exceedingly penitent, I again had him appointed. In one week from this time he secretly drank a gallon of alcohol—the other hospital liquors being out of his reach. This last misdemeanor is the cause of his final disgrace.

Thus thousands upon thousands of worthy and talented men sacrifice themselves, and destroy the peace and happiness of their families and friends by yielding to the growing evil of intemperance. But the votaries of strong drink are not confined to the sterner sex alone, as may be seen at almost every fashionable gathering, and at many a ruined home. Alas! alas! for the weakness of humanity. I sometimes grow impatient at the utter foolishness, insaneness, and wickedness, of men and women in destroying so much usefulness and happiness by cultivating a taste for alcoholic drinks.

One would think that at least professing Christians, and especially the clergy of all denominations, would eschew this evil, and lend all their influence against it; but, unfortunately, some few of these persons lead the way in setting for the rising generation an example which will do more toward luring them into the pitfall of drunkenness and perdition, and in bringing discredit on the holy name of religion itself, than all other causes combined.

Although there may be no intrinsic wrong in a Christian, or anybody else, taking a drink of intoxicating liquor when viewed in the simple act itself, yet there is a sin in so doing when he knows that a craving appetite for the same is almost sure to be generated if the habit of moderate drinking is kept up for any length of time. Besides we are enjoined by the Bible to refrain from the appearance of evil—that our brother may not be led into temptation.

If there is anything under the sun upon which I have positive convictions, it is on the dreadful evils of intemperance. I hope the time will come when the wine-cup and flowing bowl will only be known in the history of the past. Some professing Christians think they are justified in the use of alcoholic stimulants because St. Paul wrote to Timothy to take a little wine for his stomach's sake. But they should bear in mind that the latter was in ill-health, and that the former advised the wine as a medicine. There are some cases of sickness where its use is justifiable—but many of the physicians of the present day will have a fearful accountability in the next world when brought face to face with many of their forever-doomed patients, who will cry out that their sad fate was owing to the doctor's prescription of brandy or wine three or four times daily, for months and years at a time.

Orders have arrived for the Fifth Infantry to proceed further south so soon as relieved by the Seventh Infantry. The company here is one of the ten that will go. It is not known whether I am to accompany the troops or not. Some of the officers of the former regiment, being stationed at moderately pleasant frontier posts, have with them their families, from whom they must now separate. Such is army life.

Unless that little rogue, Cupid, should let his shafts pierce my heart when least expected, I shall endeavor to trudge my lonely way as heretofore, with no angelic hand to press my feverish brow when ill, or sooth my anguished soul when oppressed with harassing care; because this constant parting between husband, wife, and children, is far worse than having none from whom to separate.

For the next few years I shall be ever willing and ready to go wherever duty calls—but I hope the day is not distant when I shall be able to say good bye to the mess-pots of Uncle Sam.

June 7th.—We had a violent storm night before and last night. The rain descended in torrents. It was alarming only so far as there was danger of uprooted trees falling on our canvas domiciles. Sleeping in a tent, though disagreeable in a hurricane, is delightful in pleasant weather—unless lizards, tarantulas, mosquitoes, centipedes and snakes become too sociable. The jingle of a rattlesnake's tail is not the most musical announcement of breakfast, yet one of these monsters, six feet in length, with fifteen rattles, was killed in our mess-tent this morning—and one of his hideous relatives took shelter from the howling blasts beneath the boxes that served me as a bedstead. Doubtless these reptiles imagine that they have as good a right to this country as anybody else. Still I must protest against the freedom of their manners.

The Fifth Regiment of Infantry have received orders to concentrate at the Brazos, preparatory to the assignment of the companies to their respective stations. Portions of Seventh have already arrived in this department. The two companies which are to be stationed at this place are within a few day's march of here. The probability is that I shall remain at this post.

The appearance of so many troops in the Indian country has caused great excitement among the wild tribes. It is reported among them that the United States troops have declared war against all of the prairie Indians. The latter threaten to combine, and drive the blue-coats out of the country.

December 15th, 1851.—Several months have rolled around since I have attempted to make any record of events. During that time very few things of any interest have occurred.

The two expected companies (G and H) did not arrive until the eleventh of June. The officers were Major George Andrews, in command; Brevet-Major John C. Henshaw; Lieutenants Thomas Henry, Nicholas B. Pearce and William L. Cabell.

Captain Marcy's company, of the Fifth, remained with us a few days, and then left via Fort Washita for the Brazos. Subsequently the whole Fifth Regiment of Infantry concentrated at the latter place. Instead of being distributed at several posts the intention is now, by order of General Smith, to garrison but two new ones—one at the Brazos river, where the General's headquarters will be; and the other on the Clear Fork, of the same river. There have been two deaths among the officers of that regiment since last June—Lieutenant Patrick A. Farelly and the Colonel of the regiment, Brevet Brig.-Gen. Wm. G. Belknap. The latter died but a few weeks since, while on his way from the Brazos to Fort Washita. Being an invalid, he was conveyed in an ambulance, accompanied by a few friends, who just before reaching the latter post had occasion to absent themselves from the vehicle a short time. One of them returning in a little while found the General dead.

The corporal in charge stated that whilst the team

was moving slowly onward he heard a groan, when he immediately ran to the General—and lo! the vital spark had fled. His spirit had taken its flight to "that undiscovered country, from whose bourne no traveler returns." He has left a most interesting family to mourn his loss. May the God of mercy comfort and console them in their great and almost overwhelming affliction.

Major Andrews remained with us but a few weeks, when, in consequence of the death of Brevet Brig.-General Mathew Arbuckle, who commanded the Seventh Military Department, he was ordered to return to Fort Gibson. The General was an upright, intelligent officer; but his military career has not been very brilliant. Still he has seen a great deal of arduous frontier service. Feeble health prevented his taking a very active part in the Mexican War, which afforded an opportunity for distinction to so many of our gallant officers. Col. Henry Wilson succeeded him in command of the department.

During the past summer, when not engaged in garrison duties, and scouting expeditions among the Indians, we amused ourselves in fishing and hunting. The turbid rivers are full of buffalo-fish, suckers, eels, turtles and cat-fish. The purer streams from the hills abound in fresh water bass, sunfish, perch, and silver-sides.

The birds and animals most common to this country, that are good for food, are teal, summer and mallard duck; plover, lark, robin, prairie grouse, quail, snipe, wild geese, brant, swan, wild pigeon, wild turkey, grey and white crane, white and black tail deer, antelope,

RATTLESNAKE CAMP.—Page 86.

beaver, black bear, hare, raccoon, opossum, the grey, black and fox squirrel, and buffalo within fifteen miles; of the birds and animals not usually eatable, there are the bird of paradise, reg-winged and rusty-winged blackbird, blue-bird, buzzard, crow, dove, dipper or di-dapper, eagle, owl, prairie and fish hawk, English mocking-bird, humming-bird, king-fisher, pewee, red-bird, raven, sparrow, swallow, sap-sucker, woodpecker, whip-poor-will, bull-bat, wren, yellow-bird, mouse, gopher, prairie-dog, panther, skunk, grey and black fox, wild-cat, coyote, black and grey wolves, rat, and mustang.

My almost constant companion, in hunting, is a handsome, generous-hearted and gallant young lieutenant, who was known at West Point by the sobriquet of Nota-Bene Pearce, because his first initials are N. B., for Nicholas Bart. Being reared in Kentucky, he is, of course, at home in the saddle, with a gun on his back. Although a splendid marksman, and successful hunter, his great excitability has more than once alarmed me, and even imperiled my life.

On one occasion, as we were walking through a post-oak grove, a rabbit sprang up, and wheeled around so as to describe a part of a circle. The trees prevented Pearce from drawing a bead on his game until his line of sight almost covered me as well as the rabbit. The concussion of his gun stunned me; and for a moment I thought my left ear was torn off, but it turned out to be only a little burnt from the powder. At another time we were hunting in a dense thicket in the Wild Horse Creek bottom, when I was taken with hemorrhage from the nose. While bathing my face in the cool water of a brook, our attention was attracted by the barking of our dog a few hundred yards off. Pearce immediately dashed off to ascertain what game was held at bay by old Zeb. In a short time I heard a most fearful scream, followed instantly by the report of a gun. Then all was as silent as the grave. Fearing that he had been ambushed by lurking savages, I cautiously approached in the direction of the sound, and found the Lieutenant standing at the foot of a bluff bank reloading his gun. He motioned to me, in a very excited manner, to look at something near where I had chanced to stop; when I beheld an enormous rattle-snake lying at the foot of a tree, writhing in the last agony of death. It appears that on nearing the place where the dog was barking, Pearce suddenly came upon this huge serpent, which springing its warning rattle, and darting at his legs, caused him to leap over a fifteen feet bluff bank, yelling like an Indian. On landing out of harm's way he wheeled and fired.

On rebuking him for alarming me, he stated that having been bitten by a snake in his youth, he could not help screaming at the bare sight of this horrid reptile.

Although generous to a fault, he cannot bear the idea of any one being more successful in a hunt than himself. The natural consequence is that I occasionally make him a little envious by my nigger-luck, as he is pleased to term it. For instance, during the past summer, we started out on horseback to a hunting ground about seven miles down the Washita.

river. Not seeing anything to shoot, we were on the eve of returning, when our dogs flushed a gang of wild turkeys; some of which lit in a large cottonwood tree, about six hundred yards distant. Pearce impetuously tore through the thicket in pursuit of the game; not having on a full buckskin suit like himself, I preferred to leave the prize to him.

During his absence I discovered an enormous gang of turkeys at the head of a lake near by, quenching their thirst. Whilst crawling up for a shot I came suddenly upon another flock, so near me that it seemed impossible at first view to kill more than one, as the load of shot could not scatter much at so short a distance. I aimed so as to hit the head of one, the wing of a second, and body of a third; all three of which I killed. As the remainder rose I fired the other barrel, bringing down two more—five in one discharge of a double-barreled shotgun.

In a few minutes thereafter Pearce made his appearance with only one trophy of his late exertion, and said "dog gone you, Galen, where did you get those turkeys; I didn't hear you fire but twice?" Having explained the matter to him he was anxious to extend the hunt, but I protesting, we turned our horses' heads toward garrison. On our way thither a noble gobbler ran across the trail just ahead of us—when the Lieutenant hurriedly dismounted, and started in pursuit. His sudden action stampeded his pony, which ran off with the turkey already killed. However my friend succeeded in shooting the gobbler, and finding the runaway animal; but never fully forgave me for bringing home more game than he did.

Among the numerous small tribes of Indians who occasionally visit our post none present a more romantic history, or are more intelligent, than the Delawares and Shawnees. They are closely related to each other, having intermarried and lived together for nearly two hundred years. A small band of them, under the control of the famous guide, Black Beaver, at present occupy our deserted camp near the Canadian river—another party of them live near the Missouri river, not far from Fort Leavenworth.

They make the most trustworthy and useful guides of any Indians in the country—from the fact of their exact knowledge of all parts of the West from the Mississippi river to the Pacific ocean—having traded, hunted and trapped among nearly every tribe of wild Indians in the United States. They do not live or hunt together, as a band, but divide up into small parties of from five to ten, and roam all over the continent. They go well armed with rifles, which they know how to use to perfection. The old Mississippi rifle, carrying a half-ounce ball, is a general favorite among them.

The Delawares once lived in the territory now embraced in New Jersey, Delaware, and the eastern part of Pennsylvania; and were at one time a numerous and warlike tribe. They have been forced, by the westward march of civilization, to change their abode oftener than any other tribe of Indians in North America. The mere fact of their being thus jostled and moved about so frequently, has helped to inculcate in them an almost incurable disposition to roam.

Our command ,being composed of infantry we cannot, of course, make any extensive scouts into the wild Indian country, but frequently have to go a short distance to arbitrate between contending tribes who encamp for awhile in our vicinity. On such occasions the experience of our Delaware friends, as guides and interpreters, is invaluable. Through their assistance we were enabled lately to prevent a big fight between the Kickapoos on one side and the Witchitas and Osages on the other. The trouble arose from the latter Indians stealing from the former a number of horses. The Kickapoos returned the compliment by stealing a still greater number from the Osages and Witchitas.

The Kickapoos have recently returned from a predatory expedition, in conjunction with the notorious Seminole chief, Wild Cat, along the Mexican settlements of the Colorado. They expect to remain in the vicinity of the fort till next spring, when their usual summer trip to the southwest will be undertaken. The Kickapoo Indians are not quite so intelligent as the Delawares. They can use both bow and rifle equally well, and are as brave as Spartans. There remain of this once formidable tribe only a few hundred warriors. These, however, are more than a match for many times their number of wild Indians.

Lieutenant Mathew R. Stevenson and wife have lately arrived. The latter is accomplished and quite pretty. Of course she is a great addition to our society.

> "O fairest of creation, last and best
> Of all God's works, creature in whom excelled,
> Whatever can to sight or thought be formed,
> Holy, divine, good, amiable, or sweet."

Such is woman. What would man do without her? How wonderful her influence in all conditions of life! Her magic spell has created and crushed empires. There is no surer proof of civilization than the degree of respect in which females are held. In proof of this assertion it is only necessary to allude to well known facts. The savage treats his wife as a servant—compelling her to do all the drudgery. If he lives by hunting, it is her province to properly prepare and cook the game, and to dress the hides. If he be civilized enough to raise a patch of melons, pumpkins, and corn, his squaw has to perform all the labor of cultivation. The husband shuns all work as beneath the dignity of the hunter and warrior. Even in courtship the woman's ability to perform manual labor is sometimes considered of as much importance as her beauty and social qualifications.

A few days ago I made some inquiries of an Indian by the name of Buck, concerning his mode of life, etc. Among other questions he was asked why he married such an old squaw? His reply was:—"Young woman no good—old squaw dress skins heap." Among the Comanches the women have no voice in the selection of a husband. Her father sells her for a certain amount of goods and chattels—such as blankets, horses, etc.; no marriage ceremony whatever being performed. Among the half-civilized Indians the female's choice is often consulted. When a Choctaw desires to marry, he presents his inamorata with a deer's leg, as emblematical of his calling. If his attentions are acceptable she gives him in return an ear of corn—signifying her willingness to be his companion, and to cultivate the field for him.

CHAPTER IX.

GARRISON LIFE IN THE INDIAN TERRITORY.

An Officer Court-martialed—Another Threat by the Comanches—Rumored Massacre of Captain Marcy and party—Kickapoo War Dance—Howling of Wolves creates a Stampede—Marcy Reads his own Obituary—Visit of the Kickapoos; much sickness among them; they Importune my Assistance—Another Christmas—Deprivations of Army Officers—A Warning to Young Ladies—Little Dug's fall into a Duck Pond—The tribes of Red skins who visit the post—Choctaw Law—Murder of Dr. Ward—Desertions—Trouble with the Kickapoos, Witchitaws and Wacos—Kickapoo Ball-play—Departure of Lieutenant Garland and Wife—Rare sport at Pigeon Shooting by myself in the Mountains—The Indians must change their Habits or be Annihilated—The Soldier Jack of all Trades—More Sad News from Home.

FORT ARBUCKLE, INDIAN TERRITORY, June 20th, 1852.

LIEUTENANTS Pearce and Cabell, having been assigned to other companies, left here about a month ago. We feel very disconsolate at the loss of two such agreeable companions. Our only consolation is the arrival of Lieutenant Robert R. Garland, and his charming wife.

The harmony of our little circle has recently been marred by the arrest, and trial, before a court-martial, of Lieutenant M. R. Stevenson, upon charges preferred against him by his commanding officer, Brevet-Major J. C. Henshaw. The court convened at Fort Gibson, and honorably acquitted the Lieutenant. On receiving and approving the proceedings, the Department Commander admonished the said Henshaw to desist in future from his usual tyrannical conduct toward his subordinates. Although Major Henshaw is intelligent, polite and agreeable, he seems, for some reason or other, to be under a regimental ban—or as some would express it, placed in coventry by the other officers of his regiment. Whether justly so or not I am as yet unable to determine. The general prejudice against him destroys his usefulness, and is sure to keep him in more or less contention all the while.

The garrison has been under some excitement during the last few days, in consequence of a rumor, that the Comanches are on their way hither to drive us out of the country. It is related by the Witchitaws, who have fled to this fort for protection, that the former tribe have thrown away all the presents and medals given them from time to time by the government, and have declared war against the whites, and all small bands of Indians friendly to the latter. The alleged cause of their august displeasure is the killing of six of their tribe, a few days since, while on a marauding trip on the frontier of Texas. The Comanches have lately killed several Indians friendly to the whites; but I hardly think they will attempt an attack on this post.

July 10th.—Madam rumor now insists that the Comanches lately attacked, and completely destroyed, the command of Captain R. B. Marcy. It will be remembered that this officer has been exploring Red river from Cache creek to its source, his command consisting of one hundred and twenty men, with the following officers:—Captain George B. McClellan, Corps of Engineers; Lieutenant Updegraff, Fifth Infantry; Dr. Shumard, of Fort Smith, and Captain J. H. Strain, the Sutler of Fort Washita. The Witch taws and Wacos bring the news, and pretend to give all the particulars. Although the story is plausible it is doubtless a hoax.

July 18th.—To-day we were entertained by the Kickapoos with a war dance. They seldom have these dances unless about to be engaged in war; or after a battle. No description can portray an accurate idea of the scene, which should be seen to be appreciated. Imagine some fifty copper-colored athletic, fierce-visaged men, bedaubed most hideously with red, black and yellow paint—the red and black so arranged on the face as to give the utmost savage appearance—their long hair bedecked with vari-colored feathers—no clothing except breech-cloths, leggins and moccasins, the majority having only the first articles, neck and arms covered with bear's claws, scalps, etc.: some having buffalo horns and red flannel attached to their heads, all excitedly engaged in an irregular succession of bobbing up and down, clapping of hands, groaning, whooping, yelling, running, jumping, tumbling, bodily contortions, various pantomimic motions, accompanied by the beating of rude drums, and blowing of squaking wind instruments, and you will have a faint idea of the performance. 'Tis said that all their motions have a meaning, which, when understood by spectators, render the dance decidedly interesting. At the conclusion of this dramatical exhibition the Commissary of Subsistence gave to the Indians a beef, upon which they feasted to their hearts' content; vowing all the while a faithful allegiance to the government in the event of hostilities with the Comanches.

Last night, about one A. M., I was aroused from my slumber by a most fearful howling beneath my quarters. Springing out of bed, and grasping my rifle, I soon learned that there was no cause for alarm, as the noise proceeded from a pack of rascally wolves, who had taken shelter beneath my floor. As they had frightened me, I returned the compliment by firing off my gun, and thus creating a very laughable stampede among my uninvited guests. The uproar ended in a general garrison fright.

July 28th.—Few persons live to read their own obituaries. Captain Marcy and his companions have had this rare satisfaction. For after the majority of their friends, and the public generally, had come to the conclusion that their scalps were ornamenting the war regalia of some of the Comanche chiefs, they had the boldness to return to life again. On arriving in garrison to-day, and learning the false report of their slaughter, they were greatly amused. However, in order to relieve the anxiety of relations, friends, and the public, a messenger was despatched to Fort Smith with the news of Marcy's return—to go thence by mail to Memphis, Tennessee; from which point a telegram can be sent to Washington City.

July 30th.—Captain Marcy and McClellan, Dr. Shumard, and Mr. Suydam, left this afternoon for the States. Marcy is going to Washington City; McClellan, via St. Louis, to San Antonia, Texas. Lieutenant Updegraff started about the same time for the Brazos, with the detachment of the Fifth Infantry, which had acted as escort to the expedition.

August 5th. A party of fifty dragoons, under the command of Lieutenant George H. Stewart, and accompanied by Dr. Taylor and Lieutenant Beall, arrived here this morning. One half of the men are from Fort Graham, and the other half from Fort Worth. Being in search of Captain Marcy's party, and having struck their return trail near the Witchita village, they followed it to this place, where they will remain a few days. The detachment consists of a fine-looking body of young men.

August 6th.—Paid a visit to-day to one of the two Kickapoo villages in this neighborhood. Their lodges are built in the form of ordinary log cabins, opening at the gable-end. But instead of logs, boards, etc., they consist of a framework of upright poles, bound together by cross and top pieces—the sides and roof being covered with bark. Their beds are elevated bunks made of sticks, over which lies the ever-useful buffalo skin, which serves as covering for the body by day, and bedding at night. There are about four hundred souls in the two camps. Although they generally build their temporary villages on high ground, they do not exercise much judgment in avoiding the poisonous exhalations from swamps, low river bottoms, and marshes, by shunning such places when possible—or, when impossible, of locating to the windward—the winds in this country coming steadily from certain directions in particular seasons. Consequently they suffer terribly from malarious diseases, and their protean complications. Having no specific or effective remedies among themselves for these complaints, they often importune my assistance. I cheerfully aid the poor wretches when they show a willingness to comply with my directions. But it is no easy matter to control such a set of superstitious creatures.

August 14th.—There being no chaplain at this post, I was requested by the commanding officer to read the funeral service over a deceased soldier.

> "Heaven from all creatures hides the book of fate,
> All but the page prescribed, their present state:
> From brutes what men, from men what spirits know:
> Or who could suffer being here below?"

November 11th.—Nothing unusual has occurred during the past few months. Much sickness in garrison at present—principally malarious fevers. The season has been unusually wet—vegetation rank and abundant—conditions invariably followed in this climate by miasmatic fevers, dysentery, etc.

No change in our little social circle—except that the two lieutenants and their wives were absent a few weeks in September and October, bringing with them on their return Miss Florence Burk, who starts back this morning for Fort Washita, where her parents reside; her father being Chaplain of that post.

December 25th, .1852—Christmas in garrison is celebrated by all the demonstrations of joy and good cheer, so far as available, customary in other places. We are generally invited to the quarters of one of the married officers to partake of such refreshments as are suitable to the occasion. At this post we are denied all those delightfully pleasant church festivities common to all civilized and christian communities, for the simple reason that we have no Chaplain. Let all young ladies who are dazzled with the glare of gilt buttons at some of the fashionable parties on East, bear these, and other deprivations, in mind, before saying "yes" to the fascinating sons of Mars. Let our lawmakers, who think the life of an officer is so easy that he is worthy of but little compensation, ponder over these things also.

When speaking of a Christmas dinner at old Camp Arbuckle, in 1850, I was disposed to brag a little about the numerous dishes of fresh meat that we had on the table. A two years residence in this country with little else to eat besides game, has changed my enthusiasm a great deal in this respect, and I now almost loathe wild ducks, geese, turkeys, grouse, etc. The palate demands a greater variety of eatables, especially fresh vegetables and fruits. With the exception of a few apples, obtained from Arkansas, we never get a sight of cultivated fruits, and rarely find any of the wild varieties in this vicinity. The few wild plums, etc., that grow near here are eaten by the Indians long before maturity. Even if our pay would allow the luxury, it would be impossible to transport ripe peaches, pears, plums, cherries, and similar delicious fruits, from the States. Being very fond of such things, I miss them greatly. We are not entirely deprived of vegetables, because they can be produced in our gardens. But fruit trees require many years of growth before being large enough to bear. A friend and myself planted a young orchard near our quarters, thinking that some person might perhaps reap the benefit in the course of time. Vacating the premises shortly thereafter to a married officer, we were disgusted to find that he could see no use in providing for the wants of others who might come after us, and that he let our young trees perish for want of attention.

Most new-comers are very fond of the pecan nut, which grows in this country. When my two young friends, Lieutenants Andrew W. Evans, and Henry Douglass, first joined the post they seemed as much delighted at the sight of a full-bearing pecan tree, as boys generally are of chestnut trees. Like almost everybody else, they soon grew tired of climbing for pecans, and took a fancy for hunting. They were glad to avail themselves of my older experience in the country to escort them to the choice hunting grounds—the soldiers and Indians making game exceedingly scarce in the immediate vicinity of garrison.

Among the many amusing incidents that occurred in these trips I am tempted to relate one that happened quite recently. One of my friends, whom we call little Dug, although taught the art of riding among other things at the West Point Military Academy, has such short legs that it is impossible for him to ever gain distinction for his equestrian feats. Having a penchant for small animals, on account of their activity, and perhaps cheapness, he invested, on his arrival in this country, in a small, active, and really beautiful little pony. So, mounted on this favorite charger, he accompanied Lieutenant Evans and myself one day on a hunting trip. On passing along the margin of a pond a fine mallard duck suddenly flew up—being in the lead I turned in my saddle and fired, with the satisfaction of seeing my game fall. Killing only one duck, but hearing two splashes, I looked behind, and beheld little Dug flat in the water, and his riderless pony kicking up his saucy heels at some distance in the prairie. The scene was quite ludicrous. Our day's sport was, however, spoiled, owing to the time it took to recapture the renegade animal. On another occasion, when Evans, Douglass and I were out hunting, the former's gun got caught in the bush, and accidently went off, narrowly missing Douglass and myself.

Lieutenant Evans remained at this post but a short time, when orders, from headquarters of the army, arrived detailing him on detached service. On the 12th instant we received a batch of recruits, accompanied by two officers of the Fifth Infantry, and Doctor Thomas A. McParlin, U. S. Army, an élève of the University of Maryland. Only persons isolated like ourselves, can fully realize how pleasant it is to receive calls from congenial visitors—especially from one's own corps. The Doctor and I discussed many pleasant reminiscences of the old university, and of Baltimore, where he has recently spent some time. His service has been mostly with dragoons in New Mexico. He is now on his way to Fort McIntosh, in Texas.

February 2d, 1853.—The month of January has been decidedly monotonous. The only change in our little circle has been the departure of our former sutler, James Stevens. He has gone to try his fortune at Fort Towson, where he has just been married to a Miss Gooding. May God's blessing attend him wherever his lot may be cast. His successor at this post, Captain J. H. Strain, appears to be a gentleman, and thorough going business man. His prospects are flattering, as the command is large, and the Indian trade increasing.

The tribes of "redskins" who visit this post are Choctaws, Chickasaws, Creeks, Seminoles, Shawnees, Delawares, Kickapoos, Caddos, Wacos, Witchitaws, Osages, Keechis, Tonkawas, Comanches, etc. I have already made some allusions to the Choctaws. The Chickasaws are a very similar class of people. They own none of this Territory, but only have a right to citizenship. It appears that some twenty years ago they paid the Choctaws $500,000 for the privilege of living in their country—being subject to the Choctaw laws; and having permission to till the soil wherever they pleased, but no fee simple title of the same. A citizen can locate and change his location as often as he pleases—being at no expense for the land, and having no taxes to pay.

A few enterprising farmers could make money in the neighborhood of this fort in raising corn, which is now worth $1.50 per bushel. The post is supplied at present with this necessary article by a Colonel Borelan, of Texas. He has to transport it a long distance.

The laws among the Choctaws, though fewer, are very similar to those of the States. The old saying that "law is not always justice," is most strikingly illustrated among these Indians. Men of wealth and influence can commit crimes with almost perfect immunity.

"Plate sin in gold,
And the strong lance of justice hurtless breaks;
Arm it with rags, a pigmy straw doth pierce it."

In illustration I shall simply allude to one of many like examples: P——, living some fifty miles from here, murdered a Doctor Ward, some four years ago. The act is stated to have been a most horrible and revolting one. He, and several of his friends, waylaid the Doctor, and after beating him almost to death, lodged complaint against him to the Indian Agent, who, under false representations from his accusers, sent the Doctor out of the country, into Texas.

A short time subsequently P——, and F——, succeeded in getting the Doctor on the Choctaw side of Red River unarmed, when they clubbed him until he was apparently dead. Finding on the following morning that life was not quite extinct, P—— made his colored man knock him in the head. This same negro was afterward whipped to death for divulging the matter. A reward was offered by the proper United States judiciary officer in Texas for the arrest of the murderers—but they are still going at large. One of them was here a few days ago.

March 28th.—Quite an excitement here lately in the way of desertions. Since the paymaster paid the troops, on the first of the month, sixteen recruits have deserted. Only two have been captured so far. They escape into Texas. A detachment has been sent to-day in pursuit. The penalty for desertion is very severe. As much as I dislike to see a man whipped, it would be a satisfaction to see some of these lazy fellows severely punished. They are nearly all foreigners, and have just received from five to ten months pay, without rendering any service whatever to the government.

We have been amusing ourselves occasionally this spring by fishing. On the fourth and fifth of March, Lieutenant Garland and myself caught a fine lot of buffalo-fish with grub-worms. The largest weighed ten pounds. This fish is large and broad, and has a sucker mouth—the meat being coarse.

April 8th, 1853.—We have lately had trouble with one of the two bands of Kickapoos encamped in this vicinity. Having illegally introduced liquor into the country, they got on a big spree, and became very noisy and troublesome. The commanding officer sent a detachment of infantry to arrest such of the Indians as were known to have been guilty of bringing ardent spirits into the nation. The Kickapoos surrendered two Cayan-kashaws, but declined giving up any of their own tribe; until preparations were made to march against them in full force; when they finally submitted to the demands of the government. For awhile, however, things presented quite a warlike appearance. Had a battle ensued both bands of the Kickapoos would have united, and the troops been undoubtedly defeated. For better marksmen or braver men than these Indians are not to be found anywhere. In our dealings with the red men we always presume on what may be termed the prestige of the United States—as all partially civilized Indians know that they are likely to be punished severely if any of Uncle Sam's soldiers are killed by them.

We have just heard of some difficulty between government troops and the Witchitaws and Wacos, at Stern's Agency—not very far from here. It appears that the Witchitaws had stolen some horses from Fort Croghan. Major Henry H. Sibley, of the Second Dragoons, being on his way to the Witchitaw village to investigate the matter, met with a small band of these Indians at the agency, and took them as hostages, in order to hasten the surrender of the stolen animals. They were placed under the charge of the guard. At midnight one of the Indians rushed out and shot the sentinel dead with a pistol that he had secreted. Wildhouse, the chief, also ran out and stabbed the already lifeless body of the soldier, and was shot down by the guard. The other prisoners made their escape. Two squaws, however, returned on the following day. It is related that the chief, believing himself in danger of punishment, had previously determined to sacrifice his own life, and that of his wife and son, for the benefit of the young men of the party. Hence, at the report of the pistol, he killed his wife and son, and then thrust his knife into the corpse of the sentinel, when he met his fate. Major Sibley had no intention of punishing these Indians; and intended to have released them in a few days.

April 11th, 1853.—The Kickapoos are having a great "ball-play" at their camp beyond the Washita river. Some friends and myself have been to witness their performances. They arrange themselves into two parties. The "stakes," consisting of old clothing, buffalo robes, deer skins, bows and arrows, etc., enclosed in a sack, are put on the end of a long pole in the centre of the play-ground, which is about four hundred yards long. At each end are placed two poles, twelve feet apart, with cross-pieces at the top. The play commencing, the contestants assemble at the centre-pole; when one of the players throws up the ball, made of rags covered with buckskin, as a signal of the opening of the game. Then all is confusion doubly confounded, as each and all rush after the ball, in the greatest excitement, kicking it and knocking it with all their might, the object being to drive it between their own party poles. This effected, it constitutes one point in the game—the whole number being four. With the exception of the breech-cloth, these players are in *puris naturalibus*—and painted in the most fantastic manner.

They generally use a spoon-fashioned stick for the purpose of catching and throwing the ball, but are permitted to use their hands and feet in hurling it onward. It is astonishing how quickly they can secure the ball in this stick, and with what force they can cast it.

Bruised heads and broken limbs are common results in this exciting pastime.

May 4th, 1853.—Have just bidden farewell to Lieutenant Garland and wife, who have left for the East. In the language of the poet:—

"What words can paint the fears
When from those friends we sever,
Perhaps to part for months—for years—
Perhaps to part forever."

One peculiarity of army life is, that there are generally so few officers' families in garrison together, and this perhaps in a country where we are entirely cut off from direct communication with the rest of the world, that their intercourse with each other is that of brothers and sisters. In parting then we are moved by the same fraternal feelings—rendered doubly acute by the absence, in this wilderness, of new friends to take their places.

Although moderately contented thus far, no amount of money could induce me to remain in such a state of isolation from society for a lifetime.

May 13th, 1853.—A party of us had agreed to go to the mountains to-day to hunt pigeons. It having rained early in the morning, my friends concluded not to go. But, having been disappointed in the same manner a few mornings ago, I resolved on trying my luck alone.

After ascending the mountain, and hitching my horse so near me that the Indians could not steal him unobserved, I took my stand on one of the most favorably commanding peaks, and prepared for the sport. The prospects were at first gloomy, but brightened with the sky. It was not long ere the pigeons could be seen in every direction skimming along the surface of the hills and dales about tree-top high. Every now and then a flock came whirling by me with such rapidity that I had constantly to be on the alert, or lose my fire. I adopted the plan of shooting them on the wing, for the reason that very few lit in my vicinity; and because even when they did light, it was next to impossible to find them on account of the density of the undergrowth and foliage. Having killed as many as my horse could conveniently carry, I returned home. This being the first appearance of wild pigeons in the neighborhood, I made a general distribution of the game in garrison.

May 28th.—The sky for the last few days has been overcast with clouds. At noon to day the sun showed forth with renewed splendor and brilliancy—a refreshing breeze sprung up at the same time, which proved quite invigorating. These balmy zephyrs constitute the great redeeming quality of this climate. To-night the rattling of the windows and doors, the roaring gusts of wind, and the lightning's vivid glare, portend a fearful storm. We feel thankful to be in good, comfortable log cabins, instead of tents, on occasions like these.

Our thoughts and sympathies naturally turn to the poor, roving savages, who have no beds but Nature's, no shelter save the canopy of Heaven, no raiment save the skin of the buffalo, perhaps no food, and no hopes of obtaining sufficient for the morrow. Can these poor creatures be truly happy? They seem to be moderately so. Their wants are few, and generally easily supplied.

What a lesson to him who rolls in affluence, surrounded by all the comforts of civilized society, and is yet discontented, perhaps miserable! The old saying: that "ignorance is bliss," is strikingly exemplified in the Indian race. What unhappy souls they would be, did they properly appreciate their own true condition, and ultimate destiny on this continent. They are fast fading before the advancement of the Anglo-American race. It has been our policy from time immemorial to push the Indians further and further west, as the advancing pioneer settlements crowded upon them. But this westward migration has its limits; and these original lords of the soil will ultimately be compelled to change their habits entirely, or be annihilated.

Some of the tribes are gradually adopting the modes, habits and laws of the United States, and have proved themselves to possess considerable genius and capacity for a civilized government, others are wild and savage as the beasts upon which they subsist, and must, for many years, give us a vast deal of trouble.

May 30th.—The storm on the night of the 28th inst. raged most violently. The effects were to be seen on the following day, in the wreck of vast numbers of forest trees. It did us but little damage, except to destroy our gardens. A system of gardening has lately become a prominent feature in garrison life. A garden is allowed to each company, to the hospital, and to the commanding officer and staff, at every post. I have the superintendence of the latter two, and find the duties very agreeable.

It has for many years been customary to have gardens on a small scale, at all of the permanent fortifications. But the present Secretary of War has ordered them to be much larger than formerly. This idea is a product of the last periodical economical fit of the Government for retrenchment, and is akin to the occasional disposition to make the soldier Jack of all trades and master of none. Small gardens are essential in a hygienic point of view—large ones are unnecessary, and exhaust too much of the soldiers' time. Our government ought to have learned ere this, that a proper division of labor is a *sine qua non* in all the pursuits of life. Having already expressed myself fully on this subject, I shall say nothing more at present.

June 1st, 1853.—Have just received the sad tidings of the death of my sister-in-law, Mrs. Thomas W. Glisan. She died on the 20th of April, at the tender age of 22. Death! that sure but unwelcome visitor, has thus cast a cloud of gloom and sadness over this interesting family—

> "She is gone!—forever gone! The king of terrors
> Lays his rude hands upon her lovely limbs,
> And blasts her beauties with his icy breath."

Oh, what an unexpected and paralyzing blow this is to brother! A wife whom he idolized, to be thus stricken down in all her youth and lovliness, by the icy hand of death! Truly, life has its sorrows! Yet we must not murmur. It is the will of Him who doeth all things for the best to them for whom he careth. Our frail barks are all launched upon the stream of time, and must, sooner or later, be wafted into the ocean of eternity.

Death is no respector of persons, but seizes alike the rich and the poor, the noble, and the ignoble, the budding babe of innocence, and the grey-headed, hardened sinner; the youth full of buoyancy and hope, and the old man who is, perhaps, disgusted with the things of life, and is longing for eternity. What terror his coming sometimes produces in the bosom of families! How unexpected may be his summons! Hence it behooves us to be always ready. "For in such an hour as we know not the son of man cometh."

CHAPTER X.

INCIDENTS OF GARRISON LIFE.

Amusing Comanche scares at the Sawmill—Captain Simmons relieves Brevet-Major Henshaw—Mirage—Deer Hunting—A party of Mormons; nearly all sick; their Religion—A visit from the Comanches; the Chief is very sick; and is cured by White Man's Medicine for the first time—Fatal Encounter between Major Arnold and Doctor Steiner—A murder by Indians; and captivity of Mrs. Wilson—A general Courtmartial; a description of the several kinds of Courts—Execution of a Courtmartial Sentence—Visit from Inspector General—Ransom and Escape of the Wilson Family from the Indians.

JUNE 3D.—Paid a visit to the sawmill, four and a half miles from garrison. The owner, Mr. Willliams, has the contract for supplying the fort with lumber. He is an industrious, generous-hearted man, but fond of practical jokes. Some time ago he concluded to frighten a young man under his employment by getting up a false alarm of being attacked by the Comanches; the bugbear of this whole country. He and his accomplices raised the alarm at night by applying a slow-match to a stump well charged with powder. At the dreadful report they ran, crying the Indians are upon us.

Although it was a cold winter's night the poor dupe bolted for the mill pond, and came near drowning and freezing ere he discovered it to be a hoax. Among others who teased the poor fellow unmercifully about his stampede was a regular braggadocio—hailing from the same neighborhood in Texas. He swore that he couldn't be frightened by Indians, much less by a false alarm. As this ranting, prating bravo's boasts became intolerable, Williams concluded to put him to the test. Accordingly after making him believe that the Comanches were on their way to attack Fort Arbuckle, and exciting him to a considerable degree of fear, the conspirators, with one exception, softly rose one night, after the unsuspecting fellow had fallen asleep, and was probably dreaming of scalping knives and tomahawks, and quietly left the room.

Suddenly the report of a gun sounded upon the midnight air, then another, followed by a volley that made the welkin ring, intermingled with whooping, yelling, and the dying groans of the slain. His comrade, who was in the secret, proposed a retreat. Whereupon the frightened wretch bolted in all haste for the mill pond, and swam and dove alternately, until reaching the opposite bank, where he hid himself in a dense thicket. When he was almost chilled to death his cruel persecutors announced the joyful tidings that the enemy had been driven away. He tremblingly returned to the cabin; but not seeing all of his companions there, inquired of their whereabouts. He was told that they had been killed in the fight. Just then the fearful crack of a rifle broke the deathly stillness without, and a renewal of the attack began.

The victim climbed up the inside of the chimney, but the dreadful din without paralyzed his grip, and he fell sprawling to the bottom. This was too much for the risible organs of his persecutors, but in his abject fear he heard not their laugh.

Presently the carnage ceased, and one of the party who had lately returned from the Comanche country, came rushing in, and stated that he had been recognized by the Indians as their friend, and that they desired a parley. Being deputized to treat with the savages, he soon returned again and said that the enemy had supposed they were attacking a military post, but on being informed of their error had hastened away.

On the first of this month a party of seventeen persons, commanded by Colonel Lander, of Kentucky, passed through this place en route for California. They are driving with them 725 head of the finest cattle ever seen in this country. The route they contemplate traveling is west of north, until striking the Sante Fe, or Independence road, at Fort Atkinson. They left the States in a hurry, without even supplying themselves with subsistence or clothing. The commissary at this post issued them sufficient provisions to last to Fort Atkinson; where they anticipate replenishing their stock for the entire trip. Although the Colonel is intelligent, he has but little experience in traveling on the plains. He is likely to encounter other difficulties besides deficiency of food and clothing. The immense herds of stock that have preceded him have, in all probability, consumed nearly all of the grass along the route. The mountains will also in many places be covered with snow ere he can reach his destination. A few weeks earlier start would have enabled him to avoid all of these obstacles.

As the emigration of this year is so far ahead of him, he will be compelled, unless he can secure a military escort, to travel with his small party alone through the wild Indian country, at great risk of property and life. But what will men not endure for gold!

June 11th, 1853.—On the 4th inst., Captain Seneca G. Simmons arrived, and assumed command of the post, by virtue of his rank. This change, although perfectly proper and legitimate, sets very hard on the former commander, Brevet-Major John C. Henshaw, as he will now simply command his own company, and draw the pay and emoluments of Captain, instead of commanding the whole garrison, and drawing the double rations allowed to Post Commanders; and the pay of Major, according to his brevet rank.

June 25th, 1853.—Whilst out on a reconnoitering expedition, a short time ago, we beheld one of those strange atmospheric illusions which so often delude the huntsman and traveler. The prairie before us assumed the appearance of a beautiful lake, skirted with shady groves. A change in the air after a while dissipated this charming mirage. This singular meteorological phenomenon is very common on the Llano-estacado, a little west of here, but I have never witnessed it but twice in the Indian Territory. I saw it for the first time, in the vicinity of our old camp, near the Canadian river. Being out alone on a hunting trip, I beheld before me a herd of monstrously large animals, which resembled deer in symmetry and color, but appeared almost as large as camels.

Although having an indefinite idea of mirages, I was, for a moment, surprised and alarmed. The illusion disappeared with the fleeing of the animals, which were undoubtedly deer, magnified by a peculiar refraction of the atmosphere. Although making no allusions to deer hunting since leaving old Camp Arbuckle, I have, nevertheless, had considerable sport in this line during my sojourn at this fort, but my former enthusiasm for the amusement has abated considerably. The novice in hunting, as in the study of medicine, sometimes imagines he knows more than his preceptor. I fancy, however, that my novitiate is now passed in both of these callings, and that I am both an average physician and hunter. Although my first success in deer hunting was with a shot-gun, I now, like most all frontiersmen, use a rifle, carrying a large, or half-ounce ball, and having a plain, open back-sight. Although a much smaller ball will kill a deer if it pierce his vitals, or some large blood-vessel, yet, the larger ball is necessary to bring him down, when not struck in very vital parts. The modern, elevating back-sight is good at a target, or at very long ranges when deer are feeding, but for still-hunting, generally, it is inconvenient and almost useless, as the deer is up and off almost as soon as the sportsman halts to shoot, if not before.

A person approaching a deer lying down, should, other things being equal, move across the wind, because the animal generally turns his head from the wind, and can see the enemy approach in that direction, and is able to smell him if he come from the other side. Deer live mostly on grass, and feed early in the morning and late in the evening. These are the best periods for finding them, as it is very difficult to see them when they are lying down, because their color is similar to so many things generally found in the thickets and prairies where they make their beds. As a deer is one of the shyest animals known, it is necessary to approach him very cautiously under cover of some intervening object, or if in the level prairie, to crawl along in the grass, and stop every time the animal gives signs of alarm, by shaking his tail, or elevating his head.

I have always met with the best success in hunting these animals after a light fall of snow, which would enable me to follow their tracks, and at the same time deaden the sound of my steps. A few years ago deer could be found in vast herds in these western prairies, but they are now becoming so scarce that it is rare, indeed, that over half a dozen can be seen at a time.

We have as much sport in hunting wild geese, at the proper season, in this country, as in pursuit of any other kind of game. Especially when large flocks of them light in the low, grassy bottoms, along the Washita River. For we can frequently, by lying down on our horses, and approaching as though we intended to pass by them, come almost in gunshot range; then when they begin to slowly rise, we spur our horses at full speed in among them, and fire on the wing, bringing down from one to three at a shot. The wounded ones are very cunning and swift in hiding in the grass, ponds, or branches that chance to be near; and occasionally I have known them to dive to the bottom of the water and hold on to a root or weed, and there die like the wounded Mallard duck; but the propensity is not so common as with the latter.

July 9th, 1853.—Have been engaged for the last few days as Judge Advocate of a General Courtmartial which convened at this post on the 5th of this month. It was in session four days—during which time we tried seven cases.

One of the prisoners from Fort Towson, by the name of Wright, who was tried for abusing, striking, and disobeying a corporal of his company, made a most eloquent speech in his own defense. Why such an intelligent American as he should have enlisted as a private soldier is an enigma. He, probably, took this step in a fit of disgust at some moral or social delinquency on his part.

As previously stated, it is no rare occurrence for educated foreigners to serve a five years' enlistment merely for the purpose of employment and support until they have obtained a better knowledge of our language; but native Americans hardly ever enter the ranks in time of peace, unless they have been guilty of some misdemeanor.

July 24th.—A party of eighty Mormons arrived here on Thursday, and left to-day en route for Salt Lake City. It is composed of men, women and children—rather more males than females. They are from the vicinity of Galveston, Texas; four hundred miles a little east of south of this place; and have been two months on the way. They have had, and still have, much sickness; having lost four of their number. Had they not reached here when they did one half of the party might have died. Supposing that I would charge for my services they at first con-

AN UNBROKEN FAMILY.—Page 118.

sulted me only in their most serious cases. But after learning that my attention would be rendered gratuitously they called on me to prescribe for all the sick; who are at present convalescent, and in fair a way to recover.

I have no cause of regret in attending them free of charge, except in the case of an old ungrateful miser, who would not ask my assistance until after learning my resolution of not charging, notwithstanding his family were very ill. Although wealthy, he did not so much as thank me for my professional attention. It would not surprise me in the least that were I ever to pass through Utah in distress, and seek aid at his door, he should refuse assistance. It is stated that the close-fisted old fellow is not aware that he will be compelled to divide his treasure with his poorer Mormon brethren on his arrival into Brigham Young's dominions. It will be like taking his life to despoil him of his worldly goods.

The men and officers having a desire to hear the peculiar doctrine of the Mormons, the commanding officer requested Mr. Thomas, the Elder, to preach for us; which he did on three occasions.

He said that they believe the Protestant Bible literally, so far as it goes, but that it does not contain one half of the inspired writings. That the Book of Mormons, and the Revelations of Joe Smith, make up the deficiency. That God is in every respect made like man, except that his body contains no blood. That although his spirit fills the universe, his body has a local habitation somewhere in the heavens. That Jesus Christ was begotten by God in the same manner precisely as any human child by his father. That man, at the resurrection, resumes the identical body he had on earth, minus the blood; and claims his same wife, or wives, and children. That he can beget children in heaven in the same way they are begotten in this world. That such children become inhabitants of other spheres. They being then considered in their second condition; we being now in our first condition or estate. That the Mormon prophets have direct communication with the Lord, and can perform miracles as of old. That Joe Smith was truly an inspired man, and conversed with God as did the ancient Hebrew prophets. That they believe in a plurality of wives as a religious sentiment; not as a dictate of the passions. That they have as precedents in this faith the Jews, and two thirds of the present inhabitants of the earth. That the object of matrimony being to beget children, and bring them up in the fear of the Lord, the most pious and wealthy men should have the greater number of wives. That when any of their denomination wishes a second wife he must first ask permission of his wife or wives; then of the President of the Church, who receives a direct revelation upon the subject from God; afterward of the parents of his intended; and lastly of the lady herself.

They affirm baptism to be absolutely essential to redemption—that it literally washes out our sins. They pretend to quote the Bible in its literal sense. But I observed Mr. Thomas in his quotations of certain passages of scripture would sometimes give a literal, and as often a figurative, interpretation. He would, however, do so in such an adroit manner that his poor, deluded followers could not tell the difference. His first two sermons sounded very much like good old hardshell baptist harangues, but the last one contained the doctrinal parts of their faith.

Several of the most intelligent persons among them did not hesitate to express their utter surprise at some parts of the Mormon creed; and stated that it was the first time they had heard it; and could they retrace their steps home, they would certainly do so, but feared an attempt at returning through the wild Indian country.

September 14th, 1853.—We learn through private letters, and the public press, that United States troops are being ordered in large numbers to the Rio Grande. The move is made to counteract that of the Mexican authorities, who have thrown large bodies of troops upon that frontier.

News arrived last night that Santa Anna, with 10,000 men, had crossed the Rio Grande and taken Fort Brown—or rather Brownsville. As we are ignorant of the present relations of the two governments, we can form no idea of the truth or falsity of this rumor. It seems highly impossible that Santa Anna could have made such a movement without our government being aware of his hostile attitude. However, it is certain that our troops are being concentrated on the Rio Grande. Eight companies of the Fifth Infantry, our nearest neighbors, have received marching orders for the field of excitement. We are daily expecting orders for the same destination.

September 20th, 1853.—Notwithstanding our post is within that wide range of country claimed as a hunting ground by the Comanches, the most numerous, hostile and warlike of all the Indians of the plains, they have rarely deigned to notice us, except by threats of utter extermination unless we would remove from their country. They have a very imperfect idea of the power and greatness of the United States; but a most exalted opinion of their own prowess and magnificence. Finding that we paid no attention to their threats, and learning that we had not come into their so-called hunting ground with any hostile feelings toward them, one of their small bands made us a visit. The chief, and a few of his warriors, being prostrated while here with a severe form of malarious dysentery, were prevailed upon by some of the half-civilized Indians to try my professional skill. Happily I got them all well—whereupon the old chief thanked me for my kindness, and made me a present of a handsome pony. I at first declined the gift; but, on being assured by the interpreter that his highness would feel very much hurt at my refusal, I consented to receive it; yet subsequently gave him, in return, articles of far more value to him than the animal. Had the chief, or any of his head men, died under my treatment, his people would have believed them poisoned. As they fortunately all recovered I shall doubtless always be considered by the Comanches as a great "medicine man."

Having heard so much of their expert horsemanship we induced the chief to let a few of his young men exhibit their equestrian feats. He consented to do so if some of the officers would accompany him to a convenient spot outside of the garrison. They are undoubtedly as expert riders as any in the world.

It might be worth while to add a few more remarks, to those already made elsewhere, concerning this peculiar race of Indians. From all accounts their habits now are precisely as they were when the Spaniards first met them in 1541; except that in those early days they possessed no horses, and, of course, knew not how to ride. According to their tradition, they emigrated from South America early in the fourteenth century, and lived on the plains near the head waters of the Brazos and Colorado, in peace and happiness, until the Spaniards visited their hunting grounds and built fortifications. The Comanches believing that the Spaniards had acted in bad faith toward them, declared war, and drove the latter out of their country.

After awhile the Spaniards succeeded in getting a large number of the Indians to attend a big council at Monclovia, and having previously mined the council grounds with gunpowder, blew the unsuspecting wretches in the air—the few who were not killed by the explosion being subsequently massacred. Hence the intense hatred ever since borne by the latter towards all descendants of the Spanish race. They have many Mexican captives among them, mostly small children, who are trained to be as arrant freebooters as themselves. They usually kill all adult male prisoners. Their religion consists in an indefinite kind of faith in a Great Spirit, who can only be reached through the mediation of the sun, to whom they make known their wants; and who dispenses good and evil to the supplicants in proportion to their deeds.

A few of them believe that they will go, after dying, to a happy hunting ground—but many think that death ends their career forever. At the decease of a warrior his clothes are burnt, his war and hunting implements, best dog and favorite horse, are placed in the same grave with himself. His friends mourn his loss by howling about his last resting place for a few nights, and then change their camp for at least six moons.

November 1st, 1853.—Although considerable excitement still exists in the moving and changing of regiments; yet there are no actual, and probably will be no immediate difficulties with Mexico. That Santa Anna is raising and sending large numbers of troops to the frontier is true, but the explanation of this action now is, that they are intended to put a stop to the inroads of the Indians, who have been for a long time committing depredations in Mexico, and possibly to overawe such of the Northern provinces of the latter country as are disaffected toward the present government. We see by the papers that there has recently been an unfortunate encounter between Major Ripley A. Arnold, of the Second Dragoons, commanding Fort Graham, and Assistant Surgeon Josephus M. Steiner, of that post, in which the former was killed. Particulars not stated.

Docter Madison has written me that a party of four Indians recently robbed a wagon on the road from El Paso to Phantom Hill—shot and scalped the driver, a Mexican, leaving him apparently dead; took as prisoners a Mrs. Wilson and her two brothers-in-law (small boys), and drove off the team. There were no other persons with the vehicle at the time. Four men connected with it were absent; one of whom, a German, was a day behind with a tired horse. Two of the others had deserted, and the fourth one had gone in pursuit to recover some stolen horses. The German coming up in the night, found the wagon robbed, and the Mexican badly wounded. He dressed his wounds on the following morning, and putting him on his horse, traveled a short distance, when the animal gave out, and the Mexican was left on the roadside to die. After proceeding a short distance the German lost his road, and lay down to perish, but was picked up a few days thereafter by a detachment of dragoons, who were out scouting. The Mexican was also found still alive, although terribly mutilated, and having gone a week without food. He had managed to walk about fifty miles from the place of the massacre.

November 23, 1853.—As both my pony and horse have been lame, I have lately been compelled to do my hunting on foot. On the 10th instant I killed so many ducks and turkeys that it became necessary to send a vehicle to bring them in.

Being out hunting alone the other day my dog was pursued by a band of large wolves, who followed him close to my heels. In order to protect him it became necessary to shoot down a couple of his pursuers. Wolves, generally, are very cowardly, especially the coyote or prairie wolf; but the larger varieties do sometimes, when very hungry, become hostile.

Captain Simmons and myself caught, a few days ago in Wild Horse Creek, several of the largest catfish we have ever seen in this part of the country—one of them weighing nearly forty pounds. In one of my fishing trips not long since, it became necessary to clamber over a ledge of rocks. In so doing I unfortunately fell into a deep fissure or crevice; when, lo and behold, a water moccasin began running furiously around my legs trying to make his escape, which he finally succeeded in accomplishing, much to my satisfaction, as well as his own. The bite of this reptile is as poisonous as that of the rattle-snake.

December 16th, 1853.—A general courtmartial convened at this post on the twelfth instant—of which Major Henshaw is President, and myself Judge Advocate. It was composed of seven members; and being in session four days, tried five prisoners. A courtmartial is analagous to those civil tribunals where the judges try cases without the aid of juries. The Judge Advocate has the triplicate duties to perform of prosecutor for the government, attorney for the defence and recorder of the court. In other words, it is his duty to see that the prisoners have a fair and impartial trial; and at the same time that the military laws are properly brought to bear on every case brought before the tribunal for adjudication. There is what is called a garrison, a regimental, and a general, courtmartial. The former has cognizance of minor offences—such as drunkenness on duty, neglect of duty, unsoldier-like conduct, etc., and is generally composed of three or four members stationed at the post. The officer of the highest rank acts as president, and the junior member as recorder. The commander of the post orders the session of the garrison court, and reviews its proceedings, and either approves or disapproves its findings.

The regimental court is convened by order of the colonel of the regiment, who has authority to confirm or disapprove of the sentence.

A general court is convened by the general commanding the department or division, or the General of the Army—and sometimes by the Secretary of War. It is composed of from five to thirteen members, exclusive of the Judge Advocate, who is not considered a member of the court, and consequently has no vote in the deliberations. "The power to pardon or mitigate the punishment ordered by a court-martial is vested in the authority confirming the proceedings, and in the President of the United States. A superior military commander to the officer confirming the proceedings may suspend the execution of the sentence when, in his judgment, it is void upon the face of the proceedings, or when he sees a fit case for executive clemency. In such cases the record, with his order prohibiting the execution, shall be transmitted for the final order of the President."

The court opens by the Judge Advocate's reading the general order for its session in the presence of the prisoner, and any spectators who may choose to be present. The prisoner is then asked whether he has objections to any of the members named in the order. If he object to any member, he is required to state his objections; when the court is cleared—that is, all persons who are not members are requested to withdraw. The court then proceeds to determine whether there is sufficient cause for the challenge. If it sustains the objections, the challenged member vacates his seat—otherwise, he retains it. The Judge Advocate next swears the court, and is in his turn sworn by the President. After this the charges and specifications against the prisoner are read to him, and his plea of guilty or not guilty taken to each specification, and lastly to the charge. If he plead guilty to them all, no testimony is taken in the case, at least by the prosecution; but the prisoner may be allowed to bring forward evidence to palliate his offense. If he plead not guilty, the witnesses for the prosecution are sworn and examined as in civil courts. When the prosecution closes, the witnesses for the defense are examined in regular order.

After the testimony for the accused has been concluded, the prisoner is permitted to hand in a written defense, which may be read to the court either by himself or the Judge Advocate. The court is then closed, and proceeds to deliberate on the evidence before it, and determines the guilt or innocence of the prisoner, and pronounces the sentence accordingly. The junior member votes first, then the next in rank, and so on up to the President; or at least until two-thirds of the court vote for the same thing—this number being essential to a decision.

After the proceedings have been sent to the reviewing authority, they are published in orders to the various posts in the department; and to the whole army, if the matter had been laid before the President of the United States, which is usually the case where a commissioned officer has been tried.

January 17th, 1854.—To-day the command was marched in parade to witness the execution of a court-martial sentence on private Nower. Being tied to a tree he received fifty lashes on the bare back with a rawhide, and was then drummed out of the service. His crime was desertion—the only one for which whipping is allowed at the present time in the army.

February 27th, 1854. — On the nineteenth instant we were honored by an unexpected visit from Brevet-Lieutenant Colonel Edward R. S. Canby, Assistant Inspector-General. However well pleased he may have been with the position of the post and kindred matters, I fear his delight was not very great concerning the proficiency of the men in drilling, or even with the cleanliness of the garrison. For the fact is, that the men have been of late so pressed in erecting quarters, that they have had no time to devote to the usual garrison duties. In the review of the troops I had the honor of acting as the Colonel's Aid.

Two little boys have lately been ransomed from the Comanches, and brought to this fort. They, and their sister-in-law, Mrs. Wilson, are the three unfortunate persons whom the Indians carried off from near Phantom Hill last summer; an account of which is given a few pages back. The lady has also made her escape into New Mexico. The particulars of her cruel treatment, while with the savages, call for vengeance on the part of the government. She was a prisoner twenty-five days. For nearly a fortnight subsequent to her escape she subsisted upon hackberries; and would have perished had not a trading party of Mexicans come across her.

A fearful retribution is awaiting these Bedouins of the plains. The American people cannot much longer submit to their depredations and murders in Texas and New Mexico. We are also bound by treaty stipulations with Mexico to protect her from the marauding incursions of these Indians. This clause in the treaty has never been fully carried out by the United States. Our small army scattered as it is all over the immense frontier, is unequal to the task. The War Department has accomplished as much as possible with the few troops at its command. Congress is penny-wise and pound foolish in keeping such a diminutive force of regular soldiers on the borders of the Indian country.

AN INDIAN VILLAGE IN SUMMER.—Page 137.

CHAPTER XI.

CONTINUANCE AT FORT ARBUCKLE.

Murder of Colonel Stern, and remarkable fate of the Indians who committed the act—A visit to Caddo Village—A magnificent view from the Washita Mountains—Prairie Dogs—Climate—Our Society augmented—A curious Ceremony among the Kickapoos, and singular coincidence—Hurricane—Service of the Troops—Temporary exchange of Posts with Doctor Stone—A Suicide—To be relieved by Dr. Williams—Become Poetical.

MARCH 18TH, 1854.—On the thirteenth of this month Lieutenant Arthur D. Free, of the Second Dragoons, with a detachment of twenty men, arrived at this place. They are in pursuit of a party of Indians for the murder of Colonel Stern, Indian Agent for the Texas frontier. The Colonel and a friend were traveling in a carriage to Fort Belknap, and were murdered within six miles of that post. Their coats, baggage and mules were carried off by the murderers. The latter evidently committed the horrid deed by blows from a rifle—one being found on the spot with the barrel bent and the stock broken to pieces. A tomahawk was also used. There appeared to have been but two shots fired, one of which passed through the side of the carriage.

A detachment of dragoons took the trail of the perpetrators of this bloody act, and followed it so far as the Washita mountains, when a heavy rain erased every vestige of the same. The troops then returned to Fort Belknap—having found an arrow, a pair of moccasins, and several other articles which the murderers had left on the route. In all instances of this kind the troops employ Indians as guides. On the present occasion they had two Delawares, named Bill and Jim Shaw. A good Indian guide can follow a trail with most surprising accuracy. He can detect signs in a moment, which an inexperienced white man would find impossible to perceive even when shown him.

At Fort Belknap a clew to the murderers was gained from a party of Wacos, whom the military authorities had in custody. The first detachment of dragoons sent in pursuit being tired, a fresh and smaller one was dispatched to this post; where they arrived as before mentioned. The description of the Indians guilty of the massacre caused suspicion to rest at first upon a small party of supposed Kickapoos, who passed Nelson's house, twenty-seven miles from here, last Saturday; and offered for sale some trace chains; and who had several uniform coats, and quite a lot of money.

Black Beaver, a well known Delaware Indian, being sent for, arrived, and stated that the suspected party were Delawares, and had obtained the articles alluded to from the quartermaster at Fort Belknap. Lieutenant Free, on getting a true description of them, confirmed his statement. Beaver further said that he had been told by several Kickapoos that one of their tribe by the name of Sa-kok-wah—his two English names being Morgan and Pole-cat—and a half-breed known as Pe-a-tah-kak (half Kickapoo and Pi-an-ke-shaw), accompanied by the former's brother-in-law, a little boy, had committed the dreadful deed.

The Kickapoo chief, Mosqua, and a prominent man of the tribe by the name of Johnson being sent for by the commanding officer, the latter came promptly, and stated that the former would come after awhile. In answer to the inquiries, Johnson said that the suspected men had been in his camp for several days, but had made their escape that morning after learning that they were to be surrendered for punishment. That one of them, just previous to his getting away, had been tied to prevent his desertion.

Knowing the treachery of the Indian character, we doubted this statement at the time, but our suspicions were completely removed by the announcement yesterday morning that the Kickapoos had made every exertion to capture these men; and had succeeded in securing the half-breed, or one-eyed man, who was then being brought in. Soon after this the Kickapoos in charge of the captive arrived and stated that the fellow endeavored to make his escape, and was shot by Johnson. The corpse was brought to garrison and buried. Thus ended the career of one of them. The most desperate villain is still at large, but will doubtless be caught.

From the boy we obtained all the particulars of the murder; of which he was only a spectator. 'Tis remarkable that two strong white men, well armed, should be attacked and killed by the same number of Indians, without making some resistance. From the boy's account they must have been paralyzed with fear. For although there were two shots fired by the Indians, neither took effect. The savages rushed upon their victims with a tomahawk and empty rifle.

March 29th, 1854.—To-day the head of Sa-kok-wah, the other murderer of Colonel Stern and friend, was brought to garrison. He was killed by his own brother at Tom Pe-can's village, some forty miles north of this post. It had been agreed between Captain Simmons and Mosqua, that if Sa-hok-wah could not be brought in alive, he must be killed. And should this occur within twenty miles of here we would go out to identify the body. If further, his head was to be delivered at this post.

When Sa-kok-wah reached Pe-can's village he took dinner with his brother, and told him that he had been arrested at Mosqua's camp for killing two white men; and that subsequent to his escape he had smuggled himself into the Kickapoo camp for the night, notwithstanding a watch had been set for him, and that he lay several days in ambush near Fort Arbuckle. On being asked by his brother where he intended to go, he replied either to Missouri or the Comanche country. Then looking out of the hut and perceiving some Kickapoos coming in pursuit, he started to run; but his brother slipped up behind, and knocked him in the head with a hatchet.

Although this action of the brother appears to be savagely cruel, it is a common custom among wild Indians, and some of the partially civilized, for the nearest of kin to execute the sentence in capital crimes. This sad event ought to satisfy the government, that although the Kickapoos, like every other tribe of Indians, and every nationality of whites, have bad men among them whom their leaders cannot always control, yet they are ever willing to punish

AN INDIAN CAMP IN WINTER.—Page 137.

their culprits, or give them up for punishment, if properly approached upon the subject. It also inculcates a lesson to some of our hot-headed government officials to be calm and judicious, as well as firm, in their demands upon Indians for offences against the laws of the land.

Had Captain Simmons, instead of pursuing the temperate but decided course he did, listened to the advice of some of his juniors, and surrounded the Kickapoo camp on the first night of the arrival of the detachment of dragoons, before any explanation was made to them of our intentions, a bloody engagement would doubtless have resulted. For in the excitement of the moment they might have thought we had come to fight, or at least to intimidate, them, when their hot-blooded young men would have been up in arms in a moment. Commanders often reap the praise due their subordinates; but in this instance the conduct of Captain Seneca G. Simmons deserves high commendation.

April 6th, 1854.—The sutler and I took a trip to the Cad-do village on the twenty-eighth of last month, and were absent several days. The camp consists of about twenty-five conical lodges, made of poles covered with grass—resembling very much hay-stacks. A fire is built in the centre of each, with no outlet for the smoke except a single opening at the side, used as a door. The chief offered us the hospitality of his lodge, but we kindly told him that we preferred to eat and sleep in the open air. These Indians are almost as uncivilized as the Comanches; but are feeble in numbers and spirit.

For twenty miles of our homeward course we traveled along the summit of the Washita mountains, the geological features of which are somewhat curious. Running east and west are numerous parallel ledges of limestone rock, about eight feet apart, with intervening spaces of level ground, covered with gravel, and occasional patches of grass, and boulders of iron ore. The average height of the projections is about fifteen inches. The view of the surrounding country from one of the highest points of the mountain range is extremely beautiful.

To the south for many miles the eye rests on green, undulating prairies, bounded in the dim distance by the "cross timbers"—a belt of trees stretching for hundreds of miles through the western portions of the Indian Territory and Texas. To the north lay the charming valley of the Washita.

On this trip we saw many small villages of prairie dogs, but none of them were as large as a town we passed through last summer near Red river, some fifty miles from Fort Arbuckle. On that particular occasion we amused ourselves for hours in watching the curious antics of these interesting creatures.

The prairie dog is a small rodent animal, having a body about a foot long, and a tail two and a half inches in length. Its back and sides are of a light, dirty reddish color; and the under part of its body is of a dirty white. It has moderately long black whiskers. Its resemblance is between that of a small fice and grey squirrel. It lives in poor, dry soil, and is gregarious in its habits, throwing up mounds of earth in vast numbers in some parts of the western prairies. On approaching one of their towns it is amusing to see, on almost every mound, one of these little animals sitting on its hinder parts, with the head and fore feet upright, apparently on guard duty. They rarely permit a stranger to come within gun-shot distance.

Having heard so much of their carrying the wounded into their burrows, we were tempted to test the experiment—but relented before fully satisfying ourselves on this point, as the poor, harmless little animals looked so pitiful that we could not shoot them down out of mere scientific curiosity.

May 25th, 1854.—The weather is quite warm and sultry. A residence of several years convinces me that this climate is very enervating; and so far as malarial fevers are concerned, very sickly. I do not judge from myself, because my health is always good any and everywhere; but from my experience as a physician. If our summers were as dry as they are said to be in some parts of New Mexico, and especially on the Pacific coast, we would not feel the heat so oppressively; but as the air is frequently humid during the hottest season, the high temperature becomes exceedingly debilitating. The themometer rises in the shade as high as 101 in summer, and sometimes sinks to zero in winter.

The rain-fall is almost equally distributed between the four seasons—summer and autumn getting rather the larger share. The prevailing winds in summer are from the south; in winter from the north. There is not usually much snow—but, as before mentioned, we had quite a deep fall of it at the old camp in the winter of 1851.

The following summary of the climate is compiled

from my meteorological observations taken at this post, including the early part of 1851, as observed at the camp on the Canadian river, twenty-five miles in a direct line north of this fort:

METEOROLOGICAL OBSERVATIONS at Fort Arbuckle, Indian Territory. Latitude 34° 27′ North—Longitude 97° 09′ West of Greenwich. Altitude 1000 feet.

MONTHLY MEAN OF TEMPERATURE.	1851	1852	1853
January	39 28	36 77	41 33
February	43 11	47 07	40 68
March	54 62	53 76	51 24
April	56 96	59 77	64 26
May	69 11	70 25	66 25
June	78 03	73 71	77 35
July	81 83	78 26	79 50
August	84 55	78 04	81 81
September	77 13	69 05	74 51
October	62 80	63 11	60 77
November	45 56	45 10	52 91
December	39 47	38 82	42 44

	ANNUAL TEMPERATURE.			RAIN FALL.					WEATHER.			
Years.	Mean.	Max.	Min.	Spring.	Summ'r	Autumn	Winter.	Annual.	Fair.	Cloudy.	Rain.	Snow.
1851	61 04	101	7	5 52	4 90	6 06	7 76	24 24	251	114	57	3
1852	59 48	93	0	9 92	15 21	14 66	6 29	46 08	286	80	66	1
1853	61 08	101	10	6 67	9 14	7 53	3 34	26 68	298	67	68	4

May 31st, 1854.—On the sixth instant, Lieutenant Henry Douglass took his departure to join the Eighth Regiment of Infantry, to which he has been promoted. He is a cheerful and pleasant companion. I never saw him otherwise, except when convalescent from an attack of typhoid fever; when he became so depressed in spirits, and sensitive, that he seemed totally unlike himself. He has our best wishes for a long and prosperous life.

Our little circle has been increased by the arrival of two very agreeable demoiselles—the daughters of Major Daniel P. Whiting, of the Seventh Infantry.

On the twenty-sixth of this month, a few friends and myself paid a visit to the Kickapoo village to witness their annual ceremony of extinguishing all the fires in camp. As this last observance of their singular rite coincided with an eclipse of the sun, of which we foretold them, they became somewhat alarmed; and wondered how we could know that the sun was to be darkened on that particular day. These ignorant people have much to learn before they can appreciate how much, and yet how little, scientific men know of the mysteries of the universe.

Fort Arbuckle, June 13th, 1854.—Captain R. B. Marcy is daily expected on his way for the frontier of Texas, where he is ordered to survey a tract of country which the latter State has ceded to the United States for an Indian reservation. He will take an escort of forty men and two commissioned officers from this post. We are also daily looking for Brevet-Major Whiting's company, which is to be stationed here.

The present season has been unusually wet and stormy. About ten days ago a tornado visited portions of western Texas and the Indian Territory—sweeping everything before it. At Fort Towson many of the public buildings were unroofed, and the garrison trees blown up by the roots. It spent its greatest force in the vicinity of Gainesville, on Red river, in Texas. All of the houses were blown down, and the logs, boards and shingles scattered for miles around. A very heavy sill was carried four miles, a horse two miles, a woman three miles, a child four miles—many persons were killed—seven in one house.

June 26th, 1854.—Our command has been increased by two companies of the Seventh Infantry—making four in all—viz: C, G, H and K,—each eighty-four strong; or a total of 336 men; besides officers and families.

Captain Marcy arrived here on the twenty-first instant; and left for Texas on the twenty-fourth with an escort of forty men, under Lieutenant N. B. Pearce.

September 21st, 1854.—I have given up my quarters in garrison to one of the married officers, and am now living in a log cabin near the hospital. Very retired and convenient for study—to which I devote all my leisure time—but a little too lonely at night.

The commissioned officers belonging to this fort are Major George Andrews, Brevet-Major Theophilus H. Holmes, Brevet-Major Daniel P. Whitney, Captain Seneca G. Simmons, Brevet-Major John C. Henshaw,

Lieutenant Mathew R. Stevenson, Brevet-Captain Franklin Gardner, Brevet-Captain Wm. K. Van Bokkelen, Lieutenants Samuel B. Hayman, Henry M. Black, Robert R. Garland, N. B. Pearce, Gorden Chapin and David P. Hancock. I am the only physician. Several of the Lieutenants are on detached service.

As the married officers have their families with them, we have quite an intelligent and gay little society. Too pleasant entirely for a bachelor—so I may expect to be soon crowded out by some doctor who has a wife. But as I have served the usual time on the frontier to entitle me to a short leave of absence, a few months on East will probably be granted ere going on another tour of isolation.

A stranger in glancing over these pages might fancy, from the rare allusions made to professional duties, that I have done little else than fish, hunt, and gallop over the surrounding prairies. The fact is, that the few items dotted down in this journal are intended as a mental recreation to prevent my mind running too closely in a narrow professional groove.

I am, in medical matters, a good deal like my old friend, Judge Worthington of Baltimore, who, strolling into my office one day, as was his frequent habit, was questioned by me upon some legal cases being tried in his court of great interest to the public generally. "My friend," said he, "please do not ask me professional questions, as I have come here to get rid of the court-room and all its exhausting duties—my mind needs rest."

As the troops have fought no battles since the establishment of Fort Arbuckle, it might also be asked of what service they have been to the Government? Their mere presence had the effect of impressing upon the Indians the power and authority of the United States, and of vastly lessening the depredations of these nomadic races upon our otherwise unprotected frontier. They are here also in order to fulfill our treaty stipulations with the Choctaws, whose western limits we have kept free from the inroads of the lawless wild Indians. They have also protected emigrant parties, prevented, in a great measure, the introduction of liquor into the Indian country; and arrested, or been the means of punishing several murderers, and other fugitives from justice. Had our force been larger at the beginning; or a few companies of dragoons been stationed here, many more excursions into the wild Indian country might have been made. The number of troops is now amply sufficient for almost any emergency—still there ought to be at least one company of dragoons.

October 13th, 1854.—Been on a visit to Fort Washita—having made a mutual exchange of posts with Doctor Lyman H. Stone, from the third until the eleventh of October. Should have staid longer, but, being a witness before a court martial, was obliged to return. Had a delighful time.

Washita is garrisoned by two companies of light artillery, Brevet-Lieut. Col. Braxton Bragg in command. His military reputation is not excelled by any officer of his age in the service. He is intelligent, brave, chivalrous, and, perhaps, the best disciplinarian

PRAIRIE-DOG VILLAGE. GENERAL VIEW.—Page 138.

in the army. Not one of your *fussy old maids,* who busies himself about trifles, and allows matters of importance to pass uncared for; but is minutely exact in great things, and lets trifles take care of themselves. Has the reputation of being a Martinet; and yet there never was, perhaps, an officer more sincerely beloved and respected by his subordinates. He has charmingly pleasant manners. When conversing upon any subject of real interest to himself the expression of his countenance is truly magnetic; his bright eyes are almost dazzling.

On starting for Fort Washita, I left at my quarters, a Mr. Hinckly, late editor of the *Chickasaw Intelligencer*, who had been a guest of the post for several days. A perfect stranger to the most of us. He evidently came here with the view of addressing a young lady resident of the garrison whom he had seen at Fort Washita. From the first, I observed that he was *non compos mentis;* but was in hopes that his visit would be short, and that he might therefore not compromise himself in any way. After being here a few days, however, he deemed it expedient to remind the young lady of an alleged promise of friendship that she had formerly made him. She totally ignored it; and thus his fondest hopes were crushed. His mental excitement grew worse from this time, and when I left on the third instant, his mind was a complete wreck. Professional secrecy was then not only useless, but highly dangerous. I therefore informed the members of the garrison of his condition, and left proper directions with the hospital steward for his treatment until the arrival of Dr. Stone. On my return I was pained to learn that the poor fellow alternated from bad to worse until 4 P. M., of the 10th of this month, when he put an end to his existence by stabbing himself nine times over the region of the heart; whilst two men were in attendance upon, and one of them reading to him.

He at first attempted suicide with a pistol, which snapped, and was taken from him by the attendants. He had been divested of the knife and pistol on the eve of his first serious illness; but he succeeded in getting them from the hospital steward on the night of the suicide, by telling him that he anticipated leaving for Fort Washita early in the morning. He did, in fact, hire a man to go with him—declining to accompany Dr. Stone, who intended to start on the same day.

October 29th, 1854.—To-day we had a review and inspection of troops by the Acting Inspector-General, Brevet-Major F. N. Page, who arrived last night.

November 7th, 1854.—Have just received news that Dr. Thomas H. Williams is to relieve me at this post; when I am to proceed to Baltimore, to await instructions from the War Department. This is evidently a preliminary to a leave of absence, for which I shall apply on my arrival at that place.

I shall reach home about Christmas. Oh, how the prospect of seeing my old dear parents, brothers and sisters once more, gladdens my heart. The scenes of my youth rise up before me. How delightful the retrospective. I behold, in imagination, the native valleys and streams over which I roamed in all the buoyancy of youth:

In childhood's merry hours I used to roam,
As free as birds which flew around my home,
And built their nests in boughs of sycamore,
In beauty spread o'er stream of Linganore.
Though calmer now are manhood's colder joys,
Yet give me back awhile my boyhood toys;
My rod, my little boat, my tiny gun,
My pony bay, which lov'd so well the fun
To amble o'er the roads in nimble tread,
Or mountain trail his course less swift to thread.
Those joyous days, when rising with the sun,
I helter-skelter through the woods did run.
To shoot a rabbit, robin, or a quail;
Or on the pond my little bark did sail.
Such glee, such joy, doth come but once in life,
Then graver grow our hopes, our fears, our strife.

CHAPTER XII.

ORDERED TO BALTIMORE—TRIP THITHER.

PERRYVILE, CHOCTAW NATION, Nov. 24th, 1854.

Left Fort Arbuckle on last Tuesday for Baltimore, in company with Captain J. H. Strain, the post sutler, Doctor Williams having arrived on the Saturday previous. The doctor and I being natives of the same State, and graduates of the same institution, were mutually pleased to meet each other. Although rejoiced at the prospect of revisiting my native place, yet as the time of my departure drew near, my heart saddened at the approaching separation from old friends.

There is no society so closely bound together by all the mutual ties of association as that of the military brotherhood at a frontier post. Aside from the congeniality of education and tastes, the almost perfect isolation from the outside world deepens, in a high degree, the friendship of its members toward each other. We were accompanied a short distance on our way by several of our most intimate friends. The trip, so far, has been pleasant.

We are traveling in a Government ambulance, our baggage being in one of the wagons of an empty train returning to Fort Smith. So far we have all encamped together at night. The teamsters generally being discharged soldiers, it is really amusing to hear them relate to each other, around the camp-fire, the many little incidents connected with their army life.

There is one from Fort Arbuckle, who, although a little careful of what he says in my hearing, yet knowing that he is no longer a soldier, and that I am leaving the country, solves many little matters relating to the post which have always been a mystery to its officers — particularly as it regards the introduction of liquors into the garrison.

This secret, no man, while a private soldier, will divulge. On the contrary, he considers it a matter of principle to deceive his commander upon this point, no matter how faithful he may otherwise be. Intoxicating spirits are usually brought in the neighborhood of the post by civilians, and secreted for a few days; when they are clandestinely sold to the soldiers at exorbitant prices. It is a risky business, however. For, independent of the men, when short of funds, seizing and appropriating to their own use the whole quantity, the dealers, if caught by the proper authorities, are sure to suffer the penalty of the law.

A train of emigrants, bound for Texas, is encamped along side of us to-night. Many return after going there and finding that "distance lends enchantment to the view;" and that that country is inferior in some respects to the one left behind. On meeting these roving pioneers of the west it is generally easy to tell from what State they hail by the provincialisms made use of by them in conversation. If from Missouri, he raised "a smart chance of corn"—if from Arkansas, or Texas, "a power of cotton," or " smart chance of corn;" if from the Old Dominion, "I reckon I raised a mighty heap of tobacco last season;" "boys are peart;" "don't you think, Doc., ague makes a fellow powerful weak?" Occasionally one recognizes Jonathan from such expressions as "down East;" "By gosh, this 'ere is the biggest clearin' I ever see;" "I expect we hadn' ought to raise nothin' but wheat and rye here;" "I guess you've come arter land, ha'nt you?"

Sunday, November 26th, 1854.—Sixth day out; delightful trip so far. Nothing to mar our pleasure except the stampede of all our mules last night. Arriving in camp late they were, as usual, turned loose to graze until the teamsters could strike a fire. Leaving one man to guard the wagons, the rest of us started out in different directions to hunt the renegades; and succeeded about 10 P. M. in finding all but four. Mr. Sadler, the wagon master, and three teamsters are still absent in pursuit of them.

Came near breaking the Sabbath this morning by shooting at a large covey of quail which approached within gunshot of the camp, but suddenly recollecting that it was the Lord's day, resisted the temptation. I have ever held, and hope to be able ever to hold, the Sabbath sacred.

My hands are so chilled by the cool air that I can hardly write. But the wind is most refreshing. Oh, you weak and puny denizens of brick and mortar, could you breathe for a while, as we do, this health-inspiring breeze, it would give a new zest to your existence. Some of the scenery passed through yesterday was beautiful and picturesque—especially the broad and level prairies, interspersed occasionally with small groves of timber. On comparing my enthusiasm when first beholding these immense western meadows, a few years ago, and my present apathy upon the subject, I am forcibly reminded how soon the most lovely things of life lose their charms when seen too often.

FORT SMITH, ARKANSAS, November 29th, 1854.

Arrived here yesterday, a distance of 195 miles from Fort Arbuckle. Find the place greatly improved since I passed this way in 1850; although everything is at present at a stand-still for the want of l'argent. Judging from newspaper accounts, the distress must be general throughout the union.

LITTLE ROCK, ARKANSAS, December 6th, 1854.

After enjoying ourselves a few days at Fort Smith, we—Captain J. H. Strain, Mr. Humes and myself—left in a carriage, on the third instant, for this place, where we arrived to-day; the distance being 175 miles. We traveled mostly on the opposite side of the Arkansas River to what I did on my advent into this country; over a much better road, and in a far superior conveyance. No more public staging for me when I can conveniently hire a carriage. The soil along our route is one of the least productive we have yet seen in this country; the principal productions being cotton, corn and peaches; very large orchards of the latter. Only one or two apple orchards — it being impossible to raise good apples in this part of Arkansas. They appear to rot, or dry up, on the trees before maturity. The inhabitants generally are very poor and unthrifty.

On the second day from Fort Smith we passed an immense perpendicular bluff, three hundred feet in height, called the Dardanelles. According to tradition, some twelve years ago an Indian committed murder, and being closely pursued to the brink of this precipice, leaped over it, and was, of course, mashed to a jelly.

On the third night we stopped at Louisburgh, a very small country village. Mabie's menagerie had exhibited during the afternoon, and the place was crowded with drunken, quarrelsome people, who kept up continual rows all night; preventing us from enjoying ourselves on the soft side of a plank—or the floor of the tavern. The following are some of the principal trees observed along our route from Fort Arbuckle to this city: In the Choctaw nation—black, post and red oak, hickory, pecan, sycamore, blackjack, sweet-gum, over-cup, cottonwood. In Arkansas, the same, together with birch, honey-locust, cyprus, black and white pine.

At the house where we lodged last night we saw for the first time a young lady "dipping"—not her lovely person under water, that would have been commendable—but a stick into a snuff-bottle, and then, oh horrors! into her pretty mouth. This disgusting habit is said to be common in all classes of Arkansas society.

December 8th, 1854.—We are now gliding down White river on the Thomas P. Rea, having left Little Rock early yesterday morning in the stage for Aberdeen—where we took passage on board this vessel. The distance between the two points is sixty miles;

over the loveliest road I have seen, through a perfectly smooth and level prairie. There were sixteen passengers—nine within, and seven without. We made several very pleasant acquaintances—among others J. Knox Walker, President Polk's private secretary. We are bound for Napoleon, a distance of one hundred and seventy-five miles. White River is narrow and deep, and affords much better navigation than the Arkansas. The land on its borders is the most productive in the State; but is subject to frequent overflows.

St. Charles Hotel, New Orleans, Dec. 19th, 1854.

We arrived here on the thirteenth instant, having left Napoleon December 9th, on the steamboat I. P. Leathers, Captain Bennet. The Mississippi is very low at this season of the year—thus preventing as fine a view of the country on either side of the river as is obtained when the water is higher. We stopped at various points along the route to take in freight—mostly cotton.

In passing Vicksburg we were reminded of the notoriety it gained several years ago for lynching a band of gamblers, whom, having become so numerous as to defy the authorities, some of the most influential citizens, warned to leave within a given time, or they would be punished. Not heeding the warning, the ringleaders were taken to a neighboring hill and hung. The town was not infested with this class of men for some time thereafter. The trees lining the banks of the Mississippi from Vicksburg to New Orleans are covered with a kind of moss, much in use at present instead of hair in stuffing mattresses—a poor substitute, however.

The next most notable place to Vicksburg that we passed was Natchez; which takes its name from a tribe of Indians that once inhabited that section of the Mississippi. The French, who owned the country at the time, had much trouble with them between the years of 1720 and 1732; and on one occasion treated them very treacherously by forming a treaty of friendship, while secretly raising large forces to crush them; but only partially succeeded in their scheme. A few years subsequently the French Commandant selected one of their most flourishing villages as a site for a fort. The Indians, having been so cruelly and harshly dealt with, determined on revenge.

With this object in view, they promised the French Commander, that if he would permit them to remain at their old home until harvest, every one of them would present him with a fowl and a lot of corn. He granted their request. At the appointed time all the men of the tribes entered the fortification; and at a preconcerted signal, fell upon the unsuspecting garrison, and massacred every living soul.

The Governor immediately sent against them a large force of French and friendly Indians, who killed nearly the whole tribe. About four hundred of the survivors were taken prisoners, and sold in bondage; while the remainder were disseminated among other tribes. Each side of the Mississippi, from Napoleon down, is lined with cotton plantations until within about ninety miles of New Orleans, when the great sugar plantations are seen instead. A proper cultivation of the latter requires a much larger capital than the former. On the last day of our trip we passed a kind of horse-shoe bend in the river, which is twenty-eight miles around, and only half a mile through what is called the cut-off. The latter is used only in very high water. We have been delayed in New Orleans awaiting the departure of the steamship Empire City for New York.

So completely does a few years isolation from general society change our natural susceptibilities, that although we have been here a week the novelty and strangeness of city life impress us almost as much as though we had been reared on the great western plains, and were now paying our respects for the first time to this great emporium of the Southwest.

We have not been idle at sight-seeing since our arrival, but have visited almost every place worthy of inspection. It would be needlessly tedious to attempt a description of the various novelties that attracted our verdant attention. We saw for the first time, at the museum, wax statuary of the crowned heads of Europe, and of our own great American statesmen. The most interesting were the death-bed scenes of Webster and Calhoun; and the figures of Queen Victoria, Emperors Nicholas of Russia and Napoleon of France. We saw the unfinished Custom-house, which, when completed, will be the largest building of the kind in the Union. The walls are of granite from Maine. The architect has made a great mistake in erecting the arches supporting the brick floors too flat, considering that the building is not on a very firm foundation. In fact, numerous cracks are already visible in them, caused by the settling of the walls of the main structure.

One of the most beautiful sights of the city is its shipping; the harbor being full of all sizes and sorts of vessels from every part of the commercial world. We visited the French cemetery, located in the town. The vaults are all above ground, owing to the dampness of the earth; the city level, or grade, being three and a half feet below high water mark in the Mississippi river. Were it not for the levee extending along the river about one hundred miles, and varying from six to thirty-two feet in height, New Orleans and the surrounding country, would be inundated almost every year by the Mississippi. The embankment in front of the city is projected for some distance into the river by a series of wooden wharves.

During the hottest parts of summer the population of New Orleans is greatly reduced, by almost everybody who can spare the time and money, leaving for some more healthy climate, as the yellow fever is prevalent here every season, although epidemic only about every five years. In the winter, however, the city is full to overflowing with many thousands of strangers, and other new comers—constituting a floating population almost equal to the number of permanent citizens. It is at this time of the year, too, that the rich cotton and sugar planters come to town, to negotiate the sale of their products and spend the proceeds in luxurious living.

I have spent the most of my time in attending medical lectures at the University of Louisiana, and in examinations of the many curious pathological and anatomical specimens at the museum connected with the college; and in visiting the Charity Hospital—an immense structure, occupying a whole square, and capable of accommodating over a thousand patients. I also had the pleasure of hearing the renowned Surgeon Stone lecture, and of seeing him perform several surgical operations. He is a poor lecturer; but a bold and fearless operator.

On Sunday morning we heard the celebrated Mr. Clapp deliver a truly eloquent discourse. The church was full, but many of the audience seemed to listen to the burning words of the great preacher in a listless, sleepful manner, most surprising to us who have been so long deprived of the glorious privilege of hearing the gospel of our Lord preached in any manner, much less by the tongue of eloquence. On Sunday evening we had another intellectual and religious treat at the anniversary of the Southern Bible Society. One of the speakers, the Rev. Mr. Walker, was grandly eloquent. To-morrow morning we shall take our departure for New York.

In bidding adieu to the Valley of the Mississippi I feel how impossible it is for the finite mind to contemplate with a realizing sense of their grandeur the mighty works of the Creator, even after they are brought under general review. In contemplating the vastness of this great central valley of the North American Continent—extending as it does from the Alleghany mountains on the east, to the Rocky mountains on the west; from the Gulf of Mexico on the south, to the chain of lakes on the north; and considering the size of the mighty rivers—especially the

Mississippi—the great father of waters, one is almost appalled at the sublimity of the future greatness of this nursery of American liberty.

However diverse its population may appear at present in manners, prejudices and modes of speech corresponding to the countries from which they have come, the time is not distant when all incongruities must harmonize into one grand central whole—producing the true type of the American, with views as lofty as the mountain barriers to the east and west, and as broad and expansive as the great valley itself.

There are over twenty thousand miles of water navigation in this extensive area of the richest agricultural lands in the world. In conjunction with this it can only be a few years when this entire extent of country will be bound together, as it is now in part, by iron rails, over which will rush with almost lightning speed thousands of iron horses with lungs of fire, and breath of steam, catering to the need and comfort of a hundred millions of American freemen.

New York, December 28th, 1854.

Taking our departure from New Orleans on the twentieth in the steamship Empire City, we reached here this morning. Whilst waiting for the train, which starts for Baltimore at one P. M., I shall jot down a few of the incidents of our trip.

Not being ill for so many years, I had almost begun to think that my good fortune in this respect might attend me on the ocean as well as ashore. A most cruel deception. Although not the first, yet I was not the last, to come under the influence of seasickness. Almost every one who goes to sea has some new specific to suggest for the prevention and alleviation of this disagreeable malady. Although much relief can be obtained by following the advice of skillful and experienced physicians, who depend on no special remedies, but treat each case according to the symptoms developed, yet the unfortunate sufferers must not expect too much from medical science; as the discovery of a true specific has yet to be made.

We reached Havana, a distance of 620 miles from New Orleans at five P. M. on the twenty-second, just be fore the firing of the sun-down gun from Moro Castle. This was fortunate, as no foreign vessels are permitted to go in, or out of, the harbor between sunset and sunrise. As the Aspinwall steamer, with which ours connected, did not arrive until three P. M. on the following day, we had a splendid opportunity to see the city. We went ashore on the evening of our arrival in time to visit the opera at the Tacon theatre; which for size and grandeur is said to be excelled by only two structures of the kind in the world. It has five tiers of seats—three of which are dress circles—also an immense parquet. My fine opera glass, purchased at New Orleans, enabled me to scan with good effect the immense and brilliantly attired audience. The most noticeable feature on entering the building was the large military guard in front.

Havana is full of soldiers—the majority of the 17,000 garrisoning the Island of Cuba being stationed in and around the city. It is a very pretty sight to see them "mounting guard" with three hundred men; and grander still to witness them drill in squads of several thousands. Between the hours of eight and nine P. M. a military band discourses most delightful music in the Governor's square.

An American is struck on entering Havana with its narrow streets—like our alleys—its low houses covered with curved tiles, the convex and concave sides alternating so as to form a series of parallel grooves running from the ridge to the eaves of the roof. The windows are destitute of glass; but have instead a bowed iron grating—giving to the houses the appearance of prisons. All the hotels and public buildings have carriage houses, and horse stables, in the basements. Although kept perfectly clean, they give rise in warm weather to disagreeable odors.

The most general way of traveling in Havana is in a volante; a two-wheeled vehicle; resembling a heavy kind of chaise or gig—the tires of which are wrapped with leather to prevent noise. The horse is not driven, but ridden by a fellow in enormous boots and spurs. Almost every horse to be seen has his tail tied to one side—probably a mere fancy. Green corn, stalk and all, is the principal provender for horses. It is grown the whole year round—and, in truth, so is every other vegetable production in this climate, where frost is never seen.

On the day of our visit the thermometer stood at seventy-five degrees Fahrenheit in the shade—of course we enjoyed ice creams, iced lemonades, etc., as well as delicious tropical fruits. The shade trees around the city are charmingly beautiful, being principally palm and linden. The most beautiful trees and shrubbery are to be seen in the Bishop's garden, a mile out of the city. There are to be found the palm, the cocoa-nut, bamboo, sweet and bitter orange, lemon, mango, bread-tree, gourd-tree—together with hundreds of other varieties of lovely trees and shrubs.

Havana possesses one of the finest harbors in the world—the entrance of which is guarded by the renowned Moro Castle. This has for its foundation an immense rock, jutting out into the sea. Bold and formidable indeed must be the naval power that would attempt a forcible entrance into this harbor, when old Moro belches forth its thunders.

We left Havana on the twenty-third instant in quite a storm, which did not lull until Christmas; when we all made our appearance at a most magnificent dinner given in honor of the day by the captain. On our way we saw, for the first time, some of those dull, stupid aquatic birds called boobies. Last night the fog was so dense that the captain feared he would have to stop the steamer until it cleared up, as the cloudy weather had prevented an observation for forty hours, and he was not quite sure of his course. Still he kept on, and fortunately steered as direct to the channel in the narrows as though the sky had been clear. The surgeon declares that Captain Wendall can smell his way, as he has frequently accomplished the same feat before with his vessel when befogged.

I hope I will be able to spend a few weeks in this great city during the present winter, but must now hurry on to Baltimore, and report by letter to the Surgeon-General, and ask for a short leave of absence.

CHAPTER XIII.

HOW I SPENT MY THREE MONTHS LEAVE OF ABSENCE.

FORT WOOD, BEDLOE'S ISLAND,
NEW YORK HARBOR, April 19th, 1855.

CAPTAIN J. W. T. Gardiner and myself anticipate taking our departure to-morrow in the steamship Illinois with a detachment of recruits for the department of the Pacific.

Although my experience during the last few months has been that of hundreds of others, yet as I may some day desire to recall what now seems to me trifling events, a brief summary of how my three months leave of absence, granted me by the Secretary of War, on my reporting by letter from Baltimore on the twenty-ninth of last December, has been spent may prove of future interest. Of course the first thing done was to visit my old home at Linganore, Maryland. The joyful greetings of my dear relatives, and boyhood friends, need no record on paper, as they are indelibly fixed on the page of memory.

An absence of five years from home marks many changes. Little boys and girls have grown up to be young maidens and men. The sweet seventeens whom I met at my former visit have changed into sedate married women; or quiet, pensive young ladies, who have ceased to celebrate their birthdays. Some of my old friends have been laid beneath the cold sod, as a sad warning to those of us left behind.

'Tis singular how the little incidents of childhood are recalled to the mind in revisiting the haunts of early life; and how different a retrospective view is from the vivid pictures first engraved on the young mind. How small and insignificant appear many things now, which once seemed sublimely grand to my inexperienced observations. For instance, the mill pond near my father's farm always looked to my boyhood sight as wonderfully deep and large. On seeing it last January, just after a voyage on the ocean, it was difficult to realize that it was the same old dam in which I used to fish, swim and sail in summer; or glide over on skates in midwinter.

After revisiting my home again in March to say farewell, the pond seemed larger than it did in January, but not of the gigantic dimensions presented to my youthful eyes. We are always judging by comparison, and can only acquire liberal and expansive views of things by traveling over some other country besides our own native hills. My hotel life at the St. Nicholas, in New York, at Barnum's, in Baltimore, and Willard's, at Washington, during my temporary sojourn at these places, seemed at first grand and magnificent; but a few weeks of such life made things decidedly more commonplace. Could I, however, have been suddenly transported from either of these luxurious hotels to the miserably rough and uncouth log cabins at Fort Arbuckle, the change would have been unbearable. Yet these same log quarters once seemed to me like palaces for comfort when compared with the cold and unprotected tents, which for a long time formed our only shelter on the plains.

So now, after luxuriating like a prince for three months on my little savings of the past five years, I must gradually come down to backwoods-life again. Such are the extremes of an officer's career. But although "dressing in fine linen and faring sumptuously every day" during my short leave of absence, I have not been idle. For knowing that such an opportunity to brush up in my profession might not occur again for years, I have really devoted three fourths of my time in visiting the Baltimore, Philadelphia and New York medical colleges and hospitals, and have witnessed, and in some cases assisted, clinical operations in surgery by several of the most eminent surgeons in the United States. Such privileges have really given me more intense satisfaction than all the gay festivities to which I have had the entrée during the present winter.

At Baltimore, for instance, I saw my old professor, Nathan R. Smith, perform a few brilliant operations. At Philadelphia, Doctors Pancoast and Mutter held forth as of old; and in the city of New York I witnessed many capital operations at the City Hospital and Bellevue. But was more pleased at the opportunity of seeing an amputation by that most distinguished of all American surgeons, Valentine Mott. In the latter city the principal hospitals are too far off from the medical colleges for the students to properly avail themselves of clinical or practical medicine and surgery. This ought to be remedied by the establishment of medical schools in closer proximity to the hospitals. The University of Maryland, where I graduated, has a great advantage in this respect, as its infirmary is just across the street from the college building, and the students are permitted to hear and assist in daily clinics.

After a short visit to my Maryland friends I started to see my relations residing in the western part of the State of New York. Of course I availed myself of this opportunity of making a better acquaintance with the city of New York, which I reached on the tenth of January. Finding the St. Nicholas Hotel crowded, I was compelled to accept a room so high up toward the clouds that the rarification of the air almost made my head ache; but was accommodated with lodging lower down on the following day. Being, however, so near the attic at first, I concluded to go still higher, and get on the roof itself, in order to gain a bird's eye view of the great city and its surroundings. The sight fully repaid me for the trouble.

Mario and Grisi being the musical lions of the city, I availed myself of the first opportunity of hearing them, and getting a glimpse of Miss Coutts—the wealthy English lady accompanying them. I did not pay as much for a reserved seat as she is in the habit of paying—$800.

Barnum's Museum attracted a good deal of my attention. There, as at New Orleans, wax statuary appeared to have a prominent place. In addition to the specimens in this line seen in the latter city were the giant and giantess, Mr. and Mrs. Hale; Daniel Lambert, the fat man; and Calvin Edson, the living skeleton. The prince of humbugs, as he is called, deserves a great deal of credit for the wonderful collection of natural curiosities on exhibition at his building. A bare enumeration of the most interesting of which would be tedious and useless. The following dried specimens seemed to attract the most attention: A huge snapping turtle, obtained out of a solid rock in the State of New York; a rhinoceros harebill; a red flamingo; giant sun-fish; and Fejee mermaid. The last looks like a woman and fish combined—having the face and thorax of the former; and the abdomen and lower extremities of the latter. It is bogus of course—being an artificial preparation, manufactured so skillfully as as to deceive for a long time the public generally.

There was also on exhibition the Maine Giantess, thirty years old, weighing six hundred pounds; the female dwarf, aged eighteen, and only seventeen inches in height; also a giraffe. Barnum had two of these animals until lately—one being drowned at New Orleans whilst being put aboard a vessel for New York. "The happy family" of birds and animals together in a cage; and a fac simile of the great Portugal diamond—the original being valued at $29,625,200; attracted much attention.

Went to Grace Church on the Sunday after my arrival in the city. Couldn't help drawing a mental comparison between the fashionably-dressed audience there, and the first religious congregation I saw in Arkansas on reaching the frontier last autumn; but religion is the same, whether robed in royal purple or pauper's rags.

Remained in New York five days; and then took the cars for Cold Spring; where I left my baggage and crossed the Hudson on the ice for West Point; came within an ace of being drowned. Before venturing on the ice, I inquired whether there was any other method of reaching West Point that evening? Was assured in the negative, and cautioned not to attempt crossing until the following morning; as no one had yet dared to trust the ice.

It being part of my programme to reach the Academy that evening, I resolved to examine the ice myself. Near the shore it appeared sufficiently strong to bear most any one. So taking a pole in my hand, I determined upon the venture, and got along smoothly until near the channel, when numerous unfrozen places rendered my progress slower. On coming to ice presenting a doubtful appearance I would try its strength by a blow of my stick. In this manner I had nearly crossed the most dangerous part of the river, and began to grow more careless, when suddenly a piece of ice, on which I was standing, detached itself from the main body, and began to float down an unfrozen portion of the stream; barely affording me time to spring back out of danger. Although badly frightened, I changed my course higher up the river, and succeeded in crossing over just as darkness set in.

At the Point I was the guest of Lieutenant Thomas H. Niell, of the Fifth Infantry; Assistant Prof. of drawing at the Academy. The young officers here all mess together dressed in uniform; and by their martial appearance, and animated discussions, present a strikingly gay picture. The annual examination is going on; I had the pleasure of seeing some of the cadets examined. It would be superflous to give a description of this well known national military school.

There are just outside of the garrison two splendid

hotels, which, though empty in winter, are thronged with fashionable visitors in summer from all parts of the Union. The country surrounding West Point is picturesque and romantic. The following night I spent in Albany at the Delavan House. A peculiar feature of this hotel is white female waiters, under the superintendence of a mulatto steward. A good snow having fallen during the day the streets were merry with the jingle of sleigh-bells.

On Wednesday night I arrived in Buffalo. Here I met Lieutenant Mathew R. Stevenson of the Seventh Infantry, formerly of Fort Arbuckle, and now in the recruiting service; and received through him an invitation to a select dancing party given by the bachelors of the American Hotel; I enjoyed myself greatly. Next morning met brother Tom's law partner, Mr. George Barker, who kindly telegraphed to the former to meet me at the Dunkirk depot.

On my arrival at the latter place found Thomas waiting with his cutter and three-minute horse. My first sleigh ride in eight years. Just before getting into the sleigh, I slipped and fell on a strip of smooth ice with so much force as to almost break my cranium. There are several fine plank roads intersecting at Fredonia, where my brother resides, affording, when covered with snow, the finest sleighing it has ever been my lot to enjoy.

People living south of Mason and Dixon's line can have no idea of the rare sport afforded the denizens of the snowy North in winter, behind their fast trotting horses covered with jingling bells. Of course I visited the Niagara Falls—went thither in company with Mr. Barker and my brother. It was night when we arrived at the suspension bridge. Crossing to the Canada side, with the intention of taking lodgings at the Clifton House, we were informed that it was closed for the season; thus cutting us off from a night's view of the Falls, which is considered as wonderfully grand. Recrossing the bridge, a comfortable night's lodging was afforded us at the hotel of Colonel Cook.

The first object that attracted our attention in the morning was the suspension bridge, a stupendous structure, made both for foot and carriage passengers. A double railroad track is being constructed over head. Two immense stone towers at each end form abutments for the bridge. Over these are suspended the wire cables, which support the latter, though it is immediately held up by means of large wire ropes, dropping perpendicularly from the cables. The latter are fixed by having their ends run through massive rocks, and wedged.

From the bridge the view of the Niagara river, as it comes rolling, roaring, and foaming beneath us, is sublime in the extreme. It is a beautiful but fearful sight. A short distance below the bridge the river turns at a right angle—its waters are thus set whirling round and round, forming what is known as the whirlpool. Bodies floating down the river are here made to revolve in a circle for days ere they are permitted to go further.

We next started for the American Falls, three miles from the bridge. In crossing over to Goat Island we were shown the spot of one of the most painfully exciting scenes recorded in history—the log to which a man caught, on being washed down the rapids, and where he remained for twenty-four hours, notwithstanding the exertions of thousands of spectators to render him assistance. Finally a raft was floated by means of guiding ropes within a few feet of him. Being utterly exhausted in his efforts to spring upon it, he missed his hold and was hurled headlong over the roaring cataract below, making a last heart-rending scream as the brink of the Falls was reached.

We registered our names at the house half way across the rapids, and were soon on Goat Island. This forms a beautiful promenade in summer, when its trees are covered with foliage, instead of sleet and icicles, as at present. We were now within one hundred and fifty yards of the edge of the cataract. This space passed and the grand view lay at our feet. Yet we lingered.

"We always," says a beautiful writer, "pause before any great experience, which is the highest of its kind we can ever know. We tremble to clutch a pleasure beyond which there can be no other, when it is fairly within our grasp. We dally with our own feelings in order to prolong the thrill which precedes the supreme moment, which once known can never be experienced again."

At last the magnificently sublime sight burst upon us. The American Falls were beneath us. It would be useless to attempt a description—which has been so often made. We next visited the Horse-shoe Falls on the Canada side, a grander and more sublime sight than the other. We were not disappointed. The splendid reality equaled all the eye could wish. At the American Falls we were shown the spot where a young lady, her affianced, and a little girl, were pleasantly whiling away a bright summer's day, when the young man playfully taking the child in his arms gave her a toss as if to throw her into the rapids. She being frightened, sprang out of his arms into the stream—he of course following in order to rescue her—and the swift current bore them both over the Falls into the fathomless watery abyss below. This sad event occurred about eighteen months ago.

After being the guest of my brother for ten days, sister Eliza and I started for Maryland. The Great Central Railroad being much obstructed with snow, we took the cars at Dunkirk, on the New York and Erie road, for Elmira, a thriving town near the Pennsylvania line, situated on the Chemung, a branch of the Susquehanna river. There we left the New York and Erie railroad, and took the road leading to Philadelphia. This runs through a highly romantic country—in fact crossing the Alleghany Mountains.

Our lady passengers became very nervous as the train swept over high bridges and deep chasms. At the Quaker City we tarried a day, and visited some of the noble public buildings. Among others, Girard College and the Fairmount Water Works. The former institution was endowed, as is well known, by Stephen Girard. The requisite permit to enter is headed by an extract from the will of the endower, prohibiting all ministers of the gospel from being employed as instructors in, or from even visiting this college. Children between the ages of six and twelve are received here.

Besides the common branches of an English education, they are taught drawing, French, Spanish, and some of the higher branches of mathematics. The school now numbers about three hundred pupils. There are five buildings in all, constructed of marble. The center one is an immense structure, being surrounded by some forty-four marble columns, each nine feet in diameter and about thirty-five feet high.

One has a magnificent view of the city and surrounding country from the roof of the building. After seeing my sister safely home and remaining a few days, I returned to Baltimore, to attend medical lectures, and witness operations at the University of Maryland. On the eighteenth of February I made a visit to Washington City. After paying my respects to the Surgeon-General, Brigadier-General Thomas Lausen, and Adjutant-General Col. Samuel Cooper (as demanded by army etiquette), I visited the Capitol. Heard several fine speeches in the Senate and House. The latter is a perfect bedlam for noise and confusion.

Very few bills pass Congress on their merits alone. The great majority of those for depletion of the public treasury are got through by the influence of lobby-members—a set of agents hired by the parties interested in the passage of an act; who hang around the lobbies and drinking saloons at the Capitol, and by means of liquor, oysters, cigars, soft speeches, and sometimes money, influence the members of Congress either for or against certain bills which may be under consideration. Some of our legislators are the paid attorneys of private corporations. With few exceptions, the purest and ablest men in the country never go to Congress. We seem to be retrograding in this respect from year to year. Some of the lobbyists are paid enormously; they charge both a real and contingent fee. The first being paid whether successful or not; the second only when success crowns their manipulations.

After spending a few days in Washington, I again visited New York City, and devoted most of my time to a review of practical medicine and surgery at the clinics of New York and Bellevue Hospitals. On Sundays I of course went to church. Heard the renowned Henry Ward Beecher several times. His church, in Brooklyn, is always crowded. This gentleman has a tall, commanding figure; rather handsome, expressive features, and dark hair. His voice is soft, clear, full and powerful; gestures easy, appropriate and natural. He draws largely on beautiful similes and metaphors, and illustrations from science and natural history. The beauty, simplicity and originality of his discourses instruct and enchant his auditors. The choir, which is seated behind and above the pulpit, is very select. That which electrifies and impresses one the most, is the congregational singing by over a thousand persons.

During this visit to New York I went to see the Crystal Palace and the Croton Water Works; both stupendous and beautiful architectural productions. The former was erected three years ago as a place of exhibition for the various works of art in the civilized world. Most of the articles have either been sold or withdrawn. During the exhibition everything was examined by proper committees, and awards given according to their reports.

The building occupies a whole square, and consists of a nave and four wings, the body being surmounted by a dome. It is two stories high. Its framework is light, complex, but strong, and beautifully arranged. The sides of the building, and a large portion of the roof, are of glass. Of the few articles now on exhibition, perhaps the most interesting are the marble and bronze statuary and paintings. In the east wing is the immense bronze equestrian statue of Washington; in the south wing is the bronze statue of Webster, standing on a pedestal; and in the north wing is the Amazon on horseback—being attacked by a tiger. Of the marble statuary, the most remarkable are Christ and his Twelve Apostles. There is also a marble representation of the principal heathen gods and generals. The statues of Venus, Apollo, Paris and Cupid, are the beau-ideals of beauty and loveliness.

One of the most remarkable paintings is the "Court of Death;" it is about fifteen by twenty feet. As almost everybody has seen this picture, I shall not attempt a description or criticism of it. The picture of Orphelia is life-like, and charmingly beautiful. New York is rarely blest with many bright sunny days in winter, or early spring, but when they do come, the fair sex turn out by thousands to shop on Broadway, or promenade on Fifth Avenue. A sight of so many beautiful creatures is more pleasing than that of all the paintings on exhibition in this great city. Were all those lovely beings as angelic as they seem, what a paradise our earth would be! Man could not then be the wretched sinner that he often is.

The times have been harder in New York this winter than for many previous years—many suspensions among the large mercantile and manufacturing establishments. The poor are thus being thrown out of employment by thousands, and are holding large meetings in the park to hear exciting speeches from fanatical demagogues. Among other means of relief the City Council have established soup kitchens in various sections of the city, where the hungry poor may at least get something to prevent starvation. Calico parties have also been given for their benefit. The dresses worn on these occasions are subsequently given to the poor.

The winter has been unusually severe all over the northwest. About the middle of January there was an exceedingly deep drift of snow, seventeen miles long, on the Mississippi and Chicago Railroad, in which were buried twelve trains of cars. In some instances the passengers were under the necessity of tearing up the seats and furniture for fuel, and appropriating everything in the eating line found on board the freight cars.

Left New York March 9th for Linganore, where I took a final leave of my relatives on the twenty-sixth of the same month. Tarrying awhile in Baltimore, I arrived at Willard's Hotel in Washington April 2d. Saw there several old army friends—among others Captain R. B. Marcy, who politely invited me to call and see his family when I should return to New York. Presented a collection of dried prairie-flowers to the Smithsonian Institute. Received in return from the Secretary, Professor Baird, a letter of thanks. Called on a few ladies. Was much pleased with Miss Nina Wood, daughter of the Assistant Surgeon-General, and granddaughter of ex-President Taylor.

Sent my card to President Pierce—was honored with a few minutes' conversation. He looked care-worn and haggard. Not surprising—for if ever there was a slave to the public it is the President of the United States. He has not a moment that he can call his own. The mansion is beautiful on the out-side, but exceedingly plain within. The lord steward of the kennel in England resides in a much finer house, and receives a larger salary than our President. As the latter, however, has certain contingent ex-penses borne by the government, he can very well support the dignity of his office on $25,000 per annum. Went to the capitol; but as there were no interesting debates in either house, I took a stroll through the rotunda to see the paintings. Was charmed with Powel's master-piece—De Soto. Fer-dinand De Soto, the discoverer of the Mississippi, was one of the most remarkable men of his day. Gaining permission from the Emperor, Charles the V, he un-dertook the conquest of Florida in 1538 at his own expense. His command consisted of six hundred Spanish and Portuguese cavaliers. At the present site of Mobile he fought a sanguinary battle with the Indians. After traveling as far west as Arkansas, he attempted to descend to the Gulf of Mexico through the bayous and marshes along the banks of the Mis-sissippi river; but was attacked with a malignant fever, and died in April, 1542. There are, nowadays, few such venturesome spirits as the Spanish cavaliers of the sixteenth and seventeenth centuries.

Made a visit to the Patent Office building. Besides the many specimens of American genius, this edifice contains the National Institute—embracing one of the finest collections of curiosities in the union. The United States Exploring Expeditions have furnished a large number of splendid contributions to this museum. Perhaps there are none more curious than the collection from the Fiji Islands. Fine specimens of crockeryware; of cloth manufactured from the inner bark of trees; necklaces; bark fishing lines, with bone hooks; curious war clubs and bludgeons; a vast variety of corals—such as the cactus, fungus and rose corals—and, in fact, a coral representative of most of the floral kingdom. There are also to be seen here many stuffed fish and animals. The sea-horse and sea-lion attracting the larger share of attention from visitors.

Receiving orders from the Secretary of War to report to the General-in-chief for duty with the first detachment of recruits bound for the department of the Pacific, I left Washington on the sixth of April for Baltimore. Took leave of my friends there and reached New York on the seventh—taking a room at the Astor House. Reporting to General Winfield Scott on the ninth of April, I received orders on the eleventh to report to the superintendent of the recruiting service for duty with the detachment of recruits which is to leave here to-morrow. On leaving the city for this place I was compelled, in consequence of a gale, to stop a day at Governor's Island, where I was the guest of Colonel John J. Abercrombie, of the Second Infantry. Saw there the families of Surgeon Samuel P. Moore, Lieutenant Holdeman and others.

On the night of my arrival at this place—Fort

Wood—I was walking along the dark hall of my quarters, and stumbled down the stone stair-way leading from the basement. The fall rendered me senseless for awhile, but through the kind exertions of Lieutenant H. G. Gibson, who heard the noise, I was soon restored to my senses again. The only officer's lady at this fort is Mrs. Captain Gardiner, who will accompany her husband to the Pacific. Mrs. Major Ben. Alvord also anticipates going with us to join her husband at Fort Vancouver, Washington Territory.

CHAPTER XIV.

VOYAGE TO SAN FRANCISCO.

Sea Voyage to California—Bogus Governor—Small Pox—Railroad Scare—Wreck of the Golden Gate—Yerb Prescription for Cholera worth $1000.

STEAMSHIP ILLINOIS, April 25th, 1855.

LEFT Warren Street wharf yesterday at two P. M. with a stiff breeze from the north-east. Vessel crowded; seven hundred and fifty passengers exclusive of ship's crew. Aft there is an upper and lower cabin—forward an upper and lower steerage. The troops occupy the latter. Captain I. W. T. Gardiner, First Dragoons, Captain T. J. Craw, Top. Engineers, and myself, are in the same stateroom. Mrs. Alvord and Gardiner have another. All in the first cabin of course. A large number of women and children on board—two or three very beautiful young ladies. But oh! this seasickness. What a terrible drawback to a pretty woman. 'Tis death to all those acquired charms that render beauty so angelic. Why yesterday evening whilst old Neptune was producing his fiercest commotions (oceanic, and, per consequence, antiperistaltic) a lady absolutely inquired of me the way to the ———! She was evidently sea-green as well as seasick, or she would have found some convenient vessel in her room. On the second or third day out our seats at the table were arranged and numbered. This isn't necessary at first, as but few have nerve enough to try the odor of ship-cooked meats—and when they do are frequently glad to beat a hasty retreat. Then the slight but knowing smile of the servants, as you stagger to your room is quite aggravating.

The storm of rain and wind which we experienced in first making the ocean has passed away, and to-day is ushered in clear and beautiful. A stiff breeze from the northeast; sea not very rough, however. Our vessel is running comparatively steady as her canvass is stretched. Have seen in the dim distance quite a number of sailing vessels; some so remote that their sails only are visible. The steerage is so crowded that it is impossible to give proper medical attention to our troops.

Sunday, April 22d, 1855.—Struck the gulf stream at eleven last night; the atmosphere is consequently warmer. Early part of the night clear, with a moderate breeze. The heavens glittered with their brightest jewelry. The silvery moon gleamed her softest glances as she glided down the western plane, and Venus, though somewhat eclipsed by the queenly Luna, seemed joyously bright and sparkling.

Great are the wonders of Thy handiwork, O God; and still more wonderful Thy mercy. Permit me on this blessed day of our Redeemer to offer unto Thee thanks for Thy protecting care and mercy. The best of us are frail helpless mortals. Vouchsafe unto us an assisting and controling hand, that we may not be as lost sheep from the fold. And whilst we gaze upon this vast ocean of water may we remember it is but a drop in comparison with the ocean of eternity—and on whose boundless bosom we must all sooner or later be launched; and that it will be to us an eternity of weal, or an eternity of woe. Oh, bring us to a proper appreciation of our awful responsibility—and may we prove worthy to rank with those to whom the Lord will say, well done my good and faithful servant, enter thou into the joys of my kingdom.

April 23d, 1855.—The past twenty-four hours have been delightful—at least as far as the weather is concerned. The wind is from the northeast, and very refreshing. Sky cloudy—sea comparatively smooth. A large majority of the passengers now make their appearance at table. The children are less fretful; in short there is a general brightening up. I really felt comfortable this morning whilst seated under the fine awning, breathing the pure sea air. How delightful is the change since Saturday—then all were morose and sick, now all are cheerful. Some of the ladies have sufficiently revived to sing. Our fare is not sumptous, but substantial. The dessert is fine—tea and coffee abominable, as they always are on steamships, where all the aroma is dissipated by too much boiling. Ice is allowed us to-day. What a luxury! Saw yesterday and to-day several Mother Cary's chickens. These are only found far out at sea.

Half-past 2, P. M.—Just finished dinner—full table—first meal that all seemed to enjoy. If the weather continues calm we will begin to think sea-life endurable after all. Still cloudy. At twelve M, we were in lat. 29 degrees 52 minutes, long. 74 degrees 14 minutes, and had made in the preceding twenty-four hours two hundred and forty-one miles. As the ladies begin to show themselves at table we notice some very pretty and interesting faces.

April 24th, 1855.—Made since yesterday noon two hundred and forty-three miles. We are now distant from New York about nine hundred. Our course until yesterday evening was a point west of south—now a point east of south. In meteorological language (ten as maximum) the clearness of sky is five—force of wind three. The weather has been nearly the same since Saturday night—excepting a refreshing shower of rain at 11½ A. M. Have seen in the last twenty-four hours about half a dozen vessels. Several flying-fish have been noticed. The phosphorescence, that beautiful phenomenon of southern waters, is not yet very brilliant.

Our captain (McKinstry) is a lieutenant of the U. S. Navy. He has this command for a limited period only—agreeably to an act of congress permitting officers of the navy to command mail steamers when their services are specially required. His pay for this duty of twenty-five hundred dollars is a perquisite to his naval salary. A very clever gentleman, both intellectually and socially. As the army is a kindred branch of service he takes delight in showing us every civility and attention. We and our friends have seats near the head of his table. Our meals, therefore, are social repasts.

The troops thus far have conducted themselves remarkably well. No disturbances between them and civilians, as is frequently the case when thrown together. To the shame of the fairer *moitié du geure humaine*, however, I regret to add that the only blot upon our good deportment so far was a rumpus raised by one of the camp-women, who, having secreted liquor aboard and become intoxicated, was exceedingly boisterous and noisy. Captain G. had her confined in the baggage-room till her fillibustering propensities somewhat subsided. Have at last found a tolerable place in which to examine the sick, and have proper attention given them. The ship's surgeon, Dr. Otis, has kindly offered me his room for all cases requiring a nice examination. Lat. 25 degrees 51 minutes, long. 74 degrees 40 minutes.

April 25th, 1855.—Made two hundred and twenty-six miles in the last twenty-four hours. Latitude 22 deg. 6 min.; longitude 74 deg. 23 min. Passed, last night, the Islands known as the Wattins—and at 6½ this morning Long Island on our starboard; 9½, Crooked Island on the larboard, and are now just off Castle Island, being named from a large rock, some distance from the shore, projecting to a considerable height, and resembling a castle. All these islands contain salt works. Met three sails this morning. Had our curiosities gratified yesterday by the sight of two boobies, which sailed aloft over our vessel. At a distance they resemble fish-hawks. They are remarkable for their stupidity. Sometimes alighting on the masts of the vessel, and falling asleep, are despatched by the sailors. A beautiful bird of paradise sailed across our bow this morning—a wanderer doubtless from some neighboring isle—its plumage of a light and beautiful color.

Rising early I had the pleasure of witnessing the aerial efforts of some flying-fish. It is an interesting sight to see. them hurl aloft on the appearance of a porpoise. Sometimes light on deck; thus affording a dainty repast for the sailors. Refreshing shower this morning. Temperature growing warmer; clearness of sky remains about five; wind four. Everybody is coming out in summer apparel. Our amusements consist in chess, whist and reading. The latter is most to my taste.

April 26th, 1855—12 M.—Latitude 18 deg. 28 min.; longitude 75 deg. 20 min. Weather about the same. Moderately cloudy, with occasional showers. There was, however, a slight squall last night. At dawn made Cuba on our starboard, and Jamaica also in the dim distance. The former barely visible in consequence of the haziness of the atmosphere. Even the .latter resembled a cloud so closely that it could only be determined by its outline.

Quite an amusing hoax has just been played on some of the passengers. There is a very talkative little English Jew merchant on board, who got bruited around as being the Lieutenant Governor of Jamaica. Having made himself disagreeable to a party of gentlemen, they were disposed to "snub him," but on learning that he was a high functionary of Jamaica, one of them, Judge McAlister, of the United States District Court of California, proposed making amends by treating him with more civility and attention. He accordingly gave him a special invitation to drink wine with him. Some one of the party expressed to the Judge their incredulity of the man's holding any high official station. But he insisted that there could be no mistake about it, as Captain McKinstry had assured him of its truth. Seeing the Judge, shortly after his tete-a-tete with the Governor, we asked him how fared his excellency. He replied with much irritation—"The fellow is a contemptible humbug."

5 P. M.—Jamaica is in view; its picturesque mountains lift their lofty peaks in noble grandeur above the ocean. Oh, how I should love to exchange this monotonous ship-life for a few hours stroll over those lofty summits. So much is said of the luxury of sea air, but give me the pure mountain breeze forever. There is a dampness and sea-sick smell about everything on board ship to which I could never become reconciled. Kingston, Jamaica, though somewhat dilapidated, is said to be an interesting town. The most luscious tropical fruits abound there. The passengers are delighted at the prospect of getting on terra firma once more, and of enjoying oranges fresh from the trees. The Illinois always touches there to take in coal. Preparations are made to land—even the big gun loaded for a salute. The pilot is aboard to see us safely through the harbor. Captain McKinstry suddenly decides to keep on to Aspinwall; everybody is surprised; what can be the matter? Some suggest the probability of yellow fever or small-pox at Kingston. The Lieutenant Governor is

in a rage; swears he will sue the company for damages. The captain gives no satisfaction unless it is to the ladies, whom he tells that it would delay him too long to stop at Kingston. But *entre nous* the true reason is, that that most fearful of all diseases to encounter on a crowded vessel—the small-pox—has broken out among us, and the matter has just been reported to the captain by myself. Rather than be quarantined at Jamaica he has wisely concluded to push on to Aspinwall, where there are no regulations to prevent our landing. Knowing the terror that the announcement of small-pox would create, we have agreed to keep it secret; but at the same time guard against its spreading. We shall erect a pavilion for the man (only one as yet) on the hurricane deck, in a nice airy place, and put sentinels at the gangways. No one shall be allowed to go up.

The sick man is a soldier. As they have all been vaccinated, and are principally to themselves, a general outbreak of the disease is not apprehended. The crowded state of the vessel, however, is very favorable to its progress. I have one source of congratulation—that of having taken the precaution of vaccinating all the men before leaving Bedloe's Island. This man undoubtedly had the seeds of the disease in him previous to vaccination, as it prevailed to a slight extent at Fort Columbus some eighteen days ago. Although vaccination is not a sure preventive, it arrests the disease to a surprising extent, and modifies it in all cases.

April 27th—12 M.—The fact of small-pox being

on board is not yet discovered. Some of the knowing ones assert that the reason the Captain didn't stop at Kingston was owing to the small-pox being very prevalent there; they are accordingly delighted at our not touching at so sickly a place. Our latitude is 14 deg. 36 min.; longitude, 77 deg. 38 min; and we have come in the last twenty-four hours two hundred and fifty-six miles. Several copious showers this morning—cooling the atmosphere, but being otherwise disagreeable, as every one is compelled to crowd in the cabin.

2 P. M. — Another case of small-pox; if it should spread through the ship, what a dreadful time we shall have.

April 29th.—Latitude, 10 deg. 42 min.; longitude, 79 deg. 29 min.; two hundred and fifty-six miles since yesterday; the weather continues nearly the same, except that the wind is veering to the west. Our stateroom being on the starboard side, we now begin to get a lively breeze through the skylight, at the expense, though, of being drenched occasionally by the spray; yet this is trifling in comparison to the heat we have had to endure heretofore. Last night was the most trying. Captain C. arose, exclaiming he should die if fresh air could not be obtained. We expect to reach Aspinwall to-night, where we will leave our small-pox cases until the next detachment arrives. The news is beginning to leak out, and excites much alarm. As yet the ladies are in blissful ignorance. Some of them have been advised to be vaccinated, as the small-pox is very prevalent at Aspinwall. Among others upon whom I have just performed this operation, are

Mrs. H. and sister—very charming and intelligent ladies. They converse equally well in French, Spanish and English—and one of them has the most angelic voice I have ever heard. The husband of Mrs. H. is an invalid—a resident of San Francisco, where he amassed a princely fortune; but for the last few years he has been traveling for his health. Oh, how hard it seems for one thus surrounded by all worldly means of happiness to be doomed by the insidious progress of that most fatal of all maladies—consumption; and this, too, in the bloom and pride of early manhood.

Sunday, April 29th—7 A. M.—In the harbor of Aspinwall—got here last night at half past ten. Some difficulty in making the wharf, in consequence of the shallowness of the water, and the unmanageable state of our vessel—it being impossible to back her for some reason or other. Aspinwall contains about seven hundred inhabitants, and presents a very picturesque appearance. The surrounding country, as well as the town itself, is studded with palmettos and cocoanut trees. The buildings are few—generally frame—and belong to the Railroad Company. It is unhealthy—malarious fevers being prevalent in August and September; not so insalubrious, however, as Chagres, a point further south, where emigrants formerly crossed; it being fatal for a northerner to remain there any length of time.

After all the passengers had gone ashore last night I superintended the transfer of the two small-pox cases to a comfortable hospital near the town; this unpleasant duty was performed in a small row-boat at three o'clock at night. They were put under the care of Dr. Fish, who at first seemed reluctant to take them, as it might create an excitement in the city. It is the current report in Aspinwall this morning, that there have been forty deaths from small-pox among the troops. Great sensation! Some impostor has been imposing on the credulity of the inhabitants.

April 30th.—Left Aspinwall in the first train of cars for Panama at half past nine A. M. The civilians came in the second train a few hours afterwards. Six hours in transitu, and only forty-nine miles of railroad. This was owing to the difficulty of passing over the steep grades. At these places the engines were reversed and the train run back some distance, when the effort was renewed with increased force. At the summit, two hundred and fifty feet above the level of the Pacific Ocean, we ran back five times before succeeding. The second train, being less heavily laden, excited considerable alarm by occasionally coming up to us rather suddenly; and to add to the annoyances, our train halted within a quarter of a mile of the road's terminus in consequence of getting out of wood. In the meantime the hindmost engine came puffing up apparently, at full speed, and some gentlemen on the platform of one car cried out that we would be run into, and at the same time sprang off. This created a panic among the men—some of whom rushed for the door; others sprang out of the windows in the utmost confusion. I commended them to keep their seats—but to no purpose. When the excitement subsided, those who had run were rallied by the others for their timidity. Captain Henry W. Halleck, formerly of the Engineer Corps, and now a resident of San Francisco, and his bride, were passengers, and occupied the seat in front of Captain Cram and myself. When the stampede took place Captain Halleck was outside, but rushed for his wife, who was fortunately asleep, and did not awake until the excitement was over. Captain Gardiner and some other army people were in the car behind.

Getting out of wood at this point was owing to the carelessness of the fireman—or rather stubbornness—for being piqued at the Superintendent because he put on a second engine to assist us over the heavy grades; he neglected to fire up properly, and take in fuel at the proper time. In the States such a man would not be tolerated a single moment; but here it is impossible to relieve him under three or four weeks at least, there being no one on the Isthmus to take his place. This is only one of the thousand difficulties which the company has had to contend with in constructing such a stupendous work so far from the States.

In the first place, the physical features of the country were such as to render it almost incredible that a railroad could be constructed over it. Their workmen, some five thousand, were only to be had in the States, and other distant places—and the same difficulty obtained as it regards their material for the road and cars, which was obtained in Maine and Georgia; for although there is abundance of timber along the road, it is of too perishable a nature for the construction of a railroad. Medicines and provisions were also brought from the States.

The road cost seven millions of dollars. It runs through a picturesque country of alternate hills and dales, covered with perpetual green. Some thirty varieties of tropical plants are seen along the route: such as the cocoanut, cocoa, palmetto, orange, banana and mangrove. The latter form in many places impenetrable thickets; and one finds it impossible to unravel the mysterious involutions of trunk, root, branch and foliage—as their roots shoot into the air, and their branches into the ground—thus forming a dense jungle. Here and there are to be seen native shanties, consisting of a framework of small poles covered with palmetto leaves. The natives are indolent—subsisting mainly on fish, game and the proceeds of fruits sold to emigrants. Yesterday being Sunday we found them in their best attire. We saw a few negresses handsomely dressed, but they were evidently not natives; probably importations from the States.

Living on the Isthmus is very expensive—board is four dollars per diem at the hotels—no distinction made for children or servants; miserable fare even at this price. Vegetables on the table are *rari avi;* and stale at that. It seems to be the general wonder of travelers, crossing by this route, why some enterprising Yankees don't settle down here and try their fortunes at gardening—as vegetables are so scarce and dear, and the soil so rich. Upon inquiry, however, I find that the common garden vegetables of the States will not thrive in this climate.

As the steamer was waiting for us at Panama, we had but little time to examine that dilapidated old seaport of the United States of Colombia. This fortified city has rather a pleasing aspect from the sea, being situated on a rocky peninsula, jutting out into the Bay of Panama. Though perhaps cleaner than many Spanish-American cities, yet the odors arising from the accumulated filth in some of the streets are not like those of the attar of roses and oil of bergamot. It is built of stone in the old Spanish style. It was for many years the great centre of trade between the Pacific coast of America and Europe, but began to decline in 1740, when this trade commenced to find its channel around Cape Horn, but is now reviving again on account of the immense travel across the Isthmus to and from California.

Its harbor is good, but very shallow near the shore—necessitating large vessels to be at low tide from two to four miles out in the bay. The tides arise and fall about twenty-five feet. It commands a beautiful view of Panama Bay in front, and is overlooked in the rear by high hills. During one of the frequent revolutions in the city, General Bolivar planted his cannon on one of those heights and stormed the place. He was too far above the horizontal line for his shot to have much effect; nevertheless, the cannon's deafening roar frightened the city into capitulation.

From Panama we embarked on the John L. Stevens, Captain Pearson, commanding. She lay four miles out in the harbor, and had to be approached by row boats, and a small steamboat. It was almost impossible to get into the boats from the sandy beach without getting one's feet wet; owing to the continual swell of the sea. It was necessary to take advantage of the receding waves, and be as expeditious as possible, or the succeeding surge would drench us. It being dark when the majority of the passengers reached the steamer there was terrible confusion. The boats crowded at the gangway, each endeavoring to get precedence over the other. The pulling and hauling, and cursing and swearing, terrified the ladies greatly. The steamer is a magnificent vessel; very large and kept in perfect order; fine airy staterooms, and a promenade on the hurricane deck of three hundred and twenty feet in length; her discipline is perfect; the captain enforces his rules with much energy and strictness. Being a rough old sailor he is somewhat deficient in that cordial and gentlemanly bearing towards his passengers, which so eminently distinguishes the naval from merchant captains. Yet his constant attention to all the details of his duty inspires us with confidence. Our fare is good, but we miss the abundance of ice which was allowed us on the other side of the Isthmus. Here we pay twenty-five cents a pound for it; and not sure of getting enough even at this price.

May 1st, 1855.—Had a smooth passage yesterday. This ocean, from its calmness and placidity, is very appropriately named. The steamer is exceedingly short of servants; she even has not her usual complement, in consequence of the Golden Age not having got in before her departure. As each vessel tarries in port a fortnight it is customary to turn her servants over to the first one of the line that goes out. But even with this arrangement they are generally very scarce, owing to the fact that very few are permanently employed; simply engaging to work their passage to and from California.

Whilst at dinner yesterday (5 P. M.) news arrived of the wreck of the Golden Age. She ran on a shoal in passing between the Islands of Ke-ka-re and Quibo, pronounced Kee-bo; and, staving in her bottom, put ashore in distress. This happened at two A. M. last Sunday. A row boat was immediately dispatched for Panama, a distance of two hundred miles, for succor. But falling in with us we hurried on, and arriving at the wreck this morning at two, found the Age lying securely on a sand beach, with her bow almost out of water. The accident occurred about six hundred yards from the Island. Water began rushing in at a fearful rate, but the captain (Watkins) succeeded in reaching the shore in time to save all on board. We are now re-shipping her passengers and freight with a view of returning to Panama with them. This will detain us about three days.

It seems difficult to arrive at the particulars of the accident. It appears, however, that the Age had been detained a day over her time at San Francisco, and was endeavoring to regain the loss time, as well as make a "crack trip." In the latter particular she unfortunately succeeded. One of the principal agents, Mr. Aspinwall, was aboard, and, it is said, talking with the captain on deck when the vessel ran against the rock; it was a clear moonlight night. She has about nine hundred passengers, making in all about nineteen hundred persons on board our vessel; a perfect jam. Although we are glad to be able to afford relief to the distressed, yet a few days' delay may cause us serious inconvenience in case the small-pox reappears among us.

All the passengers are now aboard, and this immense vessel is crowded from stem to stern. Hardly a breath of air since the rain this morning. All seem exhausted from the exercise, heat and fatigue of standing up. How this great number of hungry stomachs will be able to satisfy their cravings, is more than I can tell. For the present we are put on two meals per diem. So we need complain no longer of the want of an appetite.

I should remark that the "Golden Age" was wrecked at a most fortunate point of the coast. Almost anywhere else within two hundred miles of this place she must have met a watery grave—as the shore is exceedingly bluff. The passengers amused themselves, whilst waiting for relief, in hunting monkeys and wild fruits. Many were sickened by a too free indulgence in the latter.

Wednesday, 2d—7 A. M.—Been raining and blowing all night—most everybody thoroughly uncomfortable. It would have been pleasanter for the wrecked passengers had they remained on board the "Golden Age," and the detention would only have been a day, as we met the "Panama" at four this morning in search of the former vessel. I am glad to witness so much good feeling on the part of the passengers to each other under the circumstances. Some of our passengers, it is true, can't be reconciled to so much inconvenience in order to confer so slight a benefit. Perhaps their having to wait so much longer for their meals is the most disagreeable feature of the whole. Saw a large school of porpoises rolling and pitching alongside of the vessel yesterday. The "Panama" is struggling onward some distance in our rear. The wrecked passengers were not transferred to her, as it would have made them too late for to-day's train.

May 3d.—Arrived off Panama yesterday, 12 M. The "Golden Age" passengers got ashore, and started immediately for Aspinwall. Another case of small-pox yesterday morning among the troops. I superintended the transfer of the poor fellow to a comfortable hospital, near Panama, and left him under the care of Dr. ———, formerly a surgeon to the New York Volunteers—an exceedingly pleasant person, but very punctillious in matters of honor. He has just fought a duel with a gentleman of Panama; the latter's fire tore off the shirt collar of the Doctor, who fired in the air—the seconds then interfered and amicably arranged the matter.

The steamship was unable to await the return of my party, but got under way for Tobago (twelve miles distant), even before we reached the shore. However, the agent had promised us transportation to that place in time to regain the steamer before she should finish coaling. Having seen my man comfortably cared for, the three attendants and myself made preparations for departure. On our way to the wharf, we met Dr. McNorton, the ship's surgeon, who had also been left behind. Hiring a row-boat, we started for a little steamboat, three miles out in the bay, which was taking on coal (from a vessel) for the "Stephens," and of course was bound for Tobago. When we had got about half way to her, she started for some other point. It fortunately struck us, that she was making for a lighter some two miles off, near the shore. For this point our oarsmen were directed to push with all their energy; and we fortunately reached the place just in the very nick of time—a minute later and we would have been left behind. We joined our friends on the "Stephens" about midnight. I should have added that, besides the Doctor, we fell in with another gentleman, who had also been left behind. He had gone ashore to seek a trunk (worth some $40,000 to him) which was lost. He could learn no tidings of it; it contained papers relating to a large amount of property in San Francisco.

Before leaving Panama, we went to a restaurant and got some fine oysters, which are obtained on the coast, some forty miles from that place. Also, some delicious California potatoes, which are much larger than those in the States. There is evidently quite a number of sleight-of-hand gentry abroad—several gentlemen have been robbed. Among others the ship's surgeon of $65, and a diamond ring worth $200.

May 4th, 1855.—Our course, until we got out of Panama, a distance of two hundred miles, was just a little west of south; now it is W. N. W. The weather is very warm and showery—moderately cloudy all the time—an occasional breeze.

We have at last seen the famous monster of the deep—the whale. He made his appearance within one hundred yards of the ship. Every time he came to the surface he caused the water to fly equal to a

New York fire-engine. So far our course from Panama has been within from two to ten miles of land. Some of the scenery is very beautiful. Occasionally quite a lofty mountain peak looms up in the dim distance, spurs of the Cordilleras. Taking a seat on the hurricane deck last evening I beheld the rising moon springing forth from her watery bed in full and glorious effulgence; she looked larger and brighter than ever. The most interesting sight of all (because new) was the Southern Cross. The North Star was also seen about eight degrees above the horizon.

12 o'clock, M.—Latitude 8 deg. 20 min.; longitude 83 deg. 30 min. Distance from Panama three hundred and forty-seven miles.

Sunday, May 6th, 1855.—Distance in twenty-four hours two hundred and fifty-six miles. Latitude 15 deg. 02 min; north longitude 91 deg. 39 min. west. Decidedly the warmest day of the trip. Sky hazy; no breeze, except from the motion of the ship. Ocean for a few hours this morning smooth as a mirror. But even when not affected by the wind it is in a state of undulation or gentle swell. This causes the vessel to roll a great deal. Some of the machinery getting out of gear yesterday, we were compelled to stop several times. While thus quiescent I was struck with the remarkable clearness of the ocean. Some potato peelings being thrown overboard they could be seen to the depth of thirty or forty feet. Everything considered we have cause for thankfulness in getting on so smoothly. In truth, instead of becoming disgusted with this kind of life, I really begin to enjoy it.

May 7th, 1855.—Smooth sea until eight this morning; since then rough, with a stiff breeze. Nearly everybody sea-sick. Most of those who picked up courage to go to the table this morning were glad to leave as soon as possible. The captain, like a jolly old tar, is rallying some of the faint-hearted ones about the rough weather. Says he hopes it will continue, as it gives plenty of room on the ship; most every one has retired to their rooms. As to myself I took a few spoonfuls of tea and left the table *sans ceremonie.* One cause of the roughness is our crossing the Gulf of Tehuantepec.

Considerable excitement was created yesterday by a notice on the bulletin board for all seafaring men to meet at the captain's office at one o'clock. This meeting was for the purpose of organizing parties to perform certain duties in the event of a fire, or other such emergency. Some were to command the boats; others to use the hose to extinguish the fire, others again to guard the hatchways. The excitement was increased when these parties were called on deck to go through a system of drilling. Many of the ladies were in tears, deeming that some accident was impending or apprehended to induce such precautions. Since the loss of the "Arctic" it is the custom of most commanders to prepare for such accidents as fire. To prevent unnecessary alarm, it would be advisable to state on the bulletin board the object of such preparations.

May 8th, 1855.—Our eyes were delighted with the sight of land yesterday, at three P. M. And what adds still more to the interest of the view is its being the western border of that country with which we have lately had such a bloody struggle—Mexico—a down-trodden nation—wrapped in civil discord and war. For the last two years civil carnage has cast a gloom over the land. Province after province has revolted against Santa Anna (the present self-styled Emperor). They have not acted sufficiently in concert with each other to effect anything by their movements.

To-day noon we will probably reach Acapulco, where we expect to take in coal. This place is thirteen hundred or fourteen hundred miles from Panama, and eighteen hundred or nineteen hundred from San Francisco.

Wednesday, May 9th, 1855.—Latitude 17 deg. 45 min. north; longitude 102 deg. 05 min. west. Distance from Acapulco one hundred and forty-five miles. We arrived at the latter place yesterday at noon. Left there last night at twelve. A small but beautiful harbor—about a mile long—surrounded by a lofty mountain range. The town contains some two thousand souls—is built principally of adobe, a species of sun-dried brick. It was visited December 4th, 1852, by an earthquake, which destroyed all its principal buildings.

Considerable excitement here in regard to gold mines, said to have been recently discovered in the neighborhood. Some of our steerage passengers were foolish enough to stop with the view of going to them, thus losing their passage to California. It is believed to be a speculating scheme on the part of certain American officials of this port; there may be, of course, a slight foundation for the report. To-day is exceedingly warm—no rain for several days; still in sight of the coast.

I should have added, that whilst lying in port at Acapulco, we were much amused and astonished at witnessing the Mexican boys dive; they would swim along side the steamer in crowds, and cry out, *picayune, Señor.* Some passenger would drop overboard a small silver coin, when the little fellows would rush to the spot where the piece struck the water, and by diving perpendicularly succeed almost invariably in getting it, even though it hit the water fifteen yards from them. Money, however, don't sink very rapidly in water—much less so in salt water—it always takes a kind of zigzag motion.

May 10th, 1855.—Distance since yesterday noon, 262 miles. Latitude, 19° 50′; longitude 106°. We are now crossing the mouth of the Gulf of California, and, consequently, have a pretty rough sea and refreshing breeze. Saw off our larboard yesterday afternoon a ship—the first seen in the Pacific thus far. As the sailing vessels double Cape Horn, their course is further out at sea than ours, hence our seeing them so rarely.

May 11th, 1855.—A smoother time in the Gulf than anticipated; some of the passengers were, nevertheless, sea-sick; weather sensibly cooler—in fact, pleasant. I could get quite a practice on board were it not somewhat interfering with the province of the ship's surgeon. I performed a slight operation on this gentleman himself the other day, in removing two chicots (she-koes, though vulgarly called giggers), from his big toe. These insects are very troublesome in the tropics; burrowing in the flesh, usually of the big toe, they reproduce themselves by thousands, thus creating inflammation, which ends in mortification of the whole foot if they are not removed in time.

May 12th, 1855.—Got off Cape St. Lucas at 5 P. M. yesterday; strong head wind and very rough sea; grew suddenly cool; every one donned winter clothing. Our state-room is on the starboard side, upper deck, and is one of the most airy and pleasant in the ship; three berths in it. One occupied by Captain Cram, U. S. Topographical Engineers; the other by Dr. Evans, U. S. Geologist; the third by myself. Mine being the upper one, is decidedly the most pleasant in hot weather as it gets more air from the window, but now the temperature is lower I must ask for additional bed clothing; however, I have just learned that there is an extra blanket beneath the mattress, of which I shall avail myself to-night.

Again in sight of land—probably islands near the coast. On one of them, Margarita Island, the steamer "Independence" was wrecked and burned February 16th, 1853, with the loss of nearly two hundred passengers. The total number of crew and passengers on board was four hundred and fourteen. Seven or eight steamers have been lost on this coast between Panama and San Francisco within the last six years; some from fire, but the most of them by running on shoals. There should be a law to prevent captains running so near the shore. Saw a whaling vessel this morning. This cool spell is very agreeable to the most of us.

Sunday, May 13th, 1855.—12 o'clok M.—Two hundred and twenty-three miles since yesterday noon. Latitude, 27 deg. 37 min.; Longitude, 115 deg. 7 min. One reason of our going so slowly is said to be the inferior quality of coal that we are now using; the wind is ahead also. 'Tis thought that the worst coal will be exhausted by to-morrow, when the ship will make more progress. This steamer consumes thirty-five tons a day; the "Golden Age," (double engine), seventy. It costs thirty dollars per ton; it is obtained from the Atlantic States and Europe. Six whales were seen this morning spouting alongside of our vessel; weather delightfully refreshing. Have just been introduced to a perfect treasure—ship's library—and have, consequently, discarded the miserable trash that I have heretofore been compelled to read for want of something more substantial.

May 15th, 1855.—Lofty mountains are visible in the dim distance. Their shadowy tints forcibly remind me of the following beautiful lines of Campbell:

> "Why do those cliffs of shadowy tint appear
> More sweet than all the landscape smiling near?
> 'Tis distance lends enchantment to the view,
> And robes the mountain in its azure hue."

It is almost impossible to collect one's ideas on board this noisy vessel. Even while I am writing, one of the greates bores of the ship has taken his stand close by my door with his confounded twattle. He makes acquaintanceship with everbody—inquires their history, and present objects in traveling; then gives his own. This I have heard him relate a dozen times in front of our state-room; and, usually, about four o'clock in the morning, when one most desires repose. All of our friends complain of his monotonous nasal twang; for during the course of the morning he makes his visit to every part of the ship. He professes to have been a preacher, commissioner of health, police officer, and, finally, an herb doctor. When he can command the attention of some old woman, he moves her sympathies by relating how piously his mother brought him up. According to his story, he has never been absent from home after sundown; never gone to a theatre, nor eaten an oyster supper, nor smoked, nor chewed, nor drank. Perhaps, in five minutes thereafter, you will find him taking a glass of brandy in the Surgeon's room; and one does not satisfy him, for, in the course of the day, his libations are frequent. The Doctor at first considered it a capital joke, but was finally compelled to snub him, for the old fellow exhausted nearly all his liquor. The old humbug considered the Doctor ungrateful, particularly as he had given him a "yerb prescription for the cholera, worth $1,000." The appearance of whales and porpoises are now frequent; weather delightfully cool.

CHAPTER XV.

BENICIA BARRACKS—TO PORT ORFORD, O. T.

San Francisco—Benicia Barracks—Climate—Anecdotes of Speculation—Land Titles—San Jose Lawyer and his client—Stormy Voyage to Fort Orford.

San Francisco, California, May 16th, 1855.

WE arrived here to-day at noon. The presence of Captain Gardiner being necessary aboard the steamer to keep order among the troops, I was requested to report our arrival to Brig.-General John E. Wool, the commander of the Pacific. He directed us to proceed with the troops to Benicia Barracks. Availing myself of the delay of the John L. Stevens, I took a little stroll around the city. The entrance to the bay of San Francisco, known as the Golden Gate, is formed by a great fissure in the coast range of mountains, and is only one mile and seventeen yards wide at its narrowest point. As we enter it from the ocean for the first time, its width seems much less than it really is—owing to the high steep bluffs on either side.

San Francisco is situated upon the sandy peninsula, or ridge, that separates the bay from the ocean—having the latter about four miles to the west, and the golden gate nearly the same distance in a north-westerly direction. It faces on the east the San Francisco bay, which is formed by the confluence of the San Joaquin and Sacramento rivers. This bay extends north and south parallel with the Pacific ocean, about forty miles;

being separated from the latter by the narrow peninsula just mentioned. The city possesses one of the finest harbors in the world. A few scattered houses, called Washer-woman's Bay, first present themselves on nearing the wharf, causing a feeling of disappointment; which is, however, soon dispelled on landing and seeing the many beautiful residences and noble brick and granite stores. The population is about forty-five thousand, a wonderful increase since April, 1848, when the town contained only eight hundred and fifty souls.

Although the times are hard here now, owing to the late financial panic, and croakers think the end of the city's prosperity has come, there must sooner or later be a reaction; when she will grow faster than ever. To obtain a fine view of San Francisco, and the surrounding country, it is necessary to go to the top of telegraph hill, from which eminence of two hundred and ninety feet one has a sight of portions of ten counties, the bay, the Pacific ocean, and the magical city below, destined to be the New York of the Pacific coast.

BENICIA BARRACKS, May 20th, 1855.

We reached this place on the seventeenth instant. On examining the baggage I discovered that my two trunks, containing clothing and valuable books, were missing. This was surprising, as I had been particular on arriving at San Francisco to see my baggage separated from that which was to be put out there, and took the further precaution of having it placed under the charge of a corporal. Knowing how rarely anything of this kind was recovered when left behind, I felt rather discouraged for the moment. Seeing a boat coming down the river at the time, I made for the landing, in order to secure a passage to San Francisco to hunt my trunks. Being ignorant of the path, I cut across a swampy flat, and had it rough and tug, over my patent leathers in mud and mire, for about a mile and a half. Missed her—had to wait for a second. Got to San Francisco at one and a half at night. On inquiring at the steamship company's office the following morning, had the satisfaction of finding the lost trunks, which had been taken ashore. Gross carelessness both on the part of the baggage-master and corporal.

Returning to Benicia the same day, I reported myself to the Medical Director, Surgeon Charles G. Tripler, for temporary duty at that place. These barracks are situated on an elevated rolling prairie, three quarters of a mile from the Suisun bay, right bank. The whole country is now carpeted by a luxuriant crop of wild oats. It is splendid forage for horses and cattle. Makes capital hay; but should be packed immediately after being cured, or else it becomes too dry, and loses much of its strength. Many beautiful flowers add freshness and brilliancy to the enchanting landscape. Several copious showers in the last few days; an unusual thing in this season. The Mexicans say los Yankees have changed everything—even the climate.

Near the fort is a little village of the same name. The latter is thirty miles north of San Francisco, and is situated on the north side of the Strait of Carquinez, a contraction of San Francisco bay; which is here only a mile wide. The expansion just above this point is called Suisun bay; into which the waters of the Sacramento and San Joaquin rivers empty by numerous channels, called sloughs, forming a kind of delta. The largest ocean vessels can easily reach the city of Benicia.

Things are dearer here than in San Francisco—excepting rent and board. The latter, at the American Hotel, where I am stopping is three dollars per diem. But prices are coming down, as flour and vegetables can now be purchased comparatively cheap. Certain kinds of fruits are high, and must be so for many years. A gentleman of veracity has just assured me that, feeling a desire for an apple, he asked the price of some the other day, and was told two dollars and a half each. Of course he didn't gratify his taste. In a few years fruit will be abundant, as much attention is being given to its cultivation both here and in the adjoining Territory of Oregon. Peaches and pears grow well in this State, but the best apples are raised in Oregon.

May 25, 1855.—The snow-capped Sierra Nevada is visible this morning. To the naked eye it looks like a bank of white clouds, but its outline and character are fully determined by a spyglass. This is a fine climate for flowers—which can be kept in perpetual bloom by watering. Strolling through the garden of a friend this morning, I saw a perfect paradise of sweet-williams, verbenas, geraniums, mallows, sweet peas, and many varieties of flowers peculiar to the prairies of California. One unknown species of the latter is remarkable for its propensity to spread. A single shoot will extend over a large bed in the course of a single year.

BENICIA BARRACKS, June 11th, 1855.

Having been assigned to duty at Fort Orford, Oregon Territory, I shall proceed thither in a few days. General Wool has returned from Oregon. Whilst there he fitted out an expedition for the Snake Indian country to protect emigrants from the States. It is feared that the emigration to Oregon and California will be very small this year in consequence of Indian hostilities on the plains east of the Rocky Mountains. A large force, under the command of General Harney, is being sent against the Siouxs and other troublesome tribes on that frontier. The last papers brought us accounts of several encounters between the Apaches and dragoons in New Mexico. Indian troubles in this department (the Pacific) are also quite frequent.

The coast climate of this portion of California is divided into two seasons, the dry and wet The former extending from May to November, the latter the remainder of the year. There is, properly speaking, no winter nor summer. The latter, or dry season, is, perhaps, colder than the former, and far more disagreeable, on account of the prevalence of cold winds, dense fogs and dust, which do not prevail in the wet, or winter season. The clear weather of winter is represented as delightfully balmy and pleasant. This description is more particularly applicable to San Francisco; and, perhaps, Benicia.

The almost entire absence of rain in summer is very favorable for harvesting, which is now in full blast in this vicinity. At present, one may see hundreds of persons cutting down wild oats; which, being simply cocked, is allowed to remain on the ground for weeks, and even months, without fear of its being spoiled by rain. Some haste is required in mowing it, however, as it matures very rapidly in consequence of the high winds and dry atmosphere. When I first arrived, the grass was beautifully fresh and green—it is now drying rapidly. In a few weeks some miscreant will probably set it on fire, after which the whole country will look black and barren until November, when the young oats and grass will spring up.

The old adage: "Every rose has its thorns," is as true in regard to this country and climate, as to anything else. The thorns here are fleas, which are as thick as the locusts of Egypt. It seems impossible that even Pharoah's obdurate heart could have withstood such a plague as this. I was at first rather shocked at the careless manner in which, even ladies, alluded to these insects; but a short experience taught me that the rascals would force themselves upon the attention of all; and, like many other troublesome things, soon become an engrossing subject of conversation. Perhaps, these are the only pests, as there are no venomous snakes, tarantulas, scorpions, centipedes, or mosquitoes, or, if any, but few. It is probable the latter would be troublesome, were it not for the high winds, which blow day and night, with the exception of an hour or two about sundown. These render the country particularly unpleasant for females, as they prevent their riding or promenading as much as they otherwise would.

SAN FRANCISCO, June 17th, 1855.

Left Benicia last Wednesday for this place. Will leave here on Wednesday, next, in the steamer "Columbia," for Fort Orford, Oregon. The present is a great epoch in the history of this eventful city. The recent failures of a few extensive firms, among others the banking house of Page, Bacon & Co., have created a perfect panic among business men. In addition to this, there are being brought forward for adjudication large claims, founded upon Mexican grants, for some of the land in and around San Francisco. The Bolton-Barron grant, alone, calls for three thousand acres. This claim has been allowed by the U. S. Land Commissioners; thus making Palmer, Cook & Co., who got half of it, the wealthiest men in California. It has yet to go through the Supreme Court; but as the Board acted in conformity to decisions laid down by this Honorable body, its decision may probably be sustained.

The history of the claim is, that whilst California still belonged to the Mexican Government, the latter granted to the Padre of the Dolores Mission, this amount of land, provided, he liquidated the debts of the Mission. This he complied with. When the gold fever broke out, the Padre was unable to prevent squatters from settling on his land, and accordingly sold it out. It subsequently fell into the hands of a company in Philadelphia, and the gentlemen above mentioned, who brought the present suit. The decision of the Commissioners has created great excitement, as hundreds of men are thus dispossessed of what they deemed their own. The latter have got up an association denominated "Our Homes and our Firesides," with a view of influencing the Legislature, and thus causing to be enacted a law to secure them in their rights.

There are many other large claims besides this. One, the Leidesdorff, embraces some of the finest portions of the southern part of the city. This is now before the Land Commissioners. If allowed, it will probably ruin an acquaintance of mine, Captain Folsom, Assistant Quartermaster, U. S. Army; as it will not only absorb a large portion of his estate, but establish a point in law which will compel him to loose the remainder. This gentleman was considered in the early part of last year as the largest land-holder in California, and, perhaps, in the United States. At the enormous rates at which property was then selling, his estate would have brought him a million and a half of dollars. His indebtedness was something like $200,000. Some of his judicious friends advised him to take advantage of the high prices, and dispose of enough of his estate to liquidate his debts, on which he was paying an annual interest of from thirty to forty per centum. But, like many others, his ambition was to be considered among the wealthiest land-holders in the United States, and he, therefore, held on till the present time. If his property were now forced into market it would not yield more than one quarter of its value a year ago—and there is no prospect of a reaction for a long time to come, as the prices of '54 were greatly inflated.

There is also a Mexican (native Californian) claimant for the quicksilver mines in San José (pronounced San Ho-sá) Valley, south of San Francisco some forty miles. These are considered the most productive mines in the world—at present owned by an English company. This whole valley is considered the richest and best in California. It possesses a great advantage over other sections of the State, in its numerous artificial springs, or artesian wells, which are the finest in the Union. It is said to be necessary to bore only from fifteen to thirty feet to obtain fine gushing streams; some of which throw water to the height of eight and ten feet.

It is related that a gentleman in a little village near the mines (I think San José) went to work boring an artificial spring, and that when he got down to the depth of some fifteen feet, the water rushed out in such a torrent that it was feared it would inundate the town. The City Council convened and passed an act fining the man five hundred dollars unless he put an immediate stop to the water. The poor fellow was in a dilemma, for he had tried his best, but couldn't succeed, in stemming the impetuous torrent. Finally he took the advice of a lawyer as to how he might avoid the penalty. The latter told him that if he would follow his instructions the matter could be settled in a very short time, and that his fee would be one hundred dollars. The fellow gladly embraced the proposition. His professional adviser then directed him to dig a ditch and let the water run into an adjacent ravine.

The simplicity of the thing confounded him at first. He paid the fee, however, did as advised, and of course succeeded. This is a moral for all who seek professional advice before exerting properly their own good common sense; for although this lawyer made an enemy of his client by not giving him advice more in conformity with legal custom in such cases, he undoubtedly conferred on him a greater benefit than is usually received by clients.

In connection with Captain Folsom's case, I should have added, that the rates of interest that he is paying are trifling, in comparison to the enormous sums exacted from men in reduced circumstances. A gentleman assured me that, in 1850 and 1851 he never lent a dollar for less than fifteen per cent. a month—the rates are now from two to three and a half per cent. on bond and mortgage. This demand for money seems an anomaly in a State from which there is a monthly shipment of three millions of dollars. This condition of things is, in a measure, owing to the uncertainty of titles; one is never perfectly sure that the person to whom he lends his money has an undoubted right to the property offered as surety; and, even if the title be good, there may be a previous mortgage, notwithstanding he has employed a lawyer to examine the records, for the latter are so voluminous, in consequence of the constant changes of ownership to property, that it is generally impossible to examine the matter thoroughly in the time usually devoted to such examinations in this community; hence, many who have loaned money on mortgage at three per cent. a month, wind up by losing principal and all.

This state of things has rendered capitalists timid in lending out their means on real estate security. But, independent of this, there is probably a greater demand for money in San Francisco than in any other city of its size in the world, in consequence of an unlimited system of speculation. The desire for speculation seems to have affected all professions and classes; and extends to every variety of goods or merchandise, as well as real estate. In regard to merchandise, the losses generally fall on the shipper or Eastern merchant; nine-tenths of them lose heavily. For instance, gentlemen in New York, Philadelphia or Boston, learn that a certain article is very high in San Francisco—they immediately ship immense quantities. Probably all their cargoes will arrive about the same time. The market is glutted; yet they must sell, for the expenses of a ship lying alongside of a wharf in this city are enormous. Probably the only ones that make anything out of the transaction are the jobbers; or, in some instances, the merchants to whom the cargoes may be consigned. If their instructions are to sell with as little delay as possible, and the market is dull, they sometimes buy in cargoes themselves, and by holding on awhile occasionally reap large profits.

Sometimes they find it profitable to reship it to the States, as in a recent instance, several ship loads of flour were sent to San Francisco. At the time of shipment it was buying in the latter place at forty dollars per barrel, and only worth seven dollars in New York. It was the average time of four months on the passage around Cape Horn. Its price in the meantime had gone down to seven dollars in San Francisco, and up to fifteen dollars in New York. The consignees, according to instructions, sold it, but bought it themselves, and reshipping it to the same place whence it came, realized a handsome profit. Whether they acted in good faith to the original shippers I can't say. At all events the Eastern merchants have to stand the brunt of most of the losses from wild speculations in California. It is high time for them to grow wiser by experience.

All nations are represented in San Francisco, but particularly the Jews. There are all grades of these—from the most respectable merchant, or professional man, down to the mock auction dealer. It is amusing to stroll down some of the streets after gas-light, and witness the various methods adopted by the latter class of merchants to drum up customers. A common device, is to start a band of music until a large crowd is collected, then for the mock auctioneer to mount the stand and bid off the goods as if it were really a *bona fide* auction. They thus gull large numbers of that class of people who deem everything bought at public auction must be cheap.

Occasionally, one of the initiated will step up to the auctioneer, and handing him a watch, request it to be sold, as he is pressed for money. The watch is accordingly knocked down to the highest bidder; who, when it is probably too late, discovers his magnificent gold lever (seventeen jewels), to be brass. Many a poor sailor is thus bamboozled out of his money; and the most strenuous exertions of the police are generally powerless to find out the perpetrators, from the fact that the poor dupe is usually unable to designate the precise house that sold the article. This is destined to be a large and beautiful city; its suburbs, particularly towards the Mission, are superb.

FORT ORFORD, OREGON TERRITORY, June 24th, 1855.

Leaving San Francisco on the morning of the eighteenth instant, we reached here on the evening of the 21st, after a tedious and boisterous voyage of nearly four days. The northwest head winds were so strong that we only averaged about two and a half miles per hour. On the last day out, the vessel rolled and pitched terribly; of course most everybody was sea-sick. Although so unwell as to be compelled to assume the recumbent posture while on deck, yet I greatly enjoyed the scene; for surely nothing is so sublime as the upheaving of the mighty deep in a storm. The gale began on the night of the 20th. We were suddenly awakened, and almost tossed out of our berths by a tremendous lurch and crash of the vessel; leading many to suppose she "had struck." I stood it, however, with great equanimity, as a sea-sick man will always do. When daylight dawned the sight was grand beyond description—the ocean was lashed by the wind in a terrible commotion—the billows rolled and swelled aloft as if bent on the destruction of our vessel; but of this there was not the least apprehension, as we all had had sufficient sea experience to know how difficult it is to sink a staunch ship. Her sea-sawing motions were sometimes so rapid as to almost take our breath. When struck by a cross-sea away would go chairs, basins and dishes. Our room-mate of the lower bunk was really to be pitied on one occasion of this kind. There the poor fellow lay so sick that he couldn't rise, when a sudden lurch capsized a bucket of filthy water, that the waiter was cleaning the room with, all over him. Although commiserating his pitiful condition I could not help congratulating myself on having procured a middle berth—secure from such accidents. Of course everthing that can be, is fastened down on a ship. For instance the tables, and seats for the same, are secured; but it is impracticable to tie down things which it is necessary to move constantly. The dining-table is usually covered with a movable frame-work to retain the dishes in their places; this arrangement did not suffice in the present instance.

As usual, we had some very pleasant, and a few exceedingly disagreeable persons aboard. There was a gentleman belonging to the profession of Civil Engineers, en route for Oregon, to secure a contract for surveying. Unfortunately for himself and fellow-passengers, he was very much intoxicated, and, hence, disposed to give full play to the expression of his thoughts, which being sarcastic, and generally personal, rendered his society very undesirable. He usually began his conversation by preaching forth his wonderful acquirements, which, according to his own estimation, were vast indeed. He harped principally upon the Government and her officials, *civil*, not military, and particularly the Surveyor-General of California, Major Jack Hays—who came in for the largest share of abuse; but unluckily for his auditors, he was prone before the conclusion of his discourse to identify them with the perpetrators of all his wrongs. One unfortunate fellow was disposed to quiz him, and this brought down upon himself the most sarcastic abuse I have ever heard. This gentleman was bald-pated and small-headed, and having just crossed the Isthmus, had his face burned to a blister. Mr. L—— consequently possessed a fruitful theme of discourse on phrenology. He began by asking his subject if he possessed any knowledge of this science or *any other*, and then laid down as his first proposition that men of his cranial conformation never had any intelligence; upon which he dilated with great volubility, to the merriment of every one. We could only "laugh in our sleeves," as the fellow's abuse was intolerable, and ought to have been promptly checked by the Captain, in order to prevent a disturbance. Fortunately, the abused gentleman set it all down to King Alcohol, probably deeming himself a little to blame, and bore it like a martyr—knowing, also, that a single word to Capt. Dall would have been the means of sending the intoxicated individual from the cabin to the steerage, as a nuisance. The Captain was on the eve of doing this anyway, as the man's impertinence ran wild; but he finally toned him down by taking away his liquor, and, giving him a dose of morphine, put him to sleep. Next morning he was sober, but awfully sea-sick; so we saw no more of his honor.

Near the Golden Gate was pointed out to us the spot where a splendid steamer was wrecked in 1851, on attempting to enter the harbor of San Francisco in a dense fog. We touched at Trinidad and Crescent City; the latter is a thriving little village. It is about three hundred miles from San Francisco, and sixty-two from Fort Orford. We also passed the mouth of Rogue River, famous for its Indian war in 1853.

CHAPTER XVI.

AT FORT ORFORD, OREGON.

Climate, Mines, etc., of the Oregon Coast—In Command of the Post, and Fire a National Salute—Conflict between Indian and Whites on "Battle Rock."—Fish and Game.

FORT ORFORD, OREGON TERRITORY, June 29th, 1855.

LANDING at this post on the twenty-first of this month, after a long and tedious sea voyage, *via* the Isthmus, and a short delay in California, I was vividly impressed with the exhilarating and health-inspiring influence of the air. The evergreen forests of spruce, fir, and cedar, which are still standing in all their primeval loveliness and grandeur, associated in a few places with the beautiful rhododendron, and the sweet-scented myrtle, covering mountains and vales, give a novelty and charm to the landscape unsurpassed by anything of the kind ever seen by me before.

The summer months here are delightfully cool and pleasant, but the other three seasons are checkered with fogs, cold winds, and storms of rain, and occasionally of snow. The lightning's flash and the loud thunder's rattle are in summer unseen and unheard; but the intermitting roar of old Ocean's waves dashing at regular intervals against the rock-bound shore, inspires one continually with the grandeur and sublimity of the scene.

This fort is in latitude, 42 deg. 44 min. 27 sec. north; and longitude, 124 deg. 28 min. 52 sec. west.

On reference to the Meteorological Observations of the post, I find there are in the course of a year 180 fair, 186 cloudy, and 122 rainy days, with one day of snow. The mean temperature of spring is $52\frac{26}{100}$ deg.; of summer, $58\frac{21}{100}$ deg.; of autumn $54\frac{22}{100}$ deg.; and of winter $50\frac{18}{100}$ deg.; and of the year, $53\frac{71}{100}$ of Fahrenheit. The average rainfall is in spring—$16\frac{71}{100}$ inches; in summer, $3\frac{33}{100}$ inches; in autumn, $22\frac{69}{100}$ inches; in winter, $32\frac{29}{100}$ inches, and for the year, $75\frac{02}{100}$ inches. The thermometer ranges between 79 deg. in summer, to 30 deg. above zero in winter. The climate is remarkably healthy; there are no malarious diseases. The soil is good except near the beach, but not very productive of such fruits and cereals as require warm summers.

Such garden vegetables as cabbages and potatoes thrive well; tomatoes, melons and corn hardly ever come to maturity. Peaches, plums, cherries, pears, grapes and such like fruits can not be raised to advantage. To wild berries, fruits, game and fish I shall make allusion further on after a personal inspection of the country—grass in this region is green throughout the entire year.

The principal rivers near here are the Coquille, thirty miles north; Elk, four miles north; and Rogue River, thirty miles south. The second mentioned stream received its name from the large herds of elk which range along its bottom lands. Elk meat is more largely consumed here as an article of food than beef—it is nearly as good, and much cheaper; it sells at from twelve to eighteen cents per pound, whereas good beef is worth twenty-five cents per pound.

There are two traditions as to the origin of the name

of the last mentioned river. Some assert that it took its appellation from the roguish propensities of the Indians living on its borders; whilst others maintain that rogue is a corruption of the French word rouge (or red) signifying red river, because some of its principal head branches are always turbid from a mixture of reddish clay and sand stirred up in the mining districts.

Adjoining the Military Reservation of this fort, is a little village called Port Orford, which was located or laid out in 1850, during the mania upon the subject of town sites. Having the best port between San Francisco and the Columbia River, it was thought to be an admirable spot for a large city, but like many similar attempts, it has proven a failure. For notwithstanding the additional advantages of gold having since been discovered along the sand beach for many miles above and below the town, and of the touching here of a regular mail steamer every fortnight, it still numbers only about forty houses, and one-third of these are tenantless. It has a good summer harbor, as the wind during this season is from the northwest; but in the autumn, winter and early part of spring, it is generally very dangerous for vessels to attempt to "lie to" in the harbor, or even to enter it, as the prevailing winds are then from the south, southwest, and southeast. The expenditure by the Government, some of these days, of a few millions of dollars, for a breakwater, will make this a magnificent harbor of refuge for our naval and merchant vessels, when overtaken by storms on the Northern Pacific coast.

Our post is nearly surrounded by a dense forest—

but has an expansive view of the Pacific Ocean in front. It is cut off from the beautiful Rogue River, and Willamette valleys, by the coast range of mountains—some spurs and peaks of which are very high. One of the highest points in our vicinity is "Humbug Mountain"—receiving its name from a false report of the discovery of rich gold diggings on it.

This whole coast, from San Francisco to the Russian Possessions, is thickly wooded—the principal trees are fir, cypress and cedar; the latter is only found at intervals. It makes much the best lumber, as it does not shrink and swell alternately with the dry or wet weather so much as the two other kinds, and is more durable, and makes far the best finish. It is quite abundant near this place; its market value is three or four times as much as fir or spruce. There are three saw-mills here, only one of which is at present running—the others are idle for the want of water. The one in operation is a steam mill, and turns out daily an average of fifty-five hundred feet of plank, besides many thousand laths; it employs twenty-five hands. Sawmilling is another example of our speculation. From 1847 to 1852, there was great demand for lumber, especially in San Francisco, which was then being built up of frame houses; but after the great fires there in '50 and '52, a more substantial class of buildings was erected of stone and brick—lumber was, consequently, in but slight demand. Its supply had, in the mean time, increased about twenty-fold, as a large number of persons had been induced by the enormous prices of two hundred and six hundred dollars per one thousand feet, to erect saw-mills; it is now a drug in the market.

Twelve months ago there was great excitement in regard to the discovery of gold near this place; as is usual under such circumstances large numbers of people flocked here—the majority of whom went away disappointed. The beach for many miles below and above this point has gold in it, and in some places "pays well." They who secure average claims, in point of richness, and work them properly, clear from two to seven dollars per day; but the great drawback to miners here is, that they won't let well enough alone—they are constantly leaving old claims that yield moderately well, to look out for better. Moreover, though naturally shrewd, they are easily humbugged into some castle-building, money-making, mining-operation, that promises everything and accomplishes nothing; particularly if the imposter be a foreigner, and possess some knowledge of chemical jugglery—being able by a few tricks, to convince his dupes that he has discovered some wonderful method of separating gold dust from sand, by causing it to unite more readily with mercury than by the common process, he succeeds in organizing a stock-mining company, which is to give him one third or half of the profits; thus making a very profitable operation for himself, even by the ordinary methods of mining, so long as he can keep his dupes in the dark, and hold his company together. There is a *Monsieur C.* at present humbugging some twelve or fourteen persons in this way. The affair is, however, about reaching a climax, and he will doubtless soon have to leave "these diggings," as he did those of Rogue River a short time ago. *Vive la bagatelle.*

Miners in this Territory and California are governed in their operations by what is termed the Mining Law; which, although agreeing in its general features, varies somewhat in its details in different districts. This law is a system of regulations formed by the miners themselves, and at one time governed them in almost everything criminal and civil, but is at present limited to a few points only—such as the right of ownership to claims, and the extent of ground each man is allowed by pre-emption. At some places each person is permitted to take up a claim of three hundred feet front, by fifty or one hundred deep; in others, not more than one half of this extent is granted. This only refers to pre-emption right, that is, *the title to mineral land conferred by virtue of having first "squatted on it."* One has the privilege of *buying* as many claims as he pleases.

There is not a more healthy spot on the globe than Fort Orford—the only diseases here are the result of some species of intemperance. Indeed, were it not for an occasional accident there would be no need of a physician at this post; more particularly as the command is so small—being only a detachment of twenty-five men (Company M, Third Artillery), commanded by Lieutenant A. V. Kautz, Fourth Infantry. I had more cases of sickness to attend in one day at Fort Arbuckle, during the sickly season, than I would be likely to have here in a whole year.

FORT ORFORD, July 4th, 1855.

As Lieutenant A. V. Kautz is absent on detached service I am in command of the post, and have just had the pleasure of firing a national salute of thirty one guns. To be able to appreciate our national greatness, one should travel over the Union and behold for himself the immense extent of territory now embraced in our mighty Republic; which possesses every variety of soil and climate, and more natural resources, generally, than that of any other nation on the globe; and inhabited by a people vigorous, intellectual, brave and indomitably persevering. Our past history has been a miracle to the nations of the old world; and our prospects are still more glorious. Could our forefathers have seen the fruits of the glorious cause for which they laid down their lives, their dying couches would have been replete with all the joy that earth can afford. May we never cease to commemorate this day, and to offer up thanksgiving to the Ruler of Heaven and Earth for his helping hand to our ancestors in the hour of their greatest distress. In the language of the poet I may conclude:

> "Lives there a man with soul so dead
> Who never to himself hath said,
> This is my own, my native land?"

July 5th, 1855.—We are hourly looking for the steamer "Columbia;" she always touches here, and leaves the mail, both going and returning. On her last trip down there were some four or five army officers on board—some of whom have recently received appointments in the new regiments. Among others were Captain Stoneman, Captain Whiting and Lieutenant Williams. Major Henry Prince, with some two hundred and thirty-one U. S. troops, destined for Fort Vancouver, will probably be up on the next steamer. The one they started in, the "America," was burnt on last Sunday night week, whilst stopping for a short time at Crescent City. She was totally destroyed.

In order to protect our immense western frontier, Congress passed a bill last session, adding four new regiments to the army—two of cavalry, and two of infantry. These are being rapidly filled up, and will probably be ready for the field next spring. Our troops in New Mexico are kept constantly in active service—the Apache Indian being very troublesome. An expedition of several regiments, under General Harney, has been ordered on the plains west of Kansas and Nebraska to quell Indian depredations. The Sioux have been very troublesome there within the last twelve months.

In California and Oregon disturbances occasionally occur between the settlers and Indians—a few years ago they were quite frequent. Then there were several fights in this vicinity—Captain Aldin, U. S. Army, was wounded in one of those engagements near Rogue River. Six miners were killed in another encounter on the Coquille. Shortly after this last affair, the miners in a large body went against the Indians, and killed some fifteen of them.

Within a hundred yards of garrison, and a short distance from shore, is a rock known as "Battle Rock," receiving its name from a contest which took place there in 1850, between some Americans and Indians. The former had intended landing with the view of selecting a town site, but finding the latter hostile, took up their position on the above rock, whilst their vessel—Captain Tichner's schooner—returned to San Francisco for reinforcements. The Indians made numerous attacks on the place for ten or twelve days, but being repulsed with heavy losses, finally abandoned the idea of dislodging the whites from their secure retreat. The rock being some twenty yards from shore, was rather inaccessible. A small cannon that the whites had was used with much success; and assisted more than anything else in frightening the Indians. The loss of the latter was ten or twelve. None of the former killed—a few slightly wounded. The whole party, consisting of only nine men, finally made their escape into Umpqua Valley.

July 11th, 1855.—The "Columbia" passed up last Friday, and has just gone down—having on board several army officers; some of whom are on their way to New York. Among others Lieutenant Myers and Dr. Luckley. A friend of ours, Mr. L. Blanding, of San Francisco, who has been spending a few days with us, also took passage in her this morning. Being a lawyer of some eminence, and possessing agreeable manners, his visit was very welcome to this lovely place. Our associates in this neighborhood are few indeed.

July 23th, 1855.—Lieutenant Kautz and I went a fishing yesterday in Elk River, and caught a lot of splendid trout. There are two species of this delicious fish in Oregon; one, called the mountain trout—being the same as the speckled or brook trout of the Northern States; and the other the salmon trout. The former abound in the clear mountain streams, and small fresh water lakes; the latter in the rivers and lakes near the ocean. The salmon trout are much larger than the mountain trout, and are very closely allied to the salmon itself.

This being a heavily timbered country there are, of course, very few flowers. I see no familiar ones except the yarrow, wild tansy, and strawberry; there is also a specie of wild clover which grows very abundantly. Of fruits we have the salmon-berry, thimble-berry, and sal-lalle berry. The latter resembles in appearance and taste a large variety of the huckle-berry, and affords a very delicious dessert. The thimble-berry is almost exactly like the raspberry in size and appearance, but grows on a larger and less prickly bush. Salmon-berries grow on very large shrubs, and are named from their color. They are similar in size and shape to blackberries, but not quite so palatable.

Game is very scarce in this neighborhood. The deer and elk have been frightened back into the mountains; there are a few, however, remaining. A friend has a very large pair of elk horns. It was a problem to me how the elk could run through the bushes with such immense appendages, but after seeing in what way they are adapted to the head I became convinced of their advantage—they are sloped backwards so as protect the head, neck and body from the thickets. A few panthers, martins, black bears, and otters, may be seen occasionally. There are two varieties of the latter animal—the land and sea otter. The skin of the latter is much the more valuable. There are some wolves or coyotes, but they are not often seen, and are not very troublesome, except in winter, when they lurk around the dwellings. Two varieties of foxes are also occasionally seen—the common gray and the silver gray; the last variety is prized very highly for its beautiful skin. A few squirrels, principally the small gray.

There are fewer birds here than at any place I have ever been. There are pine hens, quail, partridges (Maryland pheasant) and pigeons—and ducks and geese in winter. The harbor is dotted with sea birds—such as didappers, gulls and pelicans. There is also a large fishing hawk of the eagle species, with a white head, white on tips of tail and wings, and dark body. The pine hen is so called from always being found in the pine woods. It is almost identical with the prairie hen of the States immediately east of the Rocky Mountains; it is also known as the blue grouse. I have noticed a very beautiful bird called the blue jay—it resembles very closely the jay bird of the Middle States; but its plumage is of a much darker and more brilliant hue. The humming-bird, sparrow, cedar-bird and robin are also to be seen.

CHAPTER XVII.

FORT ORFORD—CONTINUED.

About Mining—"Drop Riffle"—Mining Excitements—Confidential Humbugs—Reticent and Lucky Miners—"For God's sake, hurry; the Lieutenant is shot."

JULY 22D, 1855.—The steamer "Columbia" stopped here on the evening of the twentieth. Lieutenants G. H. Derby and Alexander Piper, U. S. Army, were on board en route for Fort Vancouver. The former gentleman belongs to the topographical engineers, and is quite celebrated as a witty writer. His productions are usually published in a California magazine called the "Pioneer." He informs us of the death of Captain J. L. Folsom, Assistant Quartermaster, U. S. Army. He died on last Tuesday evening. He leaves a large estate.

Lieutenant Kautz has involved himself in a civil suit for putting a civilian, who had been creating distubances among the Indians on the government reserve, in the guardhouse; he confined him six days. The civil authorities have brought a suit for false imprisonment against him. He left this morning to attend his trial at Coos Bay. I am consequently in command of the post. This not being a proper duty of the medical staff, we only exercise it in the absence of all line officers. Our rank avails us in everything else but commanding. It holds good on all councils, boards, courtmartial, and in selection of quarters, etc.

Mr. Henry Tichenor and myself accompanied Mr. Kautz some ten miles up the coast. On our return we passed Cape Blanco, the most western portion of the United States territory. There are some forty miners engaged in digging gold dust on the beach at that point.

The gold is found disseminated in finely divided particles in the sand; and is separated by running the latter through a machine, consisting of a "long tom," and "drop riffle." The former is a wooden trough three feet broad, six feet long, and two inches deep, with a plate of sheet iron at one end perforated with several hundred holes. This is placed so as to form an inclined plane. At its lower end, and partly under it, is the "drop riffle." This consists of two side pieces holding a number of open boxes, one above and behind the other, like a stairway. In each of these boxes is a gate corresponding to the "rise" in a step, which can be elevated or lowered so as to be brought any required distance from the surface of the mercury in the cell of the box. A stream of water is let upon the "long tom," and the coarse sand thrown in by shovels full. The finer portions of it are washed through the sieve-like end of the "tom," and carried over the surface of the mercury in the "drop riffle." The same being brought in close contact with the mercury by means of the sliding gate or drop-board, its gold dust is thus more readily united with this metal, forming what is called an amalgam. When the mercury is sufficiently impregnated, it is poured into iron pans and the gold allowed to settle. The sediment is then placed in a linen bag and compressed; thus separating another portion of the mercury. The remainder is termed "amalgam proper," which contains about forty per centum of gold. The final step in the process is to place this into a retort, and by means of heat evaporate all the mercury. By this process very little of the latter is injured by oxidation, and it can, of course, be used again.

A constant supply of water is, in this mode of mining, necessary; and when it cannot be obtained from a stream sufficiently high to be conducted to the "tom" through a wooden trough, it is got from a shallow well by means of a carrying pump, worked either by horse or steam power—usually the former. There are some claims at Cape Blanco which "turn out very well." The best belong to a Mr. Coffee, who is said to be running through one machine, where are employed only three or four hands, about fifty dollars a day. And this, too, a regular thing.

The sand beach differs materially from what are termed solid or quartz diggings in the regularity of finding gold. In the latter it is frequently necessary to work five and six months without getting a grain, then perhaps a vein is struck which turns out hundreds of dollars a day for a short time. But sometimes a shaft is sunk at an enormous expense without yielding anything. These shafts are usually sunk in the side of a hill, down to a level with the bed of a stream where gold dust has been found in the sand. The object is to strike the original bed of gold. The gold on the beach is also much finer than that found in the placer diggings in the interior of Oregon and California.

It is very easy to get up an excitement about gold

diggings in this country. The last steamer was crowded with passengers for the newly discovered mines at Fort Colville in Washington Territory; they are represented as being vastly rich. There is doubtless much gold in that region, but, judging from the manner in which such things usually terminate in this country, about one half of those on their way there will return in a few months utterly disappointed; for the richness of mines is always exaggerated by speculators. Without going any further we will take Fort Orford as an average case, by way of illustration. About fourteen months ago a party of five or six men discovered gold at a place now called "Jackson's Diggings," some thirty miles from this place. They worked five or six weeks, but secured barely enough to compensate them for their trouble. However, they were determined on making a speculation out of it. So after securing their claims they managed to return here just about the time the steamer stopped on her way to San Francisco. Knowing that if they exhibited the gold publicly everybody would accuse them of trying to get up an excitement for speculation, it was at first confidentially shown to a few persons, who divulged the matter to their particular friends, and they in turn to theirs, until everybody learned the wonderful secret. It was represented that this gold was found after a single day's work. In a few hours everybody who could get away from Fort Orford were on their way to the mines. The merchants of this place assisted in the furor. Of course the steamship carried down glowing accounts of the richness of the mines. And 'tis said that the agents of the line got up flaming hand-bills, which were posted through the streets of San Francisco. It at least turned out gold for them; for their ship was crowded with passengers as long as the bubble lasted. Persons arrived here by hundreds; purchased pans, shovels and picks; and, for the want of other conveyance, started for the magic spot on foot. The majority being city clerks, and others of that class, who had never walked a half day in their lives, soon began to break down, and consequently to throw away such articles as they thought could be best spared. About every third man would say to his party, "Well, we want only one pick, I am going to throw mine away."

On arriving they found gold, it is true, but not enough to pay the cost of the claims. So the little bubble bursted. The discoverers, the merchants, and steamship company, being the only parties who made anything. At the present time there are not more than a dozen persons working at the place. In the significant cant of the country the "diggings have gone in."

Now for a story somewhat different, but still illustrative of the *ruse de guerre* constantly practiced in this country. A party of three men came here a short time after the above excitement, and went to work at Cape Blanco, the place spoken of above as being within eight miles of this place. After working a few days they came to the village and purchased a few articles on credit, with a promise to pay on the following week. At the appointed time the first bill was settled, and another contracted with the same limitation as to the time of settlement. Thus they worked on, as it were, from hand to mouth; and when asked how they were doing, replied, "wall, we guess we are making a living, but it is better to do this than starve."

At the expiration of some seven months these men came to the village with thirty thousand dollars, which they had got out at that spot: sold their claims at an exorbitant price, and left the country. The purchasers found the claims pretty well exhausted; and by the process then in operation could not make them pay well. But since the introduction of the drop riffle they are made to yield, on re-working, pretty good wages. And, by prospecting in the neighborhood, some of the miners have found new places, which turn out handsomely. As, for instance, that of Mr. Coffee's, alluded to above.

FORT ORFORD, July 25th, 1855.

The steamer "Columbia," Captain William Dall, touched here this morning on her downward passage; brings glorious accounts of the gold mines at Fort Colville. Almost all the settlers in the upper part of Oregon, and in Washington Territories, have started for the mines. Of course all the vessels bound from San Francisco to Oregon will, for the next four months, be crowded with passengers inflated with golden dreams.

August 2d, 1855.—There has been a coolness existing between Lieutenant K., of this post, and two persons in the village, named Smith and Sutton — the former a lawyer, the latter Justice of the Peace. Lieutenant K. started for the town to-day after dinner, and being apprehensive of an rencounter, took with him a large cane. In a short time thereafter the constable of the place, Seth Lount, came running to garrison in great perturbation, and begged me, for God's sake, to hurry down town, as the Lieutenant had been shot through the heart by Justice Sutton. My first impulse was to order a corporal's guard to assist in arresting the perpetrator of the deed, but as a few moments' delay might be the death of my friend, I of course hurried to him first. To my astonishment, on arriving I found him sitting up in a chair as composed as if nothing had happened. The whole town had concentrated there in the meantime.

On inquiry, I learned that S—— had commenced a quarrel with K——, and in the course of it had used language which the latter had construed into being called a liar, whereupon he raised his cane with the intention of striking the former, who drew a pistol and fired. Lieutenant K. immediately dropped on the floor, and on being picked up placed his hand over his heart. The bystanders, thinking the shot had taken effect in his chest, immediately sent for me. It was discovered in the meantime that the ball had not struck him—and, probably, not even grazed him. From where the ball hit the floor it is impossible that it could have passed higher up than the pelvis. Still, the expansive force of the gasses, generated by the combustion of the charge of powder in the gun, striking against the pit of the stomach, may have had something to do with the result. The most reasonable solution of the problem, however, is, that it was a nervous shock produced by the mental certainty that, if fired at with the pistol almost touching his body, death would be inevitable. The following is a case in point, taken from Guthrie's *Military Surgery:*

"During a rapid advance of part of the British Army in Portugal, one of the skirmishers suddenly came upon his adversary, with only a small bank between them; both parties presented, the muzzles of the pieces nearly touching; both fired, and both fell. The British soldier after a minute or two, thinking himself hit, but still finding himself capable of moving, got up, and found his adversary dead—on the opposite side of the bank. I saw him immediately afterwards in considerable alarm, being conscious of a blow somewhere, but which after a diligent search, proved to be only a graze on the under side of the arm; yet the certainty he was in of being killed, from the respective position of the parties, had such an effect upon him at the moment of receiving this trifling injury, as nearly to deprive him, for a short time, of his powers of volition; whereas, had the wound been received from a concealed or distant enemy, it would in all probability have been little noticed."

August 23d, 1855.—Captain T. J. Cram, U. S. Topographical Engineer; Dr. Hubbard; and Mr. Wells, editor of the *Alta California*, arrived on the "Columbia" this morning. Mr. W. having traveled all over the world, is an exceedingly well informed and entertaining gentleman. Captain C. was a fellow passenger on our trip from New York, and we are, of course, highly delighted to see him. He has come up simply on a visit. The other gentlemen are engaged in a coal speculation at Coos Bay. This mineral has been found there in large quantities; and of very good quality. It has also been discovered in other parts of this Territory, and is likely to turn out a handsome speculation to those who first succeed in bringing it to market, as all the coal heretofore used on this coast has been brought from the Eastern States or England.

I perceive that the rumor, heard here a few weeks since of Indian troubles on the Klamath River, has been confirmed. There were eleven white men killed by the Indians at last accounts. The origin of the difficulty was on the part of a few drunken Indians, who attempted to maltreat some white men.

August 26th, 1855.—General Joel Palmer, Superintendent of Indian Affairs for Oregon, and Dr. Drew, sub-agent, arrived here on the twenty-fourth instant, and left this morning for Rogue River to hold a council with the Indians of this coast, with a view of forming a treaty with them for the purchase of their possessory rights to the soil, and their removal to an Indian Reserve to be set apart for them higher up the coast.

CHAPTER XVIII.

INDIAN COUNCIL ON ROGUE RIVER.

Indian Council—A Disturbance—Two Indians and Three Whites killed—Modes, Habits, etc., of the Indians.

FORT ORFORD, WASHINGTON TERRITORY, Sept. 2d, 1855.

HAVING received a dispatch from General Palmer that a disturbance had occurred between the miners and Indians near the council grounds on Rogue river, Lieutenant Kautz and myself repaired thither, and returned on the first instant.

Leaving Fort Orford on the twenty-ninth ultimo, we arrived on the "ground" the same evening, after a journey of thirty miles over the roughest road I have ever traveled. For two thirds of the distance the rider is in constant peril of neck and limb. Woe to him if his animal makes a misstep; his journey to the bottom of some gorge would excel the velocity of steam. At one place it is necessary to ride across a stream on a *log* — a short, broad one, it is true, but still a *log*, and should your horse make a careless step a heavy tumble would be the consequence at least. In traveling up one mountain gorge it is necessary to cross a creek seventeen times in a distance of about four miles. The trail then turns abruptly westward, and the broad Pacific lies before, and three hundred feet beneath us. Yes, literally beneath us; for its bank is perpendicular, and the trail within three feet of its brink. The view is grand. Niagara itself, of which the roaring breakers below remind us, is not more sublime.

Again the road meanders through the mountains for a few miles, and then descends to the water's edge. It now continues for a few miles along the sand beach, which is admirable traveling at low tide. Here are to be seen thousands of gulls, ducks and pelicans. We were much amused at some of the latter, who had gormandized to such an extent that they could scarcely skim the waves. One old fellow was unable to surmount more than a single breaker at a time, and would occasionally be struck by its foaming crest and launched far in the rear. There is some mining done along this portion of the beach, but not much, except at the mouth of Rogue river. The gold is distributed in such minute particles through the sand that but little can be got out by the ordinary mining process. This whole coast for a hundred miles in extent will, however, be an immense field for mining some twenty years hence, when labor becomes cheaper, and machinery more perfect.

The council ground was located in a beautiful myrtle grove on the south bank of Rogue river, three miles from its mouth. The object of the council was to form a treaty with the various bands of Indians belonging to the Port Orford district, with the view of settling them, together with all other bands and tribes living on the coast of Oregon, on an Indian reserve; that is, a tract of land set aside for them exclusively—on which the whites are not permitted to reside. This system of disposing of the Indians has been for many years adopted by our government. It is the only plan to prevent their entire extermination. The manner in which it is carried out is too well known to require description. That some system of this kind is requisite is but too painfully felt by every man of sensibility and intelligence, who has ever been in our new Territories and seen how badly the Indians and whites get along together. This is more apparent on our Pacific coast than east of the Rocky Mountains. For the excitement of the gold mines has filled California and portions of Oregon more rapidly than any other parts of the United States Territory, and, consequently, brought the whites and Indians in more frequent conflict.

The donation act of Congress, which grants to actual settlers from one hundred and sixty to six hundred and forty acres of land—the amount varying according as certain provisions in the Act are complied with—when and wherever they choose to locate it, without having previously extinguished the Indian title, is another prolific source of trouble peculiar to Oregon Territory; hence the difficulties are innumerable. And what makes matters worse, some of the rougher class of miners will submit to no control in their intercourse with the Indians.

If an Indian steals anything from, or hurts one of these persons, his life is generally the forfeit. The Indians around here formerly acted upon the same principle, but their frequent conflicts with the whites have so intimidated them that they are now generally inclined to peace. They have sufficient bad and desperate fellows among them, however, to keep their bands in constant difficulty.

An instance occurred during the session of the council of a most painful character—the more so as it terminated in the death of three American citizens, together with two Indians, and came within an ace of not only breaking up all further negotiations with the Indians, but of bringing on another Rogue River war. The circumstances are these:

An Indian and a white man had a quarrel, which resulted in the latter being wounded in the shoulder by the former. The Indian fled. Captain Ben. Wright, a sub-Indian Agent, being on the treaty ground for the purpose of assembling the Indians preparatory for the treaty, happening to hear of the difficulty, and wishing to prevent further bloodshed, went personally and arrested the Indian with the view of having him properly tried, and punishing him for his misdemeanor if found guilty. At night, whilst he, some others, and the prisoner, were lying asleep in a small shanty, a shot was fired by an unknown person, which shattered the prisoner's arm. Wright having dressed his wounds, placed him between himself and the wall; thus, with his own person, affording protection to the Indian. The night passed off quietly, but as it was evident that the populace intended getting forcible possession of him in the morning with the view of hanging him, the Agent rose early and took his prisoner to the treaty ground, and there placed him in a small hut. He had scarcely done so, when the mob assembled to the number of sixty persons, armed with Colt's revolvers, and demanded the prisoner. Wright stood in the door, and by his determined manner and strong arguments, managed to keep them at bay until the arrival of a detachment of fifteen U. S. troops, who had opportunely reached the opposite side of the river; and for whom he secretly despatched a messenger. The prisoner was then turned over to their protection. The crowd hung around for some time blackguarding the soldiers, but finally dispersed.

On the following day, the twenty-seventh of August, a constable took the prisoner in charge with the intention of taking him before a magistrate some three miles down the river. At the solicitation of the constable, and request of General Palmer, General Superintendent of Indians in Oregon, who had arrived in the meantime, a corporal's guard of troops was furnished the prisoner. After the latter had been properly committed by the magistrate to stand his trial at the next term of court, he was remanded to the corporal for conveyance to prison. As the guard was ascending Rogue River late at night (moonlight) three men came alongside. The corporal ordered them to keep off, but instead of doing so they commenced firing into his boat, killing the prisoner, who was at the time between the corporal's knees, and another Indian rowing the boat.

The corporal then commanded his men to return the fire. The three men were instantly killed, each receiving a ball through his chest. The five corpses were taken to camp. The Indians fled from the council ground in consternation. An attack was expected on the general's camp by the exasperated citizens. A gentleman was dispatched to the mouth of Rogue river to explain the matter to the Vigilance Committee. On arriving there he ascertained that the three men, who had met such an untimely fate by their rashness, were to have been supported by a strong party in another boat. But this party is said to have returned home and gone to bed, after hearing the fatal shots, without even ascertaining the fate of their companions. The miners composing the Vigilance Committee were, of course, much excited, but after understanding the matter thoroughly, came to the conclusion that the soldiers acted only in the discharge of their duty. This was also the verdict of the coroner's jury, held on the deceased the following day.

The event is to be deplored. But it will probably prove a lesson to a large class of persons in this community who wish to take law into their own hands, and execute it in accordance to the dictates of interest or passion. It is probable that the Indian in this case was to blame; if so, he certainly would have met with proper punishment when tried by a jury of Americans. Why then attempt to frustrate the ends of justice by mob violence?

The Indians returned to the ground again on the thirtieth to the number of twelve hundred and twenty, and after having signed the treaty, received from the agents various presents of blankets, calicoes, kettles, shirts, pants, coats, beads, knives, hatchets, tobacco, etc. On being told that these were given them by our great Ti-hee (chief), the President of the United States, they supposed he must be a very rich man, and, of course, have a great many wives. When informed that he had only one, they were very much surprised. Their chiefs usually have as many wives as they can take care of—sometimes as high as fifteen or twenty. The men generally are permitted to have more than one. The women, on the contrary, are limited to one husband. As it is customary among all savage nations, the squaws perform all the drudgery; while the men either fish, hunt, or idle away their time in smoking. The former are said to have been chaste before the whites came among them. If so, their principles have undergone a radical change. In number the females predominate—owing to the fact of the males being killed in a larger proportion by the casualties of war, etc. They are all slaves in the strict sense of the word, and are sold like negroes among the whites. The nearest relative, such as the father, mother, brother or husband, holds the right of disposal. Two or three blankets, a canoe, or a horse, will buy any of them. Here is a wide field for the talents of the women's rights society.

I have never before seen a tribe that had not something characteristic in their dress; which usually consists of a buffalo robe, a blanket, thrown over the shoulders, buckskin moccasins, and leggins. Such is the dress of all the tribes that at present roam the prairies and deserts east of the Rocky Mountains. And such is said to have been the attire of the degenerated race of which we are now speaking. But these marks of distinction have passed away. In this whole council you couldn't perceive two Indians dressed precisely alike. One man's apparel consisted of simply a coat; another, of drawers; a third, of pants; a fourth, a jacket; a fifth, a soldier's uniform; a sixth, a pair of boots and a breech-clout, and occasionally you might see one dressed *a la American.* With the above articles they wring as many changes and combinations as the chimes of some of our fashionable church bells. One of the most amusing spectacles of all was that of a little chubby boy with a soldier's jacket, reaching to his knees, and having down its back seam a broad scarlet stripe.

The squaws adopt the same principles, or rather no principles at all, in their attire. Many of them, however, have learned to make dresses similar to those of the whites. Like all Indian women, they are passionately fond of ornaments. Some of the belles have as many as twenty strings of beads around their necks. There is a peculiar bead-like shell, about an inch long, obtained near Puget Sound, which is preferred to anything else. Instead of ear-bobs they wear dangling from the middle cartilages of their noses vari-colored shells and beads—which may be termed nose-bobs. Some of the old spinsters substitute a long painted feather stuck transversely; signifying, perhaps, that they may be easily "caught."

At the Indian villages one may sometimes see the men, and frequently the boys, in *puris naturalibus.* Not so with the females. They are never, not even the little papooses or babies, without some substitute for the fig leaf of Mother Eve. The majority of both men and women go bareheaded; though a common head-dress of the latter is a conical basket made of the inner bark of the birch tree. This also serves them for a pail, the slits being woven so closely that when swollen by moisture the vessel is perfectly water-tight. And, of course, it is also used as a basket proper—particularly to carry berries in. There are many varieties of the latter, and I am very fond of them; but to eat them when brought in these baskets sometimes requires more courage than I am master of; especially if I have previously observed the owner in the interesting occupation of searching for and eating pediculi—yes, eating them, but it is said they do it out of revenge.

Their staple article of food is the salmon, which are as plentiful in the Oregon rivers as herring and shad in the Potomac; Rogue river especially abounds in them. The agent issued them to the Indians attending the council as a substitute for beef. One haul with a seine at the mouth of the river, when the tide is setting in, is sufficient to last twelve hundred Indians a fortnight. They have some strange superstitions about these fish; and are never known to catch them until salmon-berries—which are also an article of food—are ripe; or to cut them open with a knife in dressing them—for this purpose a sharp stone is used. An infraction of this custom is an unpardonable offense to the salmon Ti-hee—chief or god. What they can't consume whilst fresh are dried for winter use. Their manner of cooking a salmon is worthy of adoption by *voyageurs*. Having dressed it properly, it is laid open longitudinally, and spread out on two sticks, arranged in the form of a cross; the longer and larger one being sharpened at one end, and stuck in the ground at a convenient distance from the fire. It thus becomes broiled much better than when cooked on a gridiron; the use of which indispensbale article of a civilized *cuisine* is as little known among them as the manufacture of flour, which they imagine is found by the white man in the beds of rivers. They usually catch salmon in weirs and cast nets. The latter is also employed in the sea in catching a species of small fish resembling sardines, which go in vast schools along the shore. Their presence is indicated by gulls and other sea-birds who hover in their vicinity. Swimming usually near the surface, they are readily secured by suddenly dipping the net under them and raising it up. But for sea-fishing a hook and line is commonly used. The latter is made of birch bark, and the former consists of a bone and nail bent at right angles to each other. When a fish is hooked he is gently drawn to the surface of the water, and a basket placed beneath to secure him.

They are also very fond of shell-fish, such as oysters, clams, muscles, etc. Their mode of cooking these, as well as their favorite kamas and cowas, is to dig a pit into which wood and stones are thrown, and a fire kindled. When the wood is consumed the articles to be cooked are thrown in upon the hot stones and covered over with dirt. They will eat any kind of animal matter, and are not particular whether it has been killed or has died a natural death. The carcass of a sea-lion floated ashore near Port Orford a short time ago. Like buzzards they gathered around it from far and near, and had a glorious feast. At the proper season berries afford them a good substitute for bread; such as the blackberry, raspberry, strawberry, salalle-berry, salmon-berry, thimble-berry, and red and black huckleberries. Those of them not living immediately on the coast subsist in part upon elk, bear and deer. But as they are notoriously lazy, and moreover have but few guns, in consequence of an Oregon law prohibiting firearms from being sold to them, their success in hunting is not very great. They are not such expert marksmen as the Indians living east of the coast range of mountains—especially the upper Rogue river and Modoc Indians. My description has reference to the Indians living on or near the coast; and especially of two tribes residing in the Port Orford district, but will apply to all those on the coast west of the coast range of mountains from the northern to the southern boundary of the Territory. There are, perhaps, three thousand, all of whom, together with most of the upper Rogue river Indians, are to be moved on one reservation twenty by seventy miles in extent. They are split up into small bands of from thirty to one hundred and fifty souls; each of which has a head man, called Ti-hee (chief), who gains control over them simply by his bravery or wealth. With few exceptions the position is neither hereditary nor elective. Their language varies in different tribes; but there is a jargon, introduced among them by the Hudson Bay Company, that they all understand. It consists of about two hundred and fifty words, taken from the English, French and Chinook Indian languages. This jargon is to them what the pantomime is to the tribes east of the Rocky Mountains; but is not an entire substitute, for the latter is used to some extent.

Like all Indians, they are very thriftless, and literally carry out the idea of letting the morrow take care of itself. Those around the white settlements will occasionally hire themselves out for a few hours or days at a time. But when eight or ten dollars are thus earned they are entirely too rich to work any more until that is exhausted.

A man is considered wealthy who possesses a few skins, blankets, a canoe, or a horse; very few of them own the latter, their usual mode of transportation being in a canoe. This is made of cedar, by first burning it out with hot stones and shaping it with a knife or hatchet. It is usually two feet broad by twelve long, but the Indians in the upper part of Oregon, and near Puget Sound, in Washington Territory, have much larger ones—some of them being sixty feet in length with a beam of eight, and are said to be beautiful specimens of naval architecture. There is nothing remarkable or peculiar in the general appearance of the coast Indians. Their height is rather below the medium. Heads will compare favorably in size with those of Anglo-Americans; retreating foreheads; nose rather inclined to flatness; thick lips, high cheek bones—and dark eyes and hair, of course. The latter is long in both sexes, and allowed to dangle down over their shoulders. The men don't seem so particular about abstracting their beards as most other Indians—some few of them even allow it to grow. Both sexes have small hands and feet. They follow the universal practice of tattooing and painting. But instead of trying to imitate nature like our belles, the squaws daub the paint on like a house painter. And when in full dress, which approximates to no dress at all, as for a dance, all the primary colors are represented on one person. We witnessed several of their balls at the council ground.

A most ludicrous sight. The spectators being seated on the ground, leaving an elliptical space in the middle for the dancers, some seventy or eighty persons will enter, and singing a he-ah......ah ..... *ah*, he-ah .... ah.... *ah*, will commence a succession of bobbing up and down, both feet at a time, body slightly bent, and limbs as rigid as marble statues. They all spring in unison—and keep pretty good time. The same dance is kept up the whole night, with proper intervals of rest. Their war dance is somewhat different.

Their houses are of the most primitive order. A single shed of bark, with a log or brush wall, and dirt floor; size usually about ten feet by twelve. In one of these are crowded from ten to fifteen persons; huddled, in bad weather, around a fire, which is invariably built in the centre of the building, with no particular outlet for the smoke. No wonder they suffer so dreadfully from sore eyes. But there is another prolific cause of this malady which needn't be mentioned in this unscientific sketch. They suffer much from consumption; and the small-pox and measles make a clean sweep whenever they appear among them. This is more owing to their method of treatment than any peculiar virulence of the disease. The patient is placed in a "sweat-house," and whilst reeking in perspiration is suddenly taken out and plunged into a stream of the coldest water that is to be found. Besides sweating they use certain kinds of herbs. But incantations are the favorite remedies. If the patient has a snake in his stomach, or be possessed of a demon in the form of a rabbit or wolf, the doctor, with grave aspect, seats himself beside the couch, and with his hands under the blanket will commence a series of gesticulations, groans, howls, and screams, until the excitement is raised to a proper pitch, then, drawing forth his hands, suddenly throws upon the floor a dead snake, wolf, or other animal. The patient being now dispossessed is expected to recover. Should the laws of nature determine otherwise, the poor doctor's life pays the forfeit, unless he can compromise the matter with the relatives by paying the value of the deceased. Being largely feed he is in honor bound to take the consequences. So it would seem that not even martyrdom itself will stay the current of quackery.

When an Indian dies he is thrown into a pit, together with all his goods and chattles. To prevent the grave being robbed these are generally injured in such a manner as to render them useless to anybody but the dead, to whom they are supposed to be indispensable in their heavenly journey. As no attempts have yet been made to enlighten these tribes upon the glorious truths of Christianity, they, of course, know nothing of the promises in the Bible. They believe in a good and evil spirit. The former is called the great Ti-hee, and reigns in heaven. His wrath is signified by hard winters, scarcity of food, and epidemics. His satisfaction by a healthy season, mild winters, and an abundance of food. Besides him there are numerous subordinate Ti-hees inhabiting particular earthly localities, and having jurisdiction over certain animals, mountains and streams. Heaven is to them either a region covered with eternal verdure—its plains and mountains teeming with elk and deer, and its crystal streams abounding in luscious salmon—according as they happen to live on the coast or in the interior.

The Indians having signed the treaty, the council was dissolved, and we all started for home, where we arrived yesterday afternoon.

CHAPTER XIX.

INDIAN WAR RUMORS.

"La grande Speculation"—Indian hostilities in Washington Territory—Defeat of Major Haller—Threatened Indian outbreak in Southern Oregon—Rumored Massacre of Lieutenant Kautz and party—Repulse of Upper Rogue River Indians by U. S. Troops under Major Fitzgerald.

SUNDAY, SEPT. 2D, 1855.—Mob law seems to be the order of the day. *La grande speculation* of Monsieur Chevalieur having turned out a failure, as predicted, a crowd of some sixty or seventy persons assembled in front of his house in Port Orford, and divided his goods and chattles *sans ceremonie*, and then voted him sixty lashes, provided he does not leave this country by the next steamer.

Monday, Sept. 3d, 1855.—The noise was kept up in the village all night. It seems that after frequent importunities Mr. Dart gave permission to some of the crowd to be "treated" at his expense. When he went to foot the bill this morning he found that the mob had run him in debt one hundred and forty dollars. It has been raining all day. The first rain we have had since May, excepting a slight shower last week.

Saturday, Sept. 9th, 1855.—Steamer arrived at four this morning. Brought Company H, Third Artillery, commanded by Lieutenant J. G. Chandler, to relieve detachment of Company M, at this post. Lieutenant

A. V. Kautz is ordered to take the latter to the Presidio; thence proceed to Fort Jones on temporary duty.

Monday, Sept. 11th, 1855.—Three men started out in the bay fishing this morning. A strong northwester springing up they were unable to manage their boat, which was gradually floating seaward. A party of staunch sailors in town perceiving their distress went to their rescue. They succeeded in saving the men, but left the boat adrift. The latter was afterwards secured by a schooner which was sent after it.

Sunday, October 14th, 1855.—The "Columbia" arrived from Portland late yesterday afternoon. She brings an account of an outbreak among the Indians in Washington Territory. For the last few months we have heard floating rumors of preparations for intended hostilities by the large Indian tribes in that section of country, but as the border settlers are somewhat like the boy in the fable, always crying wolf, we have rarely been able to tell when they really were in danger. But at present there is no doubt of an Indian war having commenced. In consequence of the reports of various persons on their way to the Colville mines having been killed by the Indians, an agent was sent out by Superintendent Joel Palmer, to ascertain their correctness, and he himself was murdered by the Indians. On this news reaching Fort Dalles, Maj. Granville O. Haller, U. S. Army, who had just got in from his expedition to the Snake Indian country, where he had been to demand the murderers of the emigrants last year, started out with a command of a hundred men to bring the murderers to an account for their atrocities. He had been out but three or four days, when a messenger brought the startling news of his command having been surrounded by the Indians at a point about twenty-five miles from the Dalles. His position was upon a hill, with ravines and thickets around him. His troops and animals had been without water for forty-eight hours. The Indians were constantly firing upon them. He was enabled to send a messenger through the ranks of the Indians in the night, who reached the Dalles Monday, October 8th, at eight P. M. Immediately on the arrival of the express at the Dalles, Lieutenant Day started with the remaining troops at that post to the succor of Maj. Haller. Maj. H. calls for large reinforcements to aid him. It is reported that a requisition has been made on the Governors of Oregon and Washington Territories for volunteers. How many is not known—some say one thousand, others five hundred.

The hostile feeling among the Indians is supposed to extend to several tribes. Proposals, it is said, have been made to all the Indians east of the Cascade range to unite in a general war of extermination against the whites. But the number that have really leagued together is not known. The Yakimas and Clikitats seem to be the prime movers in the affair. In order to induce a war spirit they report all sorts of Indian wrongs, and threaten hostilities against such tribes as will not join them. It is thought the disaffection is so widely diffused among them that one flush of victory on their part against the United States troops would induce nearly all of the tribes to unite in a general war. Hence much anxiety is felt in the result of Haller's expedition against them. They are abundantly supplied with arms and ammunition; and are thought to be good warriors; differing vastly in this respect from the Coast Indians of lower Oregon. We are expecting orders by the next steamer, which will arrive in a few days, to proceed to the seat of war.

Tuesday, October 16th, 1855.—Lieutenant August V. Kautz, Fourth Infantry, who left here with ten men about eight days ago, to survey a road between this place and Fort Lane, returned last night about twelve o'clock to get arms and ammunition for his party. He reports that on reaching the big bend of Rogue River, forty-five miles from Fort Orford, he found the settlers making port-holes in their houses, preparatory to an attack from the Indians of upper Rogue River valley. He learned from them that being advised by some friendly Indians to leave the place, as the tribes above there were hostile, but not believing the reports they started up the river to ascertain the truth of the matter. On arriving in sight of a trader's establishment they saw the building in flames, and the Indians in a war dance around it. And that they were further told by the friendly Indians that all the tribes in upper Rogue River valley had united in war against the whites. This report, together with those received from Jacksonville last mail of the disaffection of the Indians in that region in consequence, of the hanging of several of their head men at Yreka for murder, indicates that trouble is brewing in lower Oregon also. These

Indians had been arrested by the United States troops at Fort Lane, and turned over to the civil authorities of California, who, it is presumed, gave them a fair trial.

Of course everybody in this section is excited—all sorts of reports are circulating about small parties being cut off, but I have lived in an Indian country too long to put confidence in more than one twentieth part of the Indian atrocities that are reported.

October 23d, 1855.—The "Columbia" stopped this morning on her upward trip, having on board a large number of passengers, and seventy United States troops, under the command of Captain E. O. C. Ord, en route for the seat of Indian difficulties in Washington Territory. We are not ordered, for the reason, I suppose, that trouble is apprehended in this neighborhood. I see from a Yreka paper (Siskiyou County, Cal.,) that the Indians of that part of California, and in upper Rogue River valley, are truly in open hostilities. That the United States troops under Brevet-Major Edward H. Fitzgerald, of the Second Dragoons, have had an encounter with them—killing some thirty, with a loss of about ten of the soldiers. The volunteers have also had a fight with them. So it seems that a second Rogue River war is upon us. We will probably be unable to hear from the outbreak in western Oregon, and Washington Territory, until the return steamer. The Indians immediately around Port Orford are, so far, quiet. All the settlers within sixty miles of here have retired to the mouth of Rogue River and this place.

October 28th, 1855.—The steamer touched here on her downward trip this afternoon, and brings the news of Major Haller's defeat. After being surrounded by the Indians for twenty-four hours, he fought his way through their ranks—but was pursued to the Dalles—losing in the action five men, and having seventeen wounded; he also lost his howitzer. The fight lasted nearly three days. Lieutenant Day did not succeed in joining him. Success has thus added many others to the hostile tribes. It bids fair to become the greatest Indian war we have had for many years.

The Governors of Oregon and Washington Territories have called out a thousand volunteers, who will be ready for the field by the fifth of November. These, with three hundred regulars, will make a force of thirteen hundred men. Major G. J. Rains, Fourth Infantry, with five hundred men, expects to take the field against the enemy about the fifth of November. The Indians are said to be posted in large numbers near the battle field of Haller, but they will undoubtedly flee to the mountains if hard pushed.

We have received preliminary notice to get our command ready by the next steamer, to proceed to the seat of war.

CHAPTER XX.

FORT ORFORD—MORE WAR RUMORS.

Return of Kautz—His encounter with Indians—Battle of "Hungry Hill"—General Harney defeats the Sioux—A Storm—Whales in the Harbor—Christmas—Indian troubles near Puget Sound—Lieutenant Slaughter killed—Steamer "California" catching fire, and subsequently experiencing a Terrific Gale—Four Indians killed for Stealing—Two whites waylaid and killed by Indians—Slight skirmish by Volunteers—The Upper Rogue River Indians trying to incite the Coast Indians to war—Colonel Kelly's repulse of the Indians in Eastern Oregon—Upper Rogue River Indians surrounded, but escape—Good Shots—Killed Doctor Myers at three hundred yards—An Effort to separate the Coast from Hostile Indians—Rock Oysters and Sea Otter.

NOVEMBER 6TH, 1855.—A week ago news was brought here that Lieutenant Kautz and party, who were surveying a road between this place and Fort Lane, and a company from the mouth of Rogue River, who were looking out a road between that point and Yreka, were cut off by the Indians, and that the hostile bands from above were within a day's march of the village at the mouth of Rogue River, which they intended to attack—thence proceed to take Port Orford.

This rumor created a universal stampede among the whites who reside at Port Orford, and the mouth of Rogue River. Their scare alarmed the friendly Indians around here, and the few acts of precaution that they were induced to take from fear, were construed by the frightened whites as indications of hostilities. What would have been the result heaven only knows had not one of the supposed lost parties—the one from Rogue River—arrived safely home. The excitable public thus finding a part of the rumor false, were led to believe that it might all be so. The excitement has now greatly abated. It has been the cause of a good deal of inconvenience and distress to the settlers. One poor invalid, Mr. Long, was hurried down to Port Orford so rapidly that he died a few hours after his arrival. He was one of the oldest and most respected persons of this neighborhood. Everybody turned out at his funeral yesterday afternoon. There being no proper person to read the burial ceremony, I performed this solemn duty at the request of the relatives.

November 19th, 1855.—For the last fortnight the weather has been exceedingly unpleasant—raining almost incessantly, with strong winds from the southwest. We have been looking out for the mail steamer during the whole of this time, but on account of the storm she has probably been afraid to venture in. We have thus been entirely cut off from news; at least till last night; which is a great privation during these exciting times. However, the firing of cannon in the little village near here yesterday afternoon indicated something new; and on looking out of our window we found it to be a salute to the return of Lieutenant Kautz and party, who had been reported lost. This was cheering news—for we had grown very anxious about his safety—particularly as he had gone through the heart of a hostile Indian country with only ten men and a guide, and had overstaid his time three weeks.

On his way to Fort Lane, and when within forty-five miles of that .place, he accidently came upon a hostile band of Indians, who attacked him, and killed two of his men, and wounded another and himself. He made good his retreat to Bates' Station, where he arrived on the night of the twenty-fifth of October. Leaving his men there, he immediately proceeded to Fort Lane for reinforcements. Brevet-Major E. H. Fitzgerald, with sixty men of that post, was ordered to proceed against the Indians; but, on arriving at the ground, he found them so safely posted that it would have been useless to make an attack upon them with his command.

After reporting these circumstances to the commanding officer at Fort Lane, Captain Andrew J. Smith, the whole of the force at that post, about one hundred and twenty men; and some two hundred and twenty-five volunteers; were got in readiness, and marched against the Indians. They arrived on the ground on the thirtieth of October, and after fighting the Indians for nearly two days, and finding it impossible to dislodge them, gave up the attack. They intended making another effort on the ninth of this month. After this fight was over, Lieutenant Kautz and party, who had participated in it, returned to this post via Crescent City. He informs us that the mail steamer stood off that village for a short time on last Saturday, but, being unable to land either freight or passengers, proceeded on to Portland. He was informed that there were troops on board—also General Wool and staff. And that orders have been issued for the troops at this place to proceed to the scene of difficulties in Washington Territory.

Our Indian affairs are assuming a serious aspect on the other side of the mountains as well as on the Pacific coast. General Harney, with some five companies of infantry, two of cavalry, and one of artillery, met with a party of Sioux on the Blue Water river, near Fort Laramie, and routed them completely—having killed about ninety men, and taken several hundred squaws prisoners.

December 7th, 1855.—Since last writing, very little of importance has occurred in this vicinity. The Indians of this district are quiet, except at the Coquille, where there are slight indications of an outbreak. But if the settlers there act prudently they need fear no trouble for the present. We have heard nothing from the war in Washington Territory since the thirtieth of October. The troops were then on their march against the Indians, who had taken their position near the ground where Major Haller was defeated. A great fight was expected in a few days. We, of course, feel anxious to learn the result.

A mail is usually received here once a fortnight from that section of country; but an accident has occurred to the mail steamer "California," which should have been down three weeks ago. Rumor has it that she collapsed a flue, and caught fire in the Columbia river. The extent of the damage is not known. Not returning to San Francisco in due time, the steamship company sent another vessel, the "Columbia," Captain Leroy, after her. This vessel passed here last Sunday week, and should have been down six days ago. She has probably gone by in a gale. For six weeks there has scarcely been a day without a storm of wind and rain from the southwest. During the last few days it has stormed almost incessantly—accompanied by hail, thunder and lightning. The latter we have here mainly in winter; thus differing from every other climate I have ever been in. The thermometer at present ranges between thirty-five and forty.

December 24th, 1855.—We have had no mail from Portland later than the twenty-eighth of October, and no news from San Francisco since the arrival of the "Columbia" on the twenty-fifth ultimo. As these are the only two sources through which news can reach us, we have consequently been entirely cut off from the world for nearly a month. There has been more stormy weather within the past five weeks than I have ever experienced in the same length of time—in fact it has been storming almost incessantly—at least until day before yesterday. The rainfall in this month is already 19.6 inches—an unusual quantity *even* for this country. The largest measurement in any previous month, for the last three years, is said to have been sixteen inches. Last night was also colder than it has been for several years—thermometer twenty-five degrees. There has been considerable hail, and even a little snow. The mountains near here are covered with the latter. But, notwithstanding the cool state of the atmosphere, everything around looks green. The forest trees of course do, as they belong to the pine genus; and as to grass, it is even fresher than in summer. I shouldn't be surprised, however, if the frost has nipped the blossoms of the *salalle*, and *strawberries*, which were blooming a few days ago.

The storm has now lulled, and we may look for fine weather for a few days. To-day is beautiful. All nature seems to be reaminated. The larks and robins seem to enjoy it wonderfully; and even the monsters of the mighty deep appear to be aware that the elements have ceased their warfare, for they may now be seen in large numbers sporting in the harbor. 'Tis wonderful how high a whale can spout the water.

December 25th, 1855.—Christmas! This day of all others reminds us of home. Oh, how our hearts yearn for those fond ones left behind; for the many fireside *reunions* of our childhood; when we felt supremely happy if our kind mothers allowed us plenty of gingercake and lemonade. If our wants were as simple now how much happier we might be; yet, after all, there are few of us, I presume, who would be willing to exchange our present pleasures with the accompanying sorrows, for the happiness of childhood—for though our sorrows are greater our sense of pleasure is also enhanced.

'Tis curious to look back even a few years, and see what a checkered life one leads. Two years ago I ate my Christmas dinner at Fort Arbuckle, C. N.—last year on the steamship "Empire City," in the Atlantic ocean, off Cape Hatteras—and to-day on the western confines of the United States Territory. What has probably conduced more than anything else to our happiness of to-day is the arrival of the steamship "Columbia," bringing us news from the States and Washington Territory. That from the former is rather of an exciting character—as a rupture with Great Britain is seriously apprehended. The precise cause of the quarrel is not known, but from the *London Times* we learn that the British West India fleet has been suddenly increased with the ostensible purpose of preventing a fillibustering expedition, said (by the *Times*) to be fitting out in the United States against Ireland. If this be the real cause the British government is acting under a great mistake, as there is no such expedition fitting out in this country. It is to be hoped that the British and American authorities will act with prudence, and not involve the two greatest countries in the world in a protracted war.

The troops in Washington Territory have had several skirmishes with Indians since the twenty-eighth of October, routing them in every instance, but not killing many. Several officers have been killed; among others Lieutenant Wm. A. Slaughter, of the Fourth Infantry. He had had a skirmish with the Indians, whom he defeated. A few days thereafter, whilst in a hut near Fort Steilacoom, not dreaming there were any Indians near him, his small party was unexpectedly fired upon by the savages, killing him and several of his men.

It appears that the steamship "California" had a very hard time of it in her trip up the coast. The rumor of her having caught fire in the Columbia river is confirmed by Captain Wm. Dall, who was in command of her at the time. It seems that directly after crossing the bar at the mouth of the Columbia, she collapsed a flue, which accident caused the water from the boiler to leak into the furnace, thus suddenly generating so much steam that the door of the latter was forced open, and the fire was scattered in every direction. They succeeded in extinguishing the fire before much damage was done; but the ship, in the meantime, came within an ace of stranding. After being repaired at Astoria, and completing her trip to Vancouver, she was engaged by General Wool to take troops to Steilacoom—whence she proceeded to San Francisco. On her downward trip she encountered on the twenty-seventh of November, a terrific gale off the mouth of the Columbia; and came very near being foundered. The gale was from the southeast, and lasted with unabated fury for seventy hours. The engine being disabled, the ship was put under sail, and reached San Francisco after an extremely long passage of twenty-one days. Only one person drowned—the third mate.

January 3d, 1856.—The steamer "Columbia" passed down last Sunday, having gone no further than Astoria, in consequence of the Columbia River being frozen over; this is an unusual severe winter. The back country is covered with deep snow—and we have even had a few spits at this point, and the thermometer one night as low as twenty degrees above zero, Fahrenheit. The weather, however, for the last eight or ten days, has been beautiful. Exactly twenty inches of rain fell last month. No wonder the rivers have been unusually high.

The Indians in this district, with one exception, have remained quiet during the present war. The imprudence of the whites came near rendering the bands of the Coquille hostile. It seems that a rascally Englishman (Woodruff) endeavored to incite the Indians to war by telling them that the Americans intended killing them all off, and succeeded in getting them to steal some flour which had been placed under his protection. He subsequently fled to Rogue River valley. The whites on the Coquille and Coos Bay then formed a volunteer company and killed four Indians. Indian agent Ben Wright, from Port Orford, arriving in the meantime, managed to quiet the matter, and it is to be hoped that it will end without further bloodshed. Were it not for the untiring energy of the Indian agent here, supported by a company of United States troops, the Indians of this district would ere this have joined with the hostile bands in the valley.

January 7th, 1856.—Steamer "Columbia" arrived just after dark; news from the States unimportant. Brevet-Major John F. Reynolds, of company H, Third Artillery, was a passenger. He relieves Lieutenant A. V. Kautz, in command of this post; the latter is ordered to join his company at Fort Steilacoom.

January 14th, 1856.—Day before yesterday Captain Poland, commanding a company of volunteers at the big bend of Rogue River, sent an express to the Indian agent of Port Orford, stating that a party of hostile Indians had been seen in the vicinity of his fort (a block-house), and that he was nearly out of provisions. In the absence of the Indian agent, the commander of Fort Orford sent his company twenty days rations, and lent them mules to pack them.

FORT ORFORD, January 25th, 1856.

An express has just arrived from the mouth of Rogue River, bringing the news that a party, consisting of two white men and a Canadian Indian, left that place day before yesterday for the volunteer cantonment at the Big Bend—and that yesterday morning, when within eight miles of the latter place, they were waylaid by a band of hostile Indians, who fired upon them, killing the two white men, and a Shasta-Kostah Indian, who had been hired to row them up the river. The Canadian Indian made his escape, and brought the news to the mouth of the river.

It thus appears that the hostile bands of upper Rogue River are moving in this direction, and are already in the Port Orford district. As they got the better of the troops in upper Rogue River in almost every engagement since the beginning of the war, notwithstanding there were at one time twelve hundred volunteers and regulars in the field, and three hundred and fifty engaged in one battle, it is not likely we shall be able to do much with them, should they come among us in full force—at least until we are reinforced—for the whole white male population of this district, including the settlement at the mouth of

Rogue River, the volunteers at the Big Bend, citizens of Port Orford, and garrison of Fort Orford, is not more than one hundred and eighty men. A small force, even were they all prepared to fight, to act against the Indians, except in the defensive. However, it is to be hoped that we may maintain the position at the Big Bend, and also be able to get the friendly bands of that neighborhood to move nearer the coast. We may thus be enabled to prevent the hostile tribes from forcing them into their service.

January 30th, 1856.—This morning Lieutenants John G. Chandler and Drysdale, of the Third Artillery, with seventeen men, will leave this post for the mouth of the Illinois River, to remain there in charge of the provisions, and other stores, until the arrival of Captain Poland's volunteer company from their present fort at the Big Bend, which they are to abandon, in order to secure a more useful position at the mouth of the Illinois, on Rogue River, some seven miles below the Big Bend. Then Lieutenant Chandler's detachment is to proceed to the mouth of Rogue River, to assist the acting Indian agent, Jerry McGuire, in collecting all the friendly Indians in that part of the district, and removing them to Fort Orford. This is done in accordance with general instructions from the superintendent of Indian affairs of Oregon, who, foreseeing that many of the friendly tribes might be forced to take sides with those that are hostile, has ordered his assistants to keep the former separated from the latter, and even to bring the friendly bands in, and feed them if necessary.

To-day is exceedingly stormy—a strong southeast wind with rain. The troops will have a disagreeable march. I may here remark that the Indians, after killing those three men near the mouth of Illinois River the other day, made a night attack on the fort at the Big Bend in the absence of a portion of the garrison, but after shooting in the window a few times, and attempting to fire the house, went away. Two days thereafter some of the volunteers came across a few of these Indians, and firing into them, killed one man, the others retreated.

February 1st, 1856.—The detachment under Lieutenant Chandler left here day before yesterday at one P. M.—the weather being exceedingly stormy. Yesterday morning an expressman arrived from Lieutenant C., bringing an Indian prisoner and a letter. Lieutenant C. reached Half Breed's House, some twelve miles from here, the first day, with his men and animals much fatigued in consequence of the miserable roads and inclemency of the weather. At that place he met Jerry McGuire, the assistant Indian agent, with the above mentioned Indian prisoner, whom he requests shall be kept in custody for awhile, as he is suspected of being a spy. Mr. McGuire thought it better for him to accompany the troops, otherwise the friendly Indians, on seeing them, might flee to the mountains, and give much trouble. Of course his wishes were gladly complied with, as he is the best Indian interpreter on the coast, and knows all the head men belonging to the different bands. From his representation of the really serious condition of things at the mouth of the Illinois, the detachment of regulars, and the volunteers at the Big Bend, will undoubtedly unite before reaching the latter place, and march there together; for Mr. McGuire says the hostile Indians are already some fifty strong in that neighborhood, and still coming down from their headquarters further up the river.

In regard to the Indian prisoner, I may remark that he was a partner of Enas, the Canadian Indian who was with the party that was cut off near the mouth of the Illinois a few days ago. I have already mentioned that Enas brought the news of this misfortune to the mouth of Rogue River. On his arrival at the latter place the citizens were induced to let him carry an express to the volunteers at the Big Bend, informing them of what had transpired, and that a hostile band was in their vicinity. They also let him have about sixty dollars worth of gunpowder, which he said the captain of the volunteers desired him to get—for which he paid in gold slugs. Several persons offered to go with him, but he declined their company, saying that he could go more expeditiously and safely alone. Jerry McGuire (acting Indian agent) has since been at the Big Bend, and given Captain Poland the first information concerning the action of the hostile Indians in his vicinity. Enas had not arrived. Captain Poland denies having requested him to buy ammunition, or giving him any gold slugs; and as Enas possessed none himself, it is believed that he has been double dealing, and that the ammunition was purchased for the hostile Indians. Another way the latter have of getting ammunition is from the squaws kept by some of the miners.

February 2d, 1856.—This afternoon the steamer "Columbia" very unexpectedly arrived from Portland on her downward trip. We were under the impression that she passed here in a storm; but it seems she was detained for several days on a sand bar in the Columbia River. As her arrival was so unexpected, and her stay so brief, Major Reynolds was unable to transmit a communication to the headquarters of this department, informing General Wool of the excitement in this vicinity; and as we have no other mode of communication we shall have to wait for the return steamer; unless the commanding officer writes by a schooner now lying in the harbor, and bound for San Francisco in a few days. But as the prevailing winds at this season are from the south and southeast, there is no telling when she will get there. The harbor is so rough at present that she will be unable to take her cargo of lumber for some days to come. The roughness of the harbor, caused by a southeaster, is the reason why the steamer stopped so short a time.

Ben Wright, our Indian agent, arrived on the steamer this afternoon. His return will have a beneficial influence on the Indians in this district. He says that Captain Poland's volunteer company has been properly organized, and called into service by the Governor. Its strength is to be sixty men—at present it is only about twenty-two.

February 4th, 1856.—The storm has subsided. The wind has changed to the north; the sky clear and beautiful. Many unknown species of plants are to be seen blooming on the sunny slopes of the coast. The snow has disappeared on the neighboring mountains. No news from Lieutenant Chandler yet. The troops in eastern and southern Oregon are in winter quarters. They number two regiments, or twenty companies, of volunteers; and two or three companies of regulars. This number has been in the service since November last. In Washington Territory there have been seven companies of regulars (portions of the Fourth Infantry and Third Artillery) and eight companies of volunteers. In January the regular force was increased by the arrival of the Ninth Infantry, which will take the field during the ensuing spring campaign in Washington Territory and Eastern Oregon. At present the main body of them are at Fort Vancouver, and the remainder at Fort Steilacoom, Puget Sound. Since the arrival of the Ninth, Captain Keys and Ord's companies of artillery have been ordered to Benicia and the Presidio, in California. The force of regulars and volunteers that left Fort Dalles about the first of November, under Major Raines, with the hope of bringing on an engagement with the Indians near Haller's battle ground, returned after being out several weeks, in consequence of the severity of the weather. The Indians had fled from their former positions, and were not to be found in any large bodies. Some detachments of the troops, however, had a few skirmishes with small parties of Indians.

Colonel James K. Kelly, commanding another body of troops (volunteers) was more successful. He came upon a large number of the Indians near Walla Walla, in the Snake River country, and had an engagement, which lasted four days, when the Indians fled, leaving some thirty-five dead on the field, among others the famous chief of the Walla Walla's, Pee-peu-mox-a-mox. Colonel Kelly says in his report that there were probably some seventy-five of the enemy slain, as they were known to carry off many of their dead. His own loss was five or six killed and several wounded. While the difficulties were going on there, the Indians in the vicinity of Puget Sound broke out and killed some fifteen or twenty settlers. Portions of the two companies of the Fourth Infantry, stationed at Fort Steilacoom, and one or two companies of volunteers, went out against them, and finally succeeded in driving them from the neighborhood. In the several skirmishes that they had with the Indians some twelve or twenty men were killed, and several officers, among whom was Lieutenant Slaughter, Fourth Infantry, as before mentioned.

Whilst these difficulties were going on in Washington Territory and Eastern Oregon, the Indians, who had broken out in Rogue River valley, were doing a great deal of mischief; and although the number of their warriors has not at any one time been over two or three hundred, and there have been from five to fifteen hundred volunteers and regulars (a small proportion of the latter) in the field against them, yet they have in no instance been fairly whipped, except when their number was infinitely less than the whites. The fact is, the troops have insurmountable difficulties to contend with in fighting Indians in Southern Oregon. The country is so mountainous and thickly timbered, that the Indians can take their position whereever they please, which is generally impregnable, and if pushed too hard are sure to find a way of retreat. They also have many good marksmen. In a late skirmish on the Applegate, a white man, Dr. Myers, was shot at the distance of three hundred yards. In this affair the troops had, to all appearances, made sure of their foe, by surrounding a log house, in which they had secreted themselves. The former succeeded in dropping through the roof a shell, which killed two Indians; but night coming on, they concluded to keep the house surrounded till morning, and then renew the attack. During the night the Indians broke through the picket line and made their escape. On examination of the house it was found that the latter had dug pits under the floor, thus, in a measure, protecting themselves from the explosion of the shell. In almost every instance the Indians of that section have managed to evade the utmost vigilance of the troops. They came off first best at the engagement near Cow Creek, when the troops, under Colonel Ross and Captain Smith, attacked them with a force of nearly four hundred men, as mentioned on a preceding page; then again at the crossing of Rogue River, where a plan had been arranged to surround them; and lastly on the Applegate, where they certainly had them in a better position to be cut off than will soon be possessed again. Yet they have managed to kill a good number in all; and it is thought that one of the most troublesome bands (Jake's) has been entirely exterminated.

If these same Indians are really coming among us

in main force, it remains to be seen whether we shall meet with any better success than our fellow soldiers above. All we can do until reinforcements arrive, will be to keep the friendly Indians separated from the hostile Indians as far as practicable.

I may here remark that the regulars in Washington Territory and Eastern Oregon are at present commanded by Colonel George Wright—General Wool having gone to Benicia. The volunteers in Eastern Oregon have elected T. Cornelius as their colonel; Colonel Kelly, who had command whilst Colonel Nesmith was attending the Legislature, having declined a nomination. In Middle Oregon Colonel Martin commands, and in Southern Oregon the volunteer battalion have elected Bob Williams as their colonel. The appointment of Colonel Martin was made by the Governor. The elections of Colonels Cornelius and Williams have yet to receive his approval.

To-day an express was received from Lieutenant Chandler, dated February 3d, fourteen miles from the mouth of the Illinois. He had sent a request to Captain Poland for a portion of his command to join him, when they would march on to the mouth of the Illinois together. Mr. McGuire, the assistant Indian agent, was fearful all the friendly Indians would not come in. It is to be regretted that a larger force could not have been sent into that neighborhood; for the Indians of that portion of the district, seeing that the hostile Indians are the stronger party, will be induced to join them. They are totally ignorant of the power of the United States, and imagine that we are the only whites in this part of the country with whom they will have to contend.

February 7th, 1856.—I went out this afternoon and secured a fine mess of rock oysters. They are found on the seashore imbedded in solid rocks, generally of the gray sandstone species. The little cavities containing them have no communication whatever with the atmosphere except, perhaps, through the pores of the rock; unless the oyster is dead. In the latter event there are external openings. Insects probably destroy them. Their average size, shell and all, is about that of a pullet's egg, which they also resemble somewhat in shape, except they are flatter, and have a much sharper little end. I have never seen them anywhere but on this coast. They taste very much like the Chesapeake oyster, and have as fine a flavor. They are obtained by shivering the rock with a hammer.

In the cove where these oysters were obtained the sea otter is occasionally to be seen. In fact I wounded one there myself a few weeks ago, which ultimately died, and was found by the Indians. It must have died shortly after it was shot, and was then carried ashore by the tide. It is possible the one found was not mine, but as its skin had been pierced by buckshot, and I am the only one, as far as can be ascertained, who used the latter, it seems pretty evident that I killed it. But the finders are, of course, the owners.

The sea otter (*enhydra marina*) which abounds on the Pacific coast from California to Behring's Strait, is much larger than the common otter found in Europe and the eastern part of North America. Its body is about three and one half feet long—its tail fifteen inches. The general color is a beautiful maroon brown, with a brownish silver-gray to the head, neck under part of the fore legs. Its skin is considered the finest of all furs, both in texture, softness and durability; and commands as much as a hundred dollars in the markets of China, Japan, Europe and America. It lives in the ocean near the shore in winter, but in summer ascends the rivers and enters the fresh water lakes. It lives on fish, crustacea, and sea weed.

The sea otter is essentially an aquatic animal, though it can live in both air and water; although it may be found with its head, and even its body, resting on a rock, it never ventures on the dry land. When cracking a mussel shell, or playing, it swims on its back. The same position is assumed by the female whilst nursing her young, which are held pretty much as a woman holds her baby when nursing it while lying down. Her breasts also resemble the human female's. When dead the sea otter floats on the surface of the water. Many persons follow hunting it as a profession on this coast.

February 10th, 1856.—This afternoon Lieutenant Chandler arrived, having left his detachment in camp, under the command of Lieutenant Drysdale, on Rogue River, about four miles from its mouth. He, in conjunction with Captain Poland's company, and Indian agent J. McGuire, succeeded in inducing the Shasta-Costahs, and other friendly Indians in the vicinity of Big Bend, to move further down Rogue River. On the first appearance of the troops at the mouth of the Illinois, the friendly Indians took to the thicket, but were finally all got in. They reported that the hostile Indians had moved with their families up the Illinois. They will probably make that their headquarters, and thence proceed in different directions to cut off small parties. It is important that they be followed up at once, whilst their provisions are scarce, but it will be almost impossible for troops to pursue them far up the Illinois, as its banks and mountain gorges are woefully inaccessible. However, so soon as we receive reinforcements we shall doubtless take a trip against them.

February 15th, 1856.—Lieutenant Drysdale and detachment returned yesterday. The weather for the last few days has been as beautiful and mild as I ever experienced. The thermometer being generally about fifty at seven A. M., and sixty at two P. M.—wind N. W. To-night, however, the latter has changed to the S. E., and will probably give us another storm.

Major Reynolds and myself caught fourteen beautiful salmon trout in a lagoon in this vicinity yesterday; but they are not very good at this season; their flesh being soft.

CHAPTER XXI.

INDIAN TROUBLES ON ROGUE RIVER.

Uprising of Coast Indians—Terrible Massacre of Whites—Coast Settlers take refuge in temporary fortifications—Narrow escape of Dr. White, Messrs. Foster and Smith—Ten Men, sent in a rowboat with Provisions for beseiged Whites, are drowned—The Hunter Roland—Strengthening our Fortifications—A Detachment from Fort Miner nearly cut to pieces—An Exchange of Prisoners—Military Relief for Fort Miner.

MONDAY, FEB. 25TH, 1856.—Indian troubles are augmenting. Captain Ben Wright, the Indian sub-agent, Captain Poland, several volunteers, and all the settlers between this and Rogue River, except those immediately at the mouth, making about twenty-eight in all, have been massacred by the Indians.

As previously mentioned, the friendly bands from the vicinity of Big Bend of Rogue River, had been brought lower down the river, so as to keep them separated as far as possible from the hostile tribes above. Provisions were also issued them by the agent, whose intention it was to remove them, together with all the tribes in this district, to the Indian reserve selected by the superintendent last summer. The Indians seemed delighted at the idea of going on the reservation. About fifteen of Captain Poland's volunteers were kept in the neighborhood to watch their movements. On the twenty-second instant five of these attended a ball at the mouth of the river. On the same day the Indians (those brought from the

Big Bend) sent a message to Captain Wright that Enas (the traitor) was at their camp, and desired Wright to come up immediately, as he wished to have a talk with him. The latter returned answer that he would meet Enas at a half-way house; and accordingly left the same day with Captain Poland for the place of assignation. That night the ten volunteers, who were quartered in a shanty directly across the river from where the agent and Enas were to meet, heard a very suspicious noise in that direction, but did not know that anything was wrong till the following morning, when their party was attacked whilst at breakfast by an overwhelming body of savages. They immediately broke for the thicket. So far but one of them (C. Foster,) has been heard from—and he managed to reach this place. He lay secreted in a thicket near the attacked house all day Saturday, and saw sufficient of the Indian movements that day to satisfy him that all the coast Indians in that vicinity had risen against the whites. Foster says he killed two Indians with his revolver, and could have killed a third, but was afraid the report of the pistol would endanger his life. On Saturday night he left the thicket, and came as far as Euchre Creek. On coming near the ranches there he discovered them burnt, and the Euchre Indians holding a war dance. Last night he reached this place. Shortly after, a schooner arrived from the mouth of the Rogue River confirming the report of the outbreak. She left yesterday morning; she brought a list of the missing, twenty-eight in number. The nearest house burned is within fifteen miles of here.

As the Indians are vastly stronger than the whites, even though the bands between this place and the Coquille do not join them, and as they are elated by almost unprecedented success in upper Rogue River, and led on by that rascal Enas, who, from having been employed so much by the army as guide, has a perfect knowledge of this country and its most assailable points, it is feared an attack will be made on the citizens in the temporary fortifications at the mouth of Rogue River, and perhaps on this place.

12 o'clock, M.—Two men, supposed to have been killed, have found their way in—Dr. White to Rogue River, and Mr. Smith to this place. The latter states that late on the afternoon of the twenty-second, the Euchre Indians, whose encampment was near his house, came there, and told them that Seaman (both the latter and Dr. White were there on a visit), had killed two otter, and wished Warner, a partner of Mr. Smith's, to come down there immediately, and bring him two rifles. Warner, though not suspecting anything, for the Indians had been perfectly friendly, and he knew that Seaman was otter hunting, still declined to go. Shortly thereafter, the Chief came to him and said that he had found a dead otter, which had floated ashore, and wished Warner to come down and see whether it was the one which he had killed a few days previously. Warner went. Mr. Smith and the Doctor heard a shot shortly afterwards, and suspected what was up. They ran into the house, which was immediately attacked by the Indians, and set on fire. This was extinguished several times, but the latter finally succeeded in getting it in a full blaze. The two gentlemen then broke for the bushes. The bullets rattled around them, but they made their escape. Mr. Smith was from Friday night till Monday 12 o'clock M., reaching Fort Orford, a distance, by the usual trail, of only fifteen miles. Of course he kept the thicket all the way.

February 27th, 1856.—For the last few days we have been endeavoring to put our post in a condition for defence against the enemy should they attack us. Most of the buildings are made of cedar plank, and are consequently very inflammable, and afford only protection against balls. One half of the fort is surrounded by a dense forest, through which the Indians can come within pistol shot of garrison. Should the enemy arrive before we get ourselves in a defensible condition, it will be a serious matter.

Last night there were two alarms—the first one false—the second caused by a shot from a sentinel down town at four strange Indians seen hovering near. Things in this district at present are calculated to cause much vigilance and anxiety, especially as we have no chance of securing aid from a distance for some time. If the steamer gets in to-day or to-morrow, we may be able to report our condition to Col. Wright, who has probably not yet left Fort Vancouver, with all of the Ninth Regiment.

We feel much anxiety to hear from Rogue River, as large columns of smoke are plainly to be seen rising up from the vicinity of the fort erected there by the whites of that place.

February 28th, 1856.—The steamer Republic arrived here last evening. She was bound for Portland, and had gone twenty-five miles beyond Port Orford, and would not have stopped had she not caught fire, when this port was made, as it was the nearest. The fire caused but little damage. A large quantity of ammunition, intended for Vancouver and this place, was thrown overboard. By her we were enabled to inform Col. Wright of our critical position.

This morning a row-boat was dispatched to Rogue River, to learn how the settlers, who are there beseiged, are getting on. With a spy-glass, we yesterday thought we could see their fort still standing; but the shanties all along the coast seemed to have been burnt to the ground. We think that the settlers will be able to hold out till the arrival of assistance, yet it is strange the schooner has not returned.

March 1st, 1856.—This morning Mr. McGuire and another gentleman, reached here from the mouth of Rogue River. They ran a narrow escape, but the critical condition of the citizens there, rendered it absolutely necessary for an express to come through. The former states that Captain Tichenor, who left here for that place last Sunday night, was unable to get in, on account of a strong wind blowing at the time. He has probably gone to Crescent City for aid. The boat that left here day before yesterday, was capsized in attempting to land, and eight of her ten men met a watery grave. He says the Indians have burnt and destroyed all the houses and other property in that neighborhood, except the fort in which the citizens are now protected. This has been attacked several times, but as it is a good building, and situated on the sand beach, over a mile from any timber, they will probably be able to sustain themselves until the arrival of reinforcements by the next steamer, if any are sent; if not, the steamer may stop there and take them away.

The Indians are represented to be very numerous. All the upper Rouge River bands, that have given so much trouble near Jacksonville, are believed to be present, together with those who have joined them in this district. There is not a doubt from what has come to light, that the rise of all the Indians in this district has been determined on. The only thing to prevent the few bands yet professing friendship from joining the enemy, will be the timely arrival of reinforcements. We now have three small bands on the military reserve, who will remain peaceable just so long as the enemy keeps away, and no longer. But what can we do? They still profess friendship, and say they wish to live in peace with us. Surely we can't, under the circumstances, treat them otherwise than as friends. It is a difficult matter to get along with the Indians when a thirst for revenge has been awakened in their breasts, for then they know no distinction between foes or friends. All whites are then alike to them, and deep, hellish treachery and revenge becomes the motive powers of all their actions.

March 4th, 1856.—Yesterday, Roland, a celebrated hunter, came in from the Coquille. He is very inimical to the Indians, who have frequently endeavored to kill him; that is, even those now professing friendship, and for several months past there have been a few of the hostile Indians spying around in his neighborhood, three of whom followed his trail the other day.

The way he caught them in their own game is worthy of record. As has always been his custom during dangerous times, he traveled five or six miles on a certain trail, and then went off to one side and struck the same again a mile or two back, and examined it to see if he was pursued. In this way he soon discovered that three Indians were on his trail. Moving along carefully, he came up behind them and shot one; the other two broke and ran. The story is believed, because, independent of the old fellow's credibility, the action is in accordance with his character. His age is about sixty-five, and yet he can shoot better than any man in this country. A rifle in his hands is held as steadily as though it were in a vice. I could relate many daring adventures of which he is the hero, had I space to spare, but shall conclude by simply remarking that he is a second Daniel Boone. The pioneer of Kentucky must have been just such an eccentric specimen of humanity.

False alarms are the order of the night down in the village; but last night one of the sentinels there did really get a shot at an Indian spy; he was within twenty feet of him. It is not known whether the fellow was struck or not, but, judging from the manner in which he threw himself over the bank, it is thought some of the buckshot hit him. His tracks were plainly to be seen on the sand beach the next morning; also a large knife, which he had dropped, was found.

We are now enclosing a row of our principal houses in a picket fence, made of upright posts, eight feet apart, placed around in the form of a rectangular parallelogram. Boards are nailed to these both inside and outside, thus leaving a space of six inches between them, which is filled with dirt. At intervals of about thirty feet port-holes are cut to fire through; and also at suitable places there are openings of two by two and a half feet for the howitzer. A glacis will be thrown up on the outside of the fence. The latter will be completed in a few days, when the ordnance and commissary stores will be moved inside, and thus be kept secure from the enemy, who will then be unable to burn us out; and, in fact, I have no idea that they will make an attack when they perceive that we are ready for it.

The steamer is looked for to-morrow. If she brings troops they will be immediately despatched to the relief of the besieged garrison at the mouth of Rogue River.

March 7th, 1856.—The steamer from above has not yet arrived. She is two or three days behind her time. Night before last we were all put under arms about three o'clock in the morning, as it was believed by many that Indians were in the thicket just back of the garrison. When daylight broke nothing could be seen. Last night there were two false alarms down town, and one at the mill. The first was caused by a sentinel shooting at another coming to relieve him—the second by one of the pickets shooting a cow, which he mistook for an Indian—the third was the accidental discharge of his gun by a sentinel guarding the saw-mill in the vicinity of the post. This morning sixteen men arrived from Coos Bay—a coal mining region some seventy miles up the coast. They learned something had occurred down here, and came to find out the particulars. They will probably return soon to put the other settlers on their guard.

March 8th, 1856.—A row-boat has just arrived from Fort Miner, the temporary fortification of the besieged citizens at the mouth of Rogue River, and brings the following news:—

On the third or fourth instant a party of seventeen men left the fort to bring in some potatoes, about a mile distant. They had no idea that the enemy was near enough to do them any harm. A sentinel was posted in a commanding position, whilst the others put the potatoes in the wagon. Before they had finished loading, a party of Indians made an attack by first shooting the sentinel. A running fight ensued—the whites, being overpowered, were driven to the fort, with the loss of four, and two wounded. They think several of the enemy were killed—one of the chiefs among the number.

On the sixth instant an exchange of prisoners took place; the Indians giving up Mrs. ———, and her two daughters, and the whites four squaws. Mrs. ——— says the Indians put her two sons to death, but treated her and daughters well. From what she was enabled to gather from the Indians, a large number of them were killed in their attack and massacre of the volunteers. The besieged are represented as being still about one hundred strong; and have provisions for two weeks. Their fort consists of two log houses, surrounded by a high embankment of earth. They will, no doubt, be able to hold out till we can reinforce them.

It is feared an accident has occurred to the "Republic," or she would have been here several days ago, with reinforcements. The steamer from below is also due. If neither of them come in we shall all be in a perilous position; for our provisions are growing short from having to supply the distressed citizens in Port Orford, as well as the friendly Indians now on the reserve. If the latter are not fed they will leave here, and probably join the enemy at once. They say they don't wish to unite with the hostile Indians, if the whites can give them protection.

Sunday, 9th, 1856.—The steamer "Columbia" arrived last night at twelve, and brought us forty-one recruits. Major-General Wool and staff were on board. The General has ordered three bodies of regulars to proceed against the hostile Indians at Rogue River, from three different points. One hundred men, under Captain A. J. Smith, to leave Fort Lane on the eleventh instant—one hundred Crescent City on the twelfth, and seventy from this post on the thirteenth. From our proximity we shall undoubtedly reach the ground first, and may have a hard fight; for the enemy are the same (only doubly reinforced) who stood their ground against four hundred volunteers and regulars at the battle of "Hungry Hill," in upper Rogue River valley, last November.

March 11th, 1856.—The "Republic" arrived from above on the afternoon of the ninth. She brought Captain C. C. Augur's company, seventy-four men, Fourth Infantry. She was detained three days in crossing the bar of the Columbia.

VOLUNTEERS ON THE MARCH.—Page 293.

CHAPTER XXII.

CAMPAIGN AGAINST THE ROGUE RIVER INDIANS.

Troops move in three divisions against the Indians—A Skirmish at the mouth of the Illinois—The Regulars relieve a besieged Company of Volunteers, and subsequently the Citizens of Fort Miner—Skirmish at the mouth of Rogue River—Another at Macanuteeny Village—Narrow escape of two Expressmen—Captain Smith encounters the Indians near the mouth of the Illinois—An Expressman decoyed by a Spur—Skirmish with the enemy by the commands of Major Latshaw and Bruce—Pack Train captured by the Rogue River Indians—Also the Horses of Captain George's Company of Volunteers—Captain Keyes defeats the enemy at Muckle Chute Prairie—*I am Kanasket*, and I hate you"—Massacre at the Cascades.

MARCH 14TH, 1856.—Portions of Company H, Third Artillery, and G, Fourth Infantry, in all one hundred and two men, under the command of Captain Christopher C. Augur, left Port Orford this morning to act against the Rogue River Indians. The officers are Captain C. C. Augur, Fourth Infantry; Bat.-Major John F. Rignod, Third Artillery; Lieutenant Robert Macfeeby, Fourth Infantry; Lieutenant John Drysdale, Third Artillery, and myself—also some fifteen guides and packers.

It having rained on the thirteenth, and also some little to-day, the trail is muddy and slippery. It is also exceedingly hilly and rough, and lined the most of the way with thick timber. The command are obliged to march in single file. Having to wade streams, (one, Brush Creek, seventeen times) they are kept wet up to their knees.

We arrived in camp at the "Half Breed's House,"

(now vacant) ten miles from Fort Orford, about sundown. Not being able to get a good supply of pack animals, and not knowing how long we should be in the field, we have brought with us nothing but absolute necessaries—not even tents. The latter will be considered necessary before the trip is over, for I have no idea that we shall be able to return from the field for several months—in the meantime we shall probably be able to get tents. For the present, however, we must endure the weather whatever it may be. On arriving here we captured a squaw, who says she is on her way to join her tribe near Port Orford. She further states that the upper Rogue River Indians, and the coast tribes, have been quarelling, and that the former have gone up the river, taking most of the plunder with them; and that the traitor Enas is yet with the latter. Her report is considered suspicious. She will be sent to Fort Orford—to be kept awhile in custody.

Sunday, March 15th, 1856.—We came about fifteen miles yesterday over an exceedingly rough trail. The first three miles of our way lay through thick fir timber—then seven miles of dense undergrowth of chinkepin, whortleberry, large or true laurel, and rhododendron—the remainder of the trail ran through a dense growth of fir, with the exception of half a mile of peculiar species of oak, on the south hill of Euchre Creek.

The march was a hard one—several of the men and animals giving out in ascending Euchre hill, the ascent of which is three or four miles. Six mules and packs left behind; also one man. We sent back last night for the latter, but he had risen from the spot where he was last seen lying. We shall remain in camp at this place to-day, and endeavor to find the man as well as the mules. The latter are probably several miles in the rear. Yesterday our hunters killed a fat deer.

Our camp is some three or four thousand feet above the ocean, which lies plainly in view some fifteen miles to the west. The surrounding landscape is very picturesque. Some of the mountain peaks are whitened with snow, others covered with green grass. The highest points seen yesterday were Iron Mountain to the east, Bald Mountain west, and Illinois Mountain southeast. Portions of the first and second can be seen from this camp.

March 17th.—After a diligent search yesterday, we were unable to find the poor fellow we left behind. The packers were more successful, however, having found all their mules and packs, otherwise many of the command would have had no blankets to protect them from the inclemency of the weather. As it was, we all got wet from the rain. The act of sleeping on the ground of a rainy night, without tents, is not the most agreeable thing in the world.

We left the Bark Shanty camp this morning at 10 o'clock, and reached our present one at 3.30 P.M. The ascent on the side of Lobster Creek is about three miles, and so steep that pack animals can scarcely climb it. We have come eight miles, most of the way through a forest of fir timber.

From our present position, we could see Rogue River and the ocean, were it not so foggy. The fog, which lies along the water-courses many hundred feet below us, looks very beautiful, as the sun, which is setting clear, adds to its charms. The snow-capped mountains of the Illinois shine with brilliant splendor. Altogether, it is the most beautiful landscape I have ever seen.

March 19th, 1855.—Camp on north side of Rogue River, opposite the mouth of the Illinois. We arrived here yesterday at 4 P. M., having traveled fourteen miles, the most of the way through timber and dense undergrowth. On descending the mountain, immediately on Rogue River, we passed around a hill with a slope so steep, that the least misstep would have sent the rider one thousand feet below. Fortunately, no accident occurred at that point.

The view from the crest of the mountain was grand. From there we could, with our spy-glasses, see the mouth of the Illinois, on the east bank of which, near its junction with Rogue River, we also beheld Indians. We moved cautiously forward, and arriving at our present camp, and tying the animals, three detachments were sent to attack the enemy, who were seen on the opposite bank of Rogue River, only two hundred and fifty yards from our camp. One of the detachments went as close as the river would permit, and opened a fire of small arms, which was followed in a few seconds by a howitzer, under Major Reynolds. The Indians fled across the Illinois in canoes. When they got across the river in the thick timber, on the

FIGHTING THE INDIANS.—Page 283.

opposite side of Rogue River to us, they commenced a random fire upon us while we were burning their ranches, which were mostly on our side of the river. Much dried salmon and acorns were destroyed in these ranches, which constituted the Macanuteeney village. The Indians, feeling themselves secure for the time in the forest on the opposite side of the river, which is at this point only about seventy-five yards wide, and which we had no means of crossing, kept up an occasional firing during the evening, and then again early this morning, but are poor shots, or else they would have done us some injury. A few of their balls came whizzing uncomfortably near us while we were at breakfast.

It is supposed we killed four in the skirmish yesterday. Their ranches on this side of the river had every indication of having been hastily abandoned, and as there was a canoe of provisions lying on the opposite side of the river, it is thought the Indians were aware of our approach. They probably saw us when we were passing around the steep slope a few miles back. It is here we were to join the troops from Crescent City, under the command of brevet-Lieut. Col. R. C. Buchanan. He should have arrived four days ago; but from all we can now learn, it is highly probable that he has been unable to take the route indicated in General Wool's order, and has likely marched directly for the mouth of the river, to the relief of Fort Miner. As we have no idea of his whereabouts, we shall start this morning for the mouth of the river.

The Indians have been firing upon us this morning from the opposite side of Rogue River, and we have returned their fire. It would be impossible to route them from that position, unless we had some means of crossing the stream. And as we are not aware how long the besieged citizens can hold out without assistance, it is thought useless and imprudent to tarry here three or four days in building a flat boat to cross the river, and then probably be unable to bring the enemy to a fair fight.

Afternoon, March 19th, 1856.—Camp four miles from mouth of Illinois. Got here at three P. M.; men and animals nearly worn out. The hill we have just climbed, is about three miles long and very steep. Just before reaching the foot of it, there was a very high bluff bank of a ditch to ascend. Many of the pack animals fell and rolled down into the ditch, the mule on which the howitzer was packed, being among the number. Some of the saddle animals, with their riders, met with the same accident.

"*Soldiers' Camp,*" *March 20th, 1856.*—This is the same camp we made on the evening of the 17th. Indians have been seen in our rear to-day, watching our movements. The hunters killed two deer yesterday, and the same number this morning.

Late this afternoon dense columns of smoke have been seen ascending from the south bank of the mouth of Rogue River; and just at sundown two flames were observable, one succeeding the other in quick succession, and followed in about three minutes by reports like those of cannon. Colonel Buchanan has probably arrived at the mouth of the river, and had a fight with the Indians. The flashes and reports were perhaps from his howitzer, and the smoke from the burning Indian ranches. But as Captain Augur is not sure of this, he will move from here to-morrow to where the Rogue River trail turns off, and thence send an express to Fort Orford, to learn, if possible, the whereabouts of the Colonel, who may have sent some orders to the post for him.

March 22d, 1856—12 M.—We are now encamped at the junction of the Rogue River with the Illinois trail. This morning, at four A. M., an express of two men—Walker and Middleman—arrived from Colonel Buchanan, who is, with his command of one hundred and twenty men, at the mouth of Rogue River, on this side, having arrived there on the morning of the twenty-first. He had reached the opposite side on the previous evening, and had a slight skirmish with the Indians. We were right in our conjectures about the burning ranches and firing of the howitzers—it was dark, however, at the mouth of Rogue River when the latter were fired, although only sundown to us on the mountains—hence the flashes of light so plainly visible.

It appears that the Colonel's command did not leave Crescent City until the fifteenth, instead of the eleventh, as directed by General Wool; and deeming it impracticable to reach the Illinois by the route directed by the General, he marched directly for the mouth of Rogue River, where he arrived on the evening of the twentieth.

On the third day out he relieved a company of

thirty-three volunteers, who, being mounted, had gone in advance of the regulars, but were attacked by the Indians, and retreated as far as they could, and then threw themselves in a temporary breastwork, made of driftwood, on the sand beach. The Indians surrounded them there, and approached the fort by means of logs, which they rolled before them. They came boldly up within thirty yards of the volunteers, and stole all their horses. The company was kept in this perilous position for nearly two days—the numbers of the enemy constantly increasing. On the approach of the regulars the Indians retreated, having no dead on the field. The volunteers think they killed ten or fifteen; they lost one man.

The advance guard of the regulars met with a few Indians on the next day, and wounded one so badly that his comrade had to lash him on the horse. They saw no more of them after this until reaching the mouth of the river. There the main body of Indians had taken a position in a deep ditch, dug by the whites for mining purposes. Their presence was not known till they commenced firing upon the Colonel and his staff, who had gone a little in advance to select a camp. The surgeon, Dr. Hillman, had his hat knocked off, and his coat cut in two places; but no one was hurt. The troops, who had in the meantime come up, were ordered to make a charge. After the firing of a few shots, and the discharge of one or two howitzers, the enemy fled. One of the privates of the command found on his way up a piece of gold worth forty-five dollars. It was picked up on a hillside just below Pistol Creek, some twenty miles from the mouth of Roguè River.

The Colonel thinks we are at the mouth of the Illinois, and has ordered us to join him at the earliest moment—Tuesday, if possible. Captain Augur will send the express back to-night to inform the Colonel of our proximity, and that we shall march from here at twelve to-night, and endeavor to reach the point where the trail turns off to the Macanuteneey ranch by six to-morrow morning, and there await his orders. As the main body of Indians are supposed to be between that ranch and the Tututeeney village, four miles below, we may have a fight before making a junction with the Colonel.

Monday, March 24th, 1856.—Camp mouth of Rogue River. Three expressmen having been sent forward on the night of the 22d instant, to inform Col. B. of our intended movement to the vicinity of the Macanuteneey village, and of our hope of hearing from him there by six A. M. of the 23d. We took up our line of march at 1½ A. M., and reached the spot designated, by 7 A. M., and not yet hearing from Col. B. The commanding officer sent forward another expressman (McGuire), with instructions to return if possible by 10 or 11 A. M. We consequently remained there without unpacking our mules until 12 M., and receiving no information, Captain Augur ordered his command to start on for the mouth of the river. Our road was as mountainous as usual, but not so thickly timbered; the day warm; many of the men gave out. I let one of them have my horse, and consequently, had to walk ten miles over the roughest portion of the road, and in the hottest part of the day.

We passed several houses which had been plundered and burnt by the Indians, in the massacre of the 22d and 23d of February, and saw several dead bodies of the unfortunate settlers who had been so brutally murdered.

On reaching the Colonel's camp, we were informed of his intention to have sent the express back last night, and that he intended making a conjoined movement against the enemy early this morning; but as our detachment is pretty well worn down by hard marching, the movement will be postponed a day or so.

Tuesday, March 25th, 1856.—In consequence of stormy weather, we are still in camp. Small parties were sent out this morning to bury the bodies of those persons recently murdered; and the little schooner "Gold Beach" has been chartered to convey the females belonging to the Citizen Fort, to Port Orford. She left here at eleven A. M., having on board twenty-two adults and fourteen children.

March 28th, 1856.—On the afternoon of the twenty-fifth, Lieutenant Drysdale, with a small detachment, was ordered up the opposite side of the river a short distance, to reconnoitre the enemy, but returned without being able to see any Indians.

On the morning of the twenty-sixth, a detachment of troops were ordered on each side of the river, to proceed as far as Macanuteneey village, and after burning it, to return to camp. If either party fell in with the enemy, it was to have been aided, if possible, by the other.

The command on the north bank consisted of Captain E. O. C. Ord, Third Artillery; Captain Delancey F. Jones, Fourth Infantry; Lieutenant Jno. Drysdale, Third Artillery; Dr. Hillman and 115 men, being B Co. Third Artillery, and F Co. Fourth Infantry. On the south bank, Capt. C. C. Augur, Fourth Infantry, myself and about seventy men.

As it was supposed Captain Ord would have several miles further to go than Augur, the latter started an hour or two later than the former. Captain Ord's command reached the Macanuteeney village about four P. M., and not seeing any Indians proceeded at once to burn the ranches. This being accomplished he marched his men a few hundred yards up the hill; that is, back from the village, which was situated immediately on the river; and then dividing his command in two or three detachments, kept them on the lookout for Indians. A few of the men, and the guides, in the meantime endeavored to catch some horses near by, supposed to belong to the enemy. Suddenly a party of Indians rushed out from the thicket towards the troops' blankets, and fired at the men guarding them. Fortunately Lieutenant Drysdale's party, whom the Indians did not seem to be aware, was near by, met them with a heavy discharge of small arms. The enemy faltered and fell back a short distance, when Captain Ord ordered a charge, with the view of driving the enemy from their position. This was a difficult maneuver, but was handsomely accomplished. The Indians were evidently surprised at this movement—it being so different from what they had ever seen done by Americans before. So, after they were driven from their hiding places a few times, they sprang in their canoes, and crossed the river; leaving eight dead on the field. The Indians fought bravely, but are evidently bad shots; as, up to the time of their retreating, they had only wounded one soldier. The enemy being defeated, Captain Ord left for the camp at the mouth of the river, but intended going but a short distance to encamp that evening.

After marching a little ways, Sergeant Nash, of B company, whilst helping one of the men who had lagged behind the command, was fired at by an unseen foe, and wounded in the left hypochondrium. Of course no Indians could be seen. The Sergeant's wound was so dangerous as to determine the Captain to continue on to the main camp, to have him properly cared for. In the meantime Captain Augur's command proceeded up the other side of the river for four miles, when some Indians were spied a few hundred yards off, who immediately commenced whooping and yelling. We confidently expected to get a fight from the main body, whom we suspected to be lying in ambush for us. So throwing out flankers, and advance parties, as well as the nature of the country would permit, for we were marching through dense timber, we moved along briskly, but cautiously, until we got opposite the Macanuteneey village, which was seen to be burnt. We could then see a few Indians several miles ahead of us, on a high hill, but deemed it useless to attempt pursuit. Having heard a few shots in the direction of the burnt village, when we were four or five miles back, and afterwards observing a smoke rising from its site, and now seeing it burnt, we very naturally concluded that Ord had had a skirmish, and having defeated the enemy, and burnt the ranches, had returned. It was then nearly dark, we having marched ten miles instead of five—in other words the distance was just twice as far as the Colonel had been told it was. So having accomplished our orders we captured a canoe, and sending three men to camp with it, we countermarched about a mile, and then encamped for the night—with neither tents, blankets or overcoats. The clouds indicated a heavy rain, which commenced about midnight, and drenched us thoroughly. We had brought in our haversacks a cold snack—after devouring which, we slept moderately well. Our day's march on foot had been a hard one, and gave a zest to rest of any kind. Being chief of the medical staff in this command, I am, of course, entitled to horses—but the nature of the service is such as frequently to deprive everybody of the privilege of riding—thus in my case several times. About eleven o'clock at night the sentinel (and whole picket guard in that direction) hearing some one stealing up to camp, challenged and fired. Whatever, or whoever, it was, ran off—thus making a narrow escape.

Leaving camp at daylight the next morning, we reached headquarters, at the mouth of the river, by noon; and then learned that Captain Ord had arrived but a few hours previously, and had had a fight. This fight of his is the most interesting which has occurred during the Southern Oregon war—as it is the first time that Indians, when in a good position in the timber, have been driven back. It has been the custom heretofore, with the volunteers especially, on meeting with the enemy, behind trees, to take to the latter also, and pop away at an unseen foe, until all the ammunitions, or perhaps provisions, were exhausted, and then to withdraw; it being considered impossible to drive the Indians from a good position behind logs and trees.

March 29th, 1856.—As it is thought Captain Smith may be at the Big Bend of Rogue River by this time, an express of two men, Oliver Cantle and Charles Foster, was sent a few days since to communicate with him if possible; it is time they had returned. Yesterday a train of eighty pack animals, escorted by Major Reynolds with twenty men of company H, left for Fort Orford to bring provisions. Lieutenant McFeeley and Dr. Hillman accompanied them, and are to remain at Fort Orford. The former relieves the A. A. Q. M. there, Lieutenant Chandler, who will act as Colonel Buchanan's Aid. The Colonel and Lieutenant D. also went along, but will return.

The officers who have thus far reported for duty, the field with this command are:—Brevet Lieutenant-Colonel R. C. Buchanan, commanding district of Oregon and Northern California; Captain E. O. C. Ord, Third Artillery; Captain C. C. Augur, Fourth Infantry; Brevet-Major John F. Reynolds, Third Artillery; Captain Delancey Floyd Jones, Fourth Infantry; Second Lieutenant George P. Ihrie, Third Artillery; Second Lieutenant John Drysdale, Third Artillery; Dr. Hillman and myself. Dr. Hillman has been relieved from duty.

Yesterday, the little schooner "Gold Beach," from Fort Orford, being unable to enter the mouth of Rogue River, was beached a few hundred yards from camp on the opposite side of the river. Forty men were detailed to get her off, but have been unsuccessful thus far. They will, no doubt, succeed in the course of the morning.

Sunday, March 30th, 1856.—The "Gold Beach" was got off yesterday, and it is now safely anchored in the mouth of the river. The wind, which has been blowing from the southeast for the last few days, has increased to a perfect storm, accompanied by frequent showers of rain. Thanks to Colonel B., we are now permitted the shelter of tents, brought from Crescent City. It is amusing to observe the numerous seals "skylarking" and feeding in the mouth of the river; their bark is very similar to that of a dog. Sea otters may also be seen in the surf.

The expressmen sent to the Big Bend returned yesterday afternoon, not having seen or heard anything from Captain Smith's command. Their mules gave out a few miles from here, and they had to go all the way on foot. This was fortunate, perhaps, as they might otherwise have been pursued; a party of twelve or sixteen Indians on horseback having passed by them at night. As this was the night of the same day of Ord's fight with the Indians, and as they were on the trail towards the mouth of the Illinois, it is possible they were fleeing from the troops.

April 1, 1856.—Yesterday was bright and sunny; to-day the wind and rian comes in fitful blasts from the southeast, making everybody uncomfortable. We may bless our stars that we have tents—though the wind seems intent on dashing them down—the rain-drops tumble through occasionally, to let us know they are knocking without. But, after all, we feel as happy as usual. Happiness consists of a strange compound of elements. For my part, I am in as fine spirits as ever in my life. Not that I am fond of the hard and toilsome marches we have to make over these mountains, but the appreciation of rest and food afterwards is so keen and delightful. We now enjoy a slice of ham, or even pork, with as much gusto as the idle loafer in our large cities does his daintiest *bonnes bouches.*

April 5th, 1856.—The storm has intermitted—the wind being this morning from the north. 'Tis pleasant to see the sun once more. We learn that Captain Smith's command has reached Fort Orford, totally without provisions, and nearly naked. He reached the mouth of the Illinois, on the south side of Rogue River, about the twenty-second of March, and had a skirmish with a small party of Indians—probably the same Indians we drove across the river. He destroyed several ranches, and everything in them. The Indians had evidently been surprised, and ran off leaving everything behind. Two sacks of Oregon flour, and many other articles stolen by them in the massacre at the mouth of the river, were found in their huts. I feel more confident now than ever that the Indians saw our approach on the nineteenth of March, and had succeeded in conveying across the river much of their plunder before we reached the ground.

The "Columbia" touched at Port Orford on her upward trip on the morning of the ninth, at two o'clock, having on board General Wool, Colonel Ripley, Colonel Nauman and Lieutenant Arnold.

Our expressman, Captain Tichenor, on reaching Euchre Creek, eight miles from here, saw a body of Indians ahead of him—he returned to the "Half Breed's House" and got some volunteers, who happened to be there, to accompany him to within a few miles of our camp. Yesterday Captain Bledsoe, who was in Fort Orford, dispatched a messenger to tell the volunteers, who were waiting for him at the "Half Breed's Shanty," to return to Rogue River. The expressman having communicated his orders, and started on his return to Port Orford, saw lying in the trail a spur, which he dismounted to pick up, when several shots were fired at him. Jumping on his horse he hurried back and overtook the volunteers about half way between there and the Miner's Fort, which is now occupied by them. He believes he saw forty Indians. Captain Ord's company was dispatched this morning to break up this ambuscade, as it is on our only road of communication between this place and Fort Orford. The part of the trail infested by them is only seven miles from the latter fort, and consequently Captain Smith might clear the trail if we could get an express to him—but this is difficult. Captain Smith's company will be ordered to leave Fort Orford on Monday for our camp.

Major Latshaw, with one hundred volunteers, met the enemy on the twenty-third of February, on the head waters of the Coquille, and killed ten of them, with a loss of three of the former. On the twenty-third of March, Major Bruce, with two companies of volunteers, had a skirmish with the Indians between Deer Creek and the Illinois River, killing four, and losing no men. The above news comes in a Jacksonville paper, called the *Table Rock*.

The Indians have lately cut off a pack train between Crescent City and Jacksonville—killing one or two men, and taking mules, provisions and everything else—twenty-five pounds of powder included. At another point Captain George's company of mounted volunteers went out to chastise a body of Indians, whom they expected to surprise in a good place for fighting. Leaving their animals tied without any guard, they marched quietly up a hill, expecting to fall upon the enemy on the other side. After proceeding a short distance, and looking behind, they beheld the Indians running off with the troops' horses.

On the first of March a command of one hundred regulars, under Captain E. D. Keyes, Third Artillery, had an encounter with a body of Indians near Muckle Chute Prairie, on White River, in the vicinity of Puget Sound, Washington Territory. It was with the same Indians that attacked Seattle a few weeks ago. The expedition was fitted out under Lieutenant-Colonel Silas Casey, of the Ninth Infantry, who commands that district. He commanded the main force on this occasion, but sent detachments out in different directions, to concentrate near Muckle Chute Prairie.

Lieutenant A. V. Kautz, with a detachment of company A, Fourth Infantry, and H, Ninth Infantry, (the latter under the immediate command of Lieutenant D. B. McKibbin) fell in with the enemy. He immediately dispatched an express to Colonel Casey, who was supposed to be several days off. Kautz had his men in the driftwood, and the Indians theirs in the timber, until the arrival of Captain Keyes' Third Artillery, with a reinforcement of fifty men. The troops then charged, and drove the Indians from all the positions taken by them, and gained a complete victory. The regulars had one man killed, Lieutenant Kautz, and eight men wounded. The Indians carried off their dead—but the friendly Indians say the troops killed seventeen and wounded twenty—among the latter their principal chief, Leshi.

The Indians fled, and appeared to have left the neighborhood entirely. But about the tenth the picket perceived an Indian crawling up with the view of firing into camp. He fired whilst the latter was in the act of beckoning to his men to go back, and wounded him in the shoulder. He was brought into camp, and recognized as one of their principal chiefs—Kannasket. On being asked if he were not, he answered "*yes, I am Kannasket, and I hate you.*" Soon after this firing was heard, and the troops supposing an attack, one of their men shot the chief dead.

About the fifth of March, the volunteers were attacked by the Indians in the vicinity of White River. The Indians were defeated, leaving one man dead on the field. The particulars I have not learned.

On the twenty-seventh and twenty-eighth of March

the Cascades, on the Columbia River, were attacked by the Indians. Some twelve of the inhabitants were massacred; the others took refuge in a blockhouse, and were relieved in the course of two days by Colonel Wright's command of United States troops. Sixteen of the Indians were captured, and fifteen of them were to be hung. All the plunder was retaken. Two soldiers were killed and several wounded.

The Cascades is a very important place between Fort Vancouver and the Dalles. The Indians had planned their attack well, as Colonel Wright with the Ninth Regiment, had left the Dalles but a few days previously, expecting to find the enemy in an entirely different direction. The Indians, however, supposed the troops were further off than they really were.

CHAPTER XXIII.

RETURN TO PORT ORFORD — CAUSES OF INDIAN HOSTILITIES.

In the hold of a Schooner with the Hatches battened down, during a Storm—Bledsoe waylays and kills a number of Indians—Names of the Hostile Tribes—Causes of the War—Some of the Coast Indians desire Peace—General Wool and the Governors of Oregon and Washington Territories at Cross Purposes—Indians desiring to Interview an Enemy, first send an old Squaw—A Brush with the Indians at Chetcoe—An Indian lynched at Port Orford.

FORT ORFORD, April 14th, 1856.

ORDERS being issued for my return to Fort Orford to take charge of the General Hospital at that post, I left camp at the mouth of Rogue River at six P. M. yesterday, in the schooner "Gold Beach," and reached here last night about ten o'clock.

The trip was unusually disagreeable, owing to the vessel being so exceedingly small, and so crowded with passengers, besides the sick and wounded men I was taking to the General Hospital. The weather was unusually stormy and squally, and everybody seasick. This was rendered more unpleasant by the captain's keeping us all below, on account of the rain, and our being in the way on deck. The most perilous part of the trip was in coming over the bar, and through the breakers at the mouth of Rogue River. The course of the river at the mouth having changed greatly in the previous few days, it was considered a very hazardous undertaking to cross the bar for the first time, besides we were all kept below and the hatches closed, thus cutting off all chance of life to even good swimmers, in event of striking the bar and being capsized by the breakers, which were unusually heavy on account of the storm that was rising. Our captain knew nothing about sailing, never having had charge of a vessel before.

On reaching Fort Orford (eighteen miles), the captain commenced firing guns to let the people know of our arrival, so that a boat might come to us. After a few shots our signal was answered from the fort. The people down town hearing the firing, and not knowing its origin, betook themselves to their block-house, thinking the Indians close upon them.

Captain Andrew J. Smith's company, 1st Dragoons, will leave this afternoon for Rogue River. He has with him Dr. Charles H. Crane, United States Army, and First Lieutenant N. B. Sweitzer, First Dragoons. These will join Colonel Buchanan's command. Lieutenant J. C. Bonnycastle, Fourth Infantry, and Assistant Surgeon J. J. Milham, United States Army, are now at Crescent City under orders also to join the command.

FORT ORFORD, April 25th, 1856.

The steamship "Columbia" arrived yesterday morning at daybreak, and discharging about one hundred and fifteen tons of freight, most of which were army supplies, left for Portland.

April 28th, 1856.—Yesterday, Captain Augur's company escorted a mule train to this post for provisions:

a train had also left for Crescent City for supplies, escorted by Captain Floyd Jones' company. Captain Ord's company was despatched from the mouth of the river on the twenty-seventh, to reinforce Floyd Jones before he should have arrived at the most dangerous point. He did not start, however, until the return of Captain Smith and Brevet-Major Reynolds, who, with their respective companies, had been ordered up different sides of Rogue River, to scout and spy out the enemy. On the third day's march, a snow storm caught them, and the snow falling in places a foot deep, they were compelled to return to camp. A party of twelve volunteers accompanied Captain Smith on the north side of the river, some of whom left camp at daylight on the morning of the second day, and approaching Rogue River at the mouth of Lobster Creek, about one half mile from camp, perceived two canoes, with, as they supposed, twelve "bucks" and two squaws, moving down the river. The Captain (Bledsoe), ordered his men to secrete themselves behind a large rock on the bank, and fire at the Indians as they came alongside. Fortunately for their purposes, the river forms at this point a sort of eddy, which the canoes took, thus approaching within a few yards of the volunteers, and moving slowly through the eddy, they were fired upon, having several of their number killed, and the others capsized. The volunteers reloaded and killed several more, they think in all, eleven men and one squaw. The Indians' guns were lost in the water, and their canoes floated down the river, one of them lodging but a short distance below. Bledsoe, of course, desired to secure the latter, but as his detachment was too small to cope against a large body of the enemy, he prudently retired before the latter was reinforced, and joined Captain's Smith's command again, having already accomplished sufficient for one day.

April 29th, 1856.—The bands of Indians in Southern Oregon, at present in open hostilities against the whites, are: *First*—in the Port Orford district, the Shasta-Costahs, Casataneys, Tootooteeneys, Chetcos, Euchres, Joshua band. *Second*—on upper Rogue River, Taltassaneys, Applegates, (Old John's band) Shastahs, Galisecreeks, (pronounced Galeescreeks) George and Limpy's bands. The following tribes in Washington Territory and Eastern Oregon, are hostile:—the Cayuses, Clickitats, Yakimas, Chowchillas, Yumatillas, Walla Wallas and Pelouses.

In regard to the causes of the present general Indian war in the Territories of Washington and Oregon there are, and will probably always be, two opinions. Several of the Indian agents are disposed to lay the blame mostly on the whites—while the latter think that the Indians are the guilty parties. In support of the first belief, so far as it relates to the trouble in Southern Oregon, Indian agent Ambrose reports to Superintendent Joel Palmer, that the immediate cause of the outbreak was the killing, by a party of men calling themselves volunteers, of a number of friendly Indians. This statement, going broadcast over the land, is calculated to give a wrong impression as to the character of the settlers of Oregon. The truth is, that the permanent residents of the latter, and her sister Territory, Washington, have always, so far as I can learn, been particularly kind and considerate toward the red men. Being mostly frontiersmen from our Western States, having their families with them, they, aside from moral considerations, know the danger of maltreating the revengeful savage.

The Indians have among themselves a large number of reckless and bad men, who, disregarding the restraints of their chiefs, are constantly stealing from, and committing other lawless acts upon, their white neighbors, who sometimes are forced, in self-defence, to put a stop to their aggressions in other modes beside moral suasion. It is, nevertheless, undeniable that among the large floating population of miners in the two Territories, there are a few vagabond whites, who treat the Indians harshly. It is probable that the party referred to by the Indian agent were of this class. Still there is no reason for attaching the blame to either party exclusively; for the notions, habits, and moral relations, of the Indians and whites are so diametrically antagonistic that it is simply impossible for them to live side by side for many years without contentions. This has been the case ever since the earliest settlement of North America.

Whilst acts of brutality, between the two races, are usually the proximate causes of most of the disturbances, yet there are predisposing agents behind all these. Such, for instance, on the northwest coast, as the donation laws of Congress, giving away to white settlers—half breed Indians included—all of the most valuable lands in the Territories of Washington and

Oregon, without first extinguishing by treaty the possessory rights of the aborigines. So long as the latter were permitted to retire in peace to good fishing and hunting grounds, they yielded without much grumbling. In course of time, however, their new abodes became desirable to the whites, and the government was induced to make the Indians move again by offering them a moderate consideration, and future partial support for a certain number of years.

Is it not the most natural thing in the world for the red man to chafe under these repeated efforts at changing his abode from the homes and graves of his kindred? It requires but a little cruel treatment under these circumstances to kindle in his savage breast a relentless thirst for blood. When once aroused he falls upon every white person he chances to meet; treating both friend and foe alike; thus often exhibiting one of the most inhuman of all traits—base ingratitude. Worse, if possible, than that other ignoble constituent of the Indian character—treachery. The various massacres that occurred in Southern Oregon alone, at the outbreak of the present disturbance, where so many victims fell by the hands of the savage fiends, are almost enough to stifle the sympathy of philanthropists for the Indian race. Yet, as these poor heathens are not educated to the high sense of right and wrong possessed by our more enlightened people, we ought to make some allowance for their barbarous acts.

FORT ORFORD, May 2d, 1856.

Day before yesterday Mr. Olney, the Indian agent, brought to garrison an old squaw, who was found coming through Port Orford. She seemed to be in almost a dying condition from disease, fatigue, fear and hunger. A little brandy and a slice of bread were given her; of the latter she ate a few mouthfuls. Being sufficiently refreshed she informed the interpreter that she belonged to the Tootooteeneys, and had been sent by the Rogue River Indians to request the Port Orford band to tell the whites that they were tired of fighting, and desired peace; that the upper Rogue River Indians, and Enas, who had inveigled them into making war on the whites, had basely deserted them—that all their ranches and provisions were destroyed—many of their number killed and wounded, that they were nearly starving, and were desirous of peace, and were willing to come in and submit to anything the troops desired. Being put under charge of the guard, in comfortable quarters, for the night, she was, on the following morning, permitted to join the Indians on the reserve—for whether her story be true or false, the Colonel commanding the district was satisfied that all the news she could communicate to the tribes now on the military reserve would only convince them that they had better remain peaceable. Moreover she was exceedingly ill, and we were unwilling to have her die in the guard house; as the Indians might suppose she had met with foul play.

The steamer "Columbia" touched here on her downward trip yesterday. General Wool, Colonel Nauman, Major Fitzgerald, and Lieutenant Arnold—all of the army—were passengers. The General was in fine spirits; being pleased, I suppose, with the recent reports of Colonel Buchanan, and Colonel Casey, in relation to the Indians in their respective districts. Colonel C., who commands Puget Sound district, reports that many of the Indians in that district are begging for peace, and that he has succeeded in driving the remainder beyond the mountains, far away from the settlements; and what is, perhaps, as equally pleasing to the old hero, he has learned that his management of the war on this coast has been approved by the War Department. This is particularly grateful to him as he has been most bitterly censured by the Oregon press for his treatment of the volunteers, whom he refused to recognize unless they would properly enlist in the service of the United States. The Legislature of Oregon, together with Governor Curry, of the same Territory, and Governor Stevens, of Washington Territory, have all, within the past three months, petitioned the department for his recall—asserting that the General has utterly failed to render proper protection to the two Territories. I shall not discuss the matter further than to say, that, as in most matters of this kind, there seems to be right and wrong on both sides. The Governors may have made a mistake in not permitting the volunteers to be enlisted in the service of the United States; and General Wool ought to have sent an escort to protect Governor Stevens on his return from the Blackfoot country last fall, where he had been to form a treaty with them—and from whence he had to return through the enemy's country—and had to depend upon the friendly Nez Perces for an escort.

May 6th, 1856.—Yesterday Colonel Buchanan, Captain Augur, Lieutenant Chandler, with company G, Fourth Infantry, left for the mouth of Rogue River. They took with them four friendly Indians—Tagnesia, the chief of the Elk River Indians; two squaws of the same tribe, and a little Indian boy belonging to the Indian agent; and an Indian boy prisoner, who was captured near Crescent City a few weeks ago, and sent to this post for confinement. He belongs to the Pistol River Indians, who fought the volunteers on the twentieth of March. His story is confirmatory of the squaw's statement that the coast Indians are anxious to make peace.

Company G simply came up here as an escort to a pack train, which has gone down with a good supply of shoes and provisions for the troops at the mouth of the river. When it arrives, and the one from Crescent City, which has perhaps reached there before this, the Colonel will be fully prepared for an effective campaign.

If the Indians of the coast want peace, however, and will abide by his terms, he will probably have them all brought in and disarmed, preparatory to being moved on the Indian Reserve between this and the Columbia River, selected last year by General Palmer. At all events, he has taken the friendly Indians with him to send to the enemy and ascertain their wishes. One of the Indians is a very old squaw, whom the Chief intends to send to the hostile ranks first to ascertain the danger, and if there are none of the upper Indians among them, and no personal risk to be apprehended, he will then go himself. This is the universal custom of the Indians of this coast. Their oldest squaws have to go on all such dangerous errands.

May 7th, 1856.—An express arrived from Rogue River yesterday, bringing among other things, the news of a little brush between Captain Ord's company (B, Third Artillery), and the Indians at Chetco River, forty miles below the mouth of Rogue River, on the twenty-eighth or twenty-ninth ultimo. The Indians were lying-in wait for the pack train, which was being escorted to the mouth of Rogue River from Crescent City by Company F, Fourth Infantry. It was feared that the enemy might give trouble about that point, hence Col. B. wisely dispatched Captain O. from the mouth of Rogue River, to reinforce Captain Floyd Jones, ere he reached the dangerous portion of the route.

The Indians were in ambush on the north side of Chetco, prepared to attack the train as it attempted to cross. They were disconcerted by Ord's coming up on the same side, and fled. Ord gave a running fight and killed six Indians, and took a women and child prisoners. The second chief of the Chetcoes was among the slain. Ord had Seargent Smith killed and one man wounded. From the squaw prisoner, Ord learned that the Indians engaged were the Chetcoes, and about twenty-five from Rogue River. That they had been out in Smith's valley burning houses, whence they returned to Pistol River to ambuscade the train.

The expressman also learned that the Chief of the Joshuas had come down there a few days previously, persuading the Chetcoes to make peace with the whites. Thus everything goes to show that many of the Rogue River Indians desire peace; but I fear that the few citizens and volunteers we have at Port Orford, are disposed to throw obstacles in the way, for they assert their determination to shoot any and every Indian who has been known to kill a white man, either before or since the war. In accordance with these views, they yesterday tried and condemned by lynch law, an Indian belonging to the Coquille band, who have just returned from the mountains to the Government Reserve, after being stampeded a few weeks since, and having a number of their "bucks" killed by some white persons. This Indian is supposed to be one of a party of Indians who massacred two white men about two and a half years ago.

The lynch court sentenced him to be hung to-day at one P. M. It is said the Indian confesses being one of the party who committed the murder, but states that the whites have already killed four Indians for this murder, two of whom were innocent. This, according to the Indian law, should satisfy the whites; but, of course, it is no palliation by our laws, and if the Indian be guilty, he ought to be properly tried and punished, but not lynched.

CHAPTER XXIV.

REPORTS FROM THE SURROUNDING INDIAN COUNTRY.

Colonel Buchanan's command march up on each side of Rogue River with the Olive Branch in one hand, and the Sword in the other—Colonel Cornelius' Volunteers lose their horses—General Lamerick comes across the enemy at the Big Meadows—Views as to the kind of Troops necessary for Indian Service—More Peace Talk—Old George's Band—Superintendent of Indians goes to the Front—Colonel Wright's Talk with Kimiakin unsatisfactory—San Francisco Vigilance Committee—Old John's Treachery, and a bloody battle—Stampede at Port Orford—Wreck of a Vessel—Was Morrison a Knave or a Fool?—More concerning the Vigilance Committee of San Francisco—A Skirmish with the Indians four miles above the mouth of the Illinois—A Fight with the Enemy five miles below the junction of the Illinois and Rogue Rivers—The Troops victorious.

MAY 9TH, 1856.—The sentence upon the Indian prisoner above spoken of, was carried into effect. He was then buried near the foot of his gallows, on Battle Rock. The expressman, Mr. Sweat, arrived from the mouth of Rogue River yesterday afternoon. He brings the information that the troops, three hundred and forty-three in all, moved up Rogue River yesterday morning, with the olive branch in one hand, and the sword in the other. The companies of Captain Ord, Brevet-Major Reynolds, and Captain Floyd Jones, (B, Third Artillery; H, Third Artillery; F, Fourth Infantry) have started on the south side of the river; and those of Captain Smith's and Captain Augur's, (C, First Dragoons; G, Fourth Infantry) on the north side. Colonel Buchanan and

Dr. Milhau accompany the command on the south, and Dr. C. H. Crane that on the north side. Of course the captains are with their own companies.

May 17th, 1856.—By the steamer just from Portland, we learn that the First Regiment of mounted volunteers, under Colonel Cornelius, have had their horses stolen by the Indians—three hundred and ninety in all. It seems that, in accordance with the instructions of Governor Curry, the larger portion of the regiment had come in to within a few miles of the Dalles for the purpose of being disbanded. On the twenty-eighth of April they had their animals grazing about three fourths of a mile from camp under the charge of a small guard, when about fifty Yakimas, under old Kimiakin, came charging down the hill, whooping and swinging their blankets in the air—thus stampeding them all. The Indians were pursued, but without being overtaken. The number of animals lost was three hundred and fifty, which, added to the forty stolen from Fort Henrietta, on the twentieth of April, where the remainder of the regiment was stationed, makes the aggregate above mentioned. The Indians of that section were already well mounted, but now they are doubly so—having taken some of the finest horses in Oregon.

About the twenty-eighth of last month some six hundred volunteers, under General Lamerick, after seeking the upper Rogue River Indians for several weeks, came upon them at the Big Meadows; and, notwithstanding the latter numbered only about one hundred warriors, and were incumbered with their families and stock, they succeeded in making their escape after a slight skirmish. It is true that the enemy were on the opposite side of Rogue River; which, however, was fordable. From all accounts the volunteers behaved bravely, and seemed eager for a fight; but disagreed among themselves as to the best mode of making an attack. The General being powerless, according to his statement to a friend of mine, to enforce a concerted movement. Yet Messrs. Drew and Hillman, who have just come through from Jacksonville, via Crescent City, state that they saw about three hundred of the volunteers at Fort Vannois, where they had come to be disbanded, and that they were displeased with their commander for not allowing them to cross the river, so as to get at the enemy.

On the other hand, the Oregon press is filled with rumors of the great battle between the volunteers and Indians at the Meadows, with a loss of thirty or forty of the latter; which of the statements is correct, it is impossible to determine. There is a slight disposition in the Oregon newspapers to unduly extol the volunteers, and withhold from the regulars a proper share of praise.

This condition of things is the natural effect of the unfortunate dissensions between the Governors of Oregon and Washington Territories, on the one hand, and General John E. Wool, of the Army, on the other, aided also by the fact that there have been no newspaper correspondents among the United States troops to laud their actions. Although an officer of the army, I do not think myself prejudiced in asserting, that notwithstanding volunteers, composed of our hardy and brave frontiersmen, who are generally good marksmen, make far more effective troops for Indian fighting when well disciplined and under good officers, than regular soldiers, recently enlisted, and under officers fresh from the West Point Military Academy; yet the want of discipline in volunteer soldiers, frequently paralyzes their usefulness.

Taking the material as we generally find it at the period of sudden Indian outbreaks, the most valuable troops are regulars (not raw recruits), who have been taught to shoot well with rifle, aided by an equal number of sharp-shooters enlisted from the whites on the frontier, or even from friendly Indians, who are willing to obey orders, all under the command of officers experienced in Indian warfare.

Aside from the inculcation of proper discipline, the art of war, as taught at the National Military School at West Point, though well suited to civilized warfare, is badly adapted for carrying on a war with a savage foe, especially such an enemy as the upper Rogue River Indian, whose home is in the forest and mountain strongholds; who subsists on the wild fruits and animals which he finds wherever he may roam; who fights only when the advantage of position or numbers is in his favor, and vanishes when the fates are against him; who battles mostly under cover of rocks and trees, and with a deadliness of aim only to be acquired by constant practice in hunting and fighting.

The majority of regulars engaged in this war, have had more or less experience in Indian warfare, and have been drilled at target practice, until they have become average marksmen.

With the exception of the company of dragoons, who have been dismounted and allowed to retain their musketoons, the men are all armed with a musket loaded with ball and buckshot. The first named weapon is illy suited for this kind of duty, and will prove a failure if too much relied upon. The officers carry a small breech-loading rifle, with an elevating back-sight—an admirable weapon in the hands of a good marksman.

Whilst at the main camp at the mouth of Rogue River, the officers sometimes amused themselves with shooting at gulls, seals and ducks. Owing to my reputation of being a pretty good shot, I was bantered one day to try my luck at a duck swimming in the river two hundred yards from headquarters' tent, where the colonel and his staff, including myself, were standing. Regulating the elevating-sight of my rifle, for the supposed distanee, I surprised everybody by killing the duck at an off-hand shot. Perhaps I could not have done so well again in a hundred trials, yet my reputation of being a crack shot was at once established. Many a man's renown in more important matters comes upon him as suddenly and unexpectedly as mine on this occasion.

May 20th, 1856.—The schooner "Iowa," being anchored in the bay, broke her cable last night, and was driven ashore by the gale; she is likely to prove a total wreck. Yesterday afternoon a pack train of nearly two hundred animals, escorted by Company B, Third Artillery, arrived from Colonel Buchanan's command. Captain Ord states that the troops are en-

INDIANS STAMPEDING HORSES AND MULES.—Page 325.

camped at Oak Flats, on the east side of the Illinois, and five miles south of Rogue River. That the Colonel is having a talk with the coast Indians, and several of the upper Rogue River bands, who seem to be desirous of peace. He has demanded of them an unconditional surrender, except that they shall be protected if they are willing to come in and cease fighting. He does not beg them, however, to come to terms—on the contrary tells them if they want peace, and will submit to his terms, it is all right—if otherwise, to say so at once, and he is prepared to whip them into measures.

The coast Indians have already signified their assent. The upper Rogue River Indians had not arrived when the train left, but Captain Ord met Old George's band, and a part of Limpy's, five miles this side of camp. They had posted themselves on both sides of the Rogue River at the mouth of the Illinois, and were waiting to hear from Captain Smith, whom they knew, before going to the Colonel's camp. They were decidedly shy at first, and kept a position of readiness for battle in case the whites pitched into them. The chief, however, signified by a white flag that he did not wish to fight. The troops, after crossing the river, and having a short talk with them, proceeded on to this place. Old George's band is represented as a fine looking body of men, well armed and clothed. Every man had on a head-dress with a feather in the top. In fact they presented quite a military appearance. The number present was forty or fifty. Most of the coast Indians are already in the vicinity of the camp—they number several hundred warriors.

May 28th, 1856.—Oliver Cantwell came in yesterday as express from Colonel Buchanan's command, which had left Camp Oak Flats and encamped on the north side of Rogue River, four miles from the mouth of the Illinois. After Captain Ord had met George and Limpy's bands, as spoken of above, they sent word to Colonel B. that they desired to have a talk with him, but wished to see Captain Smith first. The latter accordingly took his company and went down to meet them; and on the following day Old George and Limpy marched their men to within two hundred yards of camp, and then taking twelve or fifteen as a body guard went to the Colonel and had a talk. They at first, together with the coast Indians, insisted on being permitted to remain in their present country; that they were willing to give up their arms, and do almost anything, if this request were granted them. The Colonel told them that this could not be allowed, as they had already bound themselves by treaty to go on to the reservation, and that he was determined that they should go. After three days both Old George and Limpy, of the upper Rogue River Indians, and Joshua, of the coast Indians, declared that they would go on to the reservation. The other Indians had not made up their minds on the subject when the expressman left.

The Colonel is waiting at his present camp for the arrival of the pack train with provisions from this post. This left here last Friday evening; but as it took a different route from what Colonel B. anticipated, it will cause him several days' delay in the prosecution of his plans—the first of which seems to be to send such of the tribes as are willing, to the reservation immediately. The superintendent of Indian affairs, General Joel Palmer, left with the pack train to join Colonel B., and will, no doubt, concur in all that has been done by the latter.

May 30th, 1856.—The "Columbia" arrived from Portland yesterday, she did not touch on her upward trip. The news from above is unimportant, except that the regulars, about four hundred, under Colonel Wright, had met with some twelve hundred Indians, under old Kimiakin, and had a talk, which was not satisfactory, and that a fight was consequently expected in a few days.

The most exciting news is from San Francisco. It appears that the editor of the *Evening Bulletin*, James King, was shot by James P. Casey, the editor of another evening paper, on the afternoon of the fourteenth of May, and that he died on the twentieth. The excitement was intense. A vigilance committee (the first for several years), was immediately formed to take the matter into consideration. Twenty-nine persons composed the committee proper, whose deliberations were held profoundly secret. These were supported by some twenty-nine hundred others, who were sworn to carry out all the decisions of the twenty-nine. King was buried on the twenty-second instant. On the same day, and about the same hour, Casey, his murderer, and Cora, the man who shot General Richardson a few months ago, were hanged by authority of the Vigilance Committee, after receiving a trial before this body.

It is stated that both of these men had the sympathy of such a large class of lawless men in San Francisco, that it would have been utterly useless to have gone through the mockery of a trial in the customary legal process. It is further asserted that there have been some three hundred murders committed in San Francisco during the past few years, and only three men convicted and hung; also that the Vigilance Committee is composed of the best men in the city; that even the pulpit, with scarcely a single exception, were in favor of the people's taking the matter in their own hands, as it was impossible to insure justice in any other way.

If there ever was a time when such measures were necessary, it was undoubtedly on this occasion; but all such proceedings are very sure to lead to evil. The thing may ultimately fall into the hands of vicious and lawless persons, who will do much harm. The example is a bad one.

It is alleged that King was shot by Casey, because he exposed in the *Bulletin*, some of the rascality of the latter, who was formerly in the Sing Sing Prison, New York.

June 3d, 1856.—An express of two men, Walker and Foster, arrived this morning from the troops whom they left at the Big Bend of Rogue River. The express before this, brought the news of the main camp being a few miles this side of Rogue River, near the mouth of the Illinois. Whilst remaining there awaiting for the pack train which left Fort Orford last Friday week, the Colonel sent Major Reynolds a day's travel on the trail to this post, to meet the pack train, and with instructions about getting in some of the lower Indians. About the same time Captain Andrew Smith, of the First Dragoons, was ordered to the Big Bend with his and a portion of E company, in all about ninety men, on foot, to assist in getting in old George and Limpy's bands. On arriving there, old George sent him word that the other hostile tribes had surrounded and prevented his coming in as soon as he expected, and warned Smith that the hostile bands, headed by Old John, intended attacking his camp (Smith's), and would at first attempt a little strategy, Old John to pretend that he desired peace, and wished to have a talk; in the meantime, to send into Smith's camp a body of naked, unarmed Indians, equal in number to the soldiers, and at the moment that the latter became most unsuspecting and careless, to seize upon their arms. This was to have been done at a given signal, and each Indian to grab a soldier's musket when the fight, or rather massacre, was to begin. Sure enough, on the following day, some fifty or sixty athletic Indians, naked and unarmed, came into camp, saying that Old John desired to have a talk. Smith ordered them to leave, and they did, but only went a few hundred yards and picked up their guns, which had been secreted, and commenced an attack. They were immediately joined by many others. Smith now found himself surrounded by from three to four hundred Indians, who kept firing into his camp from the morning of the twenty-eighth instant, to the afternoon of the twenty-ninth, when Captain Augur arrived on the ground with his company G, Fourth Infantry.

Smith's men raised a shout, and the two commands charged the enemy, and completely routed them. The number lost by the latter is not known, as the dead were carried off the field.

The troops had twenty-nine killed and wounded, nine killed on the field, and several deaths from severe wounds before the expressman left, which was on the thirty-first ultimo. All of the killed and wounded but five, belonged to Smith's command. Smith's position was on a rising piece of ground, surrounded by a rather open woods. He took this as the best position he could secure in the immediate neighborhood, after he had been informed of the contemplated attack. It does not appear that he had attempted to throw up any defences previous to the fight, doubtless deeming it inexpedient and bad policy. After getting Old George's warning, he dispatched a messenger to Col. Buchanan, who forthwith sent to the "Soldiers' Camp" for Reynold's company to come to headquarters, so as to enable him to dispatch reinforcements to Smith, if necessary.

When the second express arrived from the latter, stating that the Indians had surrounded and cut him off from water, etc., Captain Augur's company, which, together with Jones's F, Fourth Infantry, had been engaged in cutting a trail from opposite the mouth of the Illinois to the Big Bend, was immediately dispatched to his relief. About the same time, the Colonel was informed that the pack train was coming up on the opposite side of the river. This, instead of returning on the same trail it came to Fort Orford, had taken a much more circuitous and longer, but perhaps better one, under the circumstances, *i. e.* instead of going an almost due east course to the mouth of the Illinois, as the Colonel had anticipated, Captain Ord had crossed Rogue River forty-five miles below that point, and gone up its south side. He did this because the road was better, and because he had reasons to suppose that the Indians would attack his train if he returned on the same route that he came. However, when the Colonel was informed what route the train had taken, he kept F. Company to assist in getting it across Rogue River, near the mouth of the Illinois. When this was accomplished, and Major Reynold's company (H, Third Artillery), had arrived, the whole force marched for the Big Bend, where it was when the express left on the thirty-first.

It is pretty well ascertained, that a part of nearly all the hostile bands of Rogue River were engaged in Smith's fight, except those of George, Limpy and Joshua, and even some few of these, but against the orders of their chiefs. Had Smith not received warning from old George, every man of his command would have been butchered, and even as it was, they would all have been slain, had not Captain Augur arrived as soon as he did, for they were entirely cut off from water, and only held out as long as they did, by digging holes in the ground on the night of the twenty-eighth (the night after the first day's attack), with their tin pans, and throwing up a little embankment of dirt. It is related that the Indians charged bravely up to this temporary defence; and in one instance, a party of them crawled up and threw into the entrenchment a stick, to make the men carelessly jerk up their heads, that they might get a better shot at them. On this occasion, a little Indian boy, whom the troops had with them as an interpreter, raised himself a little, and was instantly killed. It is related that the men behaved gallantly; but as they were miserably armed with short musketoons, loaded with ball, it is believed that they did not do half the execution that might have been accomplished, had they had good rifles, or even the Government musket, loaded with buckshot and ball. The other companies were armed with the latter, but Smith's being a dragoon company, dismounted for the occasion, retained their musketoons.

The more I see of Indian fighting, the more am I convinced that the present system of arming men with musketoons or muskets, for this species of warfare, is a great error. They should have rifles, and be taught to shoot well by constant practice; and the present custom of employing soldiers while in garrison, on almost continuous hard fatigue duty, without any or very little drilling at target shooting, should be abolished.

During the fight with Captain Smith, a party of a hundred and fifty volunteers, under the command of Major Latshaw, came across George and Limpy's camps, and captured some women, children and provisions. It is asserted that but few, if any, of the warriors belonging to these chiefs, were engaged against Smith's command, but that they were only waiting to surrender; still, I presume, the volunteers were not aware of this, and it is highly probable that the proximity of the latter aided to hasten the retreat of the hostile Indians.

June 5th, 1856.—Stampedes are now the order of the day in Port Orford. As the number of men in the place is not over a dozen since the volunteers left, and the troops remaining to garrison this post are raw recruits, and number only about sixteen besides the sick, and as this is the depot of military stores, and hence a very desirable point for the enemy to capture, the people are very excitable upon the subject of Indians.

On the first instant several of the friendly Indians, who started out from here with the superintendent, General Joel Palmer, and the last pack train, returned, bringing us the first news of the fight between the troops and Indians at the Big Bend. As their sympathies are, of course, with their own race, they represented the late events in a very unfavorable light for the troops; also stated that the Chetcoes were coming up to steal away from the military reserve the Indian prisoners belonging to that tribe.

On the morning of the second a man, by the name of Parker went down the coast for about six miles to hunt some lost cattle. Shortly thereafter he came running in, and stated that he had been pursued and fired upon by a party of Indians, who followed him within sight of the village. He left his horse behind, having hitched and gone off from him a short distance when he saw the Indians. We all took our spy-glasses and looked down the coast in the direction stated, and beheld some fifteen Indians at the distance of four miles from this place. At first we could not tell whether they were marching slowly up towards the village or not. One thing we could see, however, that the advance party, on reaching what is called Rocky Point, three miles from here, waited for them behind to come up. It was now a matter of doubt whether they were hostile or not. If unfriendly, every one was satisfied that they would be supported by much larger parties coming in other directions. After they came around Rocky Point, however, and marched carelessly along the beach, we felt satisfied that they were not hostile. They turned out to be the Indian guides whom Colonel Buchanan took out with him, together with some of the Port Orford Indians, who had been at the mouth of Rogue River when the outbreak occurred; and who were previously unable to return.

Night before last some of the loafers about town, styling themselves members of the Vigilance Committee, represented to the commanding officer that two of the Indians, who arrived on the second instant, were believed to have been present at the massacre on the twenty-second of February, at the mouth of Rogue River, and wished permission to take and try them. Knowing what an excitement this would create among the Indians on the reservation, if white men were permitted to arrest every one who was supposed to have done anything since the breaking out of the troubles, and yet not having a sufficient guard to keep them away from the Indians, the commanding officer of Fort Orford had the suspected Indians placed in the guard-house, and at the same time informed the Indians that they should not be disturbed or tried before General Palmer came back. This was done to keep the mob from shooting them. That night the Chetco prisoners, numbering some twenty, deserted the reservation. It is not known, yet suspected, that the other Indians on the reservation were aware when they left, and probably assisted them—as they evidently sympathize heart and soul with their race—and are, moreover, anxious that the war should be prolonged in order that they may not be moved out of their present country.

Last night there was another stampede in Port Orford; and to-day the few settlers who had gone to mining and farming between this and Cape Blanco, ten miles up the coast, came running in. They say that Indians have been lurking in the neighborhood—and that those on the reservation are surly and cross. I am not astonished at the latter, for a few vagabond whites will not let their squaws alone, even under the present alarming state of affairs. It is a great pity that these fellows cannot be punished for their conduct—but the laws are powerless in the matter. I hope the settlers will now either stay in, or, if they go out again, remain quietly at their occupations; for this stampeding at every little excitement is just what the Indians rejoice to witness.

June 8th, 1856.—A storm of rain and wind from the southeast since day before yesterday. A schooner, the "Francisco," anchored in the bay, broke her fastenings night before last, and came ashore upon the rocks. This is the second vessel wrecked here within a few weeks. The captains may hereafter take warning, and put to sea when a southeaster springs up.

On the evening of the sixth a white man, calling

himself Morrison, was arrested in Port Orford by the citizens, and put in the guard-house at this post. He came here through the heart of the Indian country, and tells such contradictory and inconsistent stories, that it is thought by many that he has been acting with the hostile Indians, and may have come here with the view of procuring ammunition, etc., for the enemy. I am inclined, however, to believe that he is insane, and being in want of work, has ventured through the enemy's ranks alone, unarmed, and without provisions, believing himself perfectly safe in so doing. If so, he has certainly run a gauntlet that few would like to venture on. He is evidently a consummate fool or knave—it is difficult to say which.

The "Columbia" arrived yesterday, bringing no news of importance, except from San Francisco. They are having an exciting time there at present; almost equal to the reign of terror in France. The Vigilance Committee is still supreme, and supported by a majority of the clergymen, and all the papers, in the city, except the *Herald*. Nobody has been hung since the last steamer, but some twenty or thirty have been ordered out of the city. Yankee Sullivan, the celebrated prize fighter, was brought before the Vigilance Committee for trial, and whilst in custody committed suicide. Governor Johnson has issued a proclamation calling upon all good citizens to support law and order, and ordering out the State militia—that is, all young men between the ages of eighteen and twenty-five. William T. Sherman, formerly a lieutenant in the United States army, but now a banker in San Francisco, is the Major-General of militia. When the steamer left the proper authorities were busily engaged in enrolling the latter; but the call of the Governor, and order of General Sherman, had not been very promptly answered. It is to be hoped that no open collision between the authorities of the land and that of the Committee will take place, but things present an alarming aspect at this time.

June 9th, 1856.—Captain Tichenor brought an express from Colonel Buchanan's headquarters yesterday. He says the troops have had two more fights with the Indians. The first was a mere skirmish, and occurred on the fourth instant, with a party of Indians three or four miles above the mouth of the Illinois on Rogue River. The latter were engaged in fishing, and had four or five killed; the troops none. The detachment consisted of company H, Third Artillery, and Captain Bledsoe's volunteer company, under the command of Major J. C. Reynolds, United States army.

On the following day, in accordance with the instructions from Colonel Buchanan, Bledsoe's company moved down the south side of Rogue River, and Captain Augur's, company G, Fourth Infantry, the north side, and fell upon the Indians at a point some four or five miles below the mouth of the Illinois. The latter were again completely routed—sixteen of their number killed. The regulars and volunteers shared the fight equally, and each killed about the same number of Indians, with a loss of only one man, and three wounded.

CHAPTER XXV.

PLANS AND PLOTS OF THE INDIANS.

An Indian scheme to attack Fort Orford—Further indications of the Enemy growing tired of the War—More talk of Treachery and Capture of Fort Orford—George and Limpy's Bands surrender—Chief John has a Cry—Arrival of Troops and many Indians—Treachery prevented by the confinement of twelve Chiefs—Departure of a portion of the Indians for the Coast Reservation—Old John promises to come in—Captain Ord arrives with Old John's Band, and other Indians—On the Fourth of July Colonel Buchanan announces the close of the Rogue River War—Remaining Indians sent overland to the Reservation—Colonel Wright unable to make Peace with the Enemy east of the Cascade Mountains—A dangerous Sea Trip in a Canoe—San Francisco still under the control of the Vigilance Committee—United States Dragoons and Kansas Riots.

JUNE 12TH, 1856.—The people of Port Orford, and Fort Orford, have been excited for the last three days in consequence of the discovery of a plan on the part of the Indians on the military reservation here to make an attack on the fort and town. They were to be assisted by the Rogue River Indians, with whom, it is asserted, they hold constant communication. The attack to be made as soon as the weather got dry and windy—when the Indians here (who have no guns) were to pitch in with their knives and clubs; also set fire to the buildings; and the others to do all the shooting. Various circumstances go to prove this story, though it was first divulged by a squaw to the wife (a half breed) of a Frenchman. These Indians have become very impudent and saucy since the return of their chiefs from

Colonel Buchanan's camp. In fact they were sent back on account of their insolence there, where they did far more harm than good. Since returning they have repeatedly asserted that the Bostons could not subdue the Indians, and that they would not go on to the reservation. But as it is believed that their plans have been disconcerted by the last successes of the troops on the Rogue River Indians, and as it is bad policy to take harsh steps with them until it is proven beyond all shadow of doubt that they really intended to break out, the matter will be allowed to pass over; we remaining on the alert in the meantime.

June 13th, 1856.--An express from Colonel Buchanan's camp, reached here yesterday morning, with the news that the coast Indians are gradually coming in, and giving up their arms, with the view of going on the reservation.

Colonel Buchanan's whole command is on the north side of Rogue River, at three different points, and the volunteers (about three hundred), under General Lamerick, on the south side. The Indians seem to be pretty well intimidated. Just as the expressman was leaving, Old John, of the upper Rogue River Indians, sent in word that he thought his band would come in also; but the old rascal is so treacherous, that it is exceedingly difficult to judge of his sincerity. He may have another scheme in view.

The squaw who divulged the anticipated outbreak here, now asserts that the Indians intend giving up only such guns as the whites know to be in their possession, and a few old ones besides, and after they have convinced the troops of their sincerity, and got them off their guard, they are to seize the soldiers' guns, and commence a general onslaught. She says this is to be done on their arrival at this post, when the Indians now on the military reservation are to assist them. She also told the Indian Agent this morning, that spies were in the Indian camp night before last again, and that they brought several guns with them. In consequence of this report, the agent sent for the chiefs this morning, and whilst talking with them, got the commanding officer of this post to send out three or four men to examine the Indian ranches for arms, etc. In the meantime, he asked the chiefs if they had any; they said no. The guard took with them the squaw above spoken of, to point out where she thought the arms were secreted; but the Indians swarmed around her so thickly, that she afforded but little assistance. The guard, however, found two guns, which are thought to belong to the Coquille Indians, now on the reservation. As the chiefs had pretended to give up all their arms, and were found to have acted in bad faith, they were now told that it was known that they had other guns which must be brought in immediately. They finally acknowledged having a few more, which they said should be sent in this afternoon.

June 14th, 1856.—The Indians sent in the guns yesterday, as promised. This morning, the Superintendent of Indian Affairs, General Palmer, arrived from the "field." He states that Colonel Buchanan's command is on its way with two hundred and seventy-one upper Rogue River Indians, George and Limpy's bands, and four hundred and thirty-one Coast Indians. It is very doubtful whether Old John will come in. Personally, he is for war; but since a young Indian, who has been with Old Sam's band on the Indian Reservation, for a short time, was sent by the Colonel to talk with John's band, many of the latter seem anxious to quit fighting, and come in also. On Old John's hearing this, he burst out crying, and said if all his people left him, he might be compelled to come in also.

June 15th, 1856.—Colonel Buchanan, Captain Smith, Captain Augur, Doçtor Milhau, Lieutenant Chandler, Lieutenant Ihrie and Company C, First Dragoons, Companies E and G, Fourth Infantry, arrived this afternoon, with over seven hundred Indians. The latter, together with the four hundred now on the Military Reservation here, make eleven hundred, all of whom are to be moved forward to the Indian Reservation, some one hundred and twenty-five miles further up the coast, in a few days, or as soon as the Colonel can hear from the command at the mouth of Rogue River, as to whether Old John's people and the Chetcoes and Pistol River Indians are coming in. They are about the only ones now hostile on Rogue River, and number perhaps five or six hundred men, women and children. A portion of Company E, Fourth Infantry, under Lieutenant Sweitzer, having gone down Rogue River to its mouth, in canoes with the wounded, were at that point yesterday when heard from. Captain Ord and Major Reynold's companies were dispatched there this morning, from the Colonel's camp of last night, to reinforce the guard of the wounded, and bring in all the Indians who were willing to go on the reservation.

In consequence of threats by the citizens of Port Orford to shoot some of the Indians now under charge of the troops, Colonel Buchanan has issued orders to shoot any man who attempts to kill an Indian.

June 20th, 1856.—We imagined that after the main body of troops arrived, stampedes would die away at this place, but another occurred last night. Yesterday afternoon Colonel Buchanan and General Palmer were informed by several Indians — Old George among the number, whose word is believed since the information he gave Captain S. turned out to be true—that the Indians brought in here had it in contemplation to rise night before last, and attempt to kill the troops, and take the town and fort; but concluded to postpone it till last night, when the attack was to have commenced. We could not fully credit this report, but under the circumstances General Palmer deemed it prudent to cause the chiefs (some eight or ten) of the different bands to be arrested and placed in confinement for the night. Whatever their intentions may have been this put a stop to them.

Last night about two o'clock the steamer "Columbia" arrived on her upward trip, and lay here until eleven this morning. She took on board about six hundred Indians from the military reservation of this post, bound for Portland; thence by land to the Indian reservation. They were escorted by G company, Fourth Infantry, under the command of Captain Augur. The superintendent of Indian affairs, General Palmer also accompanied them. Most of these Indians belonged to the hostile bands. Those remaining here, and such as may yet be brought in, will, perhaps, be sent up in two or more detachments by land. Three of Old John's sons came in yesterday, and stated that their father's band is at the mouth of the Illinois, and that he is willing to come in. One of them was dispatched to him to-day with the request that he should come to a designated point some twelve miles from here, and surrender to Captain Ord, who is ordered to proceed from the mouth of Rogue River with his and Major Reynold's companies to that place. By the steamer we learned that the Vigilance Committee of San Francisco are still supreme—numbering some fifteen thousand men. The law and order party have been unable to offer any resistance. Several new arrests have been made since the last steamer, and many persons ordered to quit the city.

June 28th, 1856.—Captain Ord, with his and Major Reynold's companies, arrived here on the twenty-third, and left again with the same command on the following day for the "field." His orders were to proceed to a point on the Big Bend trail, some twelve miles from here, and await the arrival of Old John, who is expected to surrender to him.

Yesterday an express came in from the Captain with the information that Old John, with his whole band, would probably reach his camp in three days from day before yesterday. When the latter and the Chetcoes shall have come in, the Rogue River war may be considered closed.

July 2d, 1856.—This morning Captain Ord's command arrived, bringing in the famous Old John and his band—the terror of Southern Oregon. Ord went some twelve miles from here, and sent for Old John to come in—the latter reached his camp on the twenty-ninth ultimo, and gave up twenty-five guns—all good and in excellent order. It is supposed that he has retained a good many pistols—if so, these also will probably be taken away from him. He brings with him thirty-five men, capable of bearing arms, ninety women, and ninety children. He is about fifty-five years old—not at all prepossessing in appearance—has a resolute, discontented, and unhappy appearance. The disparity between the number of women and men, is partially owing to the fact that more of the latter have been killed in battle, but in a measure also to the habit of the men of this band marrying squaws belonging to other tribes. Being the most warlike tribe in the country they enjoy this privilege more than any other band.

July 5th, 1856.—Yesterday the grand anniversary of our National Independence was celebrated by a Federal salute of thirteen guns at dawn of day, and thirty-one at noon, and at nine P. M. by five rockets, which were sent up from the highest point of the heads, to the great admiration and astonishment of the Indians, most of whom had never seen the like before. In Port Orford thirty-one guns were fired at noon, and thirteen at sundown. The second gun at noon went off prematurely, burning the man who was ramming the charge, very severely—the ramrod was shot between his hands into the ocean. The accident was owing to his not sponging the piece before loading it. Several fights also occurred in the village. After our national salute all the officers assembled at the Colonel's quarters and partook of refreshments. We were then informed by Colonel B. that he had the pleasure of announcing the Indian war on Rogue River closed.

July 8th, 1856.—The steamer "Columbia" arrived here last evening, and left to-day at one P. M. for Portland, taking on board at this place five hundred and ninety-two Indians, (excluding infants) who are being escorted by Captain Delancy Floyd Jones' company F, Fourth Infantry, to the coast reservation. Day after to-morrow the remainder of the Indians, including Old John's band, and a portion of the Chetcoes, will also start for the same destination. They are to go by land, and will be accompanied by Major Reynold's company, H, Third Artillery, and a detachment of company E, Fourth Infantry. All the Indians of Southern Oregon, with the exception of a few stragglers, have surrendered. They number eighteen hundred persons, besides the small children.

July 12th, 1856.—Old John's band got off on the tenth instant, escorted by Major Reynold's company, and a detachment of company E, Fourth Infantry.

The officers were Major Reynolds, Doctor Milhau, Lieutenant Chandler and Lieutenant Drysdale. The troops took with them over two hundred splendid mules; one hundred and sixty of which were used as pack animals. They had provisions for themselves (ninety men) and the Indians (one hundred and twenty-five men, women and children, infants excluded,) for ninety days. Old John's party was larger than this; but some of them went up on the steamer. Most of the Chetcoes were sent by sea; the remainder of the latter are included in the above one hundred and twenty-five.

I rode out in the afternoon to Major Reynolds' first day's camp, and partook of a parting dinner with him. On the same day company C, First Dragoons, commanded by Captain A. J. Smith, started for the post to be established at the upper end of the reservation. As he was to go via Fort Lane, he went down the coast instead of up. He had with him only forty-five men—the officers are himself, Dr. C. H. Crane and Lieutenant Nelson B. Sweitzer. Companies C, and E, took a few of their convalescent wounded with them; the remainder, except two who have died since their arrival here, remain in the general hospital at this post, of which I am still in charge. When Colonel Buchanan, Captain Ord, and Lieutenant Ihrie, with company B, Third Artillery, leave here to-morrow, Lieutenant R. McFeeley and myself will be the only officers remaining at the post; and besides the sick, hospital steward, hospital attendants, and some three others, there will be no troops.

July, 13th, 1856.—The steamer "Columbia" touched this morning on her downward trip, taking on board Colonel Buchanan, Captain Ord and Lieutenant Ihrie, and Company B, Third Artillery.

By the previous steamer, we learned that Colonel Wright was still with his forces on the Natchez River, holding a council with the hostile Indians, who seemed disposed to make peace. This steamer brings the news that the Indians have all fled, and that the troops have thus far been unable to make peace or get a fight, out of them. The Colonel has gone in pursuit.

July 14th, 1856.—Judge Deady arrived here day before yesterday, to hold court at Port Orford; accompanying him was Dr. Evans, United States Geologist for Oregon. I had the pleasure of forming the acquaintance of the latter gentleman on my trip from New York to San Francisco, and was delighted to renew the same at this lonesome place, Port Orford.

The Doctor being anxious to make a geological examination of this vicinity, started for the mouth of Brush Creek yesterday morning, in a canoe, accompanied by Mr. R. W. Dunbar and myself. Our course lay across the bay of Orford, distance by water four or five miles. The ocean being calm on starting, we got along delightfully for a while; then the wind freshened from the south, blowing thus against us, our progress was extremely slow, especially as none of us knew much about managing a canoe. Dr. Evans now became seasick, and was so prostrated as to be totally unable to render any assistance. Mr. Dunbar and myself labored hard to reach our destination before the wind should become too strong; but on nearing the goal, we found the breakers too high to land. There was then no alternative but to turn about for Fort Orford again. The sea had become quite rough, particularly so near the shore. It was now my turn to be seasick, but though ill and exhausted, I felt in duty bound to assist Mr. Dunbar in navigating our frail bark. Dr. E. was entirely too much prostrated to do anything. We rigged a sail out of Mr. D.'s coat, and availed ourselves of the wind, which lasted till we had gone about a mile. As the wind was evidently about to change to the northwest, we paddled away manfully, and arrived at Fort Orford just in time to escape a strong head wind. Besides the geological examination, we had it in contemplation to fish for trout in Brush Creek. The elements blasted all our bright prospects.

July 26th, 1856.—From the nineteenth to the twenty-second, there was a strong wind from southeast, and rain at intervals, something very unusual at this season. The atmosphere is at present clear, with a northwest trade wind; thermometer 57 deg. at 7 A. M. and 65 deg. at 2 P. M. This is the ordinary July and August weather of this place. The only fruits that have yet ripened in this vicinity during the present season, are strawberries, salmon berries, black, thimble and salalle berries, first two about a month ago; the others are just in their maturity.

The steamer "Columbia" arrived on the morning of the twenty-third, bringing New York papers of the twentieth June, and San Francisco of the twenty-first

July. The Vigilance Committee is still supreme in the latter place. They have confined their action mainly to driving from the city election bullies, and others known to have been engaged in ballot-box stuffing and false voting. The most remarkable arrest by them so far, is Judge Terry, Chief Justice of the State of California. He is alleged to have stabbed a Vigilance Committee sheriff by the name of Hopkins, about the third of July. It seems that the latter had gone into the office of Dr. Ash, the Navy Agent, to arrest Reuben Maloney, for some purpose. The Doctor ordered him out; Judge Terry being present, had also something to say to him. Hopkins then sent to the Vigilance Committee for aid. In the meantime, the Judge and Maloney started for the rooms of the law and order party; but Hopkins, assisted by his friends, overtook him and seized hold of his gun; a scuffle ensued, when he was stabbed by Terry. The latter was then arrested and placed in confinement, and has since been tried by the committee, but the sentence is not yet divulged. It is supposed that if Hopkins had died, and he has been very near it, from the wound assuming an erysipelatous character, that the Judge would have been hung.

The Governor is powerless, he having called on the militia and all others to enroll themselves, and assist in putting down the committee, but has so far utterly failed. A lot of government arms sent down by his order, was seized by authority of the latter.

The last great move of the committee supporters, was to call a mass meeting, which convening, recommended among other things, that as the following officers were supposed to have been elected by fraudulent votes, they should be requested by a committee of the mass meeting, to resign, viz: Judge Freelon, Mayor Van Ness, Sheriff Scannell, District Attorney Byrne, County Clerk Hays, Recorder Kohler, Treasurer Woods, Assessor Stillman, Surveyor Gardner, Coroner Kent, Superintendent Pelton, and Justices Ryan, Chamberlain and Castree. This recommendation, among others, was adopted; but up to the departure of the "Columbia," the above government officials still held on, refusing to resign.

This committee seems to be supported by a majority of the best men in San Francisco, and it was undoubtedly originated with the best motives; but like all other opposition to the regular course of law, even though the latter may not for the time being be justly executed, will probably have an evil tendency, and might terminate in civil war.

It is a heart-rending fact that the latter is already existing in our country, but at a very different place, and impelled by other motives; I mean in Kansas Territory. There have already been several skirmishes between free-soilers and pro-slavery partisans, and the free soil town of Kansas has been burnt to the ground. It is difficult to get at the facts in the case, but it appears that the territorial sheriff, Jones, went to Kansas with a strong posse, to make some arrests. The citizens resisted, a fight ensued, and the free-soilers were compelled to leave the place, which was then burnt to the ground. The territorial officers appear to be supported by the pro-slavery party.

Colonel Summer, with a regiment of United States dragoons, is, by special orders from the President, endeavoring to quell the riots, and had up to last dates, disarmed many of the rioters, and prevented them from assembling in any very large bodies. The matter is becoming so serious, however, that it has even been debated in the Senate, whether or not the President should be recommended to send General Scott to Kansas, to quiet matters.

CHAPTER XXVI.

TO FORT YAMHILL VIA FORT VANCOUVER, CASCADES, ETC.

Packers robbed and killed by Indian Stragglers—Five bad Indians shot by a Party of Whites—Colonel Shaw routs the Enemy near Grand Ronde—Skirmish of Colonel Layton—My trip from Fort Orford to Fort Yamhill—Fort Vancouver—Hudson Bay Company—Ben. Wright—The Cascades—The Willamette Falls—Steamboat "Hoosier"—Yamhill Valley—Fort Yamhill.

FORT ORFORD, August 12th, 1856.

Sometime about the first ultimo, a pack train, accompanied by some five or six packers, left here for Crescent City. A few days thereafter, a portion of the party arrived at the latter place with the news that they had been attacked whilst asleep at night in camp, near the Chetcoe River, and two of their number killed, and some $1,500 taken. They represented it to have been done by Indians, there still being a few of the latter remaining in the mountains in that vicinity, who were left behind when the other hostile ones were taken to the reservation.

A company was raised in Crescent City, and started for the place where the murder was committed. On reaching there, they found all the mules, but no aparahoes. It was supposed that the Indians cut these up and carried them off.

On the seventh instant, whilst a few miners were "prospecting", (examining the country for gold), near the mouth of Rogue River, some twenty-five miles above where the murder was committed, an Indian came into their camp, and said that there were some very bad Indians in that vicinity, who intended killing a man by the name of Smith, living a short distance below there. Their plan was to send into Smith's camp two Indians pretending friendship, who were to fall upon and murder him. He expressed a desire to go with them, and point out a place for waylaying the Indians that were coming to Smith's, and said that afterwards he would show them where to find the others; but that they must not kill his Tilicums (relatives), among the latter.

The two Indians were accordingly watched for, two miles north of Pistol River, and fired upon, but only one was killed, the other made his escape. This was on Thursday, the seventh instant. On the following day, a party of eight white men started out at the suggestion of the Indian, who accompanied them, to waylay the other Indians, who were expected to come and look after the man who had been shot. They proceeded a short distance below the point where the latter had been killed, when the Indian guide who had gone in advance, came running back with the information that several Indians were a little in advance of them. At his suggestion, they took a good position behind a ridge, whilst he went off a few yards and showed himself to the Indians, who came towards the guide, and on reaching the place where he was standing, were fired upon, five being killed and the sixth wounded, who escaped. A little further on they saw three more, and succeeded in shooting them also; thus killing eight and wounding two.

The poor guide was accidentally severely wounded

by one of the white men in the encounter; when another, thinking, perhaps, it was better to put him out of misery, killed him.

August 13th, 1856.—The news by the "Columbia" this morning from above is very interesting. Colonel Wright, United States army, is still endeavoring to make peace with the Yakimas, and other hostile indians in that vicinity. In the meantime some volunteers, under Colonel Shaw, have had an engagement with a body of Indians at Grand Ronde Prairie, on a river of the same name. The Colonel had under him at the time one hundred and eighty mounted men; and, according to the papers, succeeded in routing the enemy. The number killed is not known. Two of his men were killed and three wounded. The skirmish occurred on the seventeenth ultimo. Two or three days previous, Major Layton, with sixty or seventy volunteers, also had a little brush with the Indians in that vicinity—and, according to his official report, there were none of the enemy killed, though he thought his detachment shot several. His loss was one or two killed, and about the same number wounded.

THE CASCADES, OREGON TERRITORY, August 25th, 1856.

Left Fort Orford August twenty-first, and arrived at Fort Vancouver, W. T., on the twenty-third. The Columbia River bar not being very rough, Captain William Dall ran his vessel in without waiting for the pilot—the latter thus losing a hundred dollars by not being ready to perform the duty. The sky being clear we enjoyed, on our trip up the Columbia, a fine view of Mount St. Helena, Mount Ranier and Mount Hood, with their snow-capped peaks, the first being 9,750, the second 12,360, and the latter 11,225 feet high.

The river bank up to the mouth of the Willamette is lined with fir and cedar; above that for a short distance, especially at Vancouver, by cottonwood, which is found wherever the river overflows. Between Vancouver and the Cascades the timber is principally fir.

I spent the Sabbath at Fort Vancouver. Was disappointed in finding my cousin, Major Pinkny Lugenbeel, of the Ninth Regiment of Infantry, absent on duty — yet had the pleasure of meeting his family. Although we have been in correspondence for a long time, and were at one period stationed within two hundred miles of each other for three years—he at Fort Gibson and I at Fort Arbuckle—still we have not met since he was a cadet at West Point; when, being on leave of absence, he visited my father's home in Maryland. I was then a mere child, but have still a vivid recollection of the gilt buttons on his uniform.

Vancouver is one of the most delightful posts in the army. It possesses an excellent, healthy climate, and commands one of the grandest landscape views in the United States. It is situated on the north bank of the Columbia River, which is at this point about sixteen hundred yards wide. In a direct line it is seventy miles from the Pacific Ocean—though the distance by the Columbia is ninety miles.

From this place I obtained the first good view of Mount Hood, the grandest mountain peak in North

America. Mount Ranier, in Washington Territory, and Mount Shasta, in California, may be a little higher, but are said not to possess such majestic beauty. The day is not distant when landscape painters, the wide world over, will delight in transferring to canvas the many charming pictures of natural scenery in the Territories of Washington and Oregon. The one who best succeeds in delineating old Mount Hood will deserve the greatest renown.

Adjoining Fort Vancouver, between it and the Columbia River, is an old trading post of the famous Hudson Bay Company. It has always been the headquarters of this great monopoly of trade in the Northwest. Here is where its Governor or chief factor had always resided until lately. This company held for many years unbounded sway over all the Indians west of the Rocky Mountains, from California to the Russian possessions in the far north.

The Hudson Bay Company commenced its operations in Canada as early as 1670, under a charter of Charles II. It had for many years of its early existence a formidable rival in the French Northwest Fur Company. The latter was in fact the pioneer in the trade in what was then known as the Territory of Oregon, embracing, at that period, the whole Pacific slope lying between the Rocky Mountains on the east, the Pacific Ocean on the west, California on the south, and Russian possessions on the north. There were many bloody conflicts between the two companies until they finally united in 1821.

The Hudson Bay Company owned at one period on this coast five trading stations and twenty-three forts.

VIEW OF MOUNT SHASTA, FROM SHASTA VALLEY.—Page 360.

It had, besides, trading parties extending into Utah, California, and Arizona, and northward all the way to the Russian American possessions. In order to facilitate commercial intercourse among the numerous bands and tribes of aborigines living in the vast extent of country in which it had an exclusive charter to trade, the Hudson Bay Company found it expedient to supply them with a common language, called the jargon, composed mainly of Chinook, with a mixture of a little French, and words coined expressly for the occasion. This jargon answers the same purpose to the Indians in Oregon that the pantomime does to the prairie tribes east of the Rocky Mountains. Merchants and Government officers, who have business relations with the Indians, find a knowledge of it very useful.

Some army friends of mine who had served in Oregon sufficiently long to learn to speak it with facility, chanced to meet at the St. Nicholas Hotel, in New York, a short while ago, and, in their conversation with each other, used the jargon altogether, much to the wonderment of bystanders, who were unable to guess their nationality.

The Hudson Bay Company, having so long held an absolute commercial control over the Territory of Oregon, began to imagine that it really had a fee simple right to the soil, or, at least, that Great Britain, through its occupancy, possessed this title. Great Britain began as early as 1818 to agitate with the United States the question of ownership; but, as no conclusion as to title could then be arrived at, it was, in a convention between the two Governments, agreed that in order to prevent disputes among themselves, the citizens and subjects of the two powers should hold a joint occupancy of the country for ten years, from October 20th, 1818. Whereupon the policy of the Hudson Bay Company was exercised in encouraging British immigration, and discouraging as much as possible, not only American traders, but all settlers from the United States.

It is stated that as many as eleven different American fur companies tried their luck in the Territory, but, owing to the overshadowing discouragement of the Hudson Bay Company, were unable to succeed.

Finally, however, Americans, through nuclei formed by missionary settlements, gained a permanent footing in the country, and though the joint occupancy of the subjects of Great Britain and the United States continued until 1846, it was then concluded in convention between the two powers that the forty-ninth degree of north latitude should be the boundary line between the possessions of the two Governments on the Pacific Coast.

Article First of said treaty reads as follows: "From the point on the forty-ninth parallel of north latitude, where the boundary laid down in existing treaties and conventions between the United States and Great Britain terminates, the line of boundary between the territories of the United States, and those of her Britanic Majesty, shall be continued westward along the said parallel of north latitude, to the middle of the channel which separates the continent from Vancouver's Island, and thence southerly through the middle of the said channel and Fuca's Straits, to the Pacific ocean; provided, however, that the navigation of the whole of the said channel and straits, south of the forty-ninth parallel of north latitude, remains free and open to both parties."

Article Second states that all that part of the Columbia River lying south of the forty-ninth parallel of north latitude, should be free to the Hudson Bay Company and British subjects trading with them.

Article Third stipulates that the possessory rights of the Hudson Bay Company and other British subjects, should be respected.

This treaty was ratified on the fifth of August, 1846. Many persons maintain that all of our Indian difficulties on this coast, have had their origin either directly or indirectly in the machinations of the Hudson Bay Company. While it is in all probability not true that the company itself, or any one of its leading officers, has ever incited the savages to war with the Americans, yet its employees were guilty of so doing.

It is a fact, however, that the Indians looked upon the members of the Hudson Bay Company as simply coming among them for purposes of trade, and not with the view of taking their land and removing them to reservations, as has always been the custom of the Americans, or " Bostons " as they called them; hence they very naturally look upon the former as friends, and the latter as enemies. The kindness of the first missionaries to the Indians, smothered for awhile their savage hatred, only to burst out when least expected, in some terrible massacre, as that of Dr. Whitman and his missionary friends by the Cayuse Indians, on the twenty-eighth of November, 1847.

The history of all such massacres, proves how unworthy the Indian is to be called the noble red man.

His treachery and ingratitude soon efface from those who know him best, all romantic notions of the elevated traits of his character, as imbibed from Cooper's novels. There are exceptions, but as a rule it will not do to rely on the friendship of an Indian towards the white man. When his savage nature is aroused, he falls on friend and foe alike. Such examples are innumerable. One of the latest is the killing of Captain Ben. Wright, the Indian Agent, in the Port Orford district, during the uprising of the Coast Indians last winter. Although it is asserted by some, that in 1850 Ben. Wright had harshly treated the Modoc Indians, on the upper Rogue River, yet after he became Indian Agent, his sympathies seem to lean, if either way, in favor of the Indian, and against the white man. He stood like a wall of adamant between the two races in their numerous quarrels on the coast, in the vicinity of Port Orford.

There are many romantic stories related of this rude, but brave and very remarkable man. He was the Kit Carson of the Pacific Coast. Whilst at Fort Vancouver, I attended church and heard the chaplain, the Rev. Dr. McCartey, preach. He is better known as the "fighting parson," from some sermons preached by him previous to accompanying the American Army in the war with Mexico. Leaving Vancouver at three P. M., twenty-fifth of August, in the steamboat "Signorita," Captain Wells, I took a trip to the Cascades, which I reached at 7½ in the evening. This portion of the river reminds me very much of the Hudson. The natural scenery is perhaps more picturesque, especially for some twenty miles below the Cascades, as this part of the river is flanked by the bluffs and peaks of the Cascade Range of mountains through which it runs. At several places the river is confined by beautiful, high, perpendicular columns of basalt, the highest being called Cape Horn, because it projects somewhat in the river. An occasional little cascade tumbling into the latter, adds to the beauty of the scenery. One of these is said to be four hundred feet high, some even call it five hundred; but I scarcely think that it is over three hundred. The Cascades proper, are nothing more than rapids, formed by the Columbia's rushing precipitately over a steep, rocky bed. They are distant one hundred and forty miles from the ocean, and about fifty from the mouth of the Willamette.

There is a portage of four and a half miles on the Washington Territory side over a good military road (not quite completed) at that point; there being a steamboat landing and a block house at each extremity; also, one of the latter about midway. At each of the block houses are stationed a small detachment of U. S. troops. It being at these three points that the Clickitat Indians made an attack last spring, killing some thirteen persons, and burning all the houses, excepting Mr. Bradford's, at the upper landing. It was at the latter point that they came so near destroying the steamboat "Mary." When the attack began, the engineer let go his boat, and, pushing out in the stream, she came within an ace of being carried over the cascades; but fortunately he, although severely wounded, was enabled to get up sufficient steam to prevent this catastrophe and start up the river. On reaching the Dalles, and giving the alarm, Colonel Wright's command immediately moved to the rescue, and drove the enemy to the mountains. Recapturing a good deal of plunder, and capturing some Indians—nine or ten of whom were subsequently hung. The enemy, on laying the plan of attack, had calculated upon Colonel Wright's command of the Ninth Infantry having taken their departure from the Dalles for the Yakima country. But it seems the Colonel's command had got but a short distance from the place when he heard of the trouble at the Cascades. The temperature of the Cascades is moderately cool in summer and cold in winter, heavy clothing being comfortable the year round.

August 26th, 1856.—I have crossed the Columbia at the Cascades to the Oregon side in a skiff, and am patiently awaiting the departure of the little steamboat "Mary" for Portland. There are but two boats plying between this and the latter place at present, connecting through the Portage with the same number above the Cascades. The river at this point is only about four hundred yards broad, running through a mountain gorge, which extends some fifteen or twenty miles. The river bottom here, including its bed, is a mile broad, and bounded on each side by almost perpendicular mountain spurs two or three thousand feet high, covered with fir. The whole aspect of the country is romantic in the extreme, and well worthy of a visit. A short distance above here is a small mountain, on which are collected several hundred Indians, who, as a body, have remained friendly during the present war—only a few of them having joined the Clickitats in their attack on the Cascades in March last.

I saw at Vancouver, Colonel George Wright, the chief in command of the United States troops now in Oregon and Washington Territories, and was informed by him that the hostile Indians of Washington and Eastern Oregon had agreed to make peace, and had thrown themselves under the protection of the troops. Old Kimiakin and other influential chiefs, however, have left their people and declined to come to terms. This may turn out a source of embarrassment. The Colonel is busily engaged in erecting block houses and forts in the Indian country east of the Cascades. He has established a new post at Walla Walla and one at Simcoe, which is in the Yakima country. It is in contemplation, also, to have a second in the latter region.

FORT YAMHILL, OREGON TERRITORY, Sept. 5th, 1856.

Leaving the Cascades on the twenty-sixth ultimo, in the steamboat "Mary," I arrived at Portland, Oregon Territory, on the same day, and took lodging at the Metropolis, kept by Mr. Keith. This is the finest hotel that I have ever seen in so small a place as Portland, a town of some 1,700 inhabitants. The city is situated on the west bank of the Willamette River, twelve miles from its mouth, and is the first in point of size and commercial importance in Oregon. With the exception of a few brick buildings, the houses are of frame, painted white. The largest, handsomest and most substantial store in the place, is owned by a colored man, by the name of Francis. The building itself is brick, and cost $8,000. The employees of the establishment are white men, the "boss" rarely showing himself.

On the twenty-eighth, I started for Oregon City, a distance of only twelve miles, in the steamboat "Portland." This is a very neat town of probably five hundred inhabitants, and is located on the east bank of the Willamette River, just below the falls. The latter, in high water, extend the whole breadth of the river in a very irregular line, and are said to be beautiful. In truth, even at the present low stage of water, they present a very picturesque appearance. The pitch of the water is about twenty feet over perpendicular basaltic rock. Immediately in the rear of the town, and extending its whole length is a steep bluff, one hundred and twenty feet high, back of which is a fine plateau. The surrounding country is thickly settled. Almost every farm contains a fine young orchard, fruit being far more valuable to the producer than grain. Wheat, for instance, is at present worth only seventy-five cents per bushel, and rapidly falling in price; whereas, apples can be sold on the trees at eight dollars per bushel.

I am informed that General McCarver has disposed of his apples this year on the trees, for $3,000. They retail in the shops at from six to twenty-five cents apiece; pears and peaches a little higher.

On Sunday I attended divine service at the Methodist Episcopal Church. On Monday I took my departure up the river in the steamboat "Hoosier," which got off just about sundown; but being unable to pass Rock Island before dark, returned, and took a fresh start early the following morning. She went about thirty miles that day, and tied up for the night, the crew and passengers, as usual, sleeping and taking

VIEW OF CAPE HORN ON THE COLUMBIA RIVER.—Page 366.

their meals on shore, there being no accommodations on board. Some ten miles from Oregon City, a plug flew out of the boat's boiler, from which all the steam escaped into the furnace, extinguishing the fire instantaneously. Fortunately, this mishap did not detain us long, as we were near a rapid, up which it would have been necessary to have "poled" the flat boat which the "Hoosier" had in tow, even had the accident not occurred. So, whilst the crew, assisted by the passengers, were getting the former over this place, the Captain succeeded in re-plugging the boiler, and steaming up again.

On the following day we reached a landing near the mouth of the Yamhill River, about eleven A. M., whence I walked to Dayton, a distance of four and a half miles, where I arrived a little after noon. The "Hoosier" reached there a little before sundown; being detained, as was anticipated, by a low stage of water in the Yamhill, rendering it necessary to use the poles frequently. She is the most miserable excuse of a steamboat that I have ever seen. The boiler and machinery are worn out, and should have been condemned years ago. It is of so ordinary a occurrence for a plug to fly out, or a flue to collapse, that it is considered of very little importance by the crew and captain, all of whom are green hands in the management of steam power.

To give a further idea of the frail character of the boat, I shall simply mention that several of the crew, getting drunk, commenced dancing, when the Captain ordered them to stop, or else they might shake down the smoke-pipe.

Dayton is on the right bank of the Yamhill, some forty miles from Oregon City by water, and twenty-four by land. It contains three or four stores, a post-office, tavern, and half a dozen dwellings. I there had the pleasure of seeing my friend, General Palmer, late Superintendent of Indian affairs in Oregon. I came from Dayton to this place on horseback, a distance of thirty miles.

The valley of the Yamhill, through which I passed, contains many pretty prairie farms, partially fenced, and having fine young orchards of a few years' growth, and moderate improvements in the way of frame cottages, which present a neat exterior, but are generally left unfinished within until building material and mechanical labor shall have become more within the reach of the owner's means. Here and there may be seen the familiar log cabin of Arkansas and Missouri. The Yamhill constitutes a small but important part of the beautiful Willamette Valley, the garden spot of Oregon. All the cereals and common garden vegetables grow here in the greatest abundance. So do most of the fruits of a temperate climate—such as apples, pears, plums, cherries, strawberries, etc. Fruit trees bear much earlier than in the States. The farms do not contain a great deal of timber, but there is an abundance of this in the Coast Range of mountains near by.

This post is located on the northern pass of the Coast Reservation, Oregon Territory, about latitude 45° north, longitude 124° west. In a direct line it is three quarters of a mile west of the South Fork of the Yamhill River, fifteen miles from the Pacific Ocean, forty-nine south of the Columbia River, and forty-five south southwest of Portland. It commands the main outlet through the Coast Range of mountains, from the Indian Coast Reservation, to the valley of the Yamhill. Its immediate position is on a gentle western slope, overlooking on the west, a small, somewhat circular valley, called the Grande Ronde, and terminating on the east and southeast by a bluff, the base of which defines a portion of the left border of the Yamhill Valley. With the exception of the latter and the Grande Ronde, the surrounding country is mountainous and thickly timbered, principally with fir, though maple, wild cherry and alder, are to be found at a few points. Near the post and down the Yamhill, are some very fine groves of white oak. There are no swamps in this vicinity, at least in summer, and the streams are all rapid, clear and pure. Malarious fevers are almost unknown here.

The post is garrisoned by a company of the First Dragoons and one of the Fourth Infantry. The commissioned officers are Captain Andrew J. Smith, (in command), Brevet Captain Oliver H. P. Taylor and James Wheeler, Jr., of the First Regiment of Dragoons, Captain Delancy Floyd Jones, of the Fourth, and Lieutenant William B. Hazen, of the Eighth Infantry, and Dr. Charles H. Crane, whom I relieve.

CHAPTER XXVII.

AT FORT YAMHILL.

Visit to the Coast—An Indian Attack upon Governor Steven's Escort—Splendid Mountain Scenery from a point near Fort Yamhill—Two Murders in Garrison—A Government Train perishes in the Snow—A Hard Trip through Deep Snow—The Indian Department and the Indians lose much Stock—The Indians threaten to return to Rogue River—Whites Stampeded—In order to stay the hand of Death, the Indians resolve to kill their Doctors—My Horse falls and rolls down a Hill—Captain Stevenson's Skirmish with the Indians in Florida—The Mormons—A Fourth of July Accident prevented by Lieutenant Sheridan—Welcker's Wedding Festivities—Mormon Troubles—Synopsis of the Weather.

FORT YAMHILL, September 16th, 1856.

I visited the coast yesterday, to see some sick men of a detachment of soldiers at that place, and returned to-day. The road is a bad one, especially in wet weather, though with a little more labor, is capable of becoming tolerably good for summer traveling. It runs through thick timber nearly all the way. Four miles from the ocean is a very high hill, commanding the best view of the Pacific I have ever seen.

Most of the Indians of the reservation being those who were lately hostile, are at present encamped immediately on the coast, near the mouth of Salmon River; the remainder are in the vicinity of the post. They are all living in tents, furnished them by the Indian Department, who contemplate giving them material for the erection of huts. They are fed by the government. Some of them seem contented, but many, especially the Upper Rogue River Indians, grumble considerably, and talk of leaving before long. I hardly think they will carry out so rash a design. Their discontent, however, suffices to get up little stampedes among the settlers occasionally; we have had two since my arrival here, in both of which it was reported that the Indians contemplated breaking out and cutting everybody's throats.

October 5th, 1856.—We have had a fortnight of delightful weather. Yesterday, however, and to-day, it has been showery. In consequence of some Calapooya Indians having left the reservation night before last, for their old homes, Captain Taylor, First Dragoons, with eighteen men, was this morning dispatched to bring them back.

Yesterday, some eighty or one hundred Klamath Indians were sent back to Klamath Lake, in Southeastern Oregon. They did not belong to this reservation. Exciting news in our Indian affairs have reached us from Walla Walla. We must await a few days for particulars.

October 6th, 1856.—By the Oregon papers, we learn that Governor Stevens, of Washington Territory, in his capacity of Indian Superintendent, was holding a council with the Indian tribes of Washington Territory, between Cascades and Bitter Root mountains. The council being held near Fort Walla Walla, was opened on the eleventh, and closed on the eighteenth of September, without being able to effect any treaty with the Indians. The following tribes were represented: John Day's Umatillas, Tyhs, Nez Perces, Des

Shutes, Walla Wallas and Cayuses. Old Kimiakin, Owhi, Qualston (Owhi's son), and the chiefs of the Spokanes and other tribes in that section, declined attending the council.

On the nineteenth, Governor Stevens, with his train of twenty-eight ox teams, and some two hundred loose animals, escorted by Captain Goff's Company (K), consisting of sixty-eight men, Washington Territory volunteers, belonging to the command of Colonel B. F. Shaw, started for the Dalles. They had proceeded but a short distance, when the Indians made an attack upon them. A corral was formed with the wagons, and the train put in a state of defence, and an express sent to Colonel Sleptoe's command of United States troops at Fort Walla Walla, for reinforcements.

About one A. M. of the twentieth, Lieutenant J. W. Davidson, with seventy men and a howitzer, arrived, when the Indians, who had kept the camp surrounded some fourteen hours, were driven off. Governor Steven' train then moved back to Fort Walla Walla, and remained there until the twenty-third, when Colonel Sleptoe gave him an escort for the Dalles.

As the Indians had burned all the grass around Fort Walla Walla, the Colonel was compelled to send the most of the Government stock with the escort as far as the Umatilla River to graze.

Thursday, October 30th, 1856.—During the last three weeks, it has rained nearly half the time, and yet the old settlers around here insist that the rainy season has not set in. It is, perhaps, a month ahead of time; to-day, however, has been beautiful and clear. Captain Delancy Floyd Jones, Lieutenant James Wheeler, Jr., and myself, availed ourselves of its charms, by ascending the top of a mountain peak, some four miles from the Fort. Having gone to its base on horseback, we dismounted, and made the ascent on foot. The height is probably a thousand or fifteen hundred feet above the surrounding valleys, and three or four thousand above the ocean. From its summit the view is magnificent. taking in the whole of the Yamhill Valley, and the snow-capped peaks of the Three Sisters, Mount Jefferson, Mount Hood, etc.

There is no news of interest from the Dalles. Col. Wright, United States Army, with the available "regular force" at his disposal, left there shortly after Governor Stevens came in, for the Walla Walla country; but what his plans are, have not yet been made public.

December 20th, 1856.—From San Francisco we learn that on the third of November, the Vigilance Committee, having surrendered the State arms to the authorities, the Governor of California withdrew his proclamation of insurrection, and the Committee are virtually disbanded.

Last night a fatal affray occurred in garrison, private Connor, of F Company, Fourth Infantry, being killed by a stab with a butcher knife in the hands of private Turner, of Company C, First Dragoons. On the 23rd of last September, a soldier of the latter company (Meehan) was beaten to death by another of the former. Stolzer, who committed the act, was tried on the 28th of last month at Dalles, in Polk county, and sentenced to a term of ten years in the Penitentiary, and to pay a fine of five dollars. Turner is now confined in the guard house at this post, and will also be tried for murder. The fact of two murders in so short a period is almost unprecedented in the United States Regular service. The parties in both instances were under the influence of "liquor" at the time—that great exciter of nine-tenths of all the crimes committed.

January 8th, 1857.—On last Friday, at 9 A. M., it commenced snowing, and continued, with short intervals, until Monday afternoon. It fell to the depth of twenty-two inches at this place; two and a half feet, eleven miles from here on the road to the Dalles; and twenty inches at the latter place; at Salem, fourteen inches; Portland, twenty-seven inches; Cascades, on last Thursday, three to six feet. It is not known how deep it is at the Dalles of the Columbia. According to the last information from that point, some nine days ago, a Government train of one hundred and twenty-five mules and horses was caught in a snow storm between the Dalles and the new post on the Simcoe, in the Yakima country, and every one perished. Such snows being unusual in this Territory, most of the farmers are without sufficient provender for their animals, many of which will perish if the snow lay long. It has melted but very little since it first fell. Night before last the thermometer was down to 15°; last night 9° of Fahrenheit.

Being compelled to go on Saturday to Dalles, thence to Salem, to get a power of attorney to send to San Francisco by the steamer due on the 10th instant, I had full benefit of the snow storm. On my return yester-

VIEW ON THE COLUMBIA RIVER NEAR THE DALLES.–Page 376.

day I found the traveling exceedingly difficult and unpleasant. The mud in the roads was, at places, very deep, and had not frozen previously to the snow, so that my horse had to wade through the depth of the two combined, or cut his limbs by following the frozen footsteps of some previous equestrian. Then again, the sloughs, sluices, and branches were covered with ice. At Salem I attended a dancing party, given at the Union Hotel, and had the pleasure of seeing all the *elite* of the town, and the "big guns" of the Oregon Legislature, which is now in session at that place. I may remark that the present is as deep a snow as has fallen in Oregon within the recollection of the oldest inhabitant—the ones of 1849 and 1853 not excepted.

January 20th, 1857.—The snow which fell between the 2nd and 5th instant lay on the ground about a fortnight without melting a great deal. Day before yesterday, however, a warm breeze sprang up from the south, accompanied with rain, which continued until this morning, when the sun shone forth for a few hours. The snow has entirely disappeared, except on the mountains, and the streams are greatly swollen. A large number of horses, belonging to the Indians, on this, the Coast Reservation, have perished during the present hard winter for want of food and shelter. And General Palmer, the former Superintendent of Indians for Oregon, it is said, has lost thirty yoke of cattle from the same cause. He had them on the reservation near the Siletz, breaking a piece of ground for the Indians, when the snow storm came on.

March 20th, 1857.—The Indians on the Coast Reservation are becoming dissatisfied. Those at the Siletz, embracing about one half of the whole number on the reservation, have lately held a council and determined to go back to their old country. They are to be joined by some of the Upper Rogue River Indians at this place. The latter during the last war were by far the most troublesome and formidable. The former consist of the tribes that lived on Lower Rogue River and the Coast, in the Port Orford District, or Curry County.

Captain Augur, the commanding officer of Fort Hoskins, near the Siletz, sent an express to Captain Taylor, of this post, for an additional company to proceed to the Siletz, and prevent, if possible, any movement on the part of the Indians. Accordingly, Company H, Fourth Infantry, under the command of Lieutenant Wheeler, First Dragoons, will start for that point today. If the Indians contemplate making any move, they will postpone it during the inclement weather. I have no idea, however, that there is any more cause for the present excitement than we have had all winter, except that the period when the Indians would be the most likely to make a move, if at all, is approaching. The settlers around here are greatly alarmed. All the whites at the agency, excepting three or four, have been frightened away. This state of things is to be deplored, for it will, undoubtedly, have a bad effect on the Indians, who may thus be reminded of doing what otherwise would not have been thought of.

April 1st, 1857.—A great day in the States for making fools of one's friends. It does not seem to be much celebrated in that mode out here. The steamer "Columbia" arrived at Portland on the 24th with New York papers of the 20th ultimo. Not much news of general importance. The most interesting item to the army, is the passage by Congress of a bill increasing the pay of officers. It gives each officer twenty dollars a month additional pay, and increases commutation value of the ration to thirty cents. Taking all grades, this is an average increase of about five hundred and fifty dollars a year to each officer.

Sunday, April 12th, 1857.—The last nine days have been delightfully mild, clear, and pleasant, with a prospect of the same continuing. The farmers are all busily engaged in plowing for their spring crops. They have heretofore usually been able to break their ground in February and March, and to put in most of their spring crop during the latter month; but the continuous wet weather prevented their so doing this season. Many express fears that from the too rapid drying of the ground it will become very hard and difficult to plough. The soil seems to be somewhat peculiar in this respect. It is probably owing to the large proportion of argillaceous matter in its composition. There is no time in the year when the grass is not green. At present it of course presents a more thrifty and growing aspect than during the cold rains and snows of winter. The valleys are now covered with beautiful flowers, golden yellow predominating, though all colors are well represented. The strawberry has been in bloom for more than a month. Great abundance of this delicious fruit is anticipated.

The Indians on the reservation near here have had another little difficulty among themselves. In consequence of so many deaths among the Upper Rogue Rivers, they recently held a council to determine who it was that had been causing them to die. What conclusion this august body came to is not known, but rumor has it that they have resolved on causing to be killed various doctors, who have been bewitching them. As a commencement, they, this morning, shot an Umpqua doctor, who, just before dying, wounded his murderer, Sambo, in the leg. There is, of course, considerable excitement among them at present, and whether the matter will end without further bloodshed remains to be seen.

April 20th, 1857.—Company F, Fourth Infantry, returned yesterday from the Siletz. The Indians at that point of the reservation, continue to be troublesome, though no outbreak has occurred, and with proper management on the part of the Indian Agent, the excitement will gradually calm down.

The Yaquina Bay, about twenty miles from the Siletz, and at the middle of the coast line of the reservation, is found to be a good and safe entrance for small vessels. The Indian Department have already landed a schooner load of provisions there for the Indians.

Lieutenant H. H. Garber, Fourth Infantry, reached here a few days ago, and will remain until F Company takes its departure. Mr. G. Clinton Gardner, lately an agent in the Quartermaster's Department at this post, and sòn of the former Surveyor-General of Oregon, having received the appointment of Assistant Surveyor and Astronomer to the Northwest Boundary Survey, left us on the eighteenth instant. He is a very intelligent and worthy young gentleman. Lieutenant William B. Hazen, Fourth Infantry, being ordered to join his regiment in Texas, bade us farewell this morning.

April 23d, 1857.—Weather continues beautiful; heavy frost (second of the season), last night; it has done much injury to the fruit. The roads are getting fine for traveling, and there is nothing I should like more than to take a daily gallop round the country, but, unfortunately, my horse is lame. On the twenty-eighth ultimo, while returning from a visit to a patient in the neighborhood, and attempting to ride over a lot of loose brush that had been thrown in a very deep mud hole, my horse sprained himself in the left hip joint; the brush was just being put down. Had I waited half an hour, until the man who was mending the road, had thrown in a sufficient quantity, the accident would not have occurred. As the horse did not go decidedly lame, I paid no attention to the matter, and foolishly attempted two days thereafter, to follow a cow trail around a very steep hill, in order to avoid the muddy road below. As ill luck would have it, on reaching the very steepest point of the trail, my horse slipped on his right hind leg, and suddenly (from pain in the left hip, perhaps,) let himself down behind, and rolled over, and continued rolling to the bottom of the hill, a distance of forty yards, and exceedingly steep.

From the suddenness of the fall, I came within an ace of being crushed to death under the saddle, but managed to extricate myself from the latter before it was too late. The horse was, of course, very much stunned; I at first thought him killed. Strange as it may appear, he escaped without a broken bone; he was badly bruised, however, and the sprain in the hip rendered worse. Being a splendid animal—worth some three hundred dollars—I regret exceedingly the accident.

May 2d, 1857.—On going to see a patient this morning, whose hand I amputated five days ago, my horse fell with me again. The fall was so great and sudden that he threw me on the ground with considerable force, but I escaped without a bruise. I was in hopes that he had recovered from the sprain received a month ago, but it seems not. After his fall I rode him some thirty miles, during such time he gave way on the left hind leg several times, but without letting himself completely down. He shows no signs of lameness, except when tramping on a rolling stone or uneven ground. I observed to-day that he does not "track" (step his hind foot straight after the fore one,) with his left hind foot, but turns it a little outwards. This is a sure sign of sprain in the hip joint.

June 14th, 1857.—The troops operating against the Florida Indians have been unable to effect much during the present winter. From the following extract of a general order of General Scott, we learn about all that has been accomplished:

"Lieutenant Edmund Freeman, Fifth Infantry, reconnoitering with a small party in the Big Cypress Swamp, near Bowleg's Town, Florida, was attacked by the Seminoles March 5th, himself and three of his men severely wounded and one man killed. Captain Carter L. Stevenson, Fifth Infantry, with his command, called, by express, from Fort Keais, twenty miles distant, came rapidly to the relief of Lieutenant Freeman's party, attacked the enemy, and, after a gallant skirmish, put them to flight, with an evident loss to the Indians, the extent of which could not be ascertained, owing to the density of the hammock."

Since then nothing has been done in that quarter, and General Harney has been ordered to turn over his command to the next in rank, and proceed to take command of a large force of cavalry and infantry about to start on the plains — destination unknown. It is surmised that they may ultimately go to Salt Lake, as the Administration is endeavoring to prevail on some one to accept the appointment of Governor of that Territory, so as to supplant Brigham Young, who threatens resistence to the United States authority if removed. It seems that the Mormons, for several years past, have practically treated the laws of the United States as a nullity—obeying no law but that of the church. Recently they have made the lives of our judicial officers there, so insecure, that several of them have resigned, Judge Drummond among others. I see, in a letter from the latter gentleman, published in the papers, in answer to some inquiries of Mrs. Gunnison, that the Mormons, in his opinion, instigated and assisted in the murder of her husband, Lieutenant Gunnison, of the United States Topographical Engineers, who was killed in or near Utah several years ago, the murder being supposed at the time to have been committed by the Indians.

The Mormons have, for several years, been applying to Congress for admission into the Union; but, as several very grave questions arise as to the propriety of admitting them with their present so-called religion, the subject has heretofore been evaded by Congress. According to the Constitution, we have no right to apply any religious test in the admission of a Territory; and, as polygamy is a part of their religion, it becomes a serious question how to dispose of the matter; for the civilized world, and the people of the United States especially, look upon this feature of Mormonism as decidedly immoral and degenerating. The question very naturally arises whether such a system as the Mormons profess can be viewed as a religion in the meaning of the Constitution. Our best interpreters of the law differ upon the subject. Hence the dilemma of Congress; and whilst the latter continues to stave off the question, the Executive is left in an embarrassing position in its dealings with this strange people. An open conflict with the United States authorities, it is feared, will result ere long.

June 15th, 1857.—On the requisition of Captain Augur, commanding Fort Hoskins, Company F, Fourth Infantry, was dispatched to the Siletz yesterday morning. It is reported that some of the Indians at that point are getting troublesome, and supposed to be on the eve of leaving the Reservation.

July 4th, 1857.--Lieutenant Philip H. Sheridan, of the Fourth Infantry, with a detachment of thirty-two men from H Company, Fourth Infantry, and D Company, Third Artillery, arrived here June 25th, and relieved Company C, First Dragoons, which, with its officers, Brevet-Captain O. H. P. Taylor and Lieutenant James Wheeler, left for Fort Walla-Walla on the 29th ultimo. Lieutenant Sheridan and myself are now the only commissioned officers at this post. In honor of the day we fired a salute of thirty-one guns at 12 M., also a shell. The sergeant in charge was on the eve of putting the latter in the howitzer with the fuse reversed. The mistake was seen and corrected by Lieutenant Sheridan, otherwise an explosion of the howitzer might have been the result.

August 6th, 1857.—For the past three months I have been kept very much engaged in making professional visits through the neighborhood. The country north and east of the post is pretty thickly settled, and I have all the difficult cases to attend within thirty miles of this place. They never send for physicians in ordinary cases.

On the 23d ultimo I concluded to give myself a few days respite, and, accordingly, started for Fort Vancouver to participate in the wedding festivities gotten up to celebrate the marriage of Lieutenant William T. Welcker, of the Ordnance Department, to Miss Katy Adair, daughter of General Adair of Astoria. There were three parties given; one by the officers' mess in garrison; another on board the United States Steamship "Active," lying off Vancouver in the Columbia

River ; and the last and most brilliant of all, by Captain Rufus Ingalls, Assistant Quartermaster United States Army. The following are some of the most prominent persons present at the latter. Captain Prevost, and Secretary of the British Navy; Lieutenants Cuyler, Bassett, and Johnson, Dr. Brown, Major Davis, Chief Engineer, Mr. Jordan and Mr. Warren, Assistant Engineers, and Mr. West, Watch Officer, all officers of the "Active," a United States Naval Steamship, Captain Shaddock and Lieutenant Mason, of the United States Revenue Service, and Mr. Archibald Campbell, the Commissioner on the part of the United States to run the Northwest Boundary, and the following army officers:—Colonel Morris, Captain Smith, Captain Waller, Captain Augur, Major Alvord, Captain Ingalls; Drs. Potts, Herndon, and DeLengle ; Lieutenants Hodges, Myers, McFeely, Mendell, Mallory, Wickliffe, Wickler, and Hughes; and the following civilians:—Messrs. Grover, Green, Stark, Kibben, Rankin, Daniels, Noble, Brooke, etc. The ladies were mostly wives of army officers, though seven or eight unmarried ones were present, among others Miss Corbett, Miss Ellen Adair, and Miss Abernethy. The supper was bountiful and gotten up in splendid style. Everything passed off delightfully. It was given on the evening of the 30th ultimo.

On the following day I took passage on the "Active" for Portland, and started the same afternoon for this post, where I arrived the next day. Mechanics are at present engaged in finishing our quarters.

The Indians on this portion of the reservation give us very little trouble, except when drunk. Notwithstanding the severity of the law, there are several vagabond white men in this vicinity who sell them liquor. They usually escape punishment on account of the difficulty of getting any one to testify against them. However, the law has one fellow in limbo, and it is to be hoped will make an example of him.

September 9th, 1857.—Weather continues delightfully pleasant, with cool, refreshing nights—splendid for sleeping. Fruit is much more abundant this year than last. Apples are now selling at from one dollar to six dollars per bushel; last year they brought from four to ten dollars. They have been ripe about a month. The farmers of Washington and Oregon Territories in consequence of the drought, have raised very light crops of grain and garden vegetables this year. The grain sowed last fall did well; but, as the preceding winter had been so severe as to kill much of the wheat, (there being no snow to protect it,) the majority of the farmers postponed sowing until spring, hoping that they would then have sufficient good weather for the purpose. The rainy season continued unusually long, however, and ceased so abruptly that the ground baked almost as hard as rock, rendering plowing impossible. Most of the grain produced this year is what is known in this country as "volunteer"—that is, such as springs up from the wastage of the preceding crop, without any cultivation whatever. Many of the farmers depend on their volunteer crops for two years in succession. But, notwithstanding the small quantity of grain produced this season, it is very low in price. This is owing to the dullness of the San Francisco market. The want of an available foreign market is one of the great drawbacks to Oregon farmers. High price of labor is the next most important. It is this last feature that renders many more advocates for slavery in this Territory than would otherwise be. Two or three years ago, one would have scarcely thought the question would ever be agitated; but now that the Territorial Convention is in session for the purpose of framing a State Constitution, the advocates for slavery are found to be quite numerous. They are, however, doubtless in the minority.

The news from the Atlantic States is not very interesting. Among the most noticeable is, that a large number of United States troops left Fort Leavenworth about the last of July, *en route* for Utah. Several battalions had started a few weeks previous for the same destination, making in all about one thousand three hundred men. A body of dragoons, intended for the expedition, is detained, for a short time, in Kansas, owing to a renewal of the excitement there between the slavery and anti-slavery party. The expedition is to be under the command of Brevet Brigadier-General W. S. Harney, so soon as he can be relieved from his Kansas duties, and joins it; and, on their arrival, they will be considered in a new department, called the Department of Utah.

The object of sending so many troops into Utah, is to enforce the United States laws, the Mormons having heretofore proved very refractory. Their great head, Young, is to be supplanted as Governor, by Colonel Cummings, who, with many other civil officers recently appointed for Utah Territory, is accompanying the expedition. Brigham Young has heretofore refused to be superseded, and has threatened resistance to the entrance of any more United States troops into his Territory. It now remains to be seen what he will do under the circumstances. Should he urge the Mormons into a general resistance, it will require a great many troops to put them down. They are now quite numerous, and have several thousand well disciplined soldiery, who, prompted by religious fanaticism and imaginary persecution, will fight desperately. They will hardly be so insane, however, as to come to an open rupture with the United States.

October 1st, 1857.—The following is a synopsis of the weather during the past year at Fort Yamhill, Oregon Territory:

1856 AND 1857.	Highest temperature.	Lowest temperature.	Average temperature.	Number of days Fair.	Number of days Cloudy.	Number of days Rain.	Number of days Snow.	Quantity of Rain —Inches.
1856.								
October	72°	29°	40. 7°	8.66	22.33	17	0	6.38
November	60°	27°	43.67°	9.33	20.66	13	2	6.63
December	53°	30°	38.88°	2	29	23	6	14.80
1857.								
January	57°	9°	38.79°	4.66	26.33	20	5	11.86
February	56°	33°	41.83°	2.33	25.66	17	4	9.03
March	63°	34°	47.42°	10.66	20.33	23	3	8.52
April	81°	35	55.48°	27	3	2	0	.10
May	91°	40°	57.27°	21	10	13	0	1.76
June	92°	45°	57.85°	20.66	9.33	10	0	1.28
July	95°	50°	61.72°	24.66	6.33	1	0	.05
August	91°	44°	60.05°	27.66	3.33	1	0	.10
September	87°	42°	57.22°	19	11	11	0	1.68
				177.62	187.30	151	20	62.19

CHAPTER XXVIII.

FORT YAMHILL—VISIT TO FORT VANCOUVER.

Loss of the Steamer "Central America"—Financial Crisis—Trouble among the Reservation Indians—Utah Expedition—An Expressman Drowned—Brigham Young more Conciliatory—Indians Moody; Chief John and Son Shackled and sent to Presidio, near San Francisco—Frazer River Mining Excitement—Rumored Fight with the Indians by the Troops under Colonel Steptoe.

October 30th, 1857.—After a tiresome professional ride through rain and mud, I am now enjoying my *otium cum dignitate* in a comfortable room before a cheerful fire, and can with feelings of perfect security listen to the howling blast and pelting rain, announcing the commencement of the rainy season. When the breeze is fresh here it usually blows a gale at sea. The Pacific is a rough and dangerous coast at this season of the year, at least that portion lying between San Francisco and Vancouver's Island. But owing to there being so few vessels on these waters it is not often we hear of any great catastrophes occurring in this part of the great watery domain. Oh, how different on the Atlantic! Almost every States' mail brings some heartrending account of disasters at sea. By the last mail comes the melancholy intelligence of the total loss of the Steamship "Central America" (late "George Law"), with over four hundred passengers, the California mail of the 20th of August, and about sixteen hundred thousand dollars in specie. She foundered at sea in a tremendous hurricane, on the 12th of September, off

Cape Hatteras. Not precisely known how many passengers were saved—one hundred were transferred to the brig "Mariner" of Boston, including all the women (twenty-six) and children, and fifty others were picked up by the Norwegian bark "Helen," after the vessel had sunk. Two of these, Messrs. R. T. Brown and John D. Derment (the latter from Oregon), had been in the water twelve hours, floating on a piece of the hurricane deck, with cork life-preservers to their persons. The Captain (Lieutenant Herndon, United States Navy) was among the lost.

There seems to be a great financial crisis taking place in the States. The ball was set in motion some two months ago by the failure of the New York branch of the Ohio Trust Company's Banking Association, and has been rolling with accelerated motion ever since. Railroad stock was the first to suffer—its depression at present being incredible. Next the banks and merchants in regular succession. The money panic is of greater severity than has occurred for many years, and alarming mercantile disasters are constantly occurring throughout the Union, but mainly in New York city.

There has lately been a little excitement among the Indians on the Coast Reservation, growing out of the killing of two Siletz Indians by Cultus Jim, of Old John's band. There being much sickness among the latter tribe, they superstitiously believed that these two men, who were medicine men or doctors, were causing it by their witchcraft. Cultus Jim accordingly waylaid and killed them—or, at least, killed one and wounded the other. A row being the consequence, the Indian

Agent, Bob Metcalf, requested all the Indians who had fire-arms to surrender them. Old John's band at first refused to comply, but subsequently promised to obey. A reinforcement of thirty troops having in the meantime arrived from Fort Hoskins, making, with those previously at the Siletz, fifty men, under the command of Lieutenant H. H. Garber. About the time that half the arms were given up by Old John, the murderer, Cultus Jim (the Chief's son), was found by the Agent, who, in company with Lieutenant Garber and a sergeant, attempted his arrest. Jim resisting and firing a pistol at Metcalf, was instantly shot by the latter and Lieutenant Garber. John subsequently threatened an attack on the troops, but things in that section seem quiet at present.

November 30th, 1857.—Our mail from the States arrived last night. The financial crisis is increasing. Nearly every bank in the Union has suspended specie payment. Corporations, merchants, etc., breaking by hundreds.

The October election in Kansas for member of the State Legislature passed off quietly. Results not yet known. United States troops were placed at all the points where riots had been apprehended between the contending parties.

The Utah Expedition continues to engross public attention. It is not yet known whether Brigham Young will offer open resistance to it or not. The leading California papers have come to the conclusion that a conflict is inevitable, as the latest accounts from Salt Lake represent the Mormons as very much excited, and preparing to resist the entrance of troops into the Territory. The advanced body of troops, seventeen hundred strong, under Colonel Albert S. Johnston, was within two days' march of Utah. Captain S. Van Vleit, Assistant Quartermaster United States Army, had been sent to Salt Lake City in advance, to ascertain from the Mormons the practicability of obtaining supplies for the troops. And it is rumored that although treated kindly, Brigham Young declined giving him any answer, but, on the contrary, delivered several belligerent sermons in his presence. I cannot believe them so fanatical as to bring on a rupture with the General Government. But *nous verrons*. There is little doubt, however, but they have been for some time instigating the neighboring Indians to acts of depredation and murder on California immigrants.

December 15th, 1857.—To-day the mortal remains of Corporal Boland, G Company, Fourth Infantry, were brought to garrison. He was drowned on the 15th instant, while attempting to swim across Mill Creek. He was carrying the mail at the time from Portland, *via* this post, to Fort Hoskins. The mule, after floating down the stream a considerable distance, found its way out, and the "mail" was recovered.

December 26th, 1857.—A general court-martial convened at this post on the 24th, and adjourned on the 25th instant. The members present were: Captain D. A. Russell, Fourth Infantry, Lieutenant Henry C. Hodges, Fourth Infantry, Lieutenant Philip H. Sheridan, Fourth Infantry, Lieutenant Nathaniel Wickliffe,

Ninth Infantry, Lieutenant Wm. T. Gentry, Fourth Infantry, and Wm. B. Hughes, Ninth Infantry. Captain David R. Jones, Assistant Adjutant-General, was Judge Advocate.

Lieutenants Hodges and Gentry left for Fort Hoskins yesterday morning, and the other gentlemen, except Sheridan, started for the same post this morning, where another court-martial is to be held—they having tarried a day to take a Christmas dinner with us. Our Christmas, by the by, went off quietly. We had the usual *sine qua non* for dinner—a fat turkey—which is a great rarity in this Territory. From the general mildness of the climate, one would suppose wild birds of this species to be abundant on this coast, but it is credibly asserted that there is not one on this side of the Rocky Mountains. Perhaps the varmints have exterminated them by destroying their eggs. The polecat, or skunk, is the most mischievous in this line; this country is overrun with them. Since the underpinning of our quarters, they have discovered that the latter affords a most pleasant and safe retreat from the rain and snow, and have, accordingly, made some very snug little subterranean passages beneath the foundation walls. They seem to take it for granted that we admire the fashionable perfume, musk, and have charitably determined to give us a benefit. I have returned the compliment by preparing for them, every night, a nice little piece of meat in a box trap, and when one is enticed into this snug little place, he is kindly conveyed some two hundred yards from the quarters, and a dose of lead gently administered from a double-barrelled shot-gun, thus demonstrating to them the falsity of the philosophical dogma, that matter is impenetrable. I have composed, in this manner, some sixteen of them, and believe that we shall, in the future, have a little rest.

It seems from the official reports of Colonel Albert S. Johnson and Colonel Alexander, that the Mormons captured and burnt three supply trains belonging to the Utah expedition, consisting in all of seventy-five wagons.

"On the morning of the 5th of October the Mormons burned two trains of Government stores on Green River and on the Big Sandy, and a few wagons belonging to Mr. Perry, Sutler of the Tenth Infantry, which were a few miles behind the latter train."—Extract from Colonel E. B. Alexander's Report to the Adjutant General, dated Camp Winfield, Utah Territory, October 9th, 1857.

This occurred on Green River, some ninety miles to the rear of the vanguard of the army under Colonel Alexander. There was no escort with these trains at the time. No one was killed—the teamsters being permitted to retain four wagons and sufficient provisions to last them to Fort Laramie, where they were ordered by the Mormons to return. At the time of this occurrence, Colonel E. B. Alexander, of the Tenth Infantry, with the advance, was at Hanes' Fork, off Green River, awaiting the arrival of the commander of the expedition, Colonel Albert S. Johnson, of the Second Cavalry. From his official letter to the Adjutant General, dated Camp Winfield, Utah Territory, October 9th, 1857, it appears that Brigham Young had directed him to return forthwith from the Territory, and had sent him his proclamation forbidding the entrance of armed forces into the same, and had, at the same time, informed him, that if the United States troops would surrender their arms and ammunition they might remain where they were for the winter, but should return to the States in the spring. The Colonel acknowledged the receipt of the Governor's letter, and informed him that the United States forces were there by instructions from the President of the United States, and that he was awaiting the arrival of the commander of the expedition, whose orders would be obeyed. He reports that he will be able to resist any attack from the Mormons, and might, perhaps, be strong enough to act on the offensive when the troops should have all come up, and that his provisions would last about six months. Colonel Johnson was met by the expressman who brought Colonel A.'s letter two hundred miles west of Fort Laramie on his way to overtake the latter.

One of the most ridiculous reports that has tended to excite the Mormons to their present state of rebellion, was that all the soldiers to be sent among them were to draw double rations in order to enable them to support a wife, who was to be seduced from the Mormons. This rumor was founded upon the fact that Harney was ordered to establish in Utah two or three double-ration posts—that is, posts where the commanding officer would be entitled to double rations. These extra rations are allowed commanding officers upon the presumption that they do most of the entertaining. A great mistake, by the by, for this is generally done by the bachelor mess.

January 14th, 1858.—Our little coterie consists at present of Captain D. A. Russell, Lieutenant P. H. Sheridan, Fourth Infantry; Messrs. Ingalls and Foster, the Sutlers; Mr. W. Holley, Acting-Assistant-Quartermaster's Clerk, and myself. We get along smoothly and pleasantly together. Our new quarters are plainly but handsomely finished, and we have taken pains to furnish them accordingly. Could our Eastern friends drop in upon us for awhile, they might be surprised at the air of comfort surrounding us. If we could always have pleasant houses like these for winter quarters, we would cheerfully campaign during the entire summer. But, oh, how checkered is army life! At this very time our military friends of the Mormon expedition are perhaps barely sheltered under canvas tents on the snow-covered plains of Utah, surrounded by enemies many times their number, who are urged on to deeds of treason, violence and blood against their race and countrymen, by the most sensual and revolting species of superstitious fanaticism that has blinded humanity since the wars of Mahomet. We are daily expecting orders to proceed thither—*i.e.*, the majority of us. Were we all to leave, another Oregon war would soon be engendered between the restless whites and dissatisfied Indians. It is not possible or necessary to send a military force from here this winter. It would perish in the mountain snows. But it can be concentrated and fully equipped to make an early start in the spring. Similar expeditions will probably be dispatched from California and the western frontier about the same time.

January 29th, 1858.—The news from the Utah Expedition, *via* the Atlantic States, is up to November 1st, and not very definite. It seems that four or five Mormons had been captured and one or two killed. They, with others, had been following in the rear of the army, stealing cattle. By the way of California, however, we have news from Salt Lake up to December 13th, 1857. The whole force under Colonel Johnston had arrived in the Territory of Utah and were posted at Fort Bridger, and other points in its vicinity. The Mormons, on abandoning, set fire to the fort; also burnt up all the grass in the neighborhood. They had stolen some twelve hundred cattle from the troops. The latter had retaliated by capturing a larger number from the Mormons. Governor Cummings issued his proclamation from Fort Bridger. It is rumored that Brigham Young had remarked in the Tabernacle that he was willing to admit Cummings, but not the troops.

April 29th, 1858.—On last Monday week, I took a trip to Portland, and also made a flying visit to Vancouver. The latter is as beautiful as ever. Of course, I mean the fort. The town is a miserable dirty village, full of liquor shops and discharged soldiers. Portland presents a very neat, flourishing appearance, and bids fair to become a large commercial city. At the latter place I succeeded in purchasing a splendid saddle and buggy horse, known all over the Territory. He is, beyond doubt, the finest saddle animal in Oregon. I got him for three hundred dollars; his value until lately has been five hundred dollars.

On Friday, Captain Russell and myself started for

home, where we arrived the following day at 4 P. M.—distance, sixty miles. We could have come through in a day had we been in a hurry.

There has been considerable excitement among the Indians on this reservation within the last fortnight. Old Sam's band of Rogue River's threatened to leave the reservation, and return to their old homes in Southern Oregon. The Rouge River's at the Siletz, and the Coast Indians, from the neighborhood of Port Orford, also declared their determination to go back. The celebrated chief, John, seemed to be the prime mover in the ferment at the Siletz. Himself and son were arrested about eight days ago, shackled, and taken to Fort Vancouver. The immediate cause of his arrest is said to be a threat to take Agent Metcalf's life. The Agent's brother, who is living with him, was wounded not long since by an Indian.

The Indians east of the Cascades are also becoming troublesome again. Nine head of cattle, belonging to a Mr. Davis, living in the vicinity of Fort Walla Walla, and thirteen head of the United States Commissioner's, at the latter place, were run off by the Palouse Indians on the 13th of April. A detachment of troops were sent in pursuit, but the Indians refused to give up the cattle. A row may be the consequence. It is also reported that two white men, on their way to the Colville mines, were killed by the Indians, not very far from Fort Walla Walla, a few weeks since.

The Willamette Valley now presents a beautiful appearance. Large crops of oats and wheat have been put in this season by the farmers, but, as is usual in this country, the harvest will probably be an expensive one, in consequence of so many persons leaving the Territory for the newly discovered mines on Fraser and Thompson's Rivers in the British possessions. A mining excitement springs up ever Summer and causes nearly all the laborers and mechanics to quit their ordinary duties, which pay them surely and well, for an uncertain livelihood in the mines.

May 27th, 1858.—We have received two Eastern mails since my last remarks—one on the 12th, the other on the 25th instant.

Congress is still harping on the subject of "bleeding Kansas," to the detriment of a vast deal of important unfinished business. It has only passed a few bills; one is for the raising of three regiments of volunteers—two for the suppression of the Mormon rebellion, the other to guard the frontier of Texas.

No late reliable news from Utah. In alluding to the Mormon difficulties, I should have added that the United States Utah forces are being reinforced by troops sent *via* Fort Leavenworth. Some started in the latter part of March—others were to go in April and the present month. General Persifer F. Smith, General William S. Harney, and Colonel E. V. Sumner, have been ordered to join the Utah Army.

The Civil Commissioners have been sent thither to hold counsel with Brigham Young, and prevent, if possible, bloodshed. They are Ex-Governor Powell, of Kentucky, and Major Ben. McCullough, of Texas.

Under date of April 29th, I mentioned the rumor of two men having been massacred near Fort Colville, in Washington Territory, and of some animals having been stolen from Fort Walla Walla by the Indians. It has since been contradicted that any men were killed, but there is no doubt as to the stealing of the cattle. The commanding officer of Fort Walla Walla, Colonel Steptoe, shortly after the stealing of the cattle by the Indians, started out into the Indian country with three companies of Dragoons, and a detachment of twenty-five Infantry. Our expressman brings a letter from an officer at Fort Vancouver stating that information has just been received, *via* express, from Fort Walla Walla, that Colonel Steptoe had had a fight with the Indians, and been defeated—losing one-half of his command, all his provisions, most of his guns, and all the horses but fifty. The news was brought to Fort Walla Walla by Indians, and was believed there, although not confirmed by any information from Colonel Steptoe or his officers. If there be any truth in the matter, it will be confirmed in a few days.

CHAPTER XXIX.

FORT YAMHILL—FINANCIAL RUIN.

Steptoe's Defeat—Chief John and Son Raise a Row on Board Ship and Get Wounded—Thirty Thousand Persons gone to Fraser River Mines—A Party of Ninety Miners under Robertson driven back by the Indians East of the Cascade Mountains—Financially Ruined—The Mormon Troubles Ended—A Campaign to be made against Confederate Indians in Eastern Washington and Oregon—Rumored Fight with the Indians by the Troops under Colonel Wright.

June 4th, 1858.—The rumor alluded to above in relation to a fight between the United States troops and Indians is partly correct. The facts are these: On the 6th ultimo, Colonel E. J. Steptoe, Ninth Infantry, started from Fort Walla Walla, in Washington Territory, for an old Hudson Bay trading post, Fort Colville, with portions of C, E, and H Companies, First Dragoons, and a detachment of twenty-five men of the Ninth Infantry, and the following officers: Captain C. S. Winder, and H. B. Fleming, Ninth Infantry, Captain O. H. P. Taylor, and Lieutenants D. McM. Gregg, James Wheeler and William Gaston, First Dragoons—in all, one hundred and fifty, besides the packers. The object of the expedition is not precisely known, but seems to have been more to give the troops some experience in campaigning than anything else. It is certain, however, that they had no idea that there would be any resistance offered them.

On leaving camp, on the morning of the 16th, they were told that the Spokanes had assembled and were ready to fight. Not believing this report, the march was continued until about eleven o'clock, when they found themselves in the presence of six hundred warriors in war costume. The command halted to have a talk. The Spokanes said they heard the troops had come out to wipe them out, and that they were ready to fight, and the troops should not cross the Spokane River. The Indians were well mounted, principally armed with rifles, and flanked the troops at a distance of one hundred yards. After some talk, Colonel Steptoe told his officers they would have to fight, but to let the Spokanes fire the first gun. The troops marched a mile, had another talk; no result except the most insulting demonstrations from the Indians. The troops were kept in the saddle three hours ready for an attack. The Indians dispersed at sunset.

On the morning of the 17th, the command started for the Palouse, marching in the following order: H Company in advance, C in the centre, with the packs, and E in the rear. About 8 A. M., Indians appeared in great numbers to the rear of the column, and just as the advance crossed a small stream, commenced firing. In twenty minutes the firing became continuous. Towards evening the troops' ammunition began to give out. Abandoning everything, they mounted their horses and left the hill at 9 P. M., and after a ride of ninety miles, mostly in a gallop, and without a rest, reached Red Wolf's crossing on Sucker River the next evening and were met by their friends, the Nez Perces. They had two officers, five men, and three friendly Indians killed, and ten men wounded—Sergeant Ball, of H Company, missing. The officers killed were

Brevet-Captain O. H. P. Taylor, and Lieutenant Gaston, First Dragoons. The former was shot through the neck ; the latter through the body. Thirty horses killed in action ; none captured by the Indians. The two howitzers were abandoned with other things. Number of Indians killed not known ; Lieutenant Gregg could count fifteen, and says the Indians acknowledged to have had forty wounded.

Captain Taylor was formerly stationed at this post, Fort Yamhill, whence he was ordered to Walla Walla about a year since. Shortly thereafter he went to the States, and returned this last Spring with his wife and two children. They had not got comfortably fixed at Fort Walla Walla ere he was ordered out on the above expedition. He was an accomplished gentleman and a gallant officer. An intimate and dear friend of mine. How sad his fate, and the bereavement of his widowed wife and orphaned children.

June 13th, 1858.—Sergeant Ball, alluded to above as missing, found his way into Fort Walla Walla some five or six days after the command returned. He was several days without food. It is now reliably reported that during the retreat of the troops, two men were left behind on account of their horses failing—Sergeant Williams (wounded) and a private soldier. They fell into the hands of the Indians, who told them to swim Snake River for their lives. They accordingly jumped in and made for the opposite shore, here some five hundred yards distant, the Indians in the meantime shooting at them. The private soldier reached the opposite shore and Fort Walla Walla in safety ; the Sergeant was supposed to have been shot in the water.

June 29, 1858.—The steamship "Pacific" arrived at Portland on the 19th instant, bringing three companies of artillery. The mail steamer reached there a few days afterwards with one more company, and the Commander of this Department, Brevet Brigadier-General Newman S. Clarke, together with his staff. Companies I and K, Third Artillery, and D, Fourth Infantry, are ordered to come up on the next steamer. E Company, Fourth Infantry, is ordered up from Fort Jones by land. The four companies of artillery already arrived are A, B, D, and M. The General's Aide-de-Camp, Lieutenant Henry H. Walker, Sixth Infantry, arrived here last Friday, and left for Fort Hoskins on Sunday—thence will return to Fort Vancouver. The object of his visit seems to be to ascertain whether any troops can be spared from either of these two posts, to join the expedition now being organized to proceed against the hostile Indians in the North. There is only one company at each of the three posts which guard the reservation—viz: at Fort Yamhill, Hoskins, and Umpqua.

Mr. W. informs us that Old John, the celebrated Rogue River chief, and son got into a row on their passage to California, in the steamer before the last. It seems that the Sergeant in charge had occasion to take them to the lower deck, when they grappled him and succeeded in securing his pistol, with which they commenced firing, both at the Sergeant and the persons who attempted to come to his rescue, whereupon one of the officers shot Old John through the nose and his son in the leg, which had to be amputated on his reaching San Francisco. It is thought that Old John and son supposed they were being taken to the lower deck to be hung—hence their conduct. It is a very unfortunate affair, and will greatly impair the confidence of the Indians in the Whites.

The Fraser River mines excitement increases. Thousands of persons are going thither from California, and hundreds from Oregon.

July 17th, 1858.—The farmers in this vicinity commenced harvesting about eight days ago, and have already cut the most of the grain sown last fall. That put in this spring is not yet mature. The crops are unusually heavy. In consequence of the late rains, and unreasonably cool weather, there is considerable smut in the wheat. The harvest is hurried through, in order that the people may go to the mines on Frazer and Thompson's Rivers, in the southern part of the British possessions. The excitement about the mines is extraordinary. It is estimated that between twenty-five and thirty thousand persons have already started thither from California, nearly all of whom are at different points in the vicinity of the mouth of Frazer River, seeking a good trail to cross the Cascade Range of mountains. Very few had, at last accounts, reached the mines; and, as speculators, particularly the steamship companies, have great interest in keeping up the excitement, it is feared the richness of the mines is overrated, and that thousands of persons have left much better mining claims in California than they will get in the north. If the reports of abundance of gold are confirmed, it will be a snug thing for that section of country, and also for our adjoining Territory,

Washington. The most intense excitement prevails about which is the best route to the gold region. Some contend for that up the Columbia River and by way of the Dalles; others say that a much shorter, and in other respects, equally as good a trail, can be found across the Cascade Range at Bellingham Bay. Oregonians, of course, go in for the former; but the present Indian hostilities on that route have hitherto prevented many from attempting to go that way. A party of about ninety men, under Captain Robertson, started from the Dalles some six weeks ago for the mines by that route, but were driven back by the Indians, with a loss of two men killed, several drowned and wounded, and all their pack animals, provisions, etc. Larger parties have since gone out with stock, and others are preparing to depart, through the same section of country. Our old friend, the ex-Superintendent of Indian Affairs, General Palmer, in one of the number. If the mines are no failure, a flourishing town must be built on this coast, in close proximity to the golden region. The great question is, where it shall be. The little town of Victoria on Vancouver's Island, in the British possessions, is at present the center of attraction. Town lots, which were not worth ten dollars previous to the excitement, are now renting there for one hundred and twenty-five dollars per month. Real estate in San Francisco, Sacramento, and throughout California is rapidly decreasing in value, in consequence of the vast drain upon the population. Flour, beef, and other provisions are rising rapidly in price in Oregon and Washington Territories. Speculators are hurrying all over the country, buying up all they can get at double what they were worth a few weeks ago.

The troops expected by the last steamer arrived at Fort Vancouver. Captain H. M. Judah's company from Fort Jones, which came up by land, will also get there to-day. Two columns are to proceed against the hostile Indians—one battalion of nine companies, being four of the First Dragoons, four of the Third Artillery, and one of the Ninth Infantry, under Colonel George Wright, is to start from Fort Walla Walla; and another of five companies, that is, three of the Ninth and two of the Fourth Infantry, under Major Robert S. Garnett, from Fort Simcoe. They expect to get off by the first of August.

There is really no news at this post of importance. A general court-martial was convened here on the 15th and adjourned on the 16th instant, of which I was Judge Advocate. The members were: Captain David A. Russell, Lieutenant Henry C. Hodges, Fourth Infantry, Lieutenant Joshua W. Sill, Ordnance Department, Lieutenant Phillip H. Sheridan, and Lieutenant William T. Gentry, Fourth Infantry. Only three cases tried—two of which were for desertion.

FORT YAMHILL, O. T., August 4th, 1858.

I am now financially a ruined man. All my savings have been lost by the carelessness of an agent. Having good health and a large though laborious private practice in the vicinity of this post, I shall work harder than ever to secure a few thousand dollars to give me a start in civil life. This can be accomplished in a year or two—then good-bye to the army, frontier isolation, and further dependence on unreliable agents. If I were now to resign, which I am half inclined to do, my practice in the Willamette Valley would soon make up my losses; but city practice, although slower in the beginning, affords a better chance for distinction in the long run—so I shall strike for that or nothing.

As my financial troubles alluded to above are analagous to those of army officers generally, who are under the necessity of employing agents to preserve their small savings, I shall give a general statement of the same:—

On coming to this coast I left a portion of my means loaned out on interest, and secured by bond and mortgage upon real estate in New York. Bringing the remainder with me, and placing it in San Francisco with an agent, who, from having once been an esteemed officer of the Army, of good financial ability, had the entire confidence of every military man in California.

This gentleman having explained to me the various methods he had under his control for investing the funds of his clients, I chose that of security by bond and mortgage upon real estate, as the safest, although yielding the smallest interest. From time to time I added a little to the amount left in his possession.

After a short service in Oregon, I learned that my agent had ceased to carry on a legitimate banking business, though this was paying him well, and had embarked pretty extensively in buying and selling of mining stock. Fully appreciating the hazardous character of mining stock speculation, I made some inquiries as to whether my money was really invested as requested, and was annoyed to find that it was not. After a tedious correspondence on the subject I succeeded in having it placed out on mortgage, as directed.

In January of last year, a friend returned from Portland with the news of my agents' failure, and added that nearly every Army officer on the Pacific Coast had thereby been plunged in penury. Seeing the necessity of preventing the note owing to me, and then nearly due, from being paid into the hands of my agent, I hastily drew up a revocation of my power of attorney to him, and appointed a new attorney. I had the new instrument executed before a neighboring Justice of the Peace. But it being essential to secure a certificate from the County Clerk, to the effect that the officer before whom the letter of attorney was executed was really a Justice of the Peace, I rode twenty-five miles through one of the deepest snows that had ever fallen in Oregon, to Dalles, the County Seat. On arriving there the office was closed. I then continued a few miles further to the residence of a lawyer, who, unfortunately, told me that in order to make my paper legal I must go eight miles further to Salem, and get the power of attorney executed before a notary public. Contrary to my own judgment I followed his advice. This extra trip took up so much of my time that on returning to the Fort I found the expressman had already departed for Portland with the mail, thus causing a detention of a fortnight more before my document could possibly go down on the steamer. On the next trip of the latter she was detained ten days by ice in the Columbia River. To add still further to my troubles, my power of attorney was returned from San Francisco, to be certified to by the County Clerk, as I had at first intended.

However, the instrument ultimately reached its destination just in time, and my funds were forwarded to my agent in New York, who was directed to invest them, together with the amount left under his supervision on my departure for the Pacific Coast, in suburban real estate in Chicago. Instead of following my instructions, he has kept the money in his own hands, and is now about to fail, leaving me the alternative of total loss, or taking worthless western lands.

August 17th, 1858.—Major B. Alvord, his brother, Mr. Vansycle, Wells, Fargo & Co.'s Express Agent at Portland, Oregon Territory, and son, arrived here on the 15th instant, and left for Fort Hoskins this morning.

The troops were paid for four months. They are entitled to their pay every two months, but the Paymaster rarely gets around so often.

We learn that the mail steamer did not reach Portland on the last trip until the 12th instant. She was detained by fogs, and by going in search of the steamship "Oregon," which ran on the rocks at Point Reyes on her last downward trip from Victoria to San Francisco. The accident is attributed to a variation in the compass—the Captain supposing he was running clear of the point some six miles, whereas he ran directly on it. There was a very dense fog at the time. As the vessel struck, many of the passengers sprang ashore, and some few are supposed to have been drowned in the effort to get on land. The engine was reversed immediately, and the steamer got to sea. She reached San Francisco in safety. The injury caused a considerable leak, but the holes were stopped with cloths, and the vessel easily kept free from water by bailing. Captain Patterson was in command.

It is now positively ascertained that there will be no war with the Mormons. The Peace Commissioners, sent to Utah by the President, arrived there about the 7th of July, and had a conference with Brigham Young and the leading Mormons, who have agreed to yield implicit obedience to the laws of the United States; in fact Brigham Young had, about a month previously, given up the seal of the Territory to his successor, Governor Cummings. Both the Governor and Commissioners went from Camp Scott to Salt Lake City unaccompanied by the army. The latter, under Brevet Brigadier-General Johnston, had, in the meantime, been reinforced to three thousand men, and replenished with supples, and all the necessary equipments for a vigorous campaign, in case the Mormons proved obdurate. Some two thousand more regular troops were also *en route* from the States. Also, Brigadier-General Harney, (promoted last spring,) who was to assume chief command—General Persifer F. Smith having died at Fort Leavenworth shortly after being ordered to Utah. In the early part of the Spring the Mormons commenced an exodus to the southern part of the Territory, with the view, as was conjectured, of seeking a new home somewhere in Mexico. They were, at last accounts, returning to their homes.

The army had not, at last dates, approached nearer the city of Salt Lake than Camp Scott. Many of the troops ordered thither have, since the first report of Governor Cummings that Young had turned over the Territorial Seal, been ordered to other points on the western frontier. One regiment of Infantry, either the Sixth or Seventh, has been ordered to Fort Walla Walla, on this coast, to aid in quelling Indian disturbances. In the meantime the Commandant of the Department has dispatched all the available troops on this coast to that section—the main body consisting of about one hundred and ninety dragoons, four hundred artillery, and ninety infantry—total, six hundred and eighty, with about two hundred camp followers, packers, wagoners, etc., or about nine companies, were to leave Walla Walla on the 15th instant; and the other column, of about five companies, under Major R. S. Garnett, were to start from Fort Simcoe about the 9th instant. The Indians, in the meantime, have been making great preparations for war, and state that they will not be subdued.

They have lately driven back several parties of miners on their way to Frazer River. Larger parties have since gone out through the same section, well armed and prepared to fight their way to the mines. The largest party, numbering over two hundred men, commanded by a Major Robertson, has gone out, *via* the Dalles and Fort Simcoe. Another party under General Joel Palmer, has taken the route a little further east, *via* the Dalles and Fort Walla Walla. Others are preparing to follow.

As it regards the mines, we have no more reliable information than we had when the excitement first commenced, from the fact of the Fraser River region being hemmed in by mountains. Many of those who shipped for the vicinity of the mouth of Fraser River, with the view of crossing the Cascade Range in that neighborhood, have returned in disgust. Thousands are, however, still awaiting at Victoria for a trail to be discovered. And it is now said that a good route has been found leading up Fraser River a short distance; thence up a northern branch, or Harrison River; thence across a few small lakes, and over only a moderately rough country to the mines. *Nous verrons.*

September 14th, 1858.—Very close and warm all day. Our expressman arrived on the 12th instant, bringing Eastern dates to August 6th.

The most important item of news is that the laying of the Atlantic Telegraph was nearly completed.

General Johnston's command marched through Salt Lake City, July —, 1858, in admirable order—not a single individual permitted to leave the ranks. His permanent camp not selected at last accounts. The Mormons were returning to their deserted homes.

There is a pretty reliable rumor that the troops under Colonel Wright met the Indians at Camp Four Lakes, and totally routed them.

CHAPTER XXX.

CLOSE OF THE INDIAN WAR IN OREGON AND WASHINGTON.

Submarine Telegraph—Total Defeat of the Indians by Colonel Wright's Command—The Indian War east of the Cascade Range at an End—Five hundred Passengers lost by the Burning of the Steamship "Austria"—Two children carried up in a Balloon—Chamberlain crossing the Plains alone with a Wheelbarrow—Nearly a fight with Old Sam's Band, whom the Troops disarm—"Tom, keep your gun, and let us shake hands in friendship."

September 23d, 1858.—Our expressman arrived from Portland yesterday. The mail reached there on the 20th. The most important news is the success of the Submarine Telegraph Cable. It will be recollected that the first submersion commenced August 5th, 1857, and resulted in a total failure. The second trial was commenced this last Summer. The telegraphic fleet consisting of three British vessels, the "Agamemnon," "Valorous," and "Gorgon," and the United States steam frigate, "Niagara," left Plymouth, England, on Thursday, June 10th, 1858. Owing to boisterous weather, the first splice was not made till the 26th of June, in mid-ocean. The cable being broken three times, and four hundred miles of it lost, the fleet put back for Queenstown, Ireland, and started from there on the final and successful trip, July 17th, 1858, and met in mid-ocean Wednesday, the 28th, made the splice at 1 P. M., and on the 29th separated, the "Agamemnon" and "Valorous" bound for Valentia, Ireland, and the "Niagara" and "Gorgon" for the Bay of Bull's Arm,

Trinity Bay, Newfoundland. Both ends through August 5th, 1858. The first communications through the cable were a message from Queen Victoria to President Buchanan, and his reply. After that, various other congratulatory messages passed between some of the high functionaries of England and the United States. At last dates the Telegraph Cable was not in perfect working order, and would not be opened to the public for several days.

"Down, down to its lowest deep—but late deemed fathomless—go the magic wires, upon which play the harmonies of whole peoples. Under the homes of the Leviathans, clustered in obscurity and mystery, where no human eye can reach, and where early faiths placed the water-gods, run these cunning devices by which nation speaks to nation, continent to continent, in the lightnings of the heavens. The old theory of distances, severances, and physical possibilities, seems destroyed, to be replaced by new combinations and consequences. The seas, storms, sucking-down argosies and armadas, are now compensated for by the prowess which seizes the deep and uses it for human purposes, declaiming in the language of nature itself —silent and sublime."

FORT YAMHILL, O. T., September 25th, 1858.

The rumored engagement of the troops under Colonel Wright with the Indians is now fully confirmed. His expedition, composed of Companies C, E, H, and I, First Dragoons, A, B, G, K and M, Third Artillery, and B and E, Ninth Infantry—being a total of five hundred and seventy men, with thirty Nez Perces Indians, acting as guides and scouts, left Fort Walla Walla, Washington Territory, in two divisions on the

7th and 15th of August, crossed Snake River on the 26th, where a post was established and placed under the charge of Brevet Major Wyse and his company, D, Third Artillery, and, after a hard march of ninety miles, and several slight skirmishes with the enemy, met a large band of Confederate Pelouse, Spokane, and Cœur d' Alene Indians, many of whom were mounted. Leaving the supplies and baggage under a guard of fifty-four men, under the command of Captain Hardie, Third Artillery, Colonel Wright, on the 1st of September, moved, with the rest of his command, against the enemy, who was posted on an eminence partly covered with timber, ready for battle. The foot troops repulsed the Indians, who were pursued by the dragoons and completely routed, with a loss of seventeen killed and many wounded. The command suffered no loss whatever. After defeating the confederate bands of the enemy at the Four Lakes, in Washington Territory, the Colonel continued his march into the hostile Indian country, and, on the 5th of September, met the same tribes of Indians, who had in the mean time, been strengthened by the Pend d' Oreilles. After a desultory and running fight of seven hours, the Indians were again put to flight, leaving dead on the field two chiefs, two head warriors, and many others killed and wounded, with no casualties to the troops, except the wounding of one man.

After a day's rest, the command pursued the Indians until they were entirely and totally dispersed, having a skirmish with them on the 8th of September, and taking from them nearly one thousand horses, many cattle, and a large quantity of provisions, grain, etc., which were destroyed. The Indians are reported to be completely demoralized, and willing to enter into stipulations for peace.

October 1st, 1858.—The following is a summary of the weather for the past twelve months at Fort Yamhill, Oregon Territory:

1857 AND 1858.	Highest temperature.	Lowest temperature.	Average temperature.	Number of days Fair.	Number of days Cloudy.	Number of days Rain.	Number of days Snow.	Quantity of Rain—Inches.
1857.								
October	76°	33°	52.43°	18.66	12.33	15	0	1.56
November	60°	27°	43.61°	13.33	16.66	15	0	7.58
December	56°	27°	42.44°	7.00	24.00	24	4	14.26
1858.								
January	52°	25°	38.43°	9.00	22.00	15	7	9.18
February	59°	13°	40.55°	10.00	18.00	15	4	9.37
March	64°	30°	43.55°	11.00	20.00	25	2	7.51
April	80°	34°	47.77°	15.33	14.66	19	0	2.66
May	80°	37°	52.87°	16.33	14.66	16	0	3.87
June	91°	46°	48.27°	18.00	12.00	7	0	2.54
July	82°	46°	59.49°	21.33	9.66	4	0	.0*
August	94°	46°	61.94°	18.33	12.66	4	0	.16
September	95°	41°	59.43°	21.33	8.66	9	0	4.02
				179.64	185.29	168	17	62.71

* Quantity inapparent.

October 27th, 1858.—Lieutenant Benjamin D. Forsyth joined this post on the 25th instant, after an absence of two years from his regiment on the recruiting service. He is quite a social addition to our little circle.

Our expressman arrived from Portland yesterday, bringing us New York dates of the 20th ultimo. The most important news to us is that the Pacific Department has been divided into the Department of California and the Department of Oregon. The former to embrace California, the latter the Territories of Oregon and Washington, excepting the Rogue River and Umpqua Districts, which are included in the Department of California. Brevet Brigadier-General Newman S. Clarke is placed in command of the latter, and Brigadier-General William S. Harney in command of the Department of Oregon. The latter's headquarters are at Fort Vancouver, where he arrived on the 24th instant.

The General came prepared to make a Winter's campaign against the Indians. He had ordered one thousand rifles of the best model, a large number of high-topped winter boots, and warm mittens, etc. On his arrival he found the war ended, and the troops coming into winter-quarters. General Clarke had taken his departure for San Francisco, and the artillery companies had been ordered by him to California. This order General Harney countermanded. It is thought the Sixth Infantry will be retained in California, on its arrival there from Utah, *en route* for Fort Walla Walla, as it is more needed there than in Oregon; besides, it is General Clarke's own regiment.

The Indian War in Oregon and Washington Territories is considered over. The troops are all nearly in. Colonel Wright hung quite a number of Spokanes and other hostile Indians, for their murders and depredations previous to the war. The notorious Qualchin among the number. He hung him on the 23d of September. His father, Ouhi, the head chief of the Clickatats, and a man of great influence among the tribes generally in that country, was taken prisoner with the view of sending him to Benicia, California.

He attempted to escape and was shot by the guard. All the murderers of Indian Agent Boland, some seven in number, have been taken and hung; some by orders of Colonel Wright, others by Major Garnett. The latter gentleman has started for the States with the remains of his wife, who died at Fort Simcoe whilst he was absent in the field. Colonel Steptoe and several other officers have also gone East on leaves of absence.

November 12th, 1858.—Colonel Joseph K. F. Mansfield, Inspector-General, arrived here on the 9th instant, and inspected the troops on the following day, and took his departure yesterday for Fort Hoskins.

He brought up New York papers of October 5th. By them we learn that the Atlantic Telegraph is out of order. No intelligent signals have been passed on it from Valencia to Newfoundlaed since September 4th, and a few days subsequently the signals failed in the opposite direction. It is supposed that one or more partial fractures have occurred in it several hundreds of miles out at sea.

The steamship "Austria," bound from Hamburg *via* Southampton to New York, was burnt on the 13th of September, nine days out, and five hundred of the six hundred passengers lost. Those saved were picked up from life-boats and buoys near the scene of the disaster. It seems that the captain, by the advice of the surgeon, had ordered the steerage to be fumigated with burning tar. The plan was to take a heated iron chain and moisten it with tar. The chain proving too hot to be held, the man let it fall and knocked over the tar-bucket. The chain ignited the tar. The passengers, in their ignorance and confusion, dashed water on the burning tar, and thus spread it all over the deck and into the magazine, which exploded. The ship was, of course, destroyed in a few minutes. Instead of throwing on water they should have smothered the tar with mattresses and blankets.

The papers also speak of a remarkable ascension of two children in a balloon. It appears that a Mr. S. M. Brooks was to have made a balloon ascension at Centralia, Illinois, sometime in September, but he being sick at the time, a Mr. Wilson went up, and after sailing sixteen miles, landed near a Mr. Harvey's. Whilst Mr. W. was engaged in conversation with some gentlemen, Mr. Harvey amused himself by putting into the balloon his two children, a girl of eight years and a lad of three, and he then let the balloon loose, intending to allow it to ascend a few yards and draw it down again by means of a rope. But the latter slipped from the hands of those holding it, and up went the balloon out of sight. It was carried eighteen miles, and, descending, lodged in the top of a tree, near a farmer's house, and was got down without any accident to the children. It seems that the little girl, after being up a long time, accidentally pulled on the rope which opens the escape valve, and, finding it lowered the balloon, kept on pulling till the latter descended. The man who first discovered their perilous predicament in the tree-top, was gazing out of his window a little before daylight to see the comet.

By the by, this reminds me that a large and beautiful comet was visible in the western heavens every evening from early in September to the middle of October. It could also be seen in the northeast and east just before daylight in the morning. There is a dispute among savans as to its identity. Some maintain that it is the comet of Charles the Fifth, which last made its appearance in 1556, others that it is a new comet, first discovered by Donati, in Italy, on the 3d of June—hence termed Donati's comet.

FORT YAMHILL, O. T., January 15th, 1859.

After an exceedingly laborious day of professional duty through mud, rain and snow, I was late last evening warming my feet with delightful anticipations of a good night's rest, which had not been my fortune for some time, when a hasty and loud knock at my door warned me that some unfortunate person needed my assistance. I was requested by the Reverend Mr. Chamberlain to hurry to his house, several miles in the country, as fast as possible, as his wife was very ill. Wishing that I was anything else but a doctor, I nevertheless obeyed the summons.

It being necessary to cross the Yamhill River, which was very high, we unsuccessfully attempted to get the ferryman to put us over, and were driven to the necessity of swimming our horses at the ford. On arriving at my patient's house, wet and cold, I tried to get a cup of hot tea or coffee, but the lady of the house being ill, and her husband in one of his insane paroxysms, this beverage could not be obtained. After a detention of a few hours I returned home again thoroughly exhausted. Such is country practice.

Mr. Chamberlain is a Methodist minister of fair education, and of agreeable, affable manners, when not insanely excited upon any subject. He believes himself to be a missionary, especially called by God to evangelize the Rogue River Indians. When this impression first took hold of him he was a resident of the State of Michigan; but suddenly leaving all of his worldly goods and his very interesting family behind, he started across the continent alone, taking his provisions along in a wheelbarrow. Of course, he replenished his supplies occasionally from the various emigrant parties that he fell in with; but steadily refused to journey with any of them. Preferring to travel alone in the wild Indian country and trust only in the Lord, who had called him to regenerate a morally dead, and physically dying, race of men and women on the far-off Pacific shores. By persistent efforts he at one time obtained the appointment of school-teacher to the Indians on the Grande Ronde Reservation, but firmly refused any remuneration from the Government. The agent wisely appropriated his salary in supporting his family, who had in the meantime arrived from the States.

The reverend gentleman would often take everything in the clothing and eating line that he could find in his house, and donate it to the Indians, who were at the time being well cared for by the Government, thus frequently leaving his wife and children destitute of the necessaries of life. Being put off the reservation by the agent, he went to Washington city without a dollar in his pocket, and by personal appeals to the Secretary of the Interior Department, got reinstated. The matter culminated, however, in his final dismissal from the reservation.

He has taken up his abode in a miserable old log cabin (where I went last night), occasionally working and preaching in the neighborhood, abiding the good time when all obstacles to his mission among his brethren, the Indians, shall have been removed. His faith and goodness of heart deserve better success than has thus far been his portion.

February 10th, 1859.—The present Winter has been as wet, muddy, and dreary as usual. There is only one company at this post, and four officers, including myself. We are all bachelors. Our life at present is very monotonous. The Indians on the reservation cause us a little excitement, by way of variety, occasionally. Being split up into numerous small bands, and located in close proximity, they consequently quarrel a good deal among themselves. The greatest source of trouble with them, arises from their superstitious notions in regard to the supposed supernatural influence of their "medicine man" in producing or curing disease. As the latter profess an absolute power in this respect, they are held responsible for the lives of their patients should nature claim her rights, and if the doctor be unwilling or unable to pay a fair valuation for the deceased, it is customary for the latter's relatives or friends to kill him. This was formerly a universal habit with the Oregon Indians, but is becoming obsolete. Nevertheless, there have been no less than five or six doctors and doctresses killed by the Indians on this reservation—Grande Ronde—since I came here, two and a half years ago. The Indian and Military Departments have endeavored to persuade them out of this absurd practice, and have lately determined to punish those who shall hereafter engage in it.

A few days ago, the Umpquas, having a doctoress they wished to have killed, hired a party of Rogue Rivers to murder her. Some nine of them, accordingly, shot her to death. The commander of this post, Captain David A. Russell, immediately sent for Sam and Louis, the respective chiefs of the Rogue River and Umpqua Indians, to have a talk about the matter. The latter obeyed the summons; but the former, not coming in time, was again sent for, and told to be here by noon of the 7th instant. He came, and was directed to return the following day with the murderers, or the troops would be sent to bring them and him, too. As the Umpquas had hired his people to commit the deed, he thought it unfair to have them held responsible for it, and, therefore, very reluctantly promised to comply. He did not return as commanded, and it was rumored that he would resist, should a force be sent to arrest them. As Old Sam's band of Rogue River Indians were known to be good shots, desperately brave, and armed with excellent rifles, we fully expected trouble.

The reason why they had not been disarmed previously, like the other Indians, was owing to their refusing to join the confederate hostile bands during the last Rogue River War, and the fact of their being the first to move on to this reservation.

A detachment of fifty men, under Lieutenant B. D. Forsythe, accompanied by Lieutenant Phillip H. Sheridan and myself, was dispatched at 3 A. M., on the 9th instant, in the midst of a snow storm, to the camp of the Indians, with orders to disarm them and arrest the principal murderers.

Owing to a difficulty in crossing the Yamhill River, which was very high, and an unexpected wearisome march over a mountain spur that lies near the camp, we did not reach the latter until broad daylight.

On arriving within a few hundred yards of the place, our force was divided into two parties. The smaller one, under Sheridan, was to dash on to the chief's shanty and arrest him. The larger, under Forsythe and myself, was to rush against the main village and disarm the inmates.

Sheridan took Old Sam completely by surprise, and made him a prisoner. Forsythe and myself, having further to go, were seen by the Indians, who at first fled for the timber near by; but soon rallied. A few shots were exchanged without effect, and a parley was agreed upon.

At the beginning of the excitement, the chief's son, a lad of twelve years, rode several times within forty yards of the soldiers, making the most insulting demonstrations. On his last attempt Forsythe declared that he would stand it no longer, and raised his rifle to fire at the little fellow, but was restrained on my hastily reminding him of the boy's extrême youthfulness.

Whilst the parley was going on, the majority of the Indians on one side, and the troops on the other, were arranged in two parallel lines, at a distance of forty yards apart. A few of the former were hidden behind their shanties, with their guns already pointed towards us. After thus standing face to face in the cold, pelting snow storm for several hours, with no prospect of a peaceful surrender on the part of the Indians, Forsythe told them his patience was exhausted, and that unless they should come to terms within five minutes he would fire upon them. Just as the time was about to expire they concluded to surrender unconditionally. We then simply disarmed those in hostile array, and arrested Shasta Jim, the chief murderer.

Old Tom, the chief's brother, is one of the noblest specimens of an Indian I have ever seen. Bold as a Spartan, and with a stentorian voice, he is the *beau ideal* of a warrior. We feel confident that he never would have yielded had he not have believed that his prisoner brother, Sam, would have been the first victim of the fight.

After the Indians had, at his command, handed over their arms, he came nobly forward and gave up his rifle to Forsythe. The latter was so impressed with his noble, soldierly bearing, that he returned him his weapon, saying, with a quivering voice and tears in his eyes, "Tom, keep your gun, and let us shake hands in friendship."

Umpqua Ellick, the main instigator of the murder, was also made a prisoner, and both he and Shasta Jim were confined in the guard-house at the garrison, at hard labor, with balls and chains attached to their legs. Sam was brought to the fort to receive a reprimand from the commanding officer, and was afterwards set at liberty.

CHAPTER XXXI.

THE INDIANS AND THEIR RELATIONS TO THE GOVERNMENT.

PORTLAND, OREGON, April 15th, 1874.

HAVING given extracts from the only part of my private journal that could be of any interest to the general reader, I shall add a few remarks on several subjects alluded to in a disconnected manner in said diary—such as the Indians and their relations to the Government—garrison society—a comparative view of the climates the southwest and northwest coast.

First, then, as to the Indians and their relations to the Government. So much has been written upon the subject of Indians by novelists and others, many of whom have never seen an Indian in their lives, excepting the few representatives of various tribes who have occasionally visited their great father at Washington, that the theme has become somewhat threadbare. I think, however, that my experience will justify a few remarks upon the question, as I have seen the Indians in all their varied grades of life, from the civilized in the interior of the State of New York, and the half-civilized in the Cherokee and Choctaw nations, down to the wild Tonkaways and Comanches of our southwestern prairies, and the Snake and Coast Indians, of Oregon. I have beheld them in health and in sickness, in peace and in war, and from a position somewhat different from that of most observers. Out of the sixteen millions of those red men who once roamed abroad over the vast area of the United States, there are now living about three hundred and forty thousand. War, pestilence, and famine have made sad havoc with these original lords of the soil; and the day is not far distant when we will hear of them only in history. It is, therefore, the duty of every one who knows anything of this fast fading race, to place it upon record for the information of future generations.

Some persons look upon the Indian as essentially a thieving, lying, cruel, relentless and murderous savage, worthy of no sympathy or love; and possessing no rights that ought to be respected, who should be shot down as a wild beast, and utterly exterminated from the face of the earth; whilst others paint him in glowing colors as possessing highly intellectual and moral qualities, and as being the innocent victim of the white man's revenge. One party denies the capability of an Indian to be civilized or Christianized, and pronounces all efforts towards this result by the Government as magnificent failures; whilst others believe that it is only necessary to explain to the Indian what civilization and Christianity are, and his whole nature is suddenly changed. Others again, think that those Indians only who hover on the border of civilization, and whose habits have been changed by long and persistent cruel treatment on the part of the whites, deserve the name of savages; that to find the red man in his faithful, honest, hospitable, noble and brave condition, it is necessary to see him in his native home, undefiled by contamination with the rest of the world.

When an Indian war occurs, a larger portion of the people of the Eastern States are too willing to believe that the right is always on the side of the poor Indian, who ought to be protected and kept out of harm's way, instead of being chastised into submission to the laws of the land. I cannot hope to reconcile or control all of these extreme views. It seem to me that the Indian, in his native state, possesses but few attributes of a noble character. He is certainly treacherous, cruel and relentless. When his savage nature is aroused, he becomes a very fiend in human form, and treacherously strikes down them who have befriended him the most, especially if they belong to the white race. Yet, that he is capable of civilization, the history of a large number of tribes most fully attests. This change cannot be effected in a day, or a month, but, in its highest degree, requires many years. Under proper instruction and treatment, he can, in process of time, be made an industrious, quiet and Christian human being.

It should not be expected that any savage race could, in the short space of one generation, become adepts in the higher degrees of civilization. The most enlightened nations on the face of the globe can hardly claim such rapid advancement. It took centuries to make the Greeks and Romans what they were in the zenith of their prosperity, or the Germans, French and English what they are at present. Why, then, should we expect impossibilities of the American aborigines? My experience goes to prove that in our Indian wars the blame is not always on either side alone. Some times bad men among the Indians kindle the flame; at other times, renegade whites.

In the mining regions of the Pacific Coast, the remote and immediate causes of hostilities are too often the abuse of the Indian women by a few bad white men. The lawless acts of the latter have served to give an unjustly bad reputation to the general population of the Pacific Coast. After an experience of nineteen years in this country, I feel proud to say, that the permanent settlers have been generally disposed to treat the Indians kindly, and that the abuse of the latter has nearly always been by a few vagabonds and desperadoes, belonging to, what is termed here, the floating population—especially in our mining regions. We must not, however, cast a stigma upon miners in general, because of the bad conduct of a few of their number, any more than we should cry down the occupants of St. Louis, Baltimore, New York, or Boston, because of the acts of lawlessness in their midst.

This calumny of cruel treatment is especially unjust to the farmers of the northwest coast. Aside from moral considerations, this class of people, having their families with them, have always been particularly careful to avoid arousing the Indian's dreadful revenge. Occasionally the cause is traceable to petty thefts on the part of the Indians, and subsequent harsh punishment from the whites. Again, it is owing to robberies or murders by bad men among the former. The prime instigators in all these troubles generally escape punishment, whilst the peaceably disposed of both races become the innocent victims of contending strife. The spirit of revenge being once aroused in the breasts of the savages, they indiscriminately and cruelly slay every white person within their reach. Then comes the counter feeling of vengeance on the part of the border settlers, who call for the extermination of the Indian race as the only salvation for themselves. It is thus, by the indiscretion or wickedness of a few men, that such intense hatred is so frequently created between our pioneer settlers and their Indian neighbors.

It is no wonder, then, that the volunteer troops, called out from the smoking ruins of their homes, and the dying shrieks of their fathers, mothers, brothers, sisters, wives, and children, in the indiscriminate slaughter by the savages that ushers in an Indian outbreak, should be a little disposed to intemperate acts against the red men. Let such of our eastern friends, who think the white man always in the wrong, be placed, for a while, under the same circumstances as are the frequently unprotected and unavenged pioneer settlers, and they will soon come to the conclusion that their sympathies should occasionally be spared for their own deeply wronged race, instead of being forever extended towards their idol, the poor Indian.

The policy of the Government in placing the Indians on reservations as fast as the white settlements encroach upon their hunting and fishing grounds is, perhaps, the most humane that could be devised, provided it is carried out faithfully and honestly by its agents. When, however, the latter are appointed because of their political principles or services to any particular party, rather than on account of their peculiar fitness for the position, the poor Indian often becomes robbed of half his rights, and the plighted faith of the Government is thereby tarnished.

The old system of political appointments in the Indian Department has been found imperfect and faulty in this respect. It remains to be seen how the plan adopted by President Grant, of removing the nominations of agents and superintendents from the political arena, and getting the various denominations of Christians to select from among themselves reliable persons for these positions, is likely to succeed. In some places this method has worked admirably well. In others it has failed, because the agents thus appointed have leaned too much on the side of mercy, and delayed too long the punishment of rebellious Indians, to the ultimate damage and loss to the Government in money and valuable lives.

I think, however, the dilly-dallying policy pursued under the influence of the Peace Commissioners in regard to the Modoc Indians, in the Winter of 1873, will for all time be a warning to Christian philanthropists, and help them to appreciate more fully their duties in the premises hereafter. Therefore, I hope that the affairs of the Indian Department, under the protection of good, Christian, and otherwise efficient men, may, after a little experience, be found to work well. If a failure be the ultimate result, then, by all means, let the Government merge the Indian into the War Department, where it once was, and from which it never ought to have been taken. There are many reasons why this should be done.

Army officers are not broken-down political hacks, who for past or future services to their party, are expected and permitted to make their short term of office pay them something beyond the mere bread and butter salary generally allowed by the Government; but gentlemen holding a life appointment of so honorable a nature that they cannot afford to have their reputations tarnished by dishonest transactions, however profitable these might be to them in a pecuniary point of view. Besides, the Indian and War Departments rarely ever agree in their lines of policy towards the Indians in times of peace or war, and when an outbreak occurs they are generally at cross-purposes, until the trouble is so far under way that nothing but millions of money and hundreds of valuable lives can stem the fury of the savage contest.

If, on the other hand, the commanding officers of the various military posts, on or adjacent to the Indian reservations; or in the country of the wild Indians on the plains, who may not yet be circumscribed in their field of roaming; were ex-officio Indian agents, the policy of the Government towards the Indians could be far more efficiently carried out. The Indians of each district would have only one white man chief to consult, instead of two, as heretofore, in regard to their wishes, and the instructions of their great father at Washington; and would soon learn that whilst the latter sympathizes with his poor red brethren of the prairies and wild forests, and desires to shield and protect them while good; yet, when his anger is kindled by their misbehavior and crimes, punishment for the guilty is certain and swift. Simplicity is a jewel in all the multifarious relations of life, but eminently so in our dealings with the Indians, who, though physically men, are intellectually little children.

Of course, there are some objections to merging the two departments into one. The Indians may not be christianized as fast as by the present system, and it may be the means of demoralizing, in course of time, the army itself; for corrupt men are pretty sure to force themselves into all positions in life where much of the public money is disbursed. The latter objection holds to some extent in the present system; but the Christian societies themselves can more easily watch their appointees than it is possible for the Government to do.

The plan commonly adopted of placing these unfortunate people on reservations, and providing for their physical and moral wants, until they can take care of themselves, is not only dictated by the common principles of humanity, but is found by experience to be the most economical and prudent mode of dealing with them.

The vast herds of buffalo which for ages have roamed over the plains, affording lodges, clothing, and food for the wild prairie tribes, have been so wantonly slaughtered by traders, sportsmen, and tourists, as well as by the improvident Indians themselves, that the latter can look to this, their natural source of physical sustenance, but a few years longer at furthest. Likewise, the deer and elk of the mountains, and the fish of the rivers of the Pacific Coast are fast disappearing; and even where they still abound, are claimed by other men, of a race antagonistic to the original owners of the soil. What then must become of these poor creatures if the Government should listen to the hue and cry of some of our people, and fail to lend a helping hand in time of need. Robbery and bloodshed would, of course, predominate along the extensive line of our frontier. For no race of men will suffer the pangs of nakedness and hunger without an effort to sustain their lives by stratagem or force, if no other means are at their command. Let them work as white men do, some would reply. But in order to work they must first be taught how, and afterwards have employment furnished them. This can only be done at the commencement on reservations, where they can be taught and induced to work for themselves. For nobody is willing to employ an uncouth savage to perform labor on his farm, or in his shop, or about his house, when he is aware that he can do nothing right except by constant watching. One might as well think of employing an insane person as an Indian fresh from the haunts of his native home, whose sense of right and wrong is, in most respects, so radically at variance with the common precepts of morality and religion. Continue to place them on reservations, and provide for their wants awhile; and even though their morals in some respects become corrupted by contact with a few bad white men, who occasionally get access to these new abodes of the red men, this cannot occur to the same extent as when they are left to shift entirely for themselves.

Having thus glanced at a few of the practical questions growing out of our relations with the Indians, it might be expected that some general allusions should be made upon the various theories in regard to the origin of this race of human beings. Are they native to the manor born? Have they a common origin with the rest of mankind, from the original parent stock in Eden, and been propagated on the American Continent by straggling parties from Asia or Europe? Are they a cross between the Asiatic or European and an original race native to this continent?

I am satisfied that no amount of traveling among the Indians can ever furnish sufficient data upon these interesting questions to satisfy conclusively the inquiring mind. Arguments of almost equal pertinence and force can be advanced upon each and all of these puzzling human problems. Some investigators claim that the Indians are a separate and distinct people from all other nations and races—springing from one or more parent stocks originating on the American Continent. Others maintain that they have their origin in common with the races of Europe and Asia, in our original ancestors, Adam and Eve; and that in some remote period in the dim past a few persons from Asia, by accident or otherwise, found their way in boats across Behring's Straits to the northwest coast of America, and thence, in due coure of time, spread their progeny all over North and South America and the adjacent islands. They adduce in support of this theory the striking resemblance in features and languages of all the tribes to each other, and claim that the language is traceable to a common root, which is exotic. A third party believe that a parent stock native to this continent has been engrafted with the ten lost tribes of Israel. They think that the character and conformation of the heads of the aborigines, and many of their customs, indicate that they have Jewish blood in their veins. The very general Indian custom of worshiping the Great Spirit—instead of stocks, and stones, and idols, as the ancient heathens and pagans did—is adduced in support of this theory. Also the facts that the Indians are divided up into tribes and bands, under the authority of captains and chiefs, and have their prophets and high priests (medicine men), and make their women in all religious festivals and ceremonies keep entirely separate from the men—like the Jews—are alleged as additional proof. They also claim a resembance in the modes of courting and marrying by the giving of presents, etc.

Some authorities would have us believe that the wild Indians of the southwestern plains, especially the Comanches, are entirely different in appearance and habits from the numerous tribes that once existed east of the Mississippi, and present a striking resemblance to the Arabs. It seems to me utterly impossible for any person, at this late period, to determine fully the origin of this singular race of human beings. The more one endeavors to inquire into the arguments in support of any particular hypothesis upon the subject, the more intricate it becomes, until, finally, we abandon the question in utter despair of any solution whatever.

The wild Indians of the prairies, east of the Rocky Mountains, hunt and fight on horseback in the open prairie; so do some of the tribes residing between those mountains and the Cascade Range. On the other hand, the tribes and bands on the Pacific Coast, west of the Cascade Mountains, live, hunt, and fight mostly on foot, and under cover of rocks and trees, like the Indians who formerly inhabited the country between the Mississippi River and the Atlantic Ocean.

Nearly all of the Indians west of the Rocky Mountains, though using the bow and arrow when the fur traders first came among them in the earlier part of this century, have learned to handle the rifle with fearful accuracy and skill. This is pre-eminently the case with those bands who formerly inhabited the country adjacent to the upper part of Rogue River and its tributaries, in southern Oregon—especially the bands of Old Sam, John, George, and Limpy—who took such a prominent part in the Rogue River war of 1855 and 1856, and were finally subdued by the troops and forced to go on the Coast Reservation, where they are at this time. It is also true of that other band of Upper Rogue River Indians, who were not parties to General Palmer's treaty of 1855, or participants in the war that subsequently followed, and who were consequently not removed on the same reservation with their neighbors, but allowed to remain a while longer in their own country. I allude to the Modocs, whose names for Indian treachery and Spartan bravery have lately attracted the attention of the civilized world.

It is said that the Comanches on the plains are slow to adopt the modern improvements in warfare, and cling tenaciously to the bow and arrow, lance and shield. The latter Indians also transport their lodges wherever they chance to roam; whereas, the Pacific Coast Indians, like the tribes which formerly inhabited the Atlantic Coast, have fixed places of abode, and cherish an abiding affection for the homes and graves of their forefathers.

This feeling was a serious obstacle in the way of removing the Indians living on the coast shortly after the Indian outbreak of 1855 and 1856; and even after they were induced to go on the reservation, situated some distance north of their places of abode, and were clothed and fed by the Government, they pined for their old homes, and would often reply, when asked by the doctor what was the matter, that their tum-tums were sick — their hearts were sick. This homesickness weighed so heavily on some of them, that they actually pined away and died.

Why is it that the Indian race is fast becoming extinct? This question has often been asked, and sometimes correctly answered. The greater causes are, of course, war, pestilence, and famine. These are positive agents of diminution or reduction; but, before entering into their discussion, it might be as well to state, that for some reason or other, the Indians, whether wild or half civilized, do not bring forth offspring as productively as the white races. This may be accounted for in a measure by the Indian mothers nursing their young for a much longer period than white women do. Still this cannot be the only reason. The power of procreation on the part of the male, bears some proportion to the natural growth of the beard. The Indians being deficient by nature in this appendage, thus bear out the general physiological law.

I do not desire to be understood that all Indians are unable to raise beard, and that is the reason why we never see them with any; but do mean to assert, that if they were to cease plucking it out—as it is the custom, because they believe it a disgrace to have it—they could not produce, to the extent of the white man, this appendage, even though they so desired. This curious fact tends towards the support of the theory, that they are nearly all a cross between a very dark and light race, being somewhat analogous in this respect to the amalgam of the Circassian and Ethiopian races. The negative cause, then, of a want of fruitful reproduction should be taken into account in estimating the reasons of the fast disappearance of this interesting people.

Among the positive causes are the three just mentioned—war, pestilence, and famine. Their incessant struggles against encroachments of the whites are not, as many suppose, the main cause of their casualties in war; for, by far, the greater number perish from the internicine strifes among themselves, band against band, tribe against tribe, especially the stronger against the weaker, might being right in their moral or ethical code. These struggles have been rendered more unequal and bloody by certain tribes learning the use of the modern deadly weapons of warfare before their enemies knew of any other means of fighting than with the primitive bow and arrow. Famine has, also, had much to do in thinning the ranks of the red men.

But, of all causes, pestilence has been, by all odds, the most destructive among them. Under this head small-pox takes the highest rank. In its successive onslaughts on these wretched people, it has swept them off by hundreds and thousands—in many instances almost exterminating entire tribes—as, for example, that nearly white, and worthy tribe, the Mandons, who once lived on the Upper Missouri River. The small-pox was introduced among them in the Summer of 1838, by the fur traders, and, in the short space of two months, all of these Indians died, with the exception of about fifty, who were subsequently enslaved by their neighboring enemies, the Riccarees. Thus, also, on the Pacific Coast, in what was then called the Territory of Oregon, seven-eighths of the Indian population living west of the Cascade Mountains fell victims to this horrible disease, between the years of 1829 and 1836.

As startling as these facts are in regard to the fatal effects of this single scourge of the human race, it is not the only unseen enemy that is wont to carry dismay and death in the Indian camp. Whooping cough, scarlet fever, typhoid and typhus fevers, epidemic dysentery, and measles, sometimes produce fearful havoc with this doomed race.

It is now, and has always been, fashionable among a large class of even refined and educated people, to sneer at the medical profession as moral lepers, who, sailing under a system of high-sounding names, suck the pecuniary life out of civilized communities without conferring any benefit. Many of them go so far as to compare the condition of the whites, who are most under the influence of wise hygienic rules, imparted by the medical profession from time to time, to that of the Indians, who, they believe, in their utter ignorance, are the most healthful, because the least doctored, race, on the face of the earth.

For the benefit of such persons allow me to say that, after an experience of many years among our red and white brothers, I am fully convinced that it is mainly from the want of a practical knowledge of such principles as our noble science inculcates, that the former suffer so much more than the latter from the ravages of disease. In time of health their modes of life in the open air, and their simple diet, conduce to robust health, as a general rule; though even here the want of a knowledge of certain plain hygienic laws frequently renders them the prey of disease. This is eminently the case in malarious districts of the great west and southwest.

When a permanent camp or a military post is about to be established anywhere in a malarious region, the medical officer seeks to have it located as far away from the low lands, river bottoms and marshes as the circumstances of the case will admit. If, however, a military necessity obliges the site to be adjacent to such unhealthy spots, the side towards the prevailing winds of Spring and early Autumn is always selected so that the malaria from those places may be wafted away from, instead of towards, the troops. The most elevated situation is also preferred, if it be to the windward of the marsh; but if to the leeward, never—unless it be so high that the winds, laden with the foul poison of the lowlands or marsh, cannot reach it; or there is no suitable place on the opposite side of the latter. The Indians, in their utter ignorance of these plain facts of medical hygiene, encamp wherever they can be most convenient to water, or the best sheltered from the storms. Some few of the bands or tribes will occasionally pitch their tents, or build their wigwams or lodges, on hills or elevated plateaux, but without regard to the location in reference to the winds and marshes. Hence, they are so often attacked by that unseen enemy, malaria, which creates more havoc in their ranks than all of their physical enemies combined.

I often saw this fact demonstrated in the southwest—especially among the roaming bands of Indians—both wild and half-civilized. Coming in from their Summer campaign on the prairies, with the view of spending the Autumn and Winter near the United States military post, and pitching their camp somewhere to the leeward of the hot-beds of malaria, just alluded to, they would soon be prostrated with the various forms of malarious fevers—such as the intermittent, or fever and ague, the remittent, the pernicious, and later in the season, the winter fever; which is generally a combination of inflammation of the lungs, typhoid and malarious fevers. Aside from the utter inability of the Indian doctors to cure these diseases, it was very evident that their causes were more active among the Indians than with the soldiers in their vicinity; mainly because their "medicine men" are ages behind their pale-face confreres in the knowledge of the principles and rules maintaining health.

It will not answer to say that the cases are not analogous, for the reason that the troops are always so much better clothed, housed and fed than the poor Indians. Whilst admitting that the difference was not so marked as far as it regards malarial fevers when the troops were compelled to live in tents, which present a better resemblance than houses do to the Indian lodges, still it was always great.

Food and clothing need not enter into the scale of comparison, because the Indians use those things which are as well adapted to their habits, in a healthy point of view, as Uncle Sam's rations and blue suits are to his soldiers. And as to the many deteriorating influences of health which the cravings of depraved appetites, or the proper duties of the two classes of persons now under consideration, produce, the prejudicial is mostly on the side of the soldiers, for whilst the Indians and the soldiers may suffer alike from the occasional use of bad whisky, the night military duties of the latter, such as being on guard, etc., expose them to the influence of malaria at a time when its poisonous effects are the most powerful; whereas the former never keep up a night watch except on occasion of danger from foes.

I might mention many other instances where the ignorance of the most common precepts of that domain of the medical science which treats of the prevention of disease, caused much sickness among the Indians; but, in order not to be tedious, shall pass it over, and shall simply state, that however deficient their skill may be in the preservation of health, it is still far more so in the means of its restoration. They are entirely ignorant, for instance, of any remedy for malarious fevers, possessing the least virtue. When the poor creatures in the vicinity of the post where I happened to be stationed, especially at Fort Arbuckle, learned, by sad experience, that but few soldiers died from the same sickness that was decimating them, they became importunate for medicine from the soldiers' doctor. Of course where I could get them to follow my directions, aid was freely rendered.

In fearful epidemics among red men, they almost always imagine either that they have been poisoned, or that some medicine man has cast a dreadful spell over them. Laboring under this infatuation they are, if not old residents of Indian reservations, where they, in time, learn better; generally shy of the pale face doctor, and can rarely be induced to take his medicine properly. Their "medicine men" depend mainly on incantations in the cure of disease, as well as in diverting any impending calamity. Yet the doctors of many bands use a kind of sweat-house, where they place the patient until the skin is almost scalded off his body, and then plunge him into the nearest stream of water, the colder the better, according to their notions. This treatment is adopted in epidemics of whooping-cough, scarlet fever, measles and small-pox, and generally with the most appalling results.

The educated white doctor uses a somewhat analogous treatment, under the name of Russian baths, for a few diseases, but never for the complaints above mentioned. Hence, again, the benefit of true medical knowledge to mankind, instead of the injurious substitutes of the poor, untutored savage, and the no less hurtful and unscrupulous nostrums of the charlatan, or mountebank, who stands on our street corners, and, with blatant mouth and oily tongue, discourses upon the so-called virtues of his wonderful medicine, beguiling thousands of people, who place confidence in his miserable falsehoods and poisonous quack compounds.

The foregoing remarks in regard to the Indians in the vicinity of Fort Arbuckle, Indian Territory, are not intended to apply to the half civilized Choctaws and Chickasaws, yet even these people were, at the time of my sojourn on their western border, many generations behind the present in medical knowledge. Occasionally a broken-down white educated physician would immigrate to their country, marry a squaw, and settle down to the practice of his profession; but, as a general rule, these people had to depend in sickness, except when near a military post, on the so-called doctors among themselves, who know little or nothing of the true principles of medicine, and that little being the cast-off garments of the old-time practice of the regular profession, when blood-letting was considered the *sine qua non* in almost all diseases.

Like Dr. Sangrado, they would draw forth the life-current from a patient until his pale lips and flickering pulse would denote imminent danger of dissolution if further loss of blood were permitted. This practice, too, they would adopt in even the lowest types of the disease, such as typhoid, typhus and winter fevers. No wonder that the mortality from these diseases was often fearfully great.

At an early period of my residence in their country, I tried to inculcate the necessity of an entirely different plan of treatment in these low forms of disease, but without any encouraging results, except in my own practice, which was confined to the neighborhood of the garrison, where there were but few settlers of any kind.

In my journal are descriptions of the modes of practice in common use among the Indians on the coast of Oregon.

For some time subsequent to their removal to the reservation they gave the white physicians much annoyance by coming for medicine only on issue or ration day, and then by taking it in a most irregular and careless manner. Very soon they generally refused to take medicine from the regularly appointed Indian physician, and sought the professional aid of myself at Fort Yamhill. Although I attended to their medical wants a great deal, and, of course, lost a patient occasionally, they never tried to harm me in the least; but when one of their own doctors failed to cure his patient, and proved unable or unwilling to pay for him in the event of his decease, they often put him to death. This practice was, after much trouble, finally abandoned, because the military authorities interfered. In surgical cases they bore pain with a wonderful degree of stoicism.

During my sojourn at Fort Yamhill I often had occasion to dress their wounds and perform upon them surgical operations. In one instance I amputated the thigh of an intelligent Indian chief, by the name of Santiam Sampson. The Indian "medicine men," who are great humbugs and very jealous of white physicians, at first predicted his death; but after his convalescence had been firmly established, they devised a cunning scheme to gain a bogus reputation for themselves, and at the same time make a little raise in a financial way. Accordingly, they informed Sampson's wife that her husband would surely die unless she paid them handsomely to "mammuck-medicine" for his recovery. The superstitious woman gave the scoundrels all of the chief's blankets, horses and other chattels, for their promised efforts in restoring him to health again. The following few nights were rendered hideous by the horrid screams and yells of these mountebanks, at a distance of two miles from where the sick man lay in hospital, unconscious of the herculean efforts that were being made by them in his behalf. At the termination of their incantations, Mrs. Sampson was informed that the evil spirit had been appeased, and that her husband would soon get well. Whereupon the affectionate woman hurried to the sick couch to impart the glad tidings to her spouse. She was amazed to find, that instead of his receiving the news with a heart overflowing with gratitude for the wonderful things that had been done for his benefit by a doting wife and wise medicine men, he seized a cudgel and commenced to beat her most unmercifully for allowing the Indian charlatans to deceive her. The hospital steward, hearing the uproar, hastened to release the poor squaw from the clutches of her enraged husband. I reported the circumstance to the commanding officer and Indian agent, who promptly made the Indian knaves restore to Sampson all his goods and chattels.

The term "mammuck-medicine," as used by these Indians, literally signifies to make a mystery, the first word meaning to make, and the second anything that is mysterious or incomprehensible.

The words "medicine" and "medicine man" are used in the northwest on both sides of the Rocky Mountains, the former being derived from the French word *medecin*, a physician or doctor. It was introduced by the French fur traders, and adopted by the Hudson Bay Company in the compilation of the "jargon," so universally used by the red men of the northwest coast.

The term "medicine man" means a little more than a doctor or physician; yet the latter is a medicine man, because he deals more or less in mysteries and

29

charms in the practice of his profession. Still, among some of the tribes on the Pacific Coast, and in the northwest, on the east side of the Rocky Mountains, there are "medicine men" who deal only in miracles and other mysteries, having nothing whatever to do in curing the sick. Anything the Indian sees that is incomprehensible to him, he calls "medicine," and any professional person among the whites, practicing an art the former does not understand, is called a "medicine man."

CHAPTER XXXII.

GARRISON SOCIETY.

PORTLAND, OREGON, April 15th, 1874.

DURING my sojourn in the army, there were very few commissioned officers who were not educated gentlemen. They were mostly *eleves* of the West Point Military Academy, with the exception of the medical staff, who, besides being graduates of respectable colleges, had to stand, prior to appointment, the most rigid of all examinations before medical boards, composed of such army surgeons as possessed the greatest experience and acquirements in their profession and the sciences generally. The varied experiences of the older officers in all phases of society, and in every part of our wide extended country, and sometimes in foreign travel, rendered them always entertaining. Even the Brevet Second Lieutenant, fresh from West Point, usually possessed an inexhaustible budget of anecdotes of that classical institution, and of the many flirtations he had experienced with the fair damsel visitors, who love so well to play the coquette with the gallant cadet or lieutenant. Although these young gentlemen fall deeply in love with almost every charming young lady whom they may chance to meet, they rarely come to garrison with a bride, for the plain reason, that their pay is insufficient to support a wife; and the girls who have rich papas do not care to exile themselves at some distant frontier post, where they can only hear the fife and drum, or, at most, a brass band, instead of choice music at the opera. Yet, occasionally, one of these gay butterflies is caught by a dashing son of Mars; and, sometimes, after a few parting tears at the shrine of fashionable frivolities, settles down in domestic life in garrison as happily as though she had been to the manor born.

Officers, however, do not commonly seek to mate with mere ball-room belles, but select women for their social, intellectual, and moral accomplishments. Hence, at posts near our large cities, or in the west, not too remote from civilization, or even on the frontier, when the garrisons are large, there is often to be found as select a society of ladies and gentlemen as at any other place. But, at forts in the center of the wild Indian country, there are few, if any, ladies to soften and charm the asperities of military life.

Under such circumstances there can, of course, be no social hops or parties to beguile dull care; no delightful drives or rides over the beautiful prairies, or fishing excursions along the charming hillside streams, accompanied by the merry laugh of God's greatest and best gift to man. After one has been for a long time thus deprived of ladies' society, he loses all power of just comparison of the relative charms of women, and, in some cases, falls in love with females altogether beneath him in social position.

When an officer thus circumstanced becomes married to an inferior person, as is sometimes the case, he commits an offence toward army society that is rarely forgiven; for the social code of ethics in garrison life is, that, as all commissioned officers and their families are really but one military brotherhood, no member of the coterie has any right to thrust upon them any uncongenial companion.

A highly accomplished young Lieutenant of my acquaintance, who was stationed at a neighboring post to Fort Arbuckle, fell in love with and married an unpolished beauty, residing at the village in his vicinity, against the protests of his most intimate friends. When he found that it was impossible for his bride to maintain her position in the society of the garrison, although the ladies were liberally disposed towards her on account of her husband, he finally concluded to send her east to receive an educational and social polish.

The black sheep in military society are the officers and their families who have been promoted from the ranks. Their generally unrefined, uncultivated and uncongenial manners, make them unwelcome members of the army circle. If they are sensibly disposed, however, these little incongruities gradually wear away. On the other hand, should the new comers, instead of trying to adapt themselves to their new sphere in society, become churlish, they are treated by the other members of the garrison as intruders. Army society is essentially aristocratic.

There is a sharp line of demarcation drawn between all commissioned and non-commissioned officers. The latter may associate with the men or private soldiers, but never with the former. The wives of the private soldiers and non-commissioned officers are denominated camp-women. There is a limited number of them allowed to each company, They act as hospital and company laundresses. There are frequently many intelligent men in the ranks. All trades and professions are sometimes represented. Even editors, doctors, and lawyers, occasionally, in a paroxysm of disgust, enlist in the army. Such men, being in the wrong element, very often cause disturbances—especially the members of the law—who are famous for breeding misunderstandings among all with whom their lot is cast. Of course this remark is not applicable to the better class of that noble profession. Many of the rank and file are educated foreigners, who, being poor, enter the service for a livelihood until they can learn the English language. There being such a medley of characters among the private soldiers, their resources for diversions, when not on duty, in the way of games, plays, theatrical displays, parties, concerts, debating societies, etc., are almost inexhaustible, even at stations far from the verge of civilization.

The commissioned officers at these out of the way posts have no such varieties of amusement. When off duty they can ride out for pleasure, go a-hunting or fishing, or remain at home to read the latest news from the States, or some interesting book, or take a social game at cards—gambling being prohibited by the army regulations. Some commanding officers are very lenient about enforcing the gambling clause in the latter. Others will permit no deviation from the letter of the law. Although playing for money by a few of the officers may have been carried on privately, without my knowledge, at all of the posts where I have been stationed, yet I never saw any of it except after the Rouge River Indian campaign of 1856.

The war being over; the paymaster having disbursed several months' pay to the command; there being no chance for the officers to get away for some time, owing to the non-arrival of the steamer; and the place insufferably dull, a few games of poker, brag and seven-up, were tolerated by the colonel commanding, who, under other circumstances, was a perfect martinet in discipline. My sleeping apartment being adjoining the room in which the so-called amusement was in full blast, I can testify as to its being conducted with perfect decorum. The losers appeared to stand their ill luck with a good deal of stoicism, until the last night of the play, when a certain quartermaster made an onslaught upon the pile, and swept the table as clean as though done by a new broom. He was very popular with the officers on his first arrival, but this brilliant *coup d' etat* seemed to lower him in their estimation. For on his departure to San Francisco on the steamer, some of them were heard to say that this gentleman was only a spectator of the play until he had acquired an insight into the peculiar method of each player, when his victory was necessarily easy and complete. Although sympathizing with these unfortunate gentlemen, I could not help thinking that their loss was a just punishment for dabbling in such questionable amusement. Social games of chess and cards are probably oftener resorted to in garrison than in civil life, to wile away the time. At Old Camp, and subsequently at Fort Arbuckle, euchre, whist and brag were the most popular of these pastimes. No betting was allowed. In lieu of money we used circular pieces of gun wadding. The playing was generally done at the quartermaster's room, but on one occasion, whilst Mrs. R. B. Marcy was at the old camp, the officers, together with her husband, proposed to play a joke upon this estimable lady by pretending to gamble in earnest. The programme being to adjourn to the captain's quarters, with a shot-bag full of quartermaster's money, and commence a game of brag, with big "antes," "I double you," etc. Although one of the conspirators against her peace of mind, I could not withstand the poor woman's look of utter amazement when we began our cruel joke, so I immediately turned State's evidence by making a full confession. Our intended joke was one of those thoughtless things that most men are sometimes led into, without thinking of the consequences.

The use of ardent spirits, in some degree, is very common in the service. My temperate habits revolted at this feature of military life more than at any other. Although fond of the taste of liquor I can hardly tell one kind from another, and have from principle alone abstained from its use all my life. Neither have I ever smoked or chewed tobacco, or dissipated in any form. Consequently I have been considered by a few of my army comrades as unsociable. But the great majority of them always respected me the more for my steady habits, even though they once in a while took a social glass.

A remarkable result of my temperate life has been an almost perfect freedom from sickness, from my earliest boyhood up to the present time. Notwithstanding I was the most delicate child of my father's family, and have been exposed to all kinds of diseases, in every variety of climate, and at places where every officer and private soldier of the garrison, and resident in the vicinity, would be stricken down several times a year with some form of malarial fever.

Many persons drank in summer to prevent affections of the bowels; in winter to keep from catching cold; in the spring and autumn to keep off the chills; at night to counteract the effects of the damp and malarial atmosphere; and were often sick. I drank not at all, and, under Providence, was always at my post of duty. It will not do to reply that my case is exceptional. The common experience of physicians, who are not so addicted to the use of spirituous liquors themselves as to render them partial and prejudiced observers, will attest the fact that intemperance predisposes to all kinds of sickness. This being so, moderate drinking, as it generally leads to the too free use of liquor, should be discarded, even though it occasionally answers a good purpose. The temporary good is nearly always transitory, and followed by permanent evil. Spirituous liquors being only a stimulant, can impart nothing permanent to the vital forces. Just in proportion to the momentary intensification of force that it gives to the system, must be the subsequent depression and abstraction of force from the person using it.

There are a few cases in medical and surgical practice where it is useful; but there being an abundance of medical substitutes, alcohol could be easily banished from the pharmacopœia without impairing in the least the doctor's power of controlling disease. The habit among a large class of the medical profession of advising, in almost all cases, the use of liquor to their patients in health and disease, is helping to fill the land with a host of intemperate men and women. If these gentlemen could only foresee the vast amount of human wretchedness that follows as the inevitable sequences of their actions, they would shudder at the fearful responsibility they are assuming. Oh, the lamentable wrecks of the brightest intellects from the use of this bane of the human race!

In whatever land, city or village we go, may be found mournful examples of the blighting influence of alcohol. It fills our hospitals, almshouses and prisons, and costs the sober, industrious taxpayers of the country millions upon millions of dollars. The expense is a trifling consideration in comparison with the misery that the use of alcoholic stimulants engenders.

In the face of these facts, it seems incomprehensible that Christian people should even tolerate, as a few of them do, the use of wine at their social gatherings. It is *there*, rather than at *saloons*, that our sons and daughters generally first learn the downward way to ruin. The advocates of strong drink quote the Bible as allowing the temperate use of wine—especially the recommendation of St. Paul, to take a little wine for his stomach's sake. But, then, the latter was somewhat of an invalid, and there may have been, in those days, no proper medicinal substitute. On the other hand, the Proverbs say: "Wine is a mocker; strong drink is raging, and whosoever is deceived thereby is not wise." Again, "Look not upon the wine when it is red, when it giveth its color in the cup, when it moveth itself aright; at the last it biteth like a serpent and stingeth like an adder." In Leviticus the following injunction is given to the priesthood: "Do not drink wine nor strong drink, thou, nor thy sons with thee, when ye go into the tabernacle of the congregation, lest ye die; it shall be a statute forever throughout your generations." In another place, the Bible says, that "It is good neither to eat flesh, nor to drink wine, nor anything whereby thy brother stumbleth, or is offended, or is made weak." If the Bible had been written nowadays, when wine is associated with so many stronger and baser compounds, it is probable that its prohibitions would have been more absolute.

Some people consider their friends unsociable if they decline to partake of a social glass. A gallant and promising young lieutenant of the army once evinced a great prejudice towards me because of my temperance principles. About ten years thereafter, a ragged man, with a red, bloated face, came into my office at Portland, Oregon, and asked me whether I had forgotten him. After a few minutes scrutiny, I recognized him as the officer alluded to above—but, oh, how changed! I almost wept for the unfortunate man. Having provided for his immediate wants, I requested him to call again in the morning. In the meantime, I learned from an officer of the army, that this poor wreck of his former self had obtained, during the rebellion, the command of a regiment of volunteers; but, owing to his dissipated habits, was dismissed from the service. He then enlisted as a private soldier; but was soon court-martialed for drunkenness, after which he deserted. Subsequently re-enlisted and deserted again; that the officers of his regiment did not care to have him taken back, as he had become an intolerable nuisance.

On learning these particulars, and ascertaining that he desired to seek employment as a clerk in the Quartermaster's Department, in San Francisco, under an officer who knew him as a lieutenant, I furnished him with a suit of clothes, and paid his passage on the steamer, obtaining from him a solemn promise never to drink any more. I have not seen him since then; but have been told that he has kept his promise, and is now an honored professor in an eastern college. Examples of this nature, excepting the reformation, are unfortunately too common both in and out of the army.

Whilst stationed at Fort Yamhill, the lamented Captain O. H. P. Taylor, who was subsequently killed in Colonel Steptoe's engagement with the Indians, and myself, became somewhat noted total abstinence men; so, of course, any little joke in that line that could be manufactured at our expense was in order. Accordingly, Lieutenant Bob McFeely, the reputed joker of the Fourth Infantry, being at a reunion of the officers at Fort Vancouver, and learning that one of the lieutenants present, who was known to be a great toper, was *en route* for Fort Yamhill to join his company, in a kind and confidential tone—loud enough, however, to be heard and duly appreciated by the whole company—told him that he would find the officers at his new post very temperate men, except Captain Taylor and Doctor Glisan, who were the hardest drinkers on the coast. The lieutenant arrived at the post fully impressed with the idea, that he would soon be under the necessity of placing us both under arrest for drunkenness.

The hardships and privations of military men have a great tendency towards cultivating habits of intemperance. Many of them are shut out for months and years from all restraining influences of a social, moral, and religious character.

The majority of the frontier posts have no chaplains, so that an officer, unless very firmly rooted in Christian principles, forgets even the prayers taught him in childhood, as did a certain military gentleman, who, on one occasion, was strolling through a canebrake, near Fort Smith, when his pathway being obstructed by a log, he nimbly bounded over the same, and suddenly found himself face to face with a huge bear. Having no weapons, and fearing to budge an inch, he concluded to try the efficacy of prayer—like our modern female temperance crusaders—but, unlike them, he had forgotten how to pray. Luckily a petition, taught him by his mother, came to his relief. So, standing bolt upright, and keeping his vigilant eyes piously turned towards bruin, he said:

"Now I lay me down to sleep,
I pray the Lord my soul to keep."

As he lived many years thereafter, it is presumed that the bear did not disturb his slumbers.

The favorite stations of young officers who disliked frontier duty, and were fond of fashionable society, were those near the large cities—as Jefferson Barracks, in the vicinity of St. Louis, Newport Barracks, opposite Cincinnati, and Fort McHenry, near Baltimore. These were famous army places, where they had the *entree* of the gayest and most fashionable circles, and could attend parties to their hearts' content, and were not expected to return the compliment, except on rare occasions, when each officer would be assessed to the amount of several months' pay, to sustain the dignity of the army, in a grand military ball. All officers, but the juniors of the medical corps, could occasionally enjoy the luxury of society in and near these civilized stations. As members of this department did not belong permanently to any regiment or garrison, but were liable for duty any and everywhere in the army, it gradually became a custom to send those recently appointed to the most distant and out of the way posts, reserving the pleasant places for the older surgeons.

Army officers rarely have an opportunity of educating their children, except by sending them to boarding schools at a great distance, the mothers frequently accompanying them as their most natural protectors; so that the husband or father is often deprived of the society of his family, even when stationed at posts not too remote or isolated for their presence. Few persons can endure this sort of life very long; hence a desire and expectation among many officers to resign when they can save enough to start them in some civil employment. This day rarely comes; for, no matter how much an officer may save whilst economizing in the far off Indian country, where there is no chance to spend his salary, a few months' leave of absence, if a bachelor, or the heavy drafts on his purse by wife and children, if married, generally succeed in keeping him a dependent on Uncle Sam's rations and money until his head is gray. Besides, the longer an officer remains in the service, the more pay and rank he receives, and the less fitted he becomes for the drudgery of civil life. The love of command, which is inherent in his very nature, also grows stronger and stronger, and he cannot reconcile himself to occupy a subordinate position in the social world, where his hard earned title of captain or major would be eclipsed by every tenth man to be met on the streets of our large cities.

Let any person try the experiment of calling out "halloo, colonel!" in a loud voice in a large crowd, assembled for any purpose in our cities, and he will be surprised at the number of responses. Hence, military men of any rank in the army soon acquire a dislike and dread of having their modest titles overshadowed by the higher sounding ones of colonel and general, so common among the militia.

There is another class of army officers, who care nothing for the comforts of home life, or of society, but who delight in roughing it on the frontier, far away from the restraints of civilization. These men are never so happy as when in the excitement of the chase, or in pursuit of a band of fleeing, horse-thieving, prairie Indians. Out of such material are our great Indian fighters made. The number of this class is very small. The duties of line officers are generally far more arduous than those of the staff corps, the Medical Department excepted. Officers of the Subsistence and Quartermaster's Departments have the easiest and most comfortable positions in the service. They are generally stationed in the large cities at the headquarters of the various military divisions and departments. The duties appertaining to these departments are conducted at frontier stations, and other distant and isolated places, by a class of officers known as acting assistant commissaries or quartermasters, being generally lieutenants of the line, and receiving a small additional pay for doing staff duty.

Our present lieutenant-general, for instance, served as acting assistant commissary and quartermaster at Fort Yamhill, in Oregon, from 1857 to 1861. Little did the then lieutenant dream, when on one occasion he confined in the guard-house of that post, an old fellow by the name of Tharpe, for peddling vegetables on the reservation, contrary to post regulations, that he would so soon acquire even a much higher title than old Tharpe derisively gave him, of Colonel Sheridan. Officers belonging to the Adjutant-Generals, Judge Advocate's, Inspector-General's, Ordnance and Pay Departments, being stationed at the headquarters of the army, military divisions and departments, are generally well provided for in the way of home comforts and opportunities of enjoying society. On the other hand, officers of the line and Medical Department, during the first half of army life, are usually stationed at out of the way frontier posts, and have, as before stated, to depend mainly on their own resources for society. This is particularly the case with infantry and cavalry officers; those of the artillery often occupy fortifications on the sea-board, and are, consequently, nearer civilization than their brethren of the other two arms of the service. A certain proportion, however, of the officers of these three corps are detailed in regular order on the recruiting service, and thereby have an opportunity of spending a few years in the large cities, where the stations for enlistments commonly are. If a bachelor is detailed for this duty, he generally returns to his regiment with a recruit who has not been required to pass the ordeal of an army regulation examination, by whose kind assistance he is enabled, in due course of time, to muster a little home infantry company of his own.

A medical officer has no such opportunities, but must remain in single blessedness all the early years of his service, or choose a wife from among the few female visitors of the married officers' families. Young medical officers are usually more able to support a wife than the juniors of the line, because they are rarely stationed at places, however remote from civilization, that they do not have more or less private practice. Jealous civil physicians have occasionally remonstrated against the army doctors practicing outside of the garrison, but without avail, because it is considered that the latter are all the more able to attend to their official duties by a little extra experience from outside practice, than though they confined their professional calls to the inmates of the garrison. Besides, if this indulgence were not allowed, the best men in the medical corps would resign, rather than depend on the pay allowed them by the Government. Even as it is, many of the most energetic of them throw up their commissions after a few years' isolation on the frontier, and try their luck in private life.

A law of Congress, passed, I believe, in 1866, stopped all new appointments, and all promotions in the Medical Department of the army. The consequence being that there is now a large deficiency of medical officers. There is no economy in this law; as a large number of contract physicians have to be employed as substitutes for the regular army surgeons, to the detriment of the service, and the injury of one of the most efficient and scientific corps in the army.

By reference to the first pages of my journal, it will be found how severe an ordeal the candidate for appointment in the medical corps has to undergo; but no such requirements are demanded of the contract doctor, who may be, and generally is, an inexperienced and unsuccessful physician.

Positions in the staff departments are much sought after by young line officers. Not solely, however, on account of the social advantages designated, but because, if only having the rank of lieutenant, they thus become promoted to at least a captaincy, except in the corps of Engineers and Ordnance Departments, where there are as low grades of rank as in the line. The two former corps are generally filled by the graduates of the West Point Military Academy, who stand near the head of the class. I believe there is not a single civil appointment in the corps of engineers. There is a vast change in this respect in the rest of the army organization within the last few years, formerly there being few officers who were not West Pointers.

The reason of this is that the late civil war has developed a large number of excellent officers, who, having had a taste of the peculiar excitement of military life, are unwilling to return to the more quiet condition of civil pursuits. It is proper that the Government, in justice to these gallant men, should avail itself of their services. But let not the fatal error be committed of appointing all such applicants, regardless of the many attributes that appertain to the conscientious and intelligent officer, or the mere fact of a person holding a commission in the regular army will no longer be a passport to the society of gentlemen, as has heretofore been the case.

Although all officers of the army are presumed to be educated gentlemen, especially if *eleves* of West Point, yet there are five corps—the engineer, ordnance, adjutant-general, military justice and medical—that bear the same relation to the other corps that Boston does to the other large cities in the Union, in an intellectual and scientific point of view.

If a young man has high military, with ultimate political aspirations, he had better serve in the line, although at first the duties are more arduous, and promotion slower; for renowned generals and future United States Presidents never come from the staff corps, no matter how the latter may distinguish themselves on the field of battle. Many of our successful and renowned generals owe much, and some of them all, of their success and fame, to a staff of scientific and brave subordinate officers.

If a young officer is full of dash, and loves a rough, active life in the saddle, he should enter one of the cavalry regiments. For even in the so-called times of peace, he will find almost continued demands for his services on our western frontier, until the last of those nomads of the prairies shall have passed to their hunting grounds beyond the setting sun. This corps was formerly called dragoons. About the year 1850 there were also several regiments of mounted riflemen and mounted infantry. Like all other things where too much is combined in one, a failure is necessarily the result. Our men cannot become at one and the same time, good infantry and effective cavalry soldiers, in the short period of one enlistment, for many reasons, one of the most important of which is the length of time required to teach them how to ride. The olden time mounted infantry used to be a laughing stock to their more experienced comrades of the dragoons or cavalry.

Having elsewhere remarked at length upon the folly of our government in some of its economical paroxysms, trying to make the army almost self-supporting, and yet requiring military impossibilities of it in the way of efficiency in every branch of service, I shall simply conclude this part of my subject by quoting the defence once made by an old soldier, who was on trial for drunkenness, that "Uncle Sam ought not to expect all the cardinal virtues for eight dollars a month."

Army officers in their intercourse with each other are punctiliously considerate and polite, and avoid, as much as possible, bickerings and quarrels. They rarely have feuds so serious that the interposition of mutual friends cannot heal. When such means fail to bring about a reconciliation, sometimes a court of inquiry or court-martial is resorted to in order to rectify the difficulty. The old practice of settling disputes by a duel is almost entirely abolished.

According to the twenty-fifth and twenty-sixth articles of war, any officer sending or accepting a challenge to fight a duel, or any second, promoter or carrier of the same must be tried by a court-martial, and, if found guilty, cashiered—that is, dismissed from the service, and prohibited from ever holding any office or trust thereafter under the Government.

Partially owing to this military law, but far more still to public opinion, which is becoming in most enlightened communities nearly unanimously opposed to duelling, the practice is rarely indulged in by officers of the army. Still, the tendency to settle disputes in this way was strong up to within the last twenty years. No matter how firmly one might be opposed on principle to the practice, he would occasionally find himself forced into this senseless and brutal method of adjustment.

Once I found myself almost in this sad predicament, and never understood precisely what happy combination of circumstances afforded me a relief. There was stationed at Fort Arbuckle, at the same time I was, a Lieutenant H., who had been promoted from the ranks for gallant services during the Mexican war. He was very quarrelsome, especially when under the influence of liquor, which was, by no means, a rare occurrence. When intoxicated, he was the terror of the regiment, and of all who came in contact with him. Of course the commonest dictates of prudence caused officers to avoid wrangling with him under such circumstances. It became necessary to send to a great distance to procure a little brandy for medical purposes, as the hospital supply had been exhausted. Unfortunately, the lieutenant heard of its arrival before anybody else, and drank it all up. The sick being greatly in need of something of the kind, I, of course, felt very much annoyed, and could have preferred charges against him, which might have resulted in his dismissal, but concluded to take no notice of the matter, either socially or officially.

Shortly after this, whilst the officers and some guests from Fort Smith were at the mess table, the lieutenant alluded to the brandy affair in such a taunting way, that I became very indignant, and used language which he deemed insulting. His first impulse seemed to be to hurl a coffee cup at my head; but, changing his mind, he abruptly left the table. When breakfast was over, I retired to my quarters in company with Lieutenant C., who was rooming with me. In a few minutes H. appeared, and, with a stern demeanor, remarked:

"So you have dared to insult me."

"Your conduct left me no alternative," was my reply; whereupon Lieutenant C. stepped forward and said:

"Gentlemen, I place you both under arrest," and persuaded H. to go to his quarters, where he was kept until duly sober, he having been drinking a little. To my surprise and delight no further notice was taken of the matter, except that we did not speak to each other for some time. It was always incomprehensible to me how I got out of the difficulty. It certainly was not on account of any personal fear, or dread of being court-martialed, on the part of Lieutenant H., for a more recklessly brave man never lived. I suspect that when he sobered off, the other officers must have convinced him of being in the wrong, and persuaded him into a generous mood. Our coolness lasted about three months, when we were reconciled in rather a singular way.

One day I had my horse side-lined, with the view of teaching him to pace. Whilst going around in a circle in a corral, with his hind and fore leg connected by a rope on each side, a little stick, on which he tramped, flew up, and, striking him on the belly, so alarmed him, that he broke out of the pen and escaped into the thicket. As I was about starting in pursuit, Lieutenant H. came galloping up with the runaway animal. Expressing my gratitude for his kindness, we made friends.

Sometime subsequently he left Fort Arbuckle for Fort Gibson, where he had been only a little while when he insulted a young officer, by throwing a glass of liquor in his face, because he declined to drink with him. The other officers of the regiment advised the insulted officer to prefer charges against the delinquent, for conduct unbecoming an officer and a gentleman, as the best means of "weeding" him out of the service. In due course of time his trial came off, and he was sentenced to be dismissed. On the proceedings reaching Washington for the action of the Secretary of War, Jefferson Davis, he failed to approve them, for the assigned reason, that the conduct of Lieutenant H. was not, in his opinion, unbecoming an officer and a gentleman. How much longer the said lieutenant remained in the army, I do not know, but understood that he subsequently resigned, to accept a colonelcy under the fillibuster, General Walker, in his attempt to subjugate Nicaragua.

In the early history of the army there was a time when staff officers possessed only assimulative, instead of real, rank. This invidious distinction between the line and staff was found, by experience, to work a great hardship upon a very meritorious class of officers, and was having the effect of driving the best of them out of the service. The members of the medical corps, from serving more constantly with the line than any other staff officers, had to stand the brunt of this unjust discrimination. It frequently happened, that highly educated gentlemen, who had grown gray in the service of their country, were placed on mixed boards and councils in a subordinate position to young brevet second lieutenants. In one instance, the veteran surgeon, Hammond, was a member of a court-martial, of which his son, fresh from West Point, was president. The wonder is, that such an outrage should have been tolerated so long. Justice finally prevailed, by Congress giving the staff corps *bona fide* rank.

On entering the service, in 1850, I found, that most of these vexatious questions, in regard to rank, had been settled. Still, there was a lingering indisposition on the part of line officers to recognize this comparatively new order of things; although they dared not depart from the letter, still, where opportunity offered, they would evade the spirit of the law. For instance, in detailing the members of a court-martial, a medical officer was generally designated as Judge Advocate, who, not being considered a real member of the court, could not claim precedence over any other officer. As, however, the position of Judge Advocate, especially of a general court-martial, was considered a very honorable, though laborious one, the doctors always yielded to the force of circumstance with a good grace.

There was one question, in regard to staff rank, that

VIEW OF MT. RANIER FROM PUGET SOUND.—Page 476.

remained for a long time unsettled. It was as to whether a staff officer, by virtue of his rank, was entitled to the command of a post, or army in the field, when he chanced to be the senior present on duty. Medical officers were very conciliatory on this point, and were loth to force an issue upon it. Members of the other staff corps felt unwilling to concede any of their supposed rights under the law, so, that the War Department was finally compelled to give a decision upon the subject; which, so far as it affected the medical corps, was, that its members might claim precedence according to rank in the selection of quarters, on councils of administration, boards of survey, court-martial, and all mixed boards, but were not entitled to the command of a post, or an army, except in the absence of all commissioned officers of the line. This ruling holds good up to the present day. Until this vexed question was settled, many methods were adopted by officers of the line to bring about a decision upon it. It is related that Captain Braxton Bragg, of "a few more grape" celebrity, chanced, at one time, to be the commanding officer and acting assistant quartermaster of a certain post. In order to test the question, Bragg, the commandante, ordered Bragg, the quartermaster, to perform a particular duty. The latter disobeying, the former placed him under arrest. The case was appealed to the Secretary of War, who decided that it was an unnecessary difficulty between the two gentlemen, and added a severe reprimand.

CHAPTER XXIII.

THE SOUTHWEST AND THE NORTHWEST.

A Comparative View of the Climate, Resources and Diseases of the Southwest, embracing the Indian Territory and Western Texas, and of the Northwest Coast, including Washington Territory and Oregon.

PORTLAND, OREGON, April 15th, 1874.

As an unusual interest is being taken by many of our own people, as well as foreign immigrants, in the great Southwest, and the new Northwest, of our extensive country, it may be worth while to summarize a few of the observations incidentally made whilst sojourning in these two sections of the United States. In so doing it will be necessary to restate some of the facts found scattered in various parts of this journal.

Whilst each of the two districts possesses attractions peculiar to itself, there is hardly anything in common, either in topography, climate, productions or diseases. One is a rolling plain, with few elevations deserving the appellation of hills or mountains. The other possessing some of the finest mountain scenery in the known world.

The one has sluggish rivulets and rivers, that wearily plod their way beneath an almost tropical sun, sometimes burrowing themselves, like the Canadian, beneath their own sandy bottoms; except at certain seasons, when, swollen by recent rains, or melting snows, from along the foothills of the Rocky Mountains, they dash madly along, overflowing their low banks for miles on each side. The other having streams and noble rivers fresh from the mountains, so cool and pure that it would seem almost impossible for a country through which they take their sprightly courses to be otherwise than healthful.

Summer in the southwest is characterized by a hot, enervating atmosphere, that creates an indisposition to mental or physical labor.

That portion of the northwest coast west of the Cascade range of mountains, has at this season a dry and refreshingly cool atmosphere, the temperature lowering as the Pacific Ocean is approached.

The balmy zephyrs of the first are laden in the spring and autumn with malaria, that manifests its deleterious influence upon the human system in various forms of fevers. The refreshing winds of the second come from the ocean, as pure as the mountain streams which they meet and embrace. Even east of the Cascade Range, where the temperature is much warmer in summer than it is west of the same, the air is so dry in summer that few suffer from the heat. There is no sultry weather on the northwest coast.

The winters in the southwest are generally mild and pleasant, with an occasional snow storm in the Indian Territory and northern portion of Texas. The same season in Oregon and Washington is as diversified as possible. Immediately along the coast the temperature is rarely below the freezing point—the rains are heavy and frequent. On the Coast Mountains there is deep snow. In the Willamette, Umpqua and Rogue River Valleys, between the coast and Cascade Range of mountains, there is much rain, with occasional snow storms, the snow melting as fast as it falls, excepting on rare occasions, when it becomes so deep that the farmers, who rarely provide much provender for their stock, are utterly astonished, and sometimes ruined by the loss of their animals. A few such examples during the last twenty-three years, have at last made this industrious, but heretofore somewhat shiftless, class of the Oregon population aware that it is true economy to lay up a supply of straw, hay, oats and corn, and build shelters for their cattle, sheep and horses, even though it might not be needed for several successive years.

The Cascade Range is, of course, whitened with snow for six months in the year; and its lofty peaks, like the Three Sisters, Mount Jefferson, Mount Hood, Mount Baker, Mount Adams, Mount St. Helen and Mount Ranier, are draped in perpetual white. 'Tis a most refreshing sight to stand on some elevated point in the Willamette Valley, on a warm summer day, and gaze upon these lovely mountains, hoary with the frosts of so many years. There they have stood for centuries, watching the progress of civilization, as westward it marched along until its vanguard has reached the utmost western limits of the American Continent. Oh, how many bloody struggles they have witnessed between the red men of the forest and the white men of the east—yea, and of internecine war among the Indians themselves.

Mount Hood looms up in rugged, awful grandeur, whilst his bride (Mount St. Helen), stands serenely above the fringe of evergreens, symmetrical and lovely as on the day she plighted her love. Why they are so cool toward each other, no one has ever dared to inquire. Their quarrel must have been fearfully unrelenting, as the Three Sisters, who were bridesmaids, have never been able to effect a reconciliation; neither have the more austere groomsmen, Mounts Jefferson, Adams and Ranier.

It is only within a few years that the latter mountain, of Washington Territory, has been recognized as higher than the majestic Mount Hood, of Oregon, and the sublime Mount Shasta, of California, its height being fourteen thousand four hundred and forty-four feet. Only a glimpse of this magnificent mountain can be had from the usual courses of travel in the Willamette Valley, and along the Columbia River, as its view is partially obstructed by St. Helen. Yet now, that we have a railroad to the Sound, tourists will have no excuse hereafter in slighting this sublime wonder of the natural world.

The day is not distant when Ranier and Hood will be selected as national signal stations, from whose lofty summits signal officers will be able to scan the broad Pacific on the west, and note the approach of foreign enemies, or observe the condition of the thousands upon thousands of vessels belonging to the merchant marine and the navy of all nations of the civilized globe, passing hither and thither, to and from the great seaports now springing up on this favored coast; and of watching on the east, north and south, the long railroad trains as they skim over the surface of this continent. Or grander still, they will be great entrepots, as well as points of observation, for the future improved methods of travel and commercial intercourse, in the way of aerial cars and ships, sailing aloft in mid-air, instead of on the earth or water.

Do not laugh, incredulous reader; remember that even more wonderful things than these have been accomplished within the last hundred years. The great inventors and discoverers have been mocked and derided as fools and idiots until their wonderful achievements have astounded the unbelieving world. We are so accustomed to these gigantic results of science, that they, even now, seem trite and commonplace. Yet, many of us, like our ancestors, think that the world is so wise; that there is no room for further knowledge or wisdom, and are slow to believe what pigmies our present great scholars, philosophers and scientific men will appear to be to their successors a few centuries hence.

Returning from our ethereal wanderings, we will make a few more allusions to our noble mountain peaks. Some of these are still living volcanoes, the most active being Mount Baker, in the northern portion of Washington Territory. Owing to the numerous and ever-varying shapes of the clouds that rest occasionally on the top of Mount Hood—like our future aerial cars will doubtless do—the inexperienced observer is too apt to report a violent state of eruption where there is none. Still, all persons who have ascended to the summit agree that sulphurous vapors are occasionally belched forth, to a slight extent, from an almost extinct crater, not far from the top. This is also true of Mount Rainier, and some, if not all, of the other peaks. There is no such mountain scenery, as that just alluded to, in the southwest.

The rolling prairies there are beautiful to behold for the first time, especially in the spring and early summer months; but beauty, when monotonous, palls upon the sight—as do certain articles of food and drink when partaken of too often. In fact, any and everything lose their charms if forced upon the attention continuously—"variety is the spice of life," is as true in landscapes and climates as in anything else. I well remember my feelings of intense delight on seeing the boundless western prairies for the first time—it seemed as though they must be the most pleasant spot on God's earth for the habitations of his people. A few days of weary travel over them, beneath a scorching sun, cooled my admiration in a wonderful degree, if so paradoxical an expression may be allowed. A few years' residence taught me to exclaim with the poet:

> "E'n were Paradise a prison,
> Still I should long to leap the crystal walls."

Man's nature is such that variety is one of his imperative wants. This variety, so far as scenery and climate are concerned, can be found on the northwest coast to a greater extent than in almost any other country in the world. It is true that her forests are forever green, and, lack to some degree, the variegated loveliness of the beautiful woods and groves of deciduous trees of many of the Atlantic States, yet she has many kinds of charming trees and shrubs besides those belonging to the *genus pinus.* The southwest is, in this respect, far behind the northwest coast, as it is almost devoid of timber, except along the water courses. The forests of Oregon are mostly distributed upon its mountain ranges and the margins of its streams. Thus the Coast Range, extending nearly north and south through the entire length of the State, and having an average breadth of twenty miles, is covered with evergreen forests of cedar, spruce, fir, sugar pine, hemlock, Oregon yew, intermixed at places with white maple, vine maple, Oregon alder, balsam tree, rhododendron, wild cherry, crab-apple; and, along the streams, cottonwood, and a kind of willow, known botanically as *salix scouleriana*, also the Oregon ash *(fraximus Oregona)*.

The Cascade Range of Mountains, extending through the whole length of Washington Territory and Oregon, parallel with the Coast Range, and distant from it about forty-five miles, is also covered with similar forests. The valley land in Oregon, lying between these two ranges of mountains, possesses a few groves of a kind of oak (*quercus garryana*) growing about fifty-five feet high, and a more diminutive scrub oak (*quercus kellogia*). A beautiful evergreen called laurel (*arbutus menziesii*) is also found in many places. As a counterpart to these magnificent forests, what do we find in the southwest? A few cotton-woods along the bottoms of the larger rivers; and overcup, pecan, sycamore, persimmon, black ash, blackberried alder and red elm, along the tributary streams, which have bottoms of greater elevation than the main rivers. On the plateaux and more elevated grounds, an occasional grove of post oak, pin oak, red oak, scrub oak, blackjack, hackberry and mesquite. In some sections no timber larger than the last-named shrub can be found.

There is such a thing as having either too little or too much timber in a country. The southwest certainly has a deficiency, and probably Washington Territory has a superabundance; but Oregon has the happy medium of just enough.

Many of the early settlers in Oregon, who hailed from the prairie country of Illinois and Iowa, where timber was exceedingly scarce, concluded to locate in the very midst of the Oregon forests, where it cost them about one hundred dollars per acre to clear and grub their land; whereas, their more sensible fellow-immigrants took up claims in the beautiful Willamette Valley, where the land is mostly prairie, with just enough of timber for firewood and fencing. The former have struggled along in comparative poverty, whilst the latter ought to be rich, if they are not, with all the advantages they have had for making money, in the finest agricultural valley in the United States. There is no other country known where the crops of cereals are so abundant and so unfailing.

This charming valley lies in what I shall call the second of the three topographical and climatographical divisions of Oregon, being separated from the first or coast district, by the Coast range of mountains; and from the third, or Eastern Oregon section, by the Cascade range--these mountains running parallel to each other in a northerly and southerly direction, through the entire length of the State, the Coast range being about four thousand, and the Cascade range about seven thousand feet high. The length of the Willamette Valley, north and south, is about one hundred and forty miles, and its width, east and west, is forty-five miles. It is characterized by a mild, uniform and healthy climate, a rich and exceedingly productive soil.

The northwest winds from the Pacific, with their cooling yet congenial influence, move gently over its surface during the summer season, making work in the open air a delightful exercise, yet not chilling the growing crops; whilst the warm southwest and southern winds of winter keep the atmosphere mild and pleasant. The Cascade range also helps to protect the valley from frost and snow. The latter, however, falls to a considerable depth occasionally.

New comers and tourists complain of our cloudy, rainy winters—Californians especially. But whilst our sister State suffers from droughts and floods alternately, five years out of every ten, the efforts of the agriculturist being thus paralyzed, Oregon has in winter her few months of rain along her valleys, and of snow in the mountains, to furnish a bountiful supply of water for her farmers and miners in the ensuing summer; with just enough of rain in spring and summer for the growth of her productions. But during harvest time the weather is dry and pleasantly warm, so that the cutting of hay and grain is a pleasant pastime, instead of irksome toil beneath a broiling sun. Owing to the dry weather, there is rarely any need of hurry about gathering the ripened grain, or of putting it in stacks, ricks or barns, to await a fitting opportunity of having it threshed.

If a farmer is not able, or does not wish, to avail himself of any of the new methods of cutting and threshing his crop in the field, he can let it stand in the shock until an opportunity offers of securing it. He may sow his wheat in June and pasture it down in the fall, or put it in during the latter season, or wait till spring, and always be sure of a good yield. Or he can harvest a cultivated crop of oats and wheat one year, and depend on what is called a volunteer crop the succeeding year—that is, a crop springing up from the wasted seed in gathering the grain, without either plowing or harrowing. This was a common method of farmers when I first came to the country, nineteen years ago. The present farmers, however, find it advantageous to till the soil, as they thus secure a sufficiently better yield over the volunteer crop to repay them for the extra labor. Besides, they may be a little conscientious about reaping the fruits of the earth except by the sweat of the brow. The early settlers had no religious scruples of this kind. They would hardly take the trouble of fencing in their claims, further than to protect their gardens and fine young orchards; notwithstanding their neighbors' cattle, as well as their own, roamed wheresoever they listed over the prairies, which were clothed with the finest of wild grass and white clover—knowing that where cattle were allowed to select their own food, they would naturally browse on the sweetest and the best, and, per consequence, would eschew the oats and wheat, and luxuriate on the sweet grass that nature had spread before them. But when the wild grass became stunted by constant and excessive pasturage, and the stock range contracted by encroaching settlements, fencing became a necessity; so that at present, the greater portions of the claims are partially, and many entirely, surrounded by fences.

The soil of this valley consists of a sandy loam, resting upon a bed of clay, and covered with a thick vegetable mold. It is watered and drained by many mountain streams of the purest water. Running through the center, from south to north, for its entire length, is the beautiful Willamette River, from which the valley takes its name. This stream empties into the noble Columbia, which forms the northern boundary of the State. The former is fed by numerous tributaries, rising on either side, the larger of which have their sources in two ranges of mountains, running parallel with, and forming the western and eastern boundaries of the valley.

The Willamette is navigable, for small steamboats, as far up as Eugene, a distance of one hundred and thirty-five miles from its mouth. One of its principal branches, the Yamhill, is navigable as far as McMinnville, a distance of twelve miles from where it enters the main stream. The valley has now two railroads—the Oregon and California, on the east side of the Willamette River, extending a distance of over two hundred miles; the Oregon Central, on the west side, being completed as far as St. Joseph, on the Yamhill River. These roads will ultimately join at Junction City, near the center of the valley, and the main road continue on from its present terminus to California, with, perhaps, a branch shooting off near Eugene, in a southeasterly course, to form a junction with the Union Pacific. Other railroads are also in contemplation. The effect of these internal improvements has been to stimulate all branches of industry in the State, and especially agriculture. Owing to this stimulus, and a more than usually favorable season, the productions of the valley during the year 1873 were increased many fold over previous years. The wheat crop alone required several hundred ships for its exportation. There were lying at one time in the harbor of Portland, the metropolis of Oregon, about twenty of these vessels, taking in cargoes of grain for foreign markets.

It has lately been acknowledged by all of the best judges, that the quality of the Willamette Valley wheat is equal, if not superior, to any in the known world. The good prices brought in the fall of 1873 and winter of 1874 gladdened the hearts and filled the pockets of the farmers, so that they felt not the effects of the money panic in the rest of the Union, and in Europe. This grain is the staple production of the Willamette Valley. Under proper cultivation, its yield to the acre is as high as sixty bushels; though the average crop, under the ordinary careless way of raising it, is, perhaps, not over thirty bushels to the acre.

The Willamette Valley contains about seven million acres of farming land, not more than one quarter of which is under cultivation. It is true that nearly all of the best lands are claimed or settled upon; yet, the farms are so large, that they are unmanageable by most of the owners, who could readily part with one half, and be the better off for so doing, as they might then properly take care of the remainder. Many of the claimants hold their lands under the donation act of Congress of 1850, which gave to every white man, half-breed Indians included, above the age of eighteen, who was a citizen of the United States, or made declaration of becoming such before a specified time, then resident of the Territory, or who became a resident prior to December 1st, 1850, three hundred and twenty acres, if a single man, and six hundred and forty acres, if married, or he became married within a year after the passage of said act—one half to himself and the other half to his wife—provided he occupied the claim four consecutive years, and otherwise complied with the terms of the act. Under the same conditions and restrictions, three hundred and twenty acres were given to such male persons described above as became residents between December 1st, 1850, and December 1st, 1853, who were married (one half to husband and the other to wife,) and half that quantity to every single man or head of a family, including widows. The effect of this law was not only to stimulate immigration, but marriages; for, in order to secure the large amount of land, many men married girls not over fourteen years of age. These hasty matrimonial alliances were often followed by evil results—not the least of which were divorces.

The early settlers had wonderful opportunities for making money, as they could raise cattle, grain, fruits and vegetables with far less labor than in any other part of the United States, and find a ready market at their very doors, from purchasers fresh from the rich gold fields of California. A few years later, the gold mines of British Columbia, Washington Territory, and Oregon, and still more recently of Montana, together with the rich gold and silver mines of Idaho Territory, furnished a constant and excellent demand for the same. These extraordinary advantages of making money by our farming population, instead of urging them into unusual activity, had generally the reverse effect; as the money came easy, it was a part of their doctrine to let it go freely. Many of them, too, would abandon their farms for the more glittering, yet far less certain, chances of wealth in the mines. Unfortunately, too, these mining excitements would generally occur in that part of the spring and summer when their crops demanded the most attention. Many a man with the "gold fever" would rush off from home, with no one left behind to take care of his claim but his wife—if he had one—if not, the place was left to itself. Generally the owner would return in the winter, worse off than when he departed, and vowing that nothing would ever induce him to be so foolish again; but, like the unfortunate drunkard, his solemn resolutions of reformation were as often broken as made.

A few shrewd farmers and traders throughout the valley have often enriched themselves by purchasing stock and farming products at an enormous sacrifice from these unfortunate mortals, who would be always on the jump for the latest gold excitement, and would sell out any and everything in a hurry in order to secure an outfit. After the farmers began to learn, from sad experience, the uncertainty of mines, and that the best gold diggings to them lay in the tillage of their own farms, they remained at home, but, for a long time, exercised little judgment in the matter of rotation of crops, and of producing such things in the greatest abundance as would likely bring the best prices, the latter being very fluctuating. The rule adopted by the majority was to raise the succeeding year in the largest quantity that which brought the most remunerative prices the year previous, the consequence being, that the market was frequently glutted by almost every product in its turn. For example, if wheat was in great demand one season, then almost every one would sow it, to the exclusion of nearly everything else, and, perhaps, overstock the market. This article falling in price, and oats becoming high, then everybody must sow a large quantity of oats, which falling in price, and wheat coming in great demand again, a large crop of this grain would be cultivated, and so on. The same system was adopted in regard to beef cattle, sheep and hogs. If bacon happened to bring a high price for one or two years, nearly every farmer would stock his place with hogs.

Mainly owing to this false system of farming and stock-raising, hogs became so abundant one year in the early days of Oregon that they had to be shot by the hundreds as a nuisance, there being no sale whatever for them. Because the climate was so mild that stock could generally subsist on the wild grass the year round, the farmers would either not produce much provender, or if raised sell it nearly all off, and even burn up their wheat and oat straw. So that when a hard winter came, which was sure to be the case every now and then, the poor animals would starve by the thousands. This careless system of farming has nearly died out, being replaced by more skill, judgment, energy and science. Scientific farming, and raising of choice breeds of stock, are fast coming into vogue. No finer varieties of sheep, cattle, chickens and horses are seen in the United States than can be found on the two extensive farms of S. G. Reed and others, a few miles up the valley.

As further evidence of the late stimulus given to agricultural pursuits in Oregon, it is only necesary to state that one of our most enterprising pioneers, R. R. Thompson, has lately introduced on his splendid farm of three thousand two hundred acres, situated in the county of Yamhill, a steam plow, imported from England at a cost of twelve thousand dollars. It works with perfect success. It is an immense implement in power and size. The two engines that run it weigh ten tons each. One of these is located at each end of the field, and works the plow by means of an attached wire cable. As fast as a furrow is finished, each engine in its turn is moved so as to let the plow enter fresh soil. There are two gangs of plows, each capable of making five furrows. One of them is placed at each end of the field. While one is working the other is raised. The alternation of this action at the end of each furrow prevents the necessity of reversing the implement. Only three men are required—one at each engine and one at the plow, which does an average work of fifteen acres per day.

The present race of agriculturists possess an advantage over the old race of pioneers, in having a more regular demand for their products, and far better facilities of transportation, and they can depend with greater certainty on having help when needed, to cultivate and harvest their crops.

After the first flush times, extending from 1850 to about 1858, the farmer could not always depend on good prices for his crop or stock, no matter what judgment he may have used in its production. Neither could he always get help, at any reasonable rate, to save his crop. Thus, prices being uncertain, labor scarce, and rarely to be depended upon, and transportation to the nearest market in wagons, slow, tedious and expensive, there is no wonder that he frequently became discouraged, and made but little effort to better his condition. The era of moderate transportation, reasonable prices for help, and a more steady market, has changed all of these things for the better. So, in our parting remarks of the pioneer farmers of Oregon, let us make due allowances for the difficulties under which they labored, and pay a passing tribute to their good common sense, rare honesty and generous hospitality.

The wonderful productions of the Willamette Valley is not confined to the cereals and grasses, but extends to all of the common varieties of fruits and vegetables. Apple, pear, plum and cherry trees begin to bear earlier here than in any other country, except California, and produce most luxuriantly. Gooseberries, strawberries, blackberries, raspberries and currants, both wild and cultivated, are abundant, large and delicious.

The early settlers of Oregon were particularly fortunate in having a fine horticultural garden, established by a Mr. Lewellen, from which to select the choicest varieties of fruit trees, shrubbery and garden seeds. Orchards of select fruit trees have for the last eighteen years been a characteristic feature of the Willamette Valley. The most remarkable thing in regard to the fruit trees of Oregon is the early age at which they begin to bear. Apple and cherry trees will commence bearing at the age of three years—other trees in a proportionately short period. They soon exhaust themselves unless kept closely pruned, and much of their fruit picked off when very small and green. Fruit-raising has made the fortunes of a great many persons throughout the State. And although the time has gone by when apples, pears and plums would sell for twelve dollars a bushel, as was the case in the palmy days of the California gold mine excitement, yet the orchardist can still make money by shipping his fruit to San Francisco and the markets, where it will bring from fifty cents to a dollar per bushel. The Oregon apples are highly prized in foreign markets. Peaches and grapes do not thrive so well in the Willamette Valley as in the more southern part of the State.

Like all the rest of the northwest coast, the Willamette Valley is rich in iron, copper, lead, coal, silver, and gold. The last two metals have not been found in such abundance as on the eastern side of the Cascade range; but the more common, and, probably, the more useful mineral, iron ore, constitutes a large portion of the hills and mountain spurs lying adjacent to river navigation, as well as near the natural routes of railroads. Close to these immense reservoirs of iron ore, coal has been discovered in inexhaustible quantities; so that furnaces, rolling mills and foundries will, in the course of a few years, make the valley resound with the busy hum of thousands of industrious mechanics and artisans. There is already one large furnace at Milwaukee, near Portland, and quite a number of foundries in the latter city.

Having described the Second District, we shall next take a glimpse at the First, or Coast District, which is a narrow strip of land, from half a mile to eight miles in width, sufficiently level for grazing or farming purposes. It is equally divided between timber and prairie lands. The soil being generally rich, especially in some of the river bottoms. Fine grass, potatoes, cabbage, and a few similar products can be raised there; but most of the ordinary vegetables, fruits and cereals do not thrive well, because of the coolness of the summers and moisture of the atmosphere. The climate is remarkably uniform, there being but little difference between the seasons.

Having said a good deal about this district in my journal, I shall add but little here. Its uniform climate, invigorating sea air, and freedom from miasma, render it the most healthful part of Oregon. It is the fashionable summer resort of persons living in the Willamette Valley, particularly of the citizens of Portland. Alsea Bay, Yaquina Bay, mouth of Salmon River, Tillamook Bay, and Clatsop Beach, being the most accessible and favorite points. Although the Coast District is in itself very narrow, yet there are numerous fertile valleys leading into the mountains along the streams that run across the coast belt into the Pacific Ocean. The soil and climate in these little valleys render them better adapted for agricultural purposes than the land immediately along the coast. Yet the numerous cosy little prairies found in the valleys afford greater advantages for the dairy business than for any other pursuit. The sands of the sea shore almost glitter with gold dust. The mountain spurs, jutting out close to the ocean, are filled with copper, iron and coal. The hills and valleys are covered with the finest fir and cedar for lumber to be found anywhere in the United States. The inlets and bays abound in oysters and salmon, and the mountain streams with speckled trout.

Some of the rivers and bays are navigable for a class of small vessels. There is an abundance of game along the coast, such as canvas-back duck, mallard duck, blue-winged teal, green-winged teal, brown crane, kildeer, plover, snipe, black brant, Canada goose, white-fronted goose, blue grouse, quail, partridge or Virginia pheasant, black tail and white tail deer, elk, brown and cinnamon bears.

It is much cooler in summer and warmer in winter in the whole of the northwest coast, lying west of the Cascade range of mountains, than in corresponding parts near the Atlantic seaboard. This is owing mainly to the facts that the prevailing winds of summer are from the northwest, and in winter from the south, southwest and southeast, and that the peculiar direction of the coast line, running from the southeast to the northwest, allows the almost uniform atmosphere of the ocean to be thus carried over the whole district, especially in winter. The cooler northwest breeze from the ocean cooling the otherwise warm temperature in summer, and the warmer southerly oceanic winds of winter rendering the otherwise cool atmosphere pleasantly mild. Another reason being that a warm current setting across from Japan, and dashing against this northwest coast, makes the water of the Pacific Ocean, and secondarily its atmosphere, of a much milder temperature in winter than that of the Atlantic in the same latitude. The nearness of the Cascade range of mountains also has its influence, by penning up, as it were, the balmy breath of the Pacific, and at the same time protecting the region in a measure from the cold blasts of the northeast.

Whilst, owing to the intervening Coast range of mountains, the climate of the Willamette Valley is not modified so much by the sea breezes as the first topographical district, yet it receives much more of them than the third region, east of the Cascade range. This is partly owing to the greater distance of the latter section from the ocean, but also to the latter chain of mountains being higher than the former. As the humid atmosphere from the ocean strikes the Coast range, the most of the moisture must be precipitated in the form of rain or snow; still, a large portion of the humidity finds its way over and through the gaps of this barrier and falls in mist or rain in the Willamette Valley. The Cascade mountains, however, are so high as to intercept the sea fogs almost entirely.

These facts account for the greater uniformity of the temperature and larger rainfall, in the first than in the second, and in the second than in the third, topographical district. The latter district, embracing the whole of Eastern Oregon, is so diversified in topographical and climatological features, as to render a comprehensive description of the same utterly impossible in this brief summary. We must content ourselves, therefore, with a few general remarks upon the subject.

This region is bounded on the west by the Cascade mountains; on the north partly by the main Columbia, and in part by Snake River, or the Lewis Fork of the Columbia River; on the east mainly by Snake River; on the south by Nevada and California—embracing an area of fifty-eight thousand square miles; consisting of immense plateaux of varying degrees of altitude, divided up by numerous mountain spurs, jutting out mostly from the Blue mountains, which run through the district from the northeast to the southwest. Although some of the streams are fringed with willow and cotton-wood, there is but little timber in this section, except on the tops of the high ridges of the mountains, where may be found cedar, larch, fir, spruce and pine.

The finest agricultural lands lie in the small valleys, and bottoms of the streams having their spring-heads in the mountains. The soil near the base of the latter is sandy and argillaceous; that of the low river bottoms, alluvial and very productive. The highlands have an ashen soil, intermixed more or less with alkaline earths and a clayey loam. All of these soils, however, will produce most of the cereals, vegetables and fruits common to a temperate zone.

This entire district is well watered by numerous mountain streams, which, however, run too deep in the ground to be generally available for irrigation; hence, as the spring and summer seasons are usually dry, the crops of the highlands often suffer from the drought. The wild grass on the high grounds grows in spots and bunches, and is called bunch-grass. It is very nutritious, and much sought after by stock, even when dry and covered with snow.

Whilst Eastern Oregon has much land that may be designated as valleys, and more still that would properly come under the designation of high, rolling prairie, there is a very great proportion of waste country in the western and central regions that is strictly volcanic. In its southern portion are many salt and fresh water lakes, the former having no apparent outlets, although receiving the supplies of considerable streams. Some of these picturesque bodies of water will compare favorably with the world-renowned Lakes of Killarney, in Ireland, and the Highland Lakes, of Scotland. One of them is called "Sunken Lake," because its surface is about eight hundred feet below the surrounding ground. Its perpendicular banks furnish only one place where the curious can descend to the enclosed fathomless limpid reservoir below. This lake region of Eastern Oregon has much good grazing and farming land, and is tolerably well watered. It has lately been the scene of one of the most remarkable struggles in the history of the world. When, in due course of time, it shall have been rendered accessible to tourists, by railroads, the lava beds of the Modoc war will attract much attention.

The diversity in altitude alone of the various little valleys in Eastern Oregon render a great difference in climate, independent of the latitude, which, of course, has its modifying influences. In many of these pleasant retreats, stock can be wintered upon the wild grass, without any other food. Yet, experience dictates to the stock raisers the necessity of always keeping a supply of provender on hand, and good shelter, for the winters are capricious, and sometimes fearfully cold, with snow so deep, that both man and beast must perish, if unprotected. During our early mining excitements, it was very common for the newspapers of the day to contain accounts of the loss of whole herds of horses, sheep and cattle, which had been driven into this country to winter, on account of the shortness of grass in the milder Willamette Valley, and because of the proximity of the mining country. But this was not the worst. Many weary miners, expressmen and traders would occasionally get blockaded by deep snows on the Blue Mountains, and even on the moderate mountain spurs and elevated prairies, so as to be cut off for months from all communication with civilization. Sometimes, too, fearful snow storms would fall upon them unexpectedly, whilst journeying in these elevated regions, freezing them to death.

By glancing at the annexed meterological table, and comparing the observations of Forts Dalles and Walla Walla—the climatic representations of Eastern Oregon—with Portland and Fort Yamhill, of the Willamette Valley, or of Fort Orford and Astoria, of the Oregon coast, it will be seen that the Third District has a much more variable climate than either of the others. Its extremes of temperature are very great. The summers are warm, and the winters, though generally only moderately cold, are sometimes as rigorous as in our New England States. It will, also, be seen that the rainfall, including the melted snow, is infinitely less than on the coast, and nothing like as great as in the Willamette Valley. In short, the climate is so entirely different from that west of the Cascade range of mountains, that those persons who are delighted with it cannot be contented in the "webfoot" country, as the Willamette Valley is derisively called, because of its frequent rains in winter.

Eastern Oregon people boast of their clear skies, of their warm summer weather, and dry snows of winter, and, although unable to produce as much wheat to the acre as is raised in the Willamette Valley, they can furnish the market with larger melons, more delicious peaches, etc. Her gold mines, too, are more extensive and much richer, thus making her essentially a mining region. The force of the winds is much greater here than in the Willamette Valley. This is particularly the case in the vicinity of the Dalles, where they drive the sand in fearful currents over the country, rendering travel, at times, anything but agreeable. All railways that may run through this section will have to be protected, at points, by sheds, to keep the sand from obstructing the trains.

Whilst these strong winds are very unpleasant near the Dalles, they are considered, in their milder form, quite agreeable to the settlers in the Walla Walla and kindred valleys. This is especially the case in the spring and autumn, when the prevailing winds from the south, southwest and southeast are quite balmy, and accompanied with sufficient showers to lay the dust, which is decidedly too omnipresent in summer.

Much more could be said of this topographical division of Oregon, as well as of the rest of the State, but the growing length of this chapter warns me to hasten on for a slight glimpse of the northern portion of the northwest—Washington Territory.

The latter is naturally divided by the Cascade range of mountains into two districts, entirely different from each other in geographical and climatological characteristics.

Its western portion is almost cut in two, from north to south by a series of straits, inlets and sounds, deep and capacious enough to hold the shipping of the world. Many persons are firm in the belief that somewhere in this Puget Sound region the future great commercial emporium of the Pacific Coast will be located. The modest little town of Tacoma, the present terminus of the Northern Pacific Railroad, is ambitious of this distinction. Portland, Oregon, however, has so many natural advantages, and such a great start over all other competitors in this line north of San Francisco, that she will doubtless continue to be the big sponge that will absorb nearly all the trade of the Great Northwest.

The western is smaller than the eastern part of Washington Territory. It is densely timbered with cedar, fir, and most of the other trees described as common to the Oregon Coast. It has but few prairies—the highest of them being sandy and gravelly. The soil in the river bottoms is mostly alluvial, rich and productive. The scarcity of good agricultural prairie land, and the abundance of the finest timber in the world, together with the bountiful supply of salmon and other fish, will for many years make this region essentially a lumbering, ship-building and fishing country. The best salmon fisheries are on the Columbia River, which divides the Territory from the State of Oregon.

The western portion of the Territory has a very uniform climate, that part of it lying between the Sound and the ocean being like the coast climate of Oregon. The district immediately east of the Sound is, of course, not so windy as the more western part. The climate may be characterized as uniform, mild, humid and healthy.

The eastern division of the Territory is similar to Eastern Oregon, but being, of course, somewhat colder in winter, on account of its more northern latitude. It is traversed by many noble streams, which empty their crystal waters into the Columbia. Although grazing and farming will be carried on to a considerable extent in this part of Washington Territory, yet her mineral wealth must continue, as heretofore, to attract the greatest attention.

It is rather a difficult task to compare the northwest with the southwest, because of the great diversity of climate in the former. I do not mean changeable climate. On the contrary, it is far more uniform than the latter; but a series of local climates, depending upon a variety of causes, such as latitude, longitude, altitude, the relative situation and proximity of each place to the Pacific ocean, to the mountain ranges, to the mountain gorges, which allow the oceanic atmosphere to pass into the valleys beyond, to the points of the compass—whether its sloping lands face the northwest, or the warmer southwest winds, and to various other circumstances too numerous to be mentioned.

Although in describing the northwest, I first divided up its more southern part (Oregon) into three topographical and climatographical districts, it has been found impossible by this method to give more than an approximate idea of the whole. Whilst the description embraces the principal characteristics of topography and climate, in regard to the coast and Eastern Oregon sections, it falls short in respect to the great valley region between these two districts; for the reason that there are lying south of the Willamette

Valley, the Umpqua and Rogue River Valleys, which though possessing many of the features of the first, are yet in some points very different. They are, of course, milder and dryer, and capable of producing some kinds of fruits and vegetables that do not thrive well in the more northern valley, especially peaches and grapes.

In order to facilitate the comparison between the southwest and northwest, I have, in the description of the various sections of the latter, omitted some of the most important features, because they are common to the whole region, and can, therefore, be the better described in an antithetical analysis of the two countries. Having already pointed out some of the contrasts in topography, I shall now allude to a few in climate.

The northwest has fewer and less destructive wind storms than the southwest, and no frightful hurricanes, which are so common in all parts of the western and southwestern States and Territories, where their courses are marked by the prostration of trees and hamlets—whirling the former in the air like so many straws. This destruction would be more marked if that region contained more forests, or habitations. What fearful catastrophies must result when all that beautiful section shall have been densely populated, with large cities scattered here and there, as centers of commerce and civilization. This is no overdrawn picture of the imagination, for hardly a year rolls over our heads that we do not read of the havoc of these western tornadoes.

From careful observations made by the Government, it is found that during the last twenty-five years only three storms of a velocity of forty-five miles an hour, have visited the northwest coast; whereas, in the old northwest, east of the Rocky mountains, such winds have been frequent, and sometimes reaching the terrible velocity of ninety-five miles an hour. Further, the southwest is subject to what is known as the "northers," or cold blasts of wind springing up suddenly from the north or northwest, sending the thermometer in a few hours from a summer temperature of 75° down almost to zero. Woe to the traveler on the prairies, if caught unprepared in such an emergency. Occasionally Government expeditions have been crippled by the loss of their mules and horses, from exposure to these chilling winds.

Captain R. B. Marcy, U. S. Army, on returning from his Sante Fe expedition in 1849, experienced one of them just before reaching the frontier settlements of Texas, with a loss of many of his animals.

In the vicinity of Fort Arbuckle, located on Wild Horse Crėek, a tributary of the False Washita River, in the Indian Territory, these "northers" occasionally appear, but not so often nor so severely as on the plains further to the southwest. However, on the 15th of March, 1854, we there witnessed a very hard one, the temperature falling in a few hours from 76° to 15°, owing to a sudden veering of the wind from the south to the northwest. These rapid changes of temperature in the southwest are more frequent in the latter part of autumn and the beginning of spring.

In Washington Territory and Oregon, a change in winter of the wind from south to north will cool the atmosphere considerably, but by no means to such an extreme as follows a similar variation of the wind in the southwest. The latter country is visited by frequent thunder storms, occurring mostly in midsummer. In that portion of the northwest lying between the Cascade range of mountains and the Ocean, thunder is rarely heard, and generally in the latter part of spring. In the section east of said range of mountains it is a little more common, but nothing like so frequent as in the Indian Territory and Western Texas.

Such a thing as sultry weather (hot and humid) is unknown in the northwest. In the southwest it is quite common, relaxing both body and mind, so as to unfit one, for the time being, for energetic employment of any kind, unless it be to fight off the numerous horrid insects and reptiles that infest the latter country, such as flies, mosquitoes, gnats, beetles, woodticks, tarantulas, scorpions, centipedes, three varieties of the rattlesnake, the ground, black and diamond cotton-mouthed moccasins—which are even more poisonous than the rattlesnake—copper-heads, adders, lizards, toads, and horned frogs, the latter being the only real innocent creatures of the whole list. This interesting reptile receives its name from the fact of having a horn protruding from the center of its head. It can live on air alone for a long time. I saw one kept in a bottle, with no water or food, for six months, without showing any evidence of diminished vitality. The most of the hideous reptiles just mentioned infest every part of the southwest. If the traveler lay his wearied head upon the grassy prairie, he often finds, on awakening in the morning, a centipede or tarantula in his boot, or a copper-head or rattlesnake nestled close by, if not beneath his blanket. The two former are almost as venomous as the latter.

The northwest is almost entirely free from these torments of the earth, having none of them, excepting flies, gnats, a few mosquitoes, and a very small number of rattlesnakes. I have only seen one of the latter since my first arrival. Whilst, during the summer season, in the southwest, one tosses restlessly and almost sleeplessly on his couch, wet with the sweaty drippings from his parboiled body, and rises in the morning more dead than alive from a want of a proper proportion of quiet, refreshing sleep, the lucky inhabitants of the northwest passes the night beneath a blanket, in a state of the most perfect security of body and mind, and awakes the next day with his muscles and brain elastic and vigorous, because the nights are always refreshingly cool and pleasant. Although our nights are always pleasantly cool, it will be seen, by reference to the annexed meteorological tables, that we sometimes have very hot days during summer in the Willamette Valley, and even hotter in Eastern Oregon; but, then, owing to the dryness of the air, the same degree of heat is not so oppressive here as in the southwest. Any one having doubts upon this subject will find, on consulting the annexed tables, how little rain falls during this part of the year in this country, and ought to know how much greater heat appears in a humid than in a dry atmosphere. If he does not, let him try the experiment for himself in a room with and without moisture. To the very few who may not understand the philosophy of this difference, I would simply state, that evaporation of the perspiration on the surface of the body has a tendency to keep the latter cool, and, that this process, other things being equal, goes on the better in a dry atmosphere, and that it is checked in exact proportion to the humidity of the air.

In the northwest we have from six to eight months tolerably dry weather, and from four to six decidedly moist. Whilst, then, the summers are delightfully pleasant, the winters, especially on the coast and in the Willamette Valley, are often dismal and gloomy. Many persons are so organized as not to be able to stand this kind of weather without a murmur; but, nine tenths of the people who remain here long enough to overcome their homesickness for the country left behind, prefer this kind of weather to a clear, cold atmosphere, with snow on the ground. Although fond of skating, and the merry jingle of sleigh bells, still I have learned to prefer the comparatively mild rainy weather to cold days, whether clear or snowy.

I have already stated, that although the climate of the Willamette Valley is generally mild in winter, yet there are, occasionally, spells of very cold or exceedingly snowy weather; so that our winters are not always like the one of 1872, when the coldest day caused the thermometer to sink to but 22° above zero. On the coast the temperature is rarely below 30° in winter, or above 22° in summer. Many persons might prefer the winters of the southwest, which are certainly dryer, and not any cooler than in the milder climatic district of Oregon, but have no advantage, in these respects, to Eastern Oregon and Washington Territory.

In regard to healthfulness, there can be no difference of opinion as to the northwest coast, being far more salubrious than the southwest. In fact, it has been proven by the Government Report of the mortality of the various States in the Union, that the Territory of Washington and the State of Oregon, are, by far, the most healthful sections of the United States.

Whilst the death-rate in Vermont, the healthiest State east of the Rocky mountains, is one in ninety-two, it is only one in one hundred and seventy-two in Oregon, and one in two hundred and twenty-eight in Washington Territory. Making due allowance for the effects naturally arising from the larger and more crowded cities in the east, still the advantage is vastly in favor of the northwest coast.

To the mind of the medical philosopher, the reason of this great dissimilarity in point of healthfulness is perfectly self-evident. Especially so, as it bears upon the comparative salubriousness of the two great regions directly under review, as both of them are nearly equal in population, size of towns and cities. As might be easily inferred from the geological, topographical and climatological characteristics of the southwest, with her rich soil, almost level surface, sluggish streams—many of which dry up in summer—frequent showers in the latter parts of spring and autumn, and hot atmosphere, there must of necessity be a vast amount of malaria generated, thus rendering the air poisonous to an extreme degree. In Oregon and Washington Territory many of these conditions are wanting. The whole aspect of the country is more mountainous; the streams come dashing from the mountain sides as cold, pure and clear as the melting snows can make them; the pure and almost steady breeze from the ocean, not only equalizes the local temperature, by lowering it in summer and elevating it in winter, but carries off the unhealthy exhalations from the soil almost as fast as generated. The surface of the ground is not covered in the autumn with any very large quantity of decaying vegetable matter, as the majority of our trees are evergreens, and the wild grasses are moderately short. As soon as decay begins in the latter, a new crop springs up, imbibing as its food the gases resulting from the decomposition of the previous production, thus purifying the atmosphere. Still, malarious or miasmatic fevers do prevail to some extent along the banks of the Willamette River and some of its tributaries, and in the low alluvial bottoms of a small extent of the noble Columbia. The coast, however, is perfectly free from all such fevers.

During a year's residence at Fort Orford, located in the latter district, I did not see a single case of any of the numerous varieties of these diseases, except in a secondary form, that is, occurring in persons who had been ill with the complaint before arriving there, or who had imbibed the poison somewhere else. The slight cases of miasmatic fevers prevalent in Oregon, are quite amenable to treatment. There are but few of its severe remittent or congestive types.

During the four years of my residence at Fort Yamhill, located on the south fork of the Yamhill River, a tributary of the Willamette, and, consequently, in the Willamette Valley, I saw hardly any of these fevers. At Portland, Oregon, they are of more frequent occurrence. But even here they are rare and mild, in comparison with the same affections in the vicinity of Fort Arbuckle, in the Indian Territory. With the single exception of myself, I never saw a person who had lived in that country four years, who had not had the intermittent, remittent or typho-malarial fever so often as to render him or her sufficiently debilitated to require a change of climate for the recuperation of health.

As may be seen by reference to the sanitary reports from the various military stations in that country, the same unhealthfulness obtains in the whole region until the dry and sandy plains are reached. Notwithstanding the great prevalence of malarious fevers in the southwest, the general mortality, except at epidemic periods, is small, owing mainly to the fact that experienced physicians have the power to control them with more promptness and certainty than any other class of maladies in the nosology. Perhaps the most fatal disease of all in that country is the "winter fever," a combination of typho-malarial fever and pneumonia. When epidemic, which is the case every few years, it sweeps off hundreds of the Indians and frontiersmen. The great mortality, however, is mainly owing to the irrational mode of treating it by many of the uneducated physicians of the country, upon the old antiphlogistic plan of depletion by blood-letting, purgatives and emetics, instead of by tonics, stimulants, etc.

Aside from the gloomy, dismal character of the long-continued cloudy and rainy weather of winter in Western Oregon and Washington Territory, there is nothing in a hygienic point of view objectionable in this season, for the temperature is rarely disagreeable, is pretty uniform, and the rains wash off a vast deal of filth and other unhealthy deposits, which accumulate during the summer, especially in the larger towns. This is preëminently the case in the city of Portland, the commercial emporium of Oregon. The miasmatic exhalations arising from the filthy back-yards and hovels of the Chinese quarters, would decimate the population of the city annually, if it were not for the thorough washing and cleansing those places receive from nature every rainy season.

With the exception of the greater prevalence in the southwest of the malarial fevers, and their multifarious complications of other diseases, I do not know but what it will compare favorably with the northwest in point of healthfulness. A majority of the usual complaints that inflict poor, perishing humanity in temperate latitudes, are found in both regions, but presenting modifications in accordance with particular local climates. The latter country can, however, thus far boast over the former in not experiencing the Asiatic cholera. This fearful complaint, at one time, even came as far as California, but did not reach the northwest. Yet, we cannot hope for an entire immunity.

There is one disease—yellow fever—that occasionally inflicts a portion of the southwest, that can, in all human probability, never find its way into this part of the United States.

In the early spring of 1852, the scurvy made its appearance among the troops at Fort Arbuckle, in the Indian Territory, owing to the want of sufficient fresh meats, vegetables and fruits in the commissary department. It being too early for garden vegetables, by my recommendation the whole neighborhood was searched in order to obtain wild onions, which were issued to the command in every conceivable shape and mode, as both food and medicine, with the most happy effects.

In explanation of the annexed meteorological table, it is necessary to state that the places designated where observations were made, are selected because of their representative character for each section or district, thus: Fort Orford and Astoria for the Oregon Coast, Fort Yamhill and Portland for the Willamette Valley, Forts Dalles and Walla Walla for Eastern Oregon and Washington Territory, Fort Steilacoom for the western part of the latter Territory, Forts Arbuckle, Chadbourne and Lancaster for the southwest. Although some of these observations were made between the years 1855 and 1859, they give as fair an idea of the climate as any later dates could possibly do. Some of the observations presented were made under my own supervision, and all by competent and reliable Government officers.

The rainfall at Fort Orford for the year 1855 of 83.40 inches, and at Astoria, in 1871, of 93.04 inches seems large, but there is no doubt as to the correctness of the observations. In this connection it may not be out of place to relate a little incident that occurred when I was stationed at Fort Arbuckle, in the year 1851. There chanced one night to be a very heavy rain for that section of country. The weather, that ever fruitful topic of conversation, being under discussion the following morning, some one inquired of me how much rain had fallen the previous twenty-four hours. I remarked "an inch and a half."

"Pshaw!" replied an old Pike, standing near, "your

tarnal thing must have leaked, for I put my bran-new boot outside the wagon on going to sleep last night, and when I got up this morning it was chuck full, and I know my boot is one foot long and two high, which would make three feet."

It is, perhaps, needless to add that the rain-gauge in use at Fort Orford and Astoria was not a boot.

METEOROLOGICAL. OBSERVATIONS.

POSITION OF STATIONS, MEAN TEMPERATURE, RANGE, QUARTERLY AND ANNUAL SUMMARY OF RAIN, ANNUAL SUMMARY OF WEATHER.

Station.	Year.	Latitude.	Lon. west from Greenwich.	Altitude.	January.	February.	March.	April.	May.	June.	July.	August.	September.	October.	November.	December.	Maximum.	Minimum.	Range.	Annual Mean.	Inches Rain.					Weather.				Barometer reduced to 32° F.			District.	
																					Spring.	Summer.	Autumn.	Winter.	Year.	Fair.	Cloudy.	Rain.	Snow.	Highest.	Lowest.	An. Mean.		
		° ′ ″	° ′ ″	Feet.																						Days.	Days.	Days.	Days.					
Fort Orford	1855	42 44 0	124 29 0	50	48.04	49.30	50.23	50.63	52.54	57.58	58.50	59.58	58.76	56.87	47.03	53.15	72	30	42	......	23.61	3.71	22.19	33.85	83.40	......	......	......	......	......	......	......	Coast.	NORTHWEST.
Fort Yamhill	1857	45 05 0	123 32 0	......	38.79	41.83	47.42	55.48	57.27	57.85	62.28	60.05	57.22	52.43	43.61	42.44	95	9	86	51.39	10.38	1.43	10.82	35.15	57.78	199	166	139	15	......	......	......	Willamette Valley.	
Do.	1858	......	......	......	38.43	40.55	43.55	48.11	52.87	56.58	59.49	61.94	59.43	47.84	43.93	35.81	94	10	84	49.04	14.04	2.76	15.34	29.92	62	175	190	165	17	......	......	......	Do.	
Do.	1859	......	......	......	37.38	38.11	40.79	45.94	51.92	62.33	58.12	60.70	57.48	52.50	38.17	34.72	89	7	82	48.19	15.77	1.21	16.87	21.78	55.63	167	198	141	31	......	......	......	Do.	
Portland	1872	45 30 0	122 27 0	57.6	36	44	48	47	57	64	68	66	59	52.6	41.6	41.9	91	22	69	62.51	5.40	1.59	16.27	32.97	56.23	144	68	146	7	30.67	29.35	30.07	Do.	
Do.	1873	......	......	......	44.4	40.6	48.1	51.3	55.9	61.5	68	67.7	61.9	49.9	47.4	37	91	17	74	63.37	7.49	1.86	13.34	27.83	50.52	152	62	144	7	30.63	29.48	30.14	Do.	
Astoria	1870	46 11 28	123 49 32	52	41.2	42.3	41	48	52.1	56.9	63.5	63.6	58.7	52.1	47.3	37.9	91	19.8	74.2	60.46	18.06	6.41	15.16	31.38	71.01	......	......	193	2	30.47	29.39	29.29	Oregon Coast.	
Do.	1871	......	......	......	43.2	40.2	44	46.7	49.5	55.4	57.4	59.1	56	51.5	44.5	39.1	79	20.2	58.8	58.66	27.31	2.99	20.59	42.15	93.04	......	......	220	3	30.69	29.05	29.98	Do.	
Do.	1872	......	......	......	40	44.3	46.9	46.2	51.6	54.1	59.3	58.7	57	52.3	42.7	41.6	98.3	27.5	50.8	59.47	19.76	3.6	13.11	42.11	78.66	......	......	193	2	30.61	29.01	30.01	Do.	
Do.	1873	......	......	......	43.7	38.9	45.3	49	51.9	55.4	59.6	60.5	57.3	49.9	47.2	37.3	82.2	24.7	57.5	59.60	24.82	7.9	8.85	36.58	78.15	......	......	184	5	30.53	29.28	30	Do.	
Dalles	1857	45 36 0	120 55 0	350	26.65	42.12	49.48	56.83	63.11	68.29	72.06	71.53	63.16	52.86	42.29	41.14	103	−10	113	54.12	3.06	1.6	8.33	16.35	29.34	221	144	64	7	......	......	......	Eastern Oregon.	
Do.	1858	......	......	......	36.78	38.33	46.50	54.29	60.21	67.92	71.85	72.78	65.27	49.91	42.82	33.94	98	− 6	104	53.33	5.97	1.7	14.96	20.94	43.63	237	128	105	13	......	......	......	Do.	
Do.	1859	......	......	......	33.38	36.74	41.67	52.26	60.15	70.13	73.81	70.59	63.35	53.19	35.05	25.21	99	− 3	102	53.79	6.05	.7	12.16	14.99	33.93	230	135	92	38	......	......	......	Do.	
Walla Walla	1857	46 3 0	118 20 0	......	27.44	39.78	46.51	50.6	60	73	70.87	75.83	65.7	55.65	39.63	38.61	99	−20	119	64.36	5.17	2.6	4.54	5.50	17.89	200	104	98	3	......	......	......	Washington Ter.	
Do.	1858	......	......	......	34.03	33.89	42.77	50.76	62.03	71.30	75.96	73.96	66.86	51.39	42.66	30.49	103	− 4	107	56.26	6.30	2.8	4	5.94	19.12	246	119	89	16	......	......	......	Do.	
Do.	1859	......	......	......	34.70	36.67	43.45	51.63	61.13	76.36	80.29	74.77	65.85	61.48	34.56	22.44	107	− 6	113	53.61	8.50	.4	6.33	2.84	18.13	265	100	63	19	......	......	......	Do.	
Steilacoom	1857	47 10 0	122 25 0	300	38.56	40.70	41.66	51.41	55.14	57.66	61.39	61.18	56.14	50.69	42.82	41.27	90	2	88	50.55	5.54	2.1	9.16	22.70	39.53	65	300	141	2	......	......	......	Puget Sound.	
Do.	1858	......	......	......	37.99	36.58	44.16	48.56	54.66	61.37	60.68	62.21	58.60	46.84	44.31	37.71	88	11	77	49.49	13.76	7.6	11.84	16.87	50.14	138	227	130	12	......	......	......	Do.	
Do.	1859	......	......	......	36.30	36.89	37.78	45.16	50.68	60.01	61.86	60.59	57.56	51.58	37.39	35.65	89	10	79	48.29	9.95	1.4	12.09	15.19	38.72	193	172	91	7	......	......	......	Do.	
Fort Arbuckle	1857	34 27 0	97 9 0	1,000	27.16	49.07	52.79	53.81	65.32	76.29	81.22	76.96	72.98	59.10	46.24	45.56	106	− 4	110	58.85	8.15	18.0	9.02	11.36	47.49	277	88	79	5	......	......	......	Indian Territory.	SOUTHWEST.
Do.	1859	......	......	......	41.74	51.08	56.83	60.11	73.19	77.93	83.88	83.05	71.87	62.73	57.92	33.36	102	0	102	62.72	7.07	7.6	10.73	2.48	27.96	270	95	78	3	......	......	......	Do.	
Fort Chadbourne	1857	32 02 0	100 5 0	2,120	30.60	52.81	56.48	55.14	69.72	79.08	82.29	81.50	72.21	61.74	49.63	45.41	104	5	99	61.88	3.01	4.4	7.74	4.91	20.07	202	163	82	1	......	......	......	Western Texas.	
Do.	1858	......	......	......	45.60	45.36	58.57	65.12	71.16	77.51	84.87	81.35	76.01	67.68	46.43	44.48	103	12	91	63.69	2.92	1.81	3.19	2.41	10.34	186	179	75	4	......	......	......	Do.	
Do.	1859	......	......	......	42.92	55.47	57.49	63.51	75.56	83.24	84.76	85.33	72.59	62.86	58.12	35.87	104	5	99	64.86	6.35	4.03	8.55	2.46	21.39	154	211	66	8	......	......	......	Do.	
Fort Lancaster	1857	30 42 0	101 25 0	2,350	39.46	55.01	60.35	59.25	71.91	79.03	80.66	81.78	78.69	63.94	50.77	45.79	106	5	101	61.63	4.87	11.39	15.72	7.60	39.58	124	241	42	2	......	......	......	Do.	
Do.	1858	......	......	......	46.81	47.82	61.17	68.54	75.92	77.09	84.14	80.79	75.02	68.48	49.33	47.38	100	14	86	64.21	6.77	13.72	2.03	5.68	28.21	225	140	36	2	......	......	......	Do.	
Do.	1859	......	......	......	45.61	58.70	61.22	68.46	80.74	85.76	86.47	87.58	76.47	65.83	58.67	38.93	105	10	95	67.37	3.85	5	4.13	1.91	24.89	267	98	28	3	......	......	......	Do.	

www.ingramcontent.com/pod-product-compliance
Lightning Source LLC
LaVergne TN
LVHW021234110826
845150LV00002B/332